THE LAW OF PROPERTY IN THE LATER ROMAN REPUBLIC

THE LAW OF PROPERTY IN THE LATER ROMAN REPUBLIC

BY

ALAN WATSON

OXFORD
AT THE CLARENDON PRESS
1968

Oxford University Press, Ely House, London W. 1

GLASGOW NEW YORK TORONTO MELBOURNE WELLINGTON
CAPE TOWN SALISBURY IBADAN NAIROBI LUSAKA ADDIS ABABA
BOMBAY CALCUTTA MADRAS KARACHI LAHORE DACCA
KUALA LUMPUR SINGAPORE HONG KONG TOKYO

PRINTED IN GREAT BRITAIN

FOR

DAVID AND ANN

PREFACE

THIS book follows the plan of my earlier ones, *The Law of Obligations in the Later Roman Republic* (Clarendon Press, 1965) and *The Law of Persons in the Later Roman Republic* (Clarendon Press, 1967). The aim has been to build up a picture of the law of property in the last two centuries of the Roman Republic by a thorough examination of all texts which are directly relevant for that period. Texts which are concerned only with an earlier or later period have been—so far as possible—omitted from the argument so that the view of late Republican law should not be obscured by preconceptions unsupported by actual evidence for that time.

The book has been greatly improved by the criticism of a large number of friends. Among lawyers, Professor R. Yaron, Mr. A. M. Honoré, and Mr. A. Dashwood read all of the typescript, and Mr. J. L. Barton read much of it. Professor Yaron, indeed, read most of the typescript at least twice. Among Roman historians, Mr. R. J. Seager read all of it, and Mr. P. A. Brunt read most of it. Far-reaching help on questions of Latin grammar came to me from Mr. R. M. Ogilvie, Miss B. I. Knott, and Mr. D. A. Malcolm. Many others gave me assistance on individual points. To all these friends I must express my deepest gratitude. Heartfelt thanks are also due to the members of the staff of Glasgow University Library, and of the Bodleian and Codrington Libraries, for their unending readiness to supply books; and, in advance, to the Clarendon Press for their famous skill and patience. Apart from final revisions, the writing of this book was completed in December 1966.

ALAN WATSON

Glasgow
July 1967

CONTENTS

Abbreviations ix

1. Kinds of *Res* 1

2. Acquisition of Ownership 16

3. *Possessio* 81

4. *Vindicatio, Actio Publiciana, Actio ad exhibendum* 91

5. Boundaries and Division 110

6. *Damnum infectum* 125

7. *Actio aquae pluviae arcendae* 155

8. Servitudes 176

9. *Usufructus* and Similar Rights 203

10. The Interdict *Quod vi aut clam* 222

11. *Donatio* 229

Index of Texts 233

Index 241

ABBREVIATIONS

AG	*Archivio giuridico.*
Beseler, *Beiträge* i–v	Beseler, *Beiträge zur Kritik der römischen Rechtsquellen* i–iv (Tübingen, 1910–20), v (Leipzig, 1931).
BIDR	*Bullettino dell'istituto di diritto romano.*
Biondi, *Successione*	Biondi, *Successione testamentaria e donazioni*, 2nd edn. (Milan, 1955).
Bonfante II. i, II. ii, III, VI	Bonfante, *Corso di diritto romano* II. i, II. ii, *La proprietà* (Rome, 1926 (i), 1928 (ii)); III, *Diritti reali* (Rome, 1933); VI *Le successioni* (Rome, 1930).
Bruns	Bruns, *Fontes iuris romani antiqui*, 7th edn. by Gradenwitz (Tübingen, 1909).
Buckland, *Textbook*	Buckland, *A Textbook of Roman Law*, 3rd edit. revised by Stein (Cambridge, 1963).
Costa, *Cicerone* i	Costa, *Cicerone giureconsulto* i, 2nd edit. (reprinted, Rome, 1964).
De Sarlo, *AV*	De Sarlo, *Alfeno Varo e i suoi digesta* (Milan, 1940).
De Zulueta, *Gaius* ii	De Zulueta, *The Institutes of Gaius, part ii, Commentary* (Oxford, 1953).
FIRA i, ii, iii	*Fontes iuris romani anteiustiniani* i–iii (Florence, 1940–3).
Index Itp.	*Index Interpolationum quae in Iustiniani Digestis inesse dicuntur* i, ii, iii, and *Supplementum* (Weimar, 1929–35).
JRS	*Journal of Roman Studies.*
Kaser, *EB*	Kaser, *Eigentum und Besitz im älteren römischen Recht*, 2nd edn. (Cologne, Graz, 1956).
Kaser, *Ius*	Kaser, *Das altrömische Ius* (Göttingen, 1949).
Kaser, *RPR* i, ii	Kaser, *Das römische Privatrecht* (Munich, 1955 (i), 1959 (ii)).
Kaser, *ZPR*	Kaser, *Das römische Zivilprozessrecht* (Munich, 1966).
Lenel, *EP*	Lenel, *Das Edictum perpetuum*, 3rd edit. (Leipzig, 1927).
Lenel, *Pal.* i. ii	Lenel, *Palingenesia Iuris Civilis* i, ii (Leipzig, 1889).
LQR	*Law Quarterly Review.*

Milan Digest	*Digesta Iustiniani Augusti*, edited by Bonfante, Fadda, Ferrini, Riccobono, and Scialoja (Milan, 1931).
RE	*Paulys Real-Encyclopädie der classischen Altertumswissenschaft* (Stuttgart, 1873–).
RHD	*Revue historique de droit*.
Rotondi, *Leges*	Rotondi, *Leges publicae populi romani* (reprinted, Hildesheim, 1966).
Schulz, *RLS*	Schulz, *Roman Legal Science* (Oxford, 1946; corrected 1953).
SDHI	*Studia et Documenta Historiae et Iuris*.
Stereotype Digest	*Corpus Iuris Civilis* i, edited by Mommsen and Krüger, 16th edn. (Berlin, 1954).
Tijd.	*Tijdschrift voor Rechtsgeschiedenis*.
TLL	*Thesaurus Linguae Latinae* (Leipzig, 1900–).
Watson, *Obligations*	Watson, *The Law of Obligations in the Later Roman Republic* (Oxford, 1965).
Watson, *Persons*	Watson, *The Law of Persons in the Later Roman Republic* (Oxford, 1967).
Yaron	Yaron, 'Reflections on *usucapio*', *Tijd.* xxxv (1967), 191 ff.
ZSS	*Zeitschrift der Savigny-Stiftung* (römische Abteilung).

1

KINDS OF *RES*

For the classification of things it is convenient to follow the classification in Gaius' Institutes since it is fuller than any we have for the Republic. This procedure may be faulted as anachronistic but the texts concerning the later Republic do show that the kinds of things which are classified in Gaius were already distinguished in our period.

Gaius primarily divides things into those *divini iuris* and those *humani iuris*.[1] Those *divini iuris* are *res sacrae* and *res religiosae*.[2] *Res sanctae* are *quodammodo divini iuris*.[3] *Res humani iuris* are either public or private.[4] Things can be further divided into corporeal and incorporeal.[5,6]

To turn first to those things which are *divini iuris* or *quodammodo divini iuris*.[7] *Res sacrae* are those things dedicated under the authority of the Roman people to the gods above; *res religiosae* are dedicated to the gods below—a thing is made *religiosus* by the act of a private individual when he buries a body in his own land provided the funeral is his concern; *res sanctae* are things such as the walls and gates of a city. These distinctions were certainly known in the Republic as Festus, s.v. *religiosus*, shows:

> Religiosus est non modo deorum sanctitatem magni aestimans sed etiam officiosus adversus homines; dies autem religiosi, quibus nisi quod necesse est nefas habetur facere, quales sunt sex et triginta atri qui appellantur, et Alliensis, atque ii, quibus mundus patet. ⟨*Religiosum ait*⟩ esse Gallus Aelius, quod homini ita facere non liceat, ut, si id faciat, contra deorum voluntatem videa⟨⟨n⟩⟩tur facere. Quo in genere sunt haec: in aedem Bonae deae virum introire; adversus auspicia legem ad populum ferre, die nefasto apud praetorem lege agere. Inter sacrum

1 G. 2. 2. 2 G. 2. 3. 3 G. 2. 8. 4 G. 2. 10.

5 G. 2. 12.

6 The other division into *res mancipi* and *res nec mancipi* is dealt with in a later chapter: *infra*, pp. 17 ff.

7 Cf. Bonfante II. i. 13 ff.

autem et sanctum et religiosum differentias bellissime refert: sacrum aedificium consecratum deo, sanctum murum qui sit circa oppidum, religiosum sepulcrum, ubi mortuus sepultus aut humatus sit satis constare ait; sed item ratione quadam et temporibus eadem videri posse, si quidem quod sacrum est, idem lege aut instituto maiorum sanctum esse putat, ut violari id sine poena non possit. Idem religiosum quoque esse, quoniam sit al⟨*i*⟩quid, quod ibi homini facere non liceat; quod si faciat, adversus deorum voluntatem videatur facere. Similiter de muro et sepulcro debere observari, ut eadem et sacra et sancta et religiosa fiant, sed quo modo ⟨⟨quod⟩⟩ supra expositum est, cum de sacro diximus.

Little is known of the jurist Aelius Gallus but he seems to have lived sometime during the last two centuries of the Republic.[1] Festus declares that Aelius Gallus brought out *bellissime* the difference between *sacrum*, *sanctum*, and *religiosum*. Gallus had said that it was generally agreed (*satis constare ait*) that a temple consecrated to a god was *sacer*, a wall round a city was *sanctum*, and a grave where a body was buried was *religiosum*. The similarity between the distinctions of Aelius Gallus and the classification of Gaius is so great that it is really impossible to doubt that as early as the time of the former these distinctions were technical in the realm of property. But, at the same time, these adjectives were used in other contexts with different meanings, e.g., *dies religiosi*, and the noun *religio* especially had a much wider meaning—Trebatius' books *de religionibus* were by no means restricted to dealing with the gods of the underworld—so that it is not surprising to find that then and later these adjectives are used in different senses even in respect of property. A good example is in Cicero, *in Q. Caecilium divinatio* I. 3.

Venisse tempus aiebant non iam ut commoda sua, sed ut vitam salutemque totius provinciae defenderem; sese iam ne deos quidem in suis urbibus ad quos confugerent habere, quod eorum simulacra sanctissima C. Verres ex delubris religiosissimis sustulisset; . . .

Cicero is talking of the desecration by Verres of the temples of the gods and he can only mean the gods above. The images (*simulacra*)

[1] Cf. Klebs, *RE* i. 492 f.; Krüger, *Geschichte der Quellen und Literatur des römischen Rechts*, 2nd edn. (Leipzig, 1912), p. 76; Kornhardt, *SDHI* xix (1953), 9 ff.

of the gods are described as *sanctissima*. Yet it would be strange if they had not been consecrated.[1] And the shrines from which these objects are taken are called *religiosissima*. Admittedly, of course, the superlatives need not carry the precise technical meanings of the positives but still, if in respect of property the positive adjectives were always used technically, it is unlikely that the superlatives would be used in this fashion by Cicero.[2] Again, in the early Empire *religiosus* can be used in this connection with respect to temples and shrines.

Aulus Gellius, *N.A.* 4. 9. 8. Masurius autem Sabinus in commentariis, quos de indigenis composuit: 'religiosum' inquit est, quod propter sanctitatem aliquam remotum ac sepositum a nobis est; verbum a 'relinquendo' dictum, tamquam 'caerimoniae' a 'carendo'. 9. Secundum hanc Sabini interpretationem templa quidem ac delubra—quia horum cumulus in vituperationem non cadit, ut illorum, quorum laus in modo extat—, quae non volgo ac temere, sed cum castitate caerimoniaque adeundum, et reverenda et reformidanda sunt magis quam involganda: 10. sed dies 'religiosi' dicti, quos ex contraria causa propter ominis diritatem relinquimus.

And in the Republic Trebatius can describe *sanctum* in this way:[3]

Sanctum est, ut idem Trebatius libro decimo Religionum refert, interdum idem quod sacrum idemque quod religiosum, interdum aliud, hoc est nec sacrum nec religiosum, est.

Here we are told that *sanctum* can mean at times the same as *sacrum*, sometimes the same as *religiosum*, and sometimes something else, neither *sacrum* nor *religiosum*. In view of this wide description of the word we cannot even be certain that where it is *aliud, hoc est nec sacrum nec religiosum* it is thought of exclusively as meaning things like city walls and gates. And to complete the confusion one might quote from the Empire Festus, s.v. *religiosum*.

Religiosum ac sacrum est, ut templa omnia atque aedes, quae etiam sacratae dicuntur; at quod per se religiosum est, non utique [*sacrum est, ut sepulcra*], quod ea non [*sacra, sed religiosa sunt*].

[1] Movable objects devoted to the worship of the gods were consecrated just as temples themselves were.

[2] On this text see also Aulus Gellius, *N.A.* 4. 9. 7.

[3] Macrobius, *Sat.* 3. 3. 5.

Res sacrae in the narrower sense were things which belonged to the gods above.

Macrobius, *Sat.* 3. 3. 2. Sacrum est, ut Trebatius libro primo de religionibus refert, quicquid est quod deorum habetur. . . .

They were outside human ownership and were to be used only in sacred ways.

Arnobius, *adversus gentes* 7. 31. operae pretium est, etiam verba ipsa depromere, quibus, cum vinum datur, uti ac supplicare consuetudo est: 'mactus hoc vino inferio esto'. 'inferio', inquit Trebatius, verbum ea causa est additum, eaque ratione profertur, ne vinum omne omnino quod in cellis atque apothecis est conditum, ex quibus illud, quod effunditur, promptum est, esse sacrum incipiat, et ex usibus eripiatur humanis. addito ergo hoc verbo solum erit, quod inferetur, sacrum nec religione obligabitur ceterum. . . .

Once consecrated, a thing belonging to the gods could not be usucapted by a human being.

Cicero, *de harusp. resp.* 14. 32. Vetera fortasse loquimur; quamquam hoc si minus civili iure perscriptum est, lege tamen naturae, communi iure gentium sanctum est ut nihil mortales a dis immortalibus usu capere possint.

According to Cicero this was not laid down by the civil law but was a rule of the *ius gentium*. In the Republic the consecration was by the pontiffs with the consent of the people which was expressed by a *lex* or *plebiscitum*.

Cicero, *ad Att.* 4. 2. 3. Cum pontifices decressent ita, SI NEQUE POPULI IUSSU, NEQUE PLEBIS SCITU IS QUI SE DEDICASSE DICERET NOMINATIM EI REI PRAEFECTUS ESSET NEQUE POPULI IUSSU AUT PLEBIS SCITU ID FACERE IUSSUS ESSET VIDERI POSSE SINE RELIGIONE EAM PARTEM AREAE mihi RESTITUI; mihi facta statim est gratulatio . . .[1]

Cicero is giving Atticus the words of the decree issued by the pontiffs at the end of the case where Cicero claimed that his house had not been properly consecrated.[2]

[1] Cf. Cicero, *de domo sua* 49. 127, 128; 53. 137. According to § 127 a law of Q. Papirius, which is otherwise unknown, enacted that there should be no consecration of any building, land, or altar, *iniussu plebis*.

[2] In general for *consecratio* see Cicero, *de domo sua*: *lex a vicanis Furfensibus templo dicta*, Bruns, no. 105 (*FIRA* iii, no. 72) of 58 B.C.

Theft of *res sacrae* was *sacrilegium*, not *furtum.*[1]

For *religiosum* in its narrow sense, Macrobius, *Sat.* 3. 3. 8. is not helpful:

. . . Servius Sulpicius religionem esse dictam tradidit quae propter sanctitatem aliquam remota ac seposita a nobis sit, quasi a relinquendo dicta, ut a carendo caerimonia.

Nor is Cicero, *Phil.* 9. 6. 14:

Atque hanc meam sententiam, patres conscripti, P. Servili sententia comprobari necesse est: qui sepulcrum publice decernendum Ser. Sulpicio censuit, statuam non censuit. Nam si mors legati sine caede atque ferro nullum honorem desiderat, cur decernit honorem sepulturae qui maximus haberi potest mortuo? Sin id tribuit Ser. Sulpicio, quod non est datum Cn. Octavio, cur quod illi datum est huic dandum esse non censet? Maiores quidem nostri statuas multis decreverunt, sepulcra paucis. Sed statuae intereunt tempestate, vetustate, sepulcrorum autem sanctitas in ipso solo est quod nulla vi moveri neque deleri potest, atque, ut cetera exstinguuntur, sic sepulcra sanctiora fiunt vetustate. 15. Augeatur igitur isto honore etiam is vir cui nullus honos tribui non debitus potest; grati simus in eius morte decoranda cui nullam iam aliam gratiam referre possumus. Notetur etiam M. Antoni nefarium bellum gerentis scelerata audacia. His enim honoribus habitis Ser. Sulpicio repudiatae reiectaeque legationis ab Antonio manebit testificatio sempiterna.

Cicero is discussing the relative merit of public statues and tombs as marks of respect for dead men. Tombs have a far greater value than statues for the latter can be destroyed but the holiness (*sanctitas*) of the former is in the ground itself and cannot be removed or destroyed by any force[2] and tombs become holier with the passing of time.

A grave became *res religiosa* when a person who had the right to do so buried a body there. This person was usually the owner.[3]

D. 10. 3. 6. 6 (Ulpian, 19 *ad ed.*). Si quis in communem locum mortuum intulerit, an religiosum fecerit videndum. et sane ius quidem inferendi in sepulchrum unicuique in solidum competit, locum autem purum alter non potest facere religiosum. Trebatius autem et Labeo

[1] For texts and discussion see Watson, *Obligations*, pp. 226 f.

[2] I do not think that this can be taken as implying that the holiness of the ground will remain even if the corpse is removed.

[3] For the situations which might arise in classical law see the texts in the Digest title, 11. 7.

quamquam putant non esse locum religiosum factum, tamen putant in factum agendum.

In this text the opinion of Trebatius is given in respect of the situation where one co-owner buries a body in a *locus purus*[1]—otherwise the text could not read *non esse locum religiosum factum*. Trebatius' view (and that of Labeo) is that one co-owner by burying a corpse on the land cannot turn the grave into a *locus religiosus*. But he does allow an *actio in factum* against him. This *actio* is presumably not decretal but that under the edict, *si quis mortuum in locum alterius intulerit vel inferre curaverit*. This edict, according to Lenel's reconstruction,[2] runs: *Si*[*ve*] *homo mortuus ossave hominis mortui in locum purum alterius aut in id sepulchrum, in quo ius non fuerit, illata esse dicentur.* [*qui hoc fecit, in factum actione tenetur et poena pecuniaria subicietur.*] Ulpian, in similar circumstances to those of D. 10. 3. 6. 6, would himself prefer to give the *actio familiae erciscundae* or *actio communi dividundo*.[3] Still, one can easily imagine that the injured co-owner would not necessarily wish the estate to be divided[4] and then he would have to have recourse to the *actio in factum*.[5]

A rather special case is discussed in Cicero, *de leg*. 2. 23. 58.

> ... Nostis extra portam Collinam aedem Honoris; aram in eo loco fuisse memoriae proditum est, ad eam cum lamina esset inventa et in ea scriptum, HONORIS, ea causa fuit, cur aedis haec dedicaretur. Sed cum multa in eo loco sepulchra fuissent, exarata sunt: statuit enim collegium locum publicum non potuisse privata religione obligari.

Thus, a public place does not become a *locus religiosus* if a private individual buries a corpse there. The date of this decision of the

[1] So we need not consider the regime of the common grave of the situation in *et sane . . . competit*: but see most recently De Visscher, *Le Droit des tombeaux romains* (Milan, 1963), p. 125; G. Longo, *Iura* xv (1964) 147 ff.

[2] *EP*, p. 226.

[3] D. 11. 7. 2. 1 (Ulpian, 25 *ad ed.*).

[4] No text for the Republic is concerned with the question of how much of the land would become *religiosus* when a body was properly buried. One cannot argue that since the XII Tables [Cicero, *de leg*. 2. 24. 61] expressly prohibited the *usucapio* of the entrance to the tomb (*forum*) it must have remained in private ownership, for the same provision forbade the *usucapio* of the *bustum* which is the term used for the place where a body is burned and buried: Festus, s.v. *bustum*.

[5] Similarly for instance in cases of *damnum iniuria datum* by one co-owner, the other might bring against him an *actio legis Aquiliae*: e.g. D. 10. 2. 16. 5; 10. 3. 10 pr.

pontiffs is unknown, but we know that a temple to Honos was erected by Q. Fabius Maximus in 233 B.C. in front of the Porta Capena,[1] and Samter suggests that the temple in front of the Porta Collina may be the oldest dedicated to Honos.[2]

Though it is not really relevant, an edict which is so closely connected with the one just mentioned that it is dealt with in the same Digest title may perhaps be best discussed here. That is the *edictum de sumptibus funerum* which Lenel reconstructs thus:[3] *Quod funeris causa sumptus factus erit, eius reciperandi nomine in eum, ad quem ea res pertinet, iudicium dabo.* There are two texts.

D. 11. 7. 14. 11 (Ulpian, 25 *ad ed.*). Si quis, dum se heredem putat, patrem familias funeraverit, funeraria actione uti non poterit, quia non hoc animo fecit, quasi alienum negotium gerens: et ita Trebatius et Proculus putat. puto tamen et ei ex causa dandam actionem funerariam.

If someone thought he was the heir and buried the *paterfamilias*, Trebatius (and Proculus) took the view that he could not bring the action under this edict because he was not intending to act on behalf of another (*quasi alienum negotium gerens*).[4] This text tells us both that the heir might be the person responsible for the burial[5] and that for expenses to be recoverable the person who undertook the burial had to be aware that he was not the person responsible.

D. 11. 7. 16 (Ulpian, 25 *ad ed.*). In eum, ad quem dotis nomine quid pervenerit, dat praetor funerariam actionem: aequissimum enim visum est veteribus mulieres quasi de patrimoniis suis ita de dotibus funerari et eum, qui morte mulieris dotem lucratur, in funus conferre debere, sive pater mulieris est sive maritus.

When a woman dies, the *veteres* would give this action against the persons who become entitled to part of the dowry.[6]

[1] Latte, *Römische Religionsgeschichte* (Munich, 1960), pp. 235 f.

[2] *RE* viii. 2, 2293.

[3] *EP*, pp. 229 ff.

[4] The substance is not affected if *hoc animo* is, as has been suggested, interpolated: cf. *Index Itp.* The question of the genuineness of *puto* to the end does not concern us: but cf. *Index Itp.*

[5] Though the person appointed by the deceased apparently had the first responsibility: for the rules as we know them in classical law see, above all, D. 11. 7. 12. 4 (Ulpian, 25 *ad ed.*).

[6] The substance is not affected by Lenel's suggestion that *dat praetor funerariam actionem* is interpolated: *Pal.* ii. 566, n. 3; followed by Krüger, *Stereotype Digest*, *ad h.l. Sive* to the end may be interpolated, as De Francisci suggests,

To judge from a text of Cicero, the burial place did not become a *locus religiosus* until the proper rites were carried out.

de leg. 2. 22. 57. . . . Declarat enim Ennius de Africano: 'Hic est ille situs.' Vere, nam siti dicuntur ii, qui conditi sunt. Nec tamen eorum ante sepulchrum est, quam iusta facta et porcus caesus est. Et quod nunc communiter in omnibus sepultis venit usu *ut* humati dicantur, id erat proprium tum in iis, quos humus iniecta cont*ex*eret, eumque morem ius pontificale confirmat. Nam priusquam in os*sa* iniecta gleba est, locus ille, ubi crematum est corpus, nihil habet religionis. Iniecta gleba tum et ill*ic* humatus est, et *sepulchrum* vocatur: ac tum denique multa religiosa iura complectitur . . .[1]

Thus, a pig had to be sacrificed and earth cast upon the human corpse.[2] It is pontifical law which determines the moment when the tomb becomes *locus religiosus*.[3]

In classical law there were two main kinds of tomb, *familiaria sepulchra* where the right to be buried there descended to the *familia*, *sepulchra hereditaria* where the right descended to the heirs.[4] The existence of both kinds seems to be attested by funerary inscriptions from the second century B.C. which read *H M H N S* meaning *hoc monumentum heredem non sequetur* and *H M H E N S* meaning *hoc monumentum heredem exterum non sequetur*.[5] These inscriptions necessarily testify to the existence of *sepulchra hereditaria* and of another regime, i.e. *sepulchra familiaria*. Cicero also tells us that it was not *fas* to bury in a grave the corpses of persons who did not belong to the *gens* and who were *extra sacra*, that is, who did not participate in its rites.[6]

Cicero further tells us of a number of provisions of the XII Tables on funerals which apparently were still in force in his own

Annali Perugia xxxii (1920) 41; the indicative would at least suggest that it should not be relied upon as going back to the *veteres*. Beseler would hold the whole text interpolated because of its 'unklassische Diktion': *ZSS* xliv (1924) 391; *ZSS* xlv (1925) 451. But it is impossible that a whole *lex* would be fabricated and attributed to a particular jurist.

[1] Cf. *de leg.* 2. 22. 55: . . . *neque necesse est edisseri a nobis . . . quo tempore incipiat sepulchrum esse et religione teneatur.*

[2] Cf. De Visscher, op. cit., p. 23. See that work also for burial rites in general.

[3] Cf. De Visscher, 'Les XII Tables et la protection des tombeaux', *Mélanges Meylan* i. 361.

[4] Cf., e.g., D. 11. 7. 5 (Gaius, 19 *ad ed. prov.*): cf. De Visscher, *Le Droit des tombeaux*, pp. 93 ff.

[5] Cf. De Visscher, op. cit., pp. 101 f.

[6] *De leg.* 2. 22. 55.

day. Of these the most important was that a dead man was not to be buried or burned within the city.[1] Certain exceptions, on account of merit, were made to this.[2] No new funeral pyre or *bustum*[3] was to be erected nearer than 60 feet to another's building without the owner's consent.[4] *Usucapio* of the entrance court of a tomb (*forum*) and of the *bustum* was prohibited.[5] Still other provisions had the function of limiting the extravagance of mourning but these are too far removed from the idea of *res religiosa* to be discussed here.[6]

The only significant text for the Republic on *res sanctae* is Festus, s.v. *religiosus* which has already been quoted and which said that the wall round a city was *sanctum*. To judge from later texts *res sanctae* did not belong to the gods but were under their protection.[7] It is probably the nature of a city wall as *res sancta* which accounts for Cicero, *de orat*. 2. 24. 100.

> Hoc in ludo non praecipitur; faciles enim causae ad pueros deferuntur; lex peregrinum vetat in murum ascendere; ascendit; hostis reppulit: accusatur. . . .

Still, not too much reliance should be placed on the text since the statutory prohibition on a peregrine to climb a wall is given as the basis for an example of typical schoolroom rhetorical problems. Such a prohibition, for Cicero's purposes, need never have existed in fact.

A *res religiosa* or *sacra* could be reconverted into private use and ownership and such a thing was termed *profana*.

> Macrobius, *Sat*. 3. 3. 4. eo accedit quod Trebatius profanum id proprie dici ait quod ex religioso vel sacro in hominum usum proprietatemque conversum est . . .

An illustration of how this could come about is given in the *lex a vicanis Furfensibus templo Iovis dicta* of 58 B.C.[8] from line 7.

[1] '*Hominem mortuum in urbe ne sepelito neve urito*': *de leg*. 2. 23. 58.

[2] Cf. Cicero, *de leg*. 2. 23. 58.

[3] Cf. *supra*, p. 6 n. 4.

[4] '*Rogum bustumve novum propius sexaginta pedes adigi aedes alienas invito domino*': Cicero, *de leg*. 2. 24. 61.

[5] Cicero, *de leg*. 2. 24. 61: *quod autem 'forum', id est vestibulum sepulchri, 'bustumve usu capi' vetat, tuetur ius sepulchrorum.*

[6] See the remaining provisions collected in Tabula X of the XII Tables: *FIRA* i. 66 ff.

[7] Cf. Kaser, *RPR* i. 321 and n. 27.

[8] Bruns, no. 105; *FIRA* iii, no. 72.

Sei quod ad eam aedem donum datum donatum dedicatumque erit, utei liceat oeti, venum dare. Ubei venum datum erit, id profanum esto. Venditio locatio aedilis esto, quem quomque veicus Furfens(is) fecerit, quod se senti*a*t eam rem sine scelere sine piaculo ⟨*vendere locare*⟩ alis ne potesto. Quae pequnia recepta erit, ea pequnia emere conducere locare dare, quo id templum melius honestius seit, liceto. Quae pequnia ad eas res data erit, profana esto, quod d(olo) m(alo) non erit factum. Quod emptum erit aere aut argento, ea pequnia, quae pequnia ad id templum data erit quod emptum erit, eis rebus eadem lex esto, quasei sei dedicatum sit.

The temple statutes lay down that a gift *datum donatum dedicatumque* to the temple may be sold and that where it is sold it is to be *profanum*. And where the gift was subjected to the *dedicatio* it would have become a *res sacra*. The money obtained by the sale may be paid out again under *emptio venditio*, *locatio conductio* or *mutuum* and, if it is, it is to be *profana*. It is reasonable to imagine that the *pecunia* here was never dedicated and that *profana* is being used simply to mean not *sacra*,[1] i.e. the purpose of the clause is simply to make it clear that the recipient of the money is to be regarded as having a good title.

Res publicae were all things owned by the state.[2] When such were stolen the offence committed was *peculatus*, not *furtum*.[3] *Res publicae* were often protected by special interdicts. Two texts on such interdicts for our period have survived.

D. 8. 5. 17. 2 (Alfenus, 2 *dig.*)[4] says that if a man builds a manure heap on a *locus publicus* against his neighbour's wall he can be compelled to remove it by an *interdictum*. Which *interdictum* is not stated, and, so far as I can discover, no modern writer has discussed the identity of this *interdictum*. In earlier times the honour was given to one of two interdicts. One suggestion was *ne quid in loco publico vel itinere fiat*.[5] Lenel's reconstruction of the edict, which is not doubted, runs as follows:[6] *Ne quid in loco publico facias inve eum locum immittas, qua ex re quid illi damni detur,*

[1] For *profanus* with this meaning see, e.g., D. 1. 8. 6. 3; 11. 7. 40.

[2] In classical law at least, things belonging to *municipia* were also designated *res publicae*: cf., e.g., Schulz, *Classical Roman Law* (Oxford, 1951), pp. 340 f.

[3] For texts and discussion see Watson, *Obligations*, pp. 226 f.

[4] Quoted and discussed *infra*, pp. 142 f.; discussed further *infra*, pp. 177 ff.

[5] Cf. the *glossa magna, ad h.l.*; Gothofredus, *ad h.l.*

[6] *EP*, p. 458.

praeterquam quod lege senatusconsulto edicto[1] *tibi concessum est. De eo, quod factum erit, interdictum non dabo.* But this interdict—at least in that form—can be excluded.[2] Although the interdict will be given where an individual will be injured[3] it is prohibitory not restitutory[4] and it is not given in respect of past behaviour.[5] Only if one were prepared to hold that the last clause was added to the interdict after the time of Alfenus and that, despite its wording as prohibitory, the praetor was prepared to use the interdict here also as restitutory[6] could one say that this is the interdict which Alfenus (or Servius) had in mind. The other interdict suggested is *quod in itinere publico factum erit, ut restituatur.*[7] That interdict runs:[8] *In via publica itinereve publico facere immittere quid, quo ea via idve iter deterius sit fiat, veto.* This interdict certainly was in existence in the time of Ofilius[9] but it cannot have been the interdict contemplated in the text. The question put to Alfenus (or Servius) did not reveal anything about the nature of the ground where the manure heap was put, so that the answer considered alternative remedies both where the land was public and where it was private. There is nothing in the question which would indicate that a *via* or *iter* was involved and so the general nature of the reply excludes the possibility that the interdict can be recommended only because the manure heap interferes with a *via publica* or *iter publicum*. But no other known interdict seems to fulfil the requirements of the circumstances. Perhaps the most likely solution is that the text envisages an interdict which was the forerunner of *ne quid in loco publico vel itinere fiat* and which was, at least to some extent, restitutory. This may have been found to be inconveniently wide in scope and so replaced.

D. 43. 8. 2. 39 (Ulpian, 68 *ad ed.*) Unde Ofilius putat eum, qui pro derelicto reliquit id opus quod fecit, si viam publicam corrupit et reliquit, non teneri hoc interdicto: non enim habet quod fecit. sed an in eum actio debeat dari, videbimus. et puto utile interdictum competere, ut, quod in via publica aedificavit, restituat.

[1] After *edicto* appeared *decretove principum* in the Empire.

[2] Cf. the *glossa magna*.

[3] D. 43. 8. 2. 2, 5.

[4] D. 43. 8. 2. 2, 7.

[5] D. 43. 8. 2. 17, 18.

[6] Because the inconvenience caused to the owner of the manure heap would be slight relative to the harm caused to the owner of the wall?

[7] Cf. the *glossa magna*.

[8] Lenel, *EP*, p. 458.

[9] D. 43. 8. 2. 39.

This text is concerned with the interdict *quod in itinere publico factum erit, ut restituatur*. Mommsen would delete *et reliquit*[1], presumably as a scribal error, and Schmidt[2] regards it as a gloss. Lenel thinks that *si* to *reliquit* is a gloss.[3] None of these suggestions affects the substance.[4] The text itself, like the surrounding fragments, is concerned with the question of who can be compelled to restore the *via publica* to its former condition. Ofilius thought that if a person constructed something on the public highway and then abandoned it (*pro derelicto reliquit*) he was not liable to the interdict. Whether the reason given in the text, *non enim habet quod fecit*, goes back to Ofilius, is Ulpian's own, or is—as Bremer[5] thinks—an interpolation does not really matter since it is difficult to see what other reason could possibly have caused Ofilius' decision.

A very particular case is discussed in D. 41. 1. 41 (Ulpian, 9 *ad ed.*).

> Statuas in civitate positas civium non esse, idque Trebatius et Pegasus: dare tamen operam praetorem oportere ut, quod ea mente in publico positum est, ne liceret privato auferre, nec ei qui posuerit. tuendi ergo cives erunt et adversus petentem exceptione et actione adversus possidentem iuvandi.

Trebatius (and Pegasus) declared that statues placed *in civitate* do not become the property of the citizens. The infinitive *oportere* shows that *dare* to *posuerit* is in indirect speech but whether it goes back to Trebatius in the Republic or only to Pegasus cannot be determined. In any event, very little for us can really be deduced from the text since we are not told to what sort of intention *ea mente* refers. A number of other texts from the Digest—none of which, however, concerns the Republic—shows that the legal position would depend on the intention of the person responsible for placing the statue *in publico* and that, moreover, there was apparently disagreement among the jurists.[6]

[1] *Digesta Iustiniani Augusti* (Berlin, 1870), ii. 567, n. 1.

[2] *Das Interdiktenverfahren der Römer* (Leipzig, 1853), p. 15, n. 6; followed, e.g., by Beretta, *Studi Albertario* (Milan, 1953) ii. 143.

[3] *Pal.*, ii. 809, n .1.

[4] Beretta's view that *sed . . . restituat* is interpolated does not concern us: loc. cit.

[5] *Iurisprudentiae Antehadrianae quae supersunt* (Leipzig, 1896), i. 342.

[6] The problem has recently been dealt with by Düll, 'Zum Recht der Bildwerke in der Antike', *Studi Betti* (Milan, 1962) iii. 131 ff. at pp. 136 ff. But this

Jurisprudentially of great interest in this connection are those things which could not be owned by individuals. There is only one text.

Cicero, *top.* 7. 32. Sed ego a vestris exemplis, nisi necessario, non recedam. Solebat igitur Aquilius, conlega et familiaris meus, cum de litoribus ageretur, quae omnia publica esse vultis, quaerentibus eis, quos ad id pertinebat, quid esset litus, ita definire, qua fluctus eluderet; hoc est quasi qui adulescentiam florem aetatis, senectutem occasum vitae velit definire; translatione utens discedebat a verbis propriis rerum ac suis. Quod ad definitiones attinet, hactenus; reliqua videamus.

Thus, according to Cicero, all *litora* are *publica.* It would be very dangerous to conclude from this that Cicero means that the sea-shore is owned by the state. Nothing more may be meant than that it is owned by no individual and can be used by everyone.[1] Cicero's main concern is not with the exact legal status of *litora.* Aquilius Gallus defined *litus* as *qua fluctus eludit.* Cicero objects to this definition because it departs from the words appropriate to the thing and to a jurist. One might also feel that the definition is not precise enough and leaves considerable room for doubt as to the extent of the sea-shore.

Things which belonged to the gods or to the state or whose use was public are sometimes called *res quorum commercium non est.*[2]

Cicero, *in Verr.* II. 3. 40. 93. Diocles est Panhormitanus, Phimes

part of his article is unsatisfactory: (*a*) What appears to be the most important text, D. 42. 5. 29 (Paul, 5 *ad leg. Iuliam et Papiam*) is not mentioned at all. (*b*) Our text, D. 41. 1. 41, is thought to be related to the situation where a private person exhibits statues temporarily on public ground under a *lex locationis.* But there is nothing at all in the text to suggest that this was the case. (*c*) In D. 43. 24. 11. 1 (Ulpian, 71 *ad ed.*) the statue has become the property of the *municipes.* The *actio furti* is given to them *quia res eorum sit quasi publicata.* This can only mean that they are the owners as if by *publicatio.* Düll's interpretation that the thing is regarded to a certain extent as the public property of the community ['es handle sich bei ihnen um eine gewissermassen als öffentliches Gut der Gemeinde anzusehende Sache (*res quasi publicata*)'] is impossible since it is completely excluded by the presence of *eorum. Eum cuius statua,* therefore, cannot mean the owner of the statue, but the person in whose honour the statue was erected. It is easy to imagine that such a person would have certain rights: cf. D. 42. 5. 29.

[1] Cf. D. 41. 1. 14 pr. (Neratius, 5 *membran.*) . . . *nam litora publica non ita sunt, ut ea quae in patrimonio sunt populi, sed ut ea, quae primum a natura prodita sunt et in nullius adhuc dominium pervenerunt:* . . .; cf. Kaser, *RPR* i. 321 f. and the references he gives.

[2] Cf. Kaser, 'Vom Begriff des "*commercium*" ', *Studi Arangio-Ruiz* (Naples, n. d.) ii. 131 ff. at pp. 161 ff.

cognomine, homo illustris ac nobilis. Arabat is agrum conductum in Segestano; nam commercium in eo agro nemini est; conductum habebat HS sex milibus. . . .

Here the absence of *commercium* is absolute; but there could also be relative absence of *commercium.*[1]

D. 31. 49. 2 (Paul, 5 *ad leg. Iuliam et Papiam*). Labeo refert agrum, cuius commercium non habes, legari tibi posse Trebatium respondisse, quod merito Priscus Fulcinius falsum esse aiebat.

Kaser correctly points out that this text and others relating to the Empire are not simply concerned with *res divini iuris* or *res publicae* but with prohibition of acquisition by the transferee. There could be various reasons for the prohibition on acquisition.

The last distinction to be dealt with in this chapter is that between corporeals, i.e. things *quae tangi possunt*,[2] and incorporeals, i.e. things *quae tangi non possunt.*[3] The distinction is found in Cicero.

top. 5. 27. Esse ea dico quae cerni tangique possunt, ut fundum aedes, parietem stillicidium, mancipium pecudem, suppellectilem penus et cetera; quo ex genere quaedam interdum vobis definienda sunt. Non esse rursus ea dico quae tangi demonstrarive non possunt, cerni tamen animo atque intellegi possunt, ut si usus capionem, si tutelam, si gentem, si agnationem definias, quarum rerum nullum subest [quasi] corpus, est tamen quaedam conformatio insignita et impressa intellegentia, quam notionem voco. Ea saepe in argumentando definitione explicanda est.

That Cicero is thinking of the distinction not simply in philosophical but also in legal terms is shown by his choice of legal concepts as his examples of incorporeal things.[4] The sole important practical effect of the distinction is that incorporeal *res nec mancipi* could not be transferred by *traditio* but required *in iure cessio*.[5,6] It is from time to time suggested[7] that since Cicero counts *paries* and *stillicidium* as corporeals then servitudes must at that time still have been regarded as corporeal. For Albanese this seems

[1] Cf. Kaser, op. cit., pp. 161, 164 ff. [2] G. 2. 13. [3] G. 2. 14.

[4] Cf. Bonfante II. i. 8 f.: Schulz claims that Cicero's definition comes from a legal source and that he is not relying upon his memory (*Principles of Roman Law* (Oxford, 1956), p. 47).

[5] G. 2. 28.

[6] Though it has to be pointed out that concepts such as *usucapio*, *gens*, *agnatio* could not be transferred at all.

[7] e.g. Albanese, *Annali Palermo* xx (1949) 364 ff.; Yaron, 227.

to be an argument for a late date for the *lex Scribonia*, which prohibited the *usucapio* of servitudes.[1] The reason for the *lex* was, in his opinion, a change in legal theory after which servitudes were considered as incorporeal.[2] But the *topica* passage should not be used in this way. It tells us nothing for the theory of servitudes. The primary meaning of *paries* is 'wall',[3] and of *stillicidium* 'dripping water';[4] in both cases a corporeal thing. When Cicero wants to talk of the servitudes he does not normally say *paries* or *stillicidium* but *ius* (or *iura*) *parietum*[5] or *stillicidiorum*.[6] There is no reason to think that Cicero in the *topica* passage is thinking of servitudes at all.

[1] But see Yaron, pp. 226 ff.

[2] Cf. *infra*, pp. 22 f.

[3] Cf., e.g., Lewis and Short, *A Latin Dictionary* (Oxford, 1879), p. 1303.

[4] Ibidem, p. 1759.

[5] *De leg.* 1. 4. 14; 2. 19. 47; *de orat.* 1. 38. 173.

[6] *De leg.* 1. 4. 14; *de orat.* 1. 38. 173. In *orator* 21. 72 he does, however, have *de stillicidiis cum apud unum iudicem dicas* when he is thinking of an action brought in respect of the servitude. But it does not follow that the meaning of Cicero is 'When you speak before one judge about the servitude right of dripping water' rather than 'When you speak before one judge about water drips'.

2

ACQUISITION OF OWNERSHIP

THE modes of acquisition of ownership fall into two groups, those which are *iuris civilis* and so are confined to citizens, and those which are *iuris gentium* and available to all. The modes in the first group are *mancipatio*, *in iure cessio*, and *usucapio*.

Mancipatio

Mancipatio was very old and was a formal act[1] of transfer of the ownership of those things which were classified as *res mancipi*. It contained an inherent warranty against eviction which was for double the sum stated in the *mancipatio* and this could not be excluded by agreement between the parties.[2] Where land mancipated had an area less than that stated in the *mancipatio*, an *actio de modo agri* lay for the value of double the difference.[3]

The form, for classical law, is described by Gaius.[4] There had to be five witnesses, Roman citizens of full age, and another person, who had the same qualifications, who held a bronze scale. The transferee grasped with his hand the thing to be mancipated—unless it were land which could be mancipated at a distance—and, holding a bronze ingot, said (where the object was a slave) '*Hunc ego hominem ex iure quiritium meum esse aio isque mihi emptus esto*

[1] For the capacity of pupils and women under *tutela* to take part in *mancipatio* see Watson, *Persons*, pp. 21 ff., 137 f., and 152; for the capacity of slaves, ibid., pp. 183 f. For texts by Plautus which seem relevant to capacity but are not really helpful, see Watson, *Obligations*, p. 75, n. 2.

[2] For the *actio auctoritatis* see Watson, *Persons*, pp. 75 ff. Other texts, Cicero, *ad fam.* 13. 8. 2; *de harusp. resp.* 7. 14, tell us nothing. The *actio* could be brought if eviction occurred within one year of the *mancipatio* or within two years if what was transferred was land: Cicero, *top.* 4. 23; *pro Caecina* 19. 54: cf. Kaser, *RPR* i. 118 f. For *auctoritas* see Mayer-Maly, 'Studien zur Frühgeschichte der *usucapio* II', *ZSS* lxxviii (1961) 221 ff., the authors he cites, and Yaron, pp. 195 ff.

[3] For this action see Watson, *Obligations*, pp. 81 ff.

[4] G. 1. 119–22.

hoc aere aeneaque libra.[1,2] He then struck the scale with the ingot and gave it to the transferor as a symbolic price. This form will also have been in operation in the later Republic. A number of texts testify to the use of the bronze as a symbolic price[3] and to the grasping with the hand.[4] That as early as the beginning of our period the piece of bronze was symbolic and was not the real price is shown by two lines of Plautus, *Truc.*, 273 f. The slave, Truculentus, asks the slave girl, Astaphium, if she wears her bronze (or brass?) rings in order to take things by *mancipatio*: *mancupion qui accipias, gestas tecum ahenos anulos? Pignus da ni ligneae haec sint quas habes Victorias.* The rings—which may be finger rings or earrings—are made of coins which portray the goddess Victoria.

No text for our period gives a list of the things which were classed as *res mancipi*. But Gaius[5] lists them for his time as slaves, oxen, horses, mules, and asses, Italic land whether built on or not, and elsewhere he adds rustic servitudes.[6] The Sabinians held that the animals in that list which were commonly broken to draught or burden were *res mancipi* from birth, but the Proculians required them actually to have been broken in.[7] If, as seems likely, there is some connection between *res mancipi* and things of which there could be *postliminium*, then Cicero, *top.* 8. 36, would suggest that the Proculian view at least was current in the later Republic.[8] Gaius' list of *res mancipi* in all probability also represents the position in our period since the class appears early to have become fixed.[9] That in the Republic provincial land was *nec mancipi* appears from G. 2. 27.

. . . *Praeterea admo*nendi sumus, *quod veteres dicebant soli Italici nexum* esse, provincialis soli nexum non *esse, hanc habere* significationem: solum

[1] It thus appears, unless the text be corrupt, that it was not necessary to state the price: but if it were not stated the *actio auctoritatis* would not lie.

[2] For the meaning of this see, above all, Prichard, 'Terminology in *Mancipatio*,' *LQR* lxxvi (1960), 412 ff.

[3] Varro, *de ling. lat.* 9. 83; cf. 5. 163: Festus, s.v. *rodus*.

[4] Cf. Varro, *de ling. lat.* 6. 85; possibly also Cicero, *ad fam.* 7. 5. 3 (*totum denique hominem tibi ita trado de manu, ut aiunt, in manum tuam istam, et victoria et fide praestantem*).

[5] G. 1. 120. Free persons could also be mancipated as in *coemptio* and *adoptio*: cf. Watson, *Persons*, pp. 24 f. and pp. 88 ff.

[6] G. 2. 29; cf. *infra*, pp. 181 ff.

[7] G. 2. 15. See now Nicosia, *Iura* xviii (1967) 45 ff., which appeared too late for consideration.

[8] Cf. Watson, *Persons*, pp. 253f.

[9] Cf. G. 2. 16.

Italicum mancipi *esse*, provinciale nec mancipi *esse*. aliter enim veteri lingua a*c*tus *vocatur, et quod illis nexus, idem nobis* est mancipa*tio*.

The correctness of the substance of the reconstruction cannot be doubted.[1] Additional evidence is to be found in Cicero, *pro Flacco* 32. 80.

Illud quaero, sintne ista praedia censui censendo, habeant ius civile, sint necne sint mancipi, subsignari apud aerarium aut apud censorem possint. In qua tribu denique ista praedia censuisti?

The *praedia* in question were in Apollonis, a town midway between Sardes and Pergamon in Lydia in the province of Asia. Cicero's question is rhetorical and the answer which he expects in the part which concerns us is that the *praedia* are not *res mancipi*. Admittedly for the benefit of his case he may be implying what is not true but his behaviour would be absurd unless provincial land generally was not *res mancipi*.[2] Although the relevant part of the text is corrupt, Cicero, *ad Att.* 15. 26. 4, shows that *mancipatio* could be made of part—and almost certainly a *pro indiviso* share is meant—of a building.[3] A further text of Cicero, *top.* 10. 45, raises the question of *mancipatio* of things which are not *res mancipi*.

Ficta etiam exempla similitudinis habent vim; sed ea oratoria magis sunt quam vestra; quamquam uti etiam vos soletis, sed hoc modo: Finge mancipio aliquem dedisse id quod mancipio dari non potest. Num idcirco id eius factum est qui accepit? aut num is qui mancipio dedit ob eam rem se ulla re obligavit? . . .

This text is taken as meaning that where there is *mancipatio* of *res nec mancipi* ownership is not transferred[4] and no liability for *auctoritas* can arise.[5] This is very reasonable since the text both speaks of a thing which cannot be given by *mancipatio* and *num*

[1] Cf. David and Nelson, *Gai Institutionum commentarii iv, Kommentar* (Leiden, 1960), pp. 252 f. See also the text from Frontinus, Book 2, printed by Bruns, ii. 86.

[2] The land could not be entered on the *census* because, being provincial, it could not be privately owned: see also Kaser, *EB*, pp. 174 ff.; Gallo, *Studi sulla distinzione fra res mancipi e res nec mancipi* (Turin, 1958), p. 23, n. 7; Jones, *Studies in Roman Government and Law* (Oxford, 1960), p. 147.

[3] See the *apparatus criticus* of Shackleton Bailey, *M. Tulli Ciceronis Epistulae* II. ii (Oxford, 1961), p. 281.

[4] e.g., Leifer, *ZSS* lvii (1937) 204 f.; Kaser, *EB*, p. 171 and n. 30.

[5] e.g. Leifer, *ZSS* lvi (1936) 149; Thormann, *Iura* v (1954) 6.

normally introduces a question which implies a negative answer.[1] None the less it is difficult not to have some doubt as to the accuracy of the first part of the proposition. It is hard to believe that, at a time when the law was as developed as it then was, *mancipatio* of a *res nec mancipi* was not treated as being a valid *traditio*.[2] Perhaps Cicero is making a mistake or it may be, though the suggestion should not be pressed, that by *id quod mancipio dari non potest*, Cicero was meaning incorporeal *res nec mancipi*. Yet another text of Cicero, *top*. 5. 28, occupies a special place in the literature of this subject.

> Atque etiam definitiones aliae sunt partitionum aliae divisionum; partitionum, cum res ea quae proposita est quasi in membra discerpitur, ut si quis ius civile dicat id esse quod in legibus, senatus consultis, rebus iudicatis, iuris peritorum auctoritate, edictis magistratuum, more, aequitate consistat. Divisionum autem definitio formas omnis complectitur quae sub eo genere sunt quod definitur hoc modo: Abalienatio est eius rei quae mancipi est aut traditio alteri nexu aut in iure cessio inter quos ea iure civili fieri possunt.

Recently Sturm devoted a book to the text from the word *abalienatio*[3] and he divided the existing theories on that part of the text into five classes and added a new theory of his own. His own theory has—rightly I think—generally been found to be not satisfactory.[4]

[1] For the construction *num . . . aut num*, cf., e.g., Cicero, *Tusc*. 3. 19: cf. Kühner–Stegmann, *Ausführliche Grammatik der lateinischen Sprache* II, 4th edn. by Thierfelder (Munich, 1962), pp. 529 f.

[2] It is sometimes said that at even quite a late date there could be no *dominium ex iure quiritium* of *res nec mancipi* [cf., e.g., the authors cited by Sturm, *Abalienatio* (Milan, 1957), pp. 36 f.], and it might be thought that Cicero means that *res nec mancipi* transferred by *mancipatio* do not give the transferee ownership *ex iure quiritium* but the *mancipatio* does operate as a *traditio*. But there is not the slightest evidence that in historical times *res nec mancipi* were incapable of being owned *ex iure quiritium*. The distinction between *iuris civilis* and *iuris gentium* modes of acquisition is not in respect of the kind of title one gets but in respect of who can use them. Thus *usucapio*, a civil mode of acquisition of ownership, is restricted to acquisition by *cives* but (*pace*, e.g. Costa, *Cicerone giureconsulto* [Rome, reprint 1964], i. 109) there is no indication that *res nec mancipi* could not be usucapted and no reason to hold that a citizen's right to a usucapted *res nec mancipi* was different from his right to a usucapted *res mancipi*: cf., e.g., Sturm, op. cit., p. 42. The emphasis in the sources for *usucapio* on land and houses (cf. Costa, loc. cit.) is not because only *res mancipi* could be usucapted. G. 2. 50 gives the explanation.

[3] Op. cit.

[4] See, e.g., the reviews by Guarino, *Labeo* iv (1958) 358 ff.; Kaser, *ZSS* lxxv (1958) 410 ff.

But he has, I feel, shown that there is no distinction in juristic usage between *abalienatio* and *alienatio*[1] and that *traditio alteri nexu* means *mancipatio*.[2] Of his criticisms of the five classes of theories on the text,[3] one alone is unconvincing, namely that of those who hold that the *topica* are not giving a definition of *abalienatio* but are limited to teaching us by which acts *res mancipi* are transferred.[4] To this class of theory he objects that if Cicero had wished to say this he would have given the text a different form and he would not have chosen as a typical *divisionum definitio* a construction where the natural order was inverted and where *est* separated the substantive from its attribute. But Cicero's choice of a legal *divisionum definitio* could well have been limited either by what he could remember (if, as he claims, he had no books with him aboard ship when composing the *topica*)[5] or by what could be found in the literature available (if he did have some books). And the form of the original text could well have depended on its context[6] and the emphasis wanted. Perhaps the text should be punctuated rather differently: *Abalienatio est, eius rei quae mancipi est, aut traditio alteri nexu aut in iure cessio*, etc. 'The act of alienation is, for a *res mancipi*, either *mancipatio* or *in iure cessio*, etc.'[7]

In iure cessio

This mode of transfer derives from a new application of the old *legis actio sacramento in rem*. Where ownership was to be transferred, the transferor and transferee appeared with the thing before the praetor, the transferee claimed the thing was his, the

[1] Op. cit., pp. 77 ff. [2] Op. cit., pp. 155 ff. [3] Op. cit., pp. 41 f.

[4] See for the supporters of this view Sturm, op. cit., pp. 37 f.

[5] On this question see, e.g., Sturm, op. cit., pp. 47 ff. The composition of the *topica* will be discussed in a later volume on *Legal Science in the Later Roman Republic*.

[6] Kaser thinks of an original context in a commentary on the word *abalienatio* as it appeared in a statute or edict, etc. which concerned only *res mancipi*: *ZSS* lxxv (1958), 411.

[7] For accessories in *mancipatio* see D. 18. 1. 40. 1 (Paul, 4 *epit. Alfeni dig.*) *infra*, pp. 186 ff.; 8. 3. 30 (idem), *infra*, pp. 184 f. Whether D. 26. 8. 12 (Julian, 21 *dig.*) is concerned with *mancipatio* or not is not clear: *infra*, pp. 78 f. No help for the law on *mancipatio* is provided by Cicero, *ad Att.* 1. 1. 3; *ad fam.* 7. 29. 1; *de harusp. resp.* 7. 14. For Varro, *de re rust.* 2. 10. 4 see *infra*, p. 21.

transferor said nothing or informally admitted the claim, and the praetor made *addictio* of the thing to the transferee.[1] When it arose is not certain but it is likely to have been in the earlier part of the Republic.[2] The scope of *in iure cessio* was very wide since it could be used for all purposes attainable by the imitation of an *actio in rem*, e.g. the transfer of ownership of both *res mancipi* and *res nec mancipi*,[3] creation of servitudes and of usufruct, cession of *tutela*, adoption, etc. There are only two texts for our period which are concerned with *in iure cessio* as a mode of transferring ownership. One is Cicero, *top.* 5. 28. The other is Varro, *de re rust.* 2. 10. 4,[4] which really tells us nothing of significance for *in iure cessio*. The paucity of texts—especially since neither of those which we have is concerned with a concrete case—may be an indication that *in iure cessio* was seldom used for the purpose of transferring ownership. Except in the case of incorporeal *res nec mancipi* there were more convenient modes of transfer.

Usucapio

Usucapio is the acquisition of ownership of a thing through possessing it without interruption for a certain period of time. It underwent vast changes between the XII Tables and classical law.[5]

Certain things could not be usucapted. *Res sacrae* could not be usucapted, nor could *res religiosae*. The former prohibition,

[1] Cf. G. 2. 24.

[2] Cf., e.g., Kaser, *EB*, p. 201. V.F. 50 (Paul, 1 *man.*) is by no means proof that *in iure cessio* goes back to the XII Tables: cf. Kaser, loc. cit. No one has, as yet, given a satisfactory explanation of the meaning in that text of *quia . . . confirmat* and it may be interpolated: cf. Wieacker, *Textstufen klassischer Juristen* (Göttingen, 1960), p. 383; Schulz, *Geschichte der römischen Rechtswissenschaft* (Weimar, 1961), pp. 218 f.; and the authors they cite. Kaser seems most recently to think that *in iure cessio* went back to the XII Tables but is not much earlier: *RPR* i, p. 43; but see *infra*, p. 93 and n. 1.

[3] There seems to be no reason to think that there ever was a time when it could not be used for the transfer of *res nec mancipi*: cf. Kaser, *EB*, p. 200.

[4] Quoted *infra*, p. 69.

[5] Whether it was originally not a mode of acquisition of ownership but a procedural rule whereby a person who had had a thing in his possession for the relevant time could defend himself against a *vindicatio* simply by proving that he had had control for that period does not concern us since it seems agreed that even before the beginning of our period it was a mode of acquisition of ownership: for literature, etc. see now Yaron, pp. 191 ff.

according to Cicero, was not laid down expressly by the *ius civile* but was a rule of the *ius gentium*.[1] For the latter prohibition the sole evidence for our period is in Cicero, *de leg*. 2. 24. 61, where he tells us that the XII Tables laid down that the entrance court of a tomb and the *bustum* could not be usucapted.[2,3] Again, under the XII Tables, the five *pedes* separating *fundi* could not be usucapted.[4]

Servitudes could be usucapted at one time but *usucapio* of them was prohibited by a *lex Scribonia*.[5] There has been considerable controversy as to whether Cicero, *pro Caecina* 26. 74, shows that *usucapio* of rustic praedial servitudes was still possible in 69 B.C., the date of that speech.

> . . . Fundus a patre relinqui potest, at usucapio fundi, hoc est finis sollicitudinis ac periculi litium, non a patre relinquitur, sed a legibus; aquae ductus, haustus, iter, actus a patre, sed rata auctoritas harum rerum omnium ab civili iure sumitur.

Despite the opposition of scholars such as Karlowa,[6] Costa,[7] and Biondi,[8] it is difficult not to follow Voigt[9] and Albanese[10] when they hold that *auctoritas* is used technically and in apposition to the preceding *usucapio fundi*. It is enough to refer to Cicero, *top*. 4. 23, with its *usus auctoritas fundi biennium est . . . sunt ceterarum rerum omnium quarum annuus est usus*, and to the *pro Caecina*, 19. 54, which has *lex usum et auctoritatem fundi iubet esse biennium*. And if *auctoritas* is being used in this way then Cicero is saying that there could be *usucapio* of the rustic praedial servitudes. Yaron[11] has a very ingenious argument to combat the deductions of Albanese from the *pro Caecina*. He points out that all that the *lex Scribonia* can have done is prohibit the creation of new servitudes by *usucapio*. It cannot

[1] *De harusp. resp*. 14. 32: quoted *supra*, p. 4.

[2] The relevant part of the text is quoted *supra*, p. 9, n. 4; cf. also pp. 8 and 6, n. 4.

[3] For the prohibition of *usucapio* of *res sacrae* and *res religiosae* in classical law see, e.g., G. 2. 48; D. 41. 3. 9 (Gaius, 4 *ad ed. prov*.).

[4] Cicero, *de leg*. 1. 21. 55: quoted and discussed *infra*, p. 111; cf. Mayer-Maly, 'Frühgeschichte II', pp. 256 ff.

[5] Cf. Rotondi, *Leges*, p. 414.

[6] *Römische Rechtsgeschichte* (Leipzig, 1901), ii. 546.

[7] *Cicerone giureconsulto* (Rome, 1964), i. 134 f.

[8] *Le servitù prediali nel diritto romano*, 2nd edn. (Milan, 1954), p. 276.

[9] *Römische Rechtsgeschichte* (Leipzig, 1892), i. p. 442 and n. 3.

[10] *Annali Palermo* xx (1949) 369 f.

[11] Yaron, pp. 226 f.

have prevented a person usucapting a piece of land from usucapting any servitudes which run with the land. Hence, he says, even if one were to admit—for the sake of argument—that Albanese's interpretation is the one to be followed, the passage would lose all specific probative force for the point in issue. Cicero could be thinking, that is, of the *usucapio* of a *fundus* and of the *usucapio* of the servitudes which were attached to that *fundus*. Though this argument seems logically impeccable the natural interpretation of Cicero's words seems to be that the servitudes are acquired as single individual things not just as parts of an estate.

Rotondi's suggested date for the *lex Scribonia*, 50 B.C., when C. Scribonius Curio was tribune of the plebs, seems quite plausible.[1] In the Empire, the jurist Paul says that servitudes are incorporeal and therefore cannot be usucapted, and it has sometimes been suggested in modern times that the *lex Scribonia* was passed to prohibit *usucapio* once it was recognized that servitudes were not corporeal.[2, 3] But although such a changed conception of the nature of servitudes might not be completely without influence, a change in theory by itself would not be enough to cause the introduction of a statute altering the practical law.[4] There must have been practical reasons for the change.[5] Again it is not clear which servitudes could be usucapted before the *lex Scribonia*. The idea that there could be *usucapio* of urban servitudes only seems now completely discredited.[6] It has also been suggested that only the four original servitudes could be usucapted[7] but there is no

[1] *Leges*, p. 414.

[2] e.g. Biondi, op. cit., p. 227.

[3] For the expression of slight doubt as to whether any servitudes ever were regarded as corporeal see *infra*, pp. 92 ff.

[4] Cf. Karlowa, op. cit. ii. 545. Also the remarks of Mayer-Maly in a different context (on G. 2. 54); 'Studien zur Frühgeschichte der *usucapio* III', *ZSS* lxxix (1962) 86 ff. at pp. 92 f. And see now Yaron, pp. 226 ff., especially at p. 228.

[5] These practical reasons are unknown, but Karlowa's suggestion has a certain plausibility. He thinks that *usucapio* of servitudes had perhaps caused so many disputes that it did not fulfil its function, namely the establishment of a legal position which was certain: loc. cit. Certainly *usucapio* of servitudes cannot have been very difficult, especially if, as seems likely, *bona fides* was not a requirement. For a rather different explanation see Yaron, pp. 226 ff.

[6] Cf. Karlowa, loc. cit.; Biondi, op. cit., p. 276.

[7] Buckland, *Textbook*, p. 265, n. 1. He refers to P.S. 1. 17. 2; D. 8. 1. 14 pr.; and 41. 3. 4. 28 for this and for the point that the *lex* may not have destroyed water rights. But, as he himself says, P.S. 1. 17. 2 does not show that such a

textual support for this. If the interpretation of *pro Caecina* 26. 74, given above is correct, then, since *aquae haustus* can be usucapted, at least all rustic praedial servitudes were capable of being usucapted. The *lex Scribonia* did not apply to the acquisition of freedom from servitudes[1] and there had to be positive *usucapio* of freedom from urban praedial servitudes.[2,3,4]

Res furtivae also could not be usucapted. There was a provision on this in the XII Tables and this was followed by a *lex Atinia*. The date of the *lex Atinia* is not known[5] but a passage of Aulus Gellius enables us to give an approximate date.

N.A. 17. 7. 1. Legis veteris Atiniae verba sunt: 'Quod subruptum erit, eius rei aeterna auctoritas esto.' 2. Quis aliud putet in hisce verbis quam de tempore tantum futuro legem loqui? 3. Sed Q. Scaevola patrem suum et Brutum et Manilium, viros adprime doctos, quaesisse ait dubitasseque utrumne in post facta modo furta lex valeret an etiam in ante facta; quoniam 'subruptum erit' utrumque tempus videretur ostendere, tam praeteritum quam futurum.

Brutus, Manilius, and Publius Scaevola dealt with the question of retroactivity of the statute and, as Daube has pointed out,[6] this they would not have done if the law had existed for a long time past. The actuality of the discussion has recently been doubted by

right could be so acquired *de novo*. Moreover, that text discusses only *aquaehaustus* and *aquaeductus*, of which the latter alone is one of the original four. I cannot see the relevance of D. 41. 3. 4. 28. D. 8. 1. 14 pr. does in fact discuss the impossibility of *usucapio* of rustic servitudes and only at the end adds that the same applies to urban servitudes. But a number of other texts discuss the four original or the rustic servitudes in general either alone or before the urban servitudes where no conclusions can be drawn as to the nature of the rules under discussion: cf., e.g., D. 8. 1. 5 pr.; 8. 1. 17. The explanation lies simply in the historical order of development of the servitudes.

1 Cf. D. 41. 3. 4. 28(29).

2 D. 8. 2. 7 (Pomponius, 26 *ad Quintum Mucium*): quoted and discussed *infra*, pp. 181 ff.

3 Although we have here a case of *usucapio* of an incorporeal right without *bona fides* it should not be deduced from this that the *lex Scribonia* was not passed—at least partly—because of a change in the theory of the nature of servitudes. It should be noticed that *usucapio* of freedom from a servitude is a very special case in that the *usucapio* is an additional requirement to the rule that servitudes were lost by non-use.

4 For Cicero, *top.* 5. 27 see *supra*, pp. 14 f.

5 For the various suggestions which have been made see now Yaron, pp. 216 ff.

6 *Cambridge Law Journal* vi (1936–8) 233, n. 44.

Mayer-Maly, who suggests that the *lex Atinia* may have become the paradigm case on the retroactivity of statutes.[1] But this does not quite seem to fit the grammar of the passage in question. The verb *valeret* must have been in the present tense in Quintus Mucius, and that verb governs not only *in post facta furta* but also *in ante facta furta*. The question therefore was 'Whether the law applies only to future thefts or also to past thefts?' The present tense in the discussion in respect of thefts committed before and after the *lex* is difficult to explain if the discussion is only of the paradigm case. If for the *lex Atinia* the question were merely theoretical one might have expected either 'Whether the law applies only to future thefts or did also apply to thefts before the statute?'[2] or more likely 'Whether the law applied only to future thefts or also to thefts before the statute?' Manilius was praetor in 155 B.C., consul in 149. Brutus was praetor in 142 B.C. Publius Scaevola was praetor in 136, consul in 133 B.C. Thus, a date around the middle of the second century B.C. seems indicated.[3,4] Cicero's view seems to have been that the *lex Atinia* was not retroactive.

in Verr. II. 1. 42. 109. De iure vero civili si quis novi quid instituit, is non omnia quae ante acta sunt rata esse patietur? Cedo mihi leges Atinias, Furias, Fusias, ipsam, ut dixi, Voconiam, omnis praeterea de iure civili: hoc reperies in omnibus statui ius quo post eam legem populus utatur. . . .

Of the known *leges Atiniae* it would appear that only for our present statute would the question of retroactivity be in any way relevant.[5] So presumably Cicero is thinking of our statute. When one considers the use Cicero is making of this statute—he puts it at the

[1] 'Studien zur Elementarliteratur über die *usucapio*', *Studi Betti* iii. 488 f.; 'Frühgeschichte III', pp. 100 f.

[2] Attraction of the two verbs into the present tense, though no doubt possible, is quite unlikely.

[3] Cf. Yaron, pp. 214 ff.

[4] Aulus Gellius in §§ 4–8 continues with the opinion of the first-century B.C. grammarian, P. Nigidius, on the grammatical question, but this adds nothing to our knowledge of the law.

[5] The others are: *lex Atinia* (or *Acilia*) *de coloniis quinquede ducendis*, cf. Rotondi, *Leges*, pp. 266 f.; *Lex Marcia Atinia de pace cum Philippo facienda*, cf. Rotondi, op. cit., p. 267; *lex Atinia de tribunis plebis in senatum legendis*, cf. Rotondi, op. cit., pp. 330 f.

head of the list—it seems reasonable to imagine that the view which prevailed was that the *lex Atinia* was not retroactive.[1]

We know the wording of the main provision of the *lex Atinia* from Aulus Gellius, namely *Quod subruptum erit, eius rei aeterna auctoritas esto*. This provision was restricted by a further clause.

D. 41. 3. 4. 6 (Paul, 54 *ad ed.*). Quod autem dicit lex Atinia, ut res furtiva non usucapiatur, nisi in potestatem eius, cui subrepta est, revertatur, sic acceptum est, ut in domini potestatem debeat reverti, non in eius utique, cui subreptum est. igitur creditori subrepta et ei, cui commodata est, in potestatem domini redire debet.

Thus, the *lex* declared that there was to be no *usucapio*, *nisi in potestatem eius, cui subrepta est revertatur*.[2] Paul tells us that it was settled that this clause meant that for *usucapio* the thing had to return *in domini potestatem*. No text indicates how the provision was interpreted in the Republic.

Before the *lex Atinia* was passed, a provision of the XII Tables governed the question of *usucapio* of *res furtivae*. The main source of our knowledge of these is Gaius' Institutes.[3]

2. 45. Sed aliquando etiamsi maxime quis bona fide alienam rem possideat, non tamen ill*i* usucapio procedit, velut si qui*s* rem furtivam aut vi possessam possidea*t*; nam furtivam lex XII tabularum usucapi prohibet, vi possessam lex Iulia et Plautia.

2. 49. Quod ergo vulgo dicitur, furtivarum rerum et vi possessarum usucapionem per lege*m* XII tabularum prohibitam esse, non eo pertinet ut n*e ipse* f*ur quive* per vim *possi*det usucapere *po*ssit (nam huic ali*a* ratione usucapio non competit, quia scilicet mala fide possidet), sed nec ullus alius, quamquam ab eo bona fide emerit, usucapiendi ius habeat.

There has been a wide variety of opinions on the nature of the XII Tables' provision[4] but there are, I want to suggest, two fixed

[1] No argument to the contrary can be drawn from the fact that it is in Cicero's interest that the statutes he refers to were not retroactive, because if the *lex Atinia* as it was understood was not in his favour he did not need to refer to it.

[2] Cf., e.g., Bruns, p. 47, n. 10; Voci, *Modi di acquisto della proprietà* (Milan, 1952), p. 164.

[3] But see also D. 41. 3. 33 pr. (Julian, 44 *dig.*); J. 2. 6. 2; Theoph. 2. 6. 2; all of which refer both to the *lex Atinia* and the XII Tables; cf. now Yaron, p. 216, n. 59 and the references he gives. In general I agree with the negative side of Mayer-Maly's investigation into the scope of the XII Tables' provision ('Frühgeschichte II', pp. 264 ff.), so that no real attempt need be made here to examine these earlier views; cf. also Yaron, p. 217.

[4] For these, see most recently Yaron, pp. 217 ff.

points which can help to limit future discussions. The first emerges from the texts of Gaius and we must remember that he was an expert on the XII Tables and wrote a commentary on them. We can be sure[1]—though it has been doubted—that the XII Tables did contain some clause prohibiting *usucapio* of things which had been stolen. But much more significant is the fact that Gaius takes the XII Tables as being the basis of the law on this point in his own day (*prohibet* in § 45) and does not even mention the *lex Atinia*,[2] This must mean either that the rule of the XII Tables was similar to the law in force after the *lex Atinia* or at least that the wording of the XII Tables was such that it could be so interpreted by Gaius. The second fixed point is that since the discussion by Publius Mucius, Manilius, and Brutus on the retroactivity of the *lex Atinia* cannot be entirely pointless, there must have been a substantial difference between the law in force before the *lex Atinia* and the provisions of that statute. Situations where *usucapio* was now no longer to be possible must have been established by the statute. It is this point which is against the view that the innovation of the statute was that *res furtivae* could be usucapted once they had returned to the person from whom they were taken.[3,4] Only two of the many solutions proposed for the substance of the XII Tables' provision are in harmony with these fixed points. The first is that of Mommsen,[5] which was reshaped by Daube[6] and accepted in principle with certain hesitation by Kaser[7] and Mayer-Maly.[8] This is that the XII Tables simply prohibited *usucapio* by the *fur* but did not generally prohibit the *usucapio* of *res furtivae*. A clause of the XII Tables which declared that a *fur*

[1] Cf. now Yaron, p. 218.

[2] Cf. Mayer-Maly, op. cit., p. 267: 'Nun ist es auffallend daß Gaius von der *lex Atinia* nichts weiß.' But he seems to draw no conclusions from this observation.

[3] For those who hold this view, see Mayer-Maly, op. cit., p. 268, n. 213.

[4] Cf. Mayer-Maly, op. cit., pp. 268 f.; Yaron, p. 218.

[5] *Römisches Strafrecht* (Berlin, 1899), p. 756, n. 1: 'Am nächsten liegt die Annahme. . . .'

[6] '*Furtum proprium* and *furtum improprium*', *Cambridge Law Journal* vi (1936–8) 217 ff.: '. . . is probable for several reasons' (p. 231).

[7] *ZSS* lxviii (1951) 168 ff.: '. . . die mir manches für sich zu haben scheint'; *RPR* i, pp. 119 f.: 'Am ehesten . . .'; *BIDR* lxv (1962) 89 ff.

[8] Op. cit., pp. 264 ff.: 'Solche Erklärung hat in der Tat viel für sich. Als völlig gesichert kann sie freilich nicht gelten'; p. 269: '. . . den höchsten Wahrscheinlichkeitsgrad erreicht.'

could not usucapt could explain the formulation of G. 2. 49. Gaius could be trying to interpret the clause as meaning that *res furtivae* could not be usucapted by means of the argument that the clause cannot have its apparent meaning since *usucapio* by the thief is anyhow, for a different reason, impossible.[1] But various difficulties for this view have been suggested both by Kaser and Mayer-Maly themselves and now by Yaron. Kaser (before he accepted the theory) thought it implausible that in early law a person suing for the return of a thing would have to prove that the defendant was a thief; it should be enough, he thinks, that the plaintiff proved that the thing had been stolen from him by anyone.[2] Mayer-Maly, in his turn, observed that G. 2. 45 refers to the things, not to the thief, and that there is no source which indicates a prohibition of *usucapio* which was restricted to the thief. Again, he finds it rather doubtful that it would have been thought necessary to lay down expressly that the thief could not usucapt. Yaron adds a further objection,[3] namely that it would be difficult to account for an extension of the early prohibition by the *lex Atinia* since any such extension would be unfavourable to commerce. The second theory which fits our two fixed points is that of Yaron himself.[4] He considers that the XII Tables' provision did prohibit the *usucapio* of *res furtivae* but that in the course of time the jurists, in the interests of commerce, relaxed the rules. This development, he suggests, should be looked at in the light of other changes in *usucapio* such as the introduction of the requirement of *bona fides*. The *lex Atinia* then would be the conservative reaction putting back the clock in the name of morality, ancient wisdom, and so on. But against this suggestion it should be observed that Yaron makes no attempt to show how the jurists relaxed the express provision of the XII Tables. It is difficult to see how the provision could have been got rid of in practice since one would expect it to have been

[1] But Daube's suggested reconstruction of the clause as *adversus furem aeterna auctoritas* (op. cit., p. 232) was not accepted by Kaser (*ZSS* lxviii (1951) 168 ff.) or by Mayer-Maly (op. cit., p. 269, n. 217). Kaser now tends to accept Daube's reconstruction: *BIDR* lxv (1962) 90.

[2] *EB*, p. 96.

[3] Yaron, p. 220.

[4] Yaron, pp. 223 ff. He stresses that his views 'do not pretend to be more than a hypothesis'.

appealed to frequently.[1] Moreover, even if in practice the provision of the XII Tables tended to be ignored, if the *lex Atinia* merely reaffirmed the provision of the XII Tables, could the jurists really discuss whether the *lex Atinia* was retroactive?[2]

A special question on *usucapio* of *res furtivae* is raised by D. 41. 10. 4 pr. (Pomponius, 32 *ad Sab.*).

Si ancillam furtivam emisti fide bona, [quodque *ins. Mommsen*] ex ea natum et apud te conceptum est ita possedisti, ut intra constitutum usucapioni tempus cognosceres matrem eius furtivam esse, Trebatius omni modo, quod ita possessum esset, usucaptum esse. ego sic puto distinguendum, ut, si nescieris intra statutum tempus, cuius id mancipium esset, aut si scieris neque potueris certiorem dominum facere, aut si potueris quoque et feceris certiorem, usucaperes: sin vero, cum scires et posses, non feceris certiorem, contra esse: tum enim clam possedisse videberis, neque idem et pro suo et clam possidere potest.

The *Trebatius* of the text becomes *Neratius* in the Greek version which appears in the *Ἑξάβιβλος* of Harmenopoulos.[3] But despite arguments to the contrary, especially those of Riccobono,[4] the presumption must be that *Trebatius* is the correct reading.[5] We are concerned with the text really only so far as *usucaptum esse*. This part of the text is not in perfect form—*quodque* has to be inserted and the verb which *Trebatius* governs is not given—but apart from the interpolation of *constitutum usucapioni tempus* for *annum* the sentence appears to be genuine.[6] Trebatius held that if in good faith you bought a stolen slave girl and while she was under your control she conceived and bore a child, and during the period of *usucapio* you discovered that the mother was *furtiva*, the child will be usucapted.[7] The decision of Trebatius corresponds to that generally held by later jurists.[8] This text also shows that

[1] Cicero, *Phil.* 3. 6. 16 does not aid our knowledge of the *lex Atinia*.

[2] Though Yaron should not be understood to assume formal reaffirmation.

[3] 3. 3. 92.

[4] 'Sul fr. 4 pr. D. *pro suo* e la versione greca riportata da Armenopulo', now in *Scritti di diritto romano* (Palermo, 1957), i. 337 ff.

[5] Cf. Kaser, '*Partus ancillae*', *ZSS* lxxv (1958) 156 ff. at p. 176 and n. 97. For the literature see Kaser, op. cit., p. 176, n. 97.

[6] Ibidem, p. 176. But earlier interpolations had been suggested.

[7] For *omni modo* see *infra*, p. 30.

[8] Cf. Kaser, op. cit., pp. 165 ff. (especially p. 176) and the texts of classical jurists which he gives.

with respect to *usucapio*, as was the case with *ususfructus*,[1] the child born to a slave woman was not regarded as *fructus* since the *fructus* of something possessed in good faith did not have to be usucapted but automatically became the property of the possessor.[2] *Omni modo* in the text has given rise to some difficulty. Thus, it contributed to Riccobono's view that *Trebatius* was an error for *Neratius*.[3] And Kaser says:[4] 'The old dispute as to the rule *partus ancillae in fructu non est* was settled even in the time of Trebatius. But if there were still jurists at that time who wanted the *partus ancillae* treated as fruit, then even in their view the acquirer would become owner, but at once and without the need for *usucapio*. Perhaps one should interpret *omni modo*, "in any event", in this sense.' But there is a simpler explanation. *Omni modo* should be given its normal meaning, 'in every case', or 'in all circumstances', and is simply saying that for Trebatius there are no qualifications to the rule he is propounding. The *omni modo* is explicable in terms of the remainder of the text from *ego sic puto distinguendum*, where various distinctions are drawn. *Omni modo* stresses the difference between the absolute view of Trebatius and the qualified view of the later jurist, and the words probably are to be attributed to the author of the second part of the text, whether one wishes to regard the writer as Pomponius or someone else.[5]

G. 2. 45 also tells us that the *usucapio* of things taken by violence was prohibited by the *lex Iulia et Plautia*. The *lex Plautia* appears to date from between 78 and 63 B.C.[6] It is probably safe to presume that moveable *res vi possessae* counted as *res furtivae* and that as such could not be usucapted even before the *lex Plautia*,[7] but the *lex Plautia*'s provision may have been more specifically concerned with the *usucapio* of land occupied by force. The *lex Iulia* may be

[1] Cf. *infra*, pp. 214 ff.

[2] Cf. Kaser, op. cit., pp. 165 ff.

[3] Op. cit., p. 340.

[4] Op. cit., p. 176, n. 97.

[5] For D. 49. 15. 27 (Iavolenus, 9 *ex post. Lab.*), which also shows that *res furtivae* could not be usucapted, see Watson, *Persons*, p. 254.

[6] Cf. Rotondi, *Leges*, pp. 377 f.

[7] This could explain why in G. 2. 49 we are told that it is commonly said that *usucapio* of *res vi possessae* was prohibited by the XII Tables. But the text has been held corrupt. See now, however, David and Nelson, *Gai Institutionum commentarii iv, Kommentar* , pp. 266 f.

of Julius Caesar—he seems to have been responsible for a possible one around 46 B.C.[1]—or of Augustus.[2]

There were restrictions on the *usucapio* of things belonging to persons of restricted capacity but these have been dealt with in a previous volume.[3]

In classical law in general a person who wanted to usucapt had to have begun his possession of the thing in good faith and to have a *iustus titulus* for his possession. There is very wide agreement that in early law neither *bona fides* nor *iusta causa* was required.[4] We have no real indication as to the time when *bona fides* and *iusta causa* began to be demanded but the dominant view which regards the second century B.C. as quite likely seems plausible.[5] Again, there is considerable controversy as to the relationship between *bona fides* and *iusta causa*.[6] Van Oven, for instance, regards the two elements as forming a unity.[7] Kaser thinks that *bona fides* is later and developed out of the requirement of *iusta causa*.[8] And Voci has suggested that *bona fides* is the earlier.[9] Even for *bona fides* itself, a question of priority has been raised: De Visscher has argued that at first *bona fides* was not required in all cases of *usucapio* but only in those where the transferor was not the owner, and so not where there was simply *traditio* of a *res mancipi*.[10]

But when *bona fides* and *iusta causa* became requirements for *usucapio*, certain cases continued to exist where *bona fides* was not necessary. These were *usucapio pro herede*, *usureceptio*, *usucapio* of freedom from urban servitudes, and probably, though there is no

[1] Cf. Rotondi, *Leges*, pp. 422 f.

[2] Of about 17 B.C.: cf. Rotondi, op. cit., pp. 450 f.

[3] Watson, *Persons*: for *res* of a *pupillus*, pp. 137 f., of a *mulier* under *tutela*, pp. 21 ff. and 152; for D. 41. 3. 34 (Alfenus Varus, 1 *dig. a Paulo epit.*), see p. 179. [Other texts are V.F. 1; Cicero, *ad Att.* 1. 5. 6; D. 26. 8. 4; 41. 4. 2. 8.]

[4] See, most recently, Yaron, pp. 214 f., especially for his treatment of the differing opinion of Mayer-Maly, 'Frühgeschichte III', pp. 97 f.

[5] For this and the other periods which have been suggested see Yaron, p. 214; and see *infra*, pp. 48 ff.

[6] Again for this see Yaron, loc. cit.

[7] *Tijd.* xvi (1939) 434.

[8] *EB*, pp. 296 ff. According to Wubbe, the opinions of Van Oven and Kaser are not mutually exclusive: *Tijd.* xxviii (1960) 14, n. 5.

[9] Op. cit., pp. 210 ff.: *contra*, Mayer-Maly, *RE* ix A i, 1114 ff.

[10] *SDHI* xxii (1956) 104; *SDHI* xxiii (1957) 33: cf. Mayer-Maly, op. cit., 1113.

real evidence, *usucapio* of servitudes.[1] *Usucapio* of servitudes was abolished by the *lex Scribonia*, probably of 50 B.C.[2] *Usucapio* of freedom from servitudes is a very special case. Here and here alone is *usucapio* not a privilege granted to the person allowed to acquire but an additional burden placed upon him since rustic servitudes, the older type, were lost by non-use and the owner of the servient tenement did not have to usucapt freedom from the servitude positively. In the circumstances, it is probably unwise ever to draw conclusions from *usucapio libertatis* for the general nature of *usucapio*.[3] The remaining two cases, *usucapio pro herede* and *usureceptio*, have another feature in common—which, however, does not apply to *usureceptio ex praediatura*—namely, that land is usucapted after one year instead of after the usual two years.[4]

According to Gaius 2. 54 one could at one time usucapt the *hereditas* itself, and that after one year. And he uses this fact to explain why land forming part of an inheritance could still be usucapted after one year. The *usucapio* of a *hereditas* itself is usually thought to have disappeared quite early. The arguments are drawn from Cicero, *de legibus*.

de leg. 2. 19. 48. Exposite haec iura pontificum auctoritate consecuta sunt, ut, ne morte patris familias sacrorum memoria occideret, iis essent ea adiuncta, ad quos eiusdem morte pecunia venerit. hoc uno posito, quod est ad cognitionem disciplinae satis, innumerabilia nascuntur, quibus implentur iuris consultorum libri. quaeruntur enim, qui astringantur sacris. heredum causa iustissima est; nulla est enim persona, quae ad vicem eius, qui e vita emigrarit, propius accedat. deinde, qui morte testamentove eius tantundem capiat, quantum omnes heredes. id quoque ordine; est enim ad id, quod propositum est, adcommodatum. tertio loco, si nemo sit heres, is, qui de bonis, quae eius fuerint, cum

[1] It is from time to time suggested that *usucapio pro derelicto* is another instance of *usucapio* where *bona fides* is not necessary: e.g. Kaser, *EB*, p. 297, n. 12; Mayer-Maly, loc. cit. But it never seems to be so described in the sources and this modern construction may depend on too juristic an attitude to positive requirements for *usucapio*. It is hard to believe that a man is not acting *bona fide* when he takes control of a thing which he thinks has been freely and willingly discarded by its owner, but which, in fact, has been discarded by a non-owner.

[2] Cf. *supra*, pp. 22 f.

[3] Cf. *supra*, p. 24 and n. 3.

[4] Of course even if one felt that *usucapio libertatis* should not be regarded as a very special case, it would not be relevant for this point.

moritur, usu ceperit plurimum possidendo. quarto, qui, si nemo sit, qui ullam rem ceperit, de creditoribus eius plurimum servet. 49. extrema illa persona est, ut is, si qui ei, qui mortuus sit, pecuniam debuerit neminique eam solverit, proinde habeatur, quasi eam pecuniam ceperit.

Cicero is setting out the pontifical rules which existed in his time for determining who had the obligation of performing the *sacra* of a deceased *paterfamilias*. These rules he learnt from Quintus Mucius Scaevola,[1] and they replaced even older pontifical rules:

de leg. 2. 20. 49. Haec nos a Scaevola didicimus, non ita descripta ab antiquis. nam illi quidem his verbis docebant: tribus modis sacris adstringi, aut hereditate, aut si maiorem partem pecuniae capiat, aut, si maior pars pecuniae legata est, si inde quippiam ceperit.

Many modern writers have tended to think of these rules as emanating from pontifical edicts and decrees[2,3] but there is no evidence to suggest such an origin. Indeed, Cicero's language, with its *hoc uno posito . . . innumerabilia nascuntur* in § 48 and *descripta ab antiquis*[4] in § 49 strongly suggests that the pontifical rules derive not from enactments but from a series of pontifical decisions in specific cases.[5] Support for this view would also seem to come from the linking in opinion on a particular point of Tiberius Coruncanius (who was active around 250 B.C.), of Publius Scaevola (who was *pontifex maximus* around 130 B.C.), and of *ceteri* by Cicero in *de leg.* 2. 21. 52.

Hoc ego loco multisque aliis quaero a vobis, Scaevolae, pontifices maximi et homines meo quidem iudicio acutissimi, quid sit quod ad ius pontificium civile appetatis; civilis enim iuris scientia pontificium quodam modo tollitis. nam sacra cum pecunia pontificum auctoritate, nulla lege coniuncta sunt. itaque si vos tantum modo pontifices essetis, pontificalis maneret auctoritas, sed quod idem iuris civilis estis peritissimi, hac scientia illam eluditis. placuit P. Scaevolae et Ti. Coruncanio, pontificibus maximis, itemque ceteris, eos, qui tantundem caperent, quantum omnes heredes, sacris alligari.

[1] Cf. *de leg.* 2. 19. 47 ff.

[2] For these writers see now Franciosi, *Usucapio pro herede* (Naples, 1965), p. 133, nn. 1, 2.

[3] For the forms which priestly declarations of the law might take see Schulz, *Roman Legal Science* (Oxford, 1946), p. 16.

[4] The MSS. variations here do not affect the point.

[5] For this view see now Franciosi, op. cit., pp. 133 ff.

The total impression gained is of a development by case-law where it is possible to distinguish sharply between the position in the time of Cicero and Quintus Mucius and the position at some non-specific time in the past. From § 52 we can probably conclude that this time in the past was before the pontificate of Tiberius Coruncanius.[1] For Coruncanius and the others referred to, persons who took as much (*tantundem*) as all the heirs were to be liable for the *sacra*. This corresponds to what one might call the second provision of the later stage of development, but the earlier stage of development demanded that such a person take a greater share (*maior pars*). Whether we can know much more about the dating of the two sets of rules is doubtful. Mayer-Maly, who thinks that the rules derive from pontifical decrees, would date the older rather from the fourth century B.C. than from the period between 300 and 250 B.C. because the subject-matter of the inheritance is called *pecunia* and one still had to reckon with 'Legatentestamente', i.e. wills which appointed no heir but distributed the inheritance among legatees. But the use of the word *pecunia* in this sense is no indication of extreme antiquity of the pontifical rule. We have no knowledge of when this use of the word *pecunia* became obsolete and the extremely conservative retention of technical terms in full use is a well-known characteristic of both priests and jurists.[2] Nor is there any need to feel that 'Legatentestamente' were still in existence. Mayer-Maly says that the formulation of the earlier decree only sets out that more than half of the *pecunia* be divided into legacies and that nothing is said about the appointment of the

[1] Cf., above all, Bruck, *Über römisches Recht im Rahmen der Kulturgeschichte* (Berlin, Göttingen, Hamburg, 1954), pp. 28 f.; Mayer–Maly, 'Frühgeschichte III', p. 96, who thinks in terms of pontifical decrees; see also the authors cited by Mayer-Maly, op. cit., p. 95. Voci, who also thinks of decrees, thinks that Coruncanius was himself the author of the later decree: *Diritto ereditario romano* (Milan, 1960), i. 116.

[2] And see Cicero, *top*. 6. 29: *Sic igitur veteres praecipiunt: cum sumpseris ea quae sint ei rei quam definire velis cum aliis communia, usque eo persequi, dum proprium efficiatur, quod nullam in aliam rem transferri possit. ut haec 'hereditas est pecunia'. commune adhuc; multa enim genera pecuniae. adde quod sequitur: 'quae morte alicuius ad quempiam pervenit'. nondum est definitio; multis enim modis sine hereditate teneri pecuniae mortuorum possunt. unum adde verbum: 'iure'. iam a communitate res diiuncta videbitur, ut sit explicata definitio sic: 'hereditas est pecunia quae morte alicuius ad quempiam pervenit iure.' nondum est satis; adde: 'nec ea aut legatu testamento aut possessione retenta'. confectum est.*

heir.[1] But these rules, as formulated in § 49 also talked about someone becoming liable, *hereditate*, for the *sacra*. There seems no reason to think that at the time when these rules came into existence the use of the word *hereditas* was restricted to an inheritance descending upon intestacy. Nor is it clear why one should believe that by *aut, si maior pars pecuniae legata est* wills where there was no appointment of an heir were meant. Likewise, the connection between the view of Coruncanius and the relative part of the later pontifical position does not indicate that the whole later position dates from a time shortly after that pontiff. But it has been suggested that Coruncanius does not deserve the credit of having held the view attributed to him by Cicero.[2] The argument is that the *tantundem*-rule presupposes the existence of the limitation introduced by the *lex Voconia* of 169 B.C. that no one legatee could take by legacy more than the heir or all the heirs together instituted in the last will. But this is not so. Certainly, if under the older position Cicero's *si maior pars pecuniae legata est* refers (as one would think) to a legacy to one person, that particular rule would have no practical value after the *lex Voconia* in respect of inheritances within the scope of that clause of the statute,[3] but that is no reason for thinking that the pontiffs could not have created their *tantundem*-rule—which is perfectly reasonable in the context of *sacra*—before the passing of the statute.

Further evidence for the development of the later pontifical position is in Cicero, *de leg.* 2. 20. 50.

> Sed pontificem sequamur. videtis igitur omnia pendere ex uno illo, quod pontifices cum pecunia sacra coniungi volunt isdem ferias et caerimonias adscribendas putant. atque etiam dant hoc Scaevolae, cum est partitio, ut, si in testamento deducta scripta non sit ipsique minus ceperint, quam omnibus heredibus relinquatur, sacris ne alligentur. in donatione hoc idem secus interpretantur, et, quod pater familias in eius donatione, qui in ipsius potestate est, adprobavit, ratum est; quod eo insciente factum est, si id is non adprobat, ratum non est.

The Scaevolae—hence not Quintus Mucius alone but also Publius—considered the situation where legatees voluntarily take less than

[1] Op. cit., p. 94.

[2] Cf. Franciosi, op. cit., pp. 137 ff.

[3] Perhaps only very large inheritances came under the statute: cf. the author's forthcoming *The Law of Succession in the Later Roman Republic*, chapter 12.

all the heirs. *Omnes heredes* must refer to the second rule of the later pontifical position.

The importance of the dating for us is that the third part of the later pontifical position concerns *usucapio pro herede* and the word *plurimum* would seem to indicate that what is under consideration is not *usucapio* of the whole *hereditas* but *usucapio* of individual things.[1] Obviously, the argument would seem to be, for pontiffs concerned with the obligations of the *sacra*, *usucapio hereditatis* would have been much more significant than *usucapio* of individual things so that silence here can be taken as showing that *usucapio hereditatis* was obsolete.[2] But if this argument is correct all that one

[1] Cf. Mayer-Maly, op. cit., p. 91.

[2] *Pace* Mayer-Maly, even if one accepts for the sake of argument that the rules did result from two pontifical decrees nothing more can be learnt from them for the history of *usucapio pro herede*. He thinks that in the earlier decree *aut si maiorem partem pecuniae capiat* refers (exclusively or at least mainly) to *usucapio pro herede* (op. cit., p. 93) and that the person who usucapts is bound to perform the *sacra* rather than one who takes by legacy (*aut si maior pars pecuniae legata est*); whereas in the later decree legatees appear in second place, those usucapting only in third place. Hence, he concludes (op. cit., pp. 94 f.), that the later decree shows that persons usucapting were coming to be regarded more and more as interlopers. But under the earlier decree there can be no question of any such significance in the order between him who *maiorem partem pecuniae capiat* and the person who takes a legacy. First of all, there are good reasons for suspecting the originality of at least part of *aut si maior pars pecuniae legata est, si inde quippiam ceperit*. Lenel thinks, for grammatical and substantive reasons, that *si maior pars pecuniae legata est* is a gloss (*Essays in Legal History*, edited by Vinogradoff (Oxford, 1913), p. 131 and n. 3; but see Korošeć, *Die Erbenhaftung* (1927), p. 103, n. 2; Mayer-Maly, op. cit., p. 94, n. 31). If Lenel is right, then there can be no question of significance in the order. Bruck very reasonably thinks that *si inde quippiam ceperit* was added during the development of the pontifical rule and was intended to stop a legatee trying to avoid his responsibilities for the *sacra* by taking only a smaller part of his legacy (op. cit., p. 28). If this is correct then these two provisions of the decree are not arranged in the order of liability for the *sacra*. The two cases would be mutually exclusive. There could not, at the same time, be a situation where one person usucapted a *maior pars pecuniae* while another took the *maior pars pecuniae* by legacy. Whatever one may think of the suggestions of Lenel and Bruck, it is difficult to accept that at the time of the decree the meaning of this provision was that anyone who took anything, however little, by legacy became liable for the *sacra* but only if the greater part of the inheritance were left as legacies. But if one accepts that this was, in fact, the meaning of the provision then it becomes reasonable to make liable beforehand that person who took the *maior pars pecuniae* whether he took it by *usucapio pro herede* or by *donatio mortis causa*. On this approach one cannot exclude the possibility that *donatio mortis causa* was under discussion at least as much as *usucapio pro herede*. [This for Simonius, *Die Donatio mortis causa im klassischen römischen Recht* (Basle, 1958), p. 37, against Mayer-Maly, op. cit., p. 93.] And if this is so, one can no longer see so much significance in the change

can say is that *usucapio hereditatis* was obsolete in the time of Quintus Mucius. There is no evidence that this particular rule of the later pontifical position was accepted earlier. On the other hand, one can put no other *terminus post quem* for it since this second position was developing as early as Coruncanius.

But despite the foregoing, two texts of Cicero, *pro Flacco* 34. 85 and *ad Att.* I. 5. 6, make it very likely that *usucapio hereditatis* still existed in his time.[1] The first text is by far the stronger and for its proper interpretation it must be set in its context.

34. 84. At enim Androni Sextilio gravis iniuria facta est et non ferenda, quod, cum esset eius uxor Valeria intestato mortua, sic egit eam rem Flaccus quasi ad ipsum hereditas pertineret. In quo quid reprehendas scire cupio. Quod falsum intenderit? Qui doces? 'Ingenua', inquit, 'fuit.' O peritum iuris hominem! Quid? ab ingenuis mulieribus hereditates lege non veniunt? 'In manum', inquit, 'convenerat.' Nunc audio; sed quaero, usu an coemptione? Usu non potuit; nihil enim potest de tutela legitima nisi omnium tutorum auctoritate deminui. Coemptione? Omnibus ergo auctoribus; in quibus certe Flaccum fuisse non dices. 85. Relinquitur illud quod vociferari non destitit, non debuisse, cum praetor esset, suum negotium agere aut mentionem facere hereditatis. Maximas audio tibi, L. Luculle, qui de L. Flacco sententiam laturus es, pro tua eximia liberalitate maximisque beneficiis in tuos venisse hereditates, cum Asiam provinciam consulari imperio obtineres. Si quis eas suas esse dixisset, concessisses? Tu, T. Vetti, si quae tibi in Africa venerit hereditas, usu amittes an tuum nulla avaritia salva dignitate retinebis? at istius hereditatis iam Globulo praetore Flacci nomine petita possessio est. Non igitur impressio, non vis, non occasio, non tempus, non imperium, non secures ad iniuriam faciendam Flacci animum impulerunt.

At this point of his speech Cicero is defending his client, Flaccus, against the charge that when a certain married woman, Valeria, died intestate Flaccus acted as if the inheritance belonged to him though he was not entitled to it. After ironically dismissing the possibility that Valeria was in the *manus* of her husband, Cicero considers the possibility that Flaccus' accuser who was entitled to

of order between the earlier and later decrees, since *donatio mortis causa* would seem to appear again in the second rule of the later decree.

[1] See, e.g., Bonfante VI. 224 f.; Albanese, *Studi Palermo* XX (1949) 400 f.: for others who take this view see the references given by Franciosi, op. cit., p. 162, n. 87.

the *hereditas* did not press his claim at the time because he was then praetor and it was not proper for him *suum negotium agere*. Cicero then asks T. Vettius whether, if any *hereditas* came to him in Africa, he would lose it *usu*, or whether he would keep it without greed and preserving his honour. Now this question to Vettius about losing an inheritance *usu* is put with direct reference to the argument that Flaccus has acted as though the *hereditas* of Valeria belonged to him. The relevant point is the acquisition or loss by *usucapio* of an *hereditas*, not of individual things forming part of the *hereditas*. Against this interpretation of the text,[1] it is not enough to say that the text is irrelevant for our purposes because it does not directly refer to the acquisition of an *hereditas* but to its loss, and that *hereditatem usu amittere* does not necessarily imply that the *hereditas* as such was lost and could mean that the individual things were lost as a result of *usucapio* of them. What is at issue for Cicero is that his client is said to have acted *quasi ad ipsum hereditas pertineret*, not that he has usucapted or attempted to usucapt individual things. For this very reason, too, it is irrelevant to point out[2] that even today the word 'eredità', 'inheritance' is misused. In what is fundamentally under discussion there is no scope for Cicero to be misusing the word *hereditas*. Likewise, Costa's point[3] that the passage referring to *hereditatem usu amittere* might be dominated by the local graecizing rules which later concurred to form *longi temporis praescriptio* misses the mark because Cicero's main concern is with the question of acquisition *usu* of an inheritance by Flaccus. That Cicero can treat this accusation against his client, at this point, as being about *usucapio hereditatis* must show that *usucapio hereditatis* was still in existence in 59 B.C. when the speech was written, though of course it does not prove that in fact the accusation against Flaccus was in respect of *usucapio hereditatis*. Cicero, however, it will be noticed, nowhere attempts to argue that *usucapio hereditatis* would in any event have given the inheritance of Valeria to Flaccus but rather denies that there was

[1] For the contrary view see Franciosi, *Usucapio pro herede*, pp. 162 f. and the references he gives, p. 162, n. 88.

[2] As Franciosi does in respect of *hereditatem usu amittere*: op. cit., p. 163, n. 89.

[3] *Cicerone giureconsulto*, p. 238.

any *usucapio hereditatis* and this would seem to be a clear indication that at this time *usucapio hereditatis* was regarded as morally unjustified. It may be thought on general grounds that it is implausible to hold that *usucapio hereditatis*, i.e. *usucapio* of an incorporeal, could be in existence as late as 59 B.C., but this suggested implausibility loses all force if, as was argued above, *usucapio servitutis* continued until it was abolished by statute probably in 50 B.C.[1] The other text of Cicero is *ad Att.* 1. 5. 6.

> De Tadiana re mecum Tadius locutus est te ita scripsisse, nihil esse iam quod laboraretur, quoniam hereditas usu capta esset. Id mirabamur te ignorare, de tutela legitima, in qua dicitur esse puella, nihil usu capi posse.

This text certainly does talk of a *hereditas* being usucapted, but if it stood alone its value for us would be doubtful, since one could not exclude the possibility that Cicero was using his words inexactly.[2]

The argument from *pro Flacco* 34. 85 and *ad Att.* 1. 5. 6 demands a reconsideration of *de leg.* 2. 19. 48. It seems that one should argue that *tertio loco, si nemo sit heres, is, qui de bonis, quae eius fuerint, cum moritur, usu ceperit plurimum possidendo*, though framed in terms of *usucapio pro herede* also covers *usucapio hereditatis*. After all, a person who by *usucapio* acquires the complete inheritance as a unit can certainly be said to take *plurimum*. The only real argument against this approach, I think, might be that *usucapio hereditatis* would be—for sacral purposes—a much more significant situation than *usucapio pro herede*, and that if *usucapio hereditatis* then existed it would be surprising that it was not specifically listed separately. But it may well have been the case that *usucapio hereditatis* was in practice relatively uncommon. It is easy to imagine that *usucapio pro herede* would be of frequent occurrence but not so easy to think that it would often happen that someone who was not the heir would take the necessary steps—whatever they might have been—to become accepted as the heir. If *usucapio hereditatis* was rare—and it has been suggested that *pro Flacco*

[1] *Supra*, pp. 22 f.

[2] See most recently Franciosi, op. cit., pp. 113 f. and the authors he cites. For other aspects of the text see now Watson, *Persons*, p. 137.

34. 85 shows that it was regarded as morally reprehensible—then this could explain why no express mention is made of it in *de leg.* 2. 19. 48. On this view there is no proof that *usucapio hereditatis* was obsolete before the time of Seneca.[1]

Gaius in 2. 55 says that *usucapio hereditatis* (which he describes as *tam improba*) was allowed because the *veteres* wanted inheritances to be accepted promptly so that there should be persons to carry on the *sacra* and that the deceased's creditors might have someone from whom they might recover what was owed them. The texts just examined from Cicero's *de legibus* give this account —and especially the first explanation of the rule—considerable plausibility. But no doubt these explanations account for the survival of *usucapio pro herede* when other cases of *usucapio* without *bona fides* were disappearing rather than for the original existence of *usucapio hereditatis* or *pro herede*. They will have come into being long before *bona fides* and *iusta causa* were demanded for *usucapio*. This practical explanation for the survivial of *usucapio pro herede* will also help us to understand why in this case land could be usucapted after only one year. Gaius in 2. 54 says that land could here be usucapted in one year because in earlier times the *hereditas* itself was usucapted after one year through the possession of things forming part of the *hereditas*, and that when later it was held that an *hereditas* itself could not be usucapted, *usucapio* after one year of everything—including land—forming part of an inheritance survived. But this explanation, at least in a simple form, is impossible. At the time when there could be *usucapio hereditatis* it must also have been possible to usucapt the individual things forming part of an *hereditas*.[2] There is no indication anywhere that this was one of the rare cases in early law where *usucapio* was not possible. When a piece of land forming part of an inheritance was then seized, the period of *usucapio* should originally have been, one would think, the usual two years. When it was established that

[1] *De benef.* 6. 5. 3.

[2] So apparently Kaser, *RPR* i. 92. But Franciosi holds (*Usucapio pro herede*, pp. 166 f.) that because D. 41. 5. 2. 2 (Julian, 44 *dig.*) shows that *usucapio pro herede* was in existence in the time of Servius *usucapio hereditatis* was then obsolete. D. 41. 5. 2. 2 and *Vat. Fr.* 294, though very relevant to *usucapio pro herede*, are fully discussed in connection with the maxim *nemo sibi ipse causam possessionis mutare potest*: *infra*, pp. 50 ff.

there could no longer be *usucapio hereditatis* but only *usucapio pro herede* one would not expect that rules pertaining to the former only would be made to apply to the latter. Where such a transfer of rules did occur, as in the period of time for usucapting land, this must have been due to a particular desire for such a result. And a very good practical reason can be given. The purpose of *usucapio pro herede* is not to benefit the person who takes the property but to compel the heir to accept the inheritance reasonably quickly and to take over the responsibilities for the *sacra* and debts of the deceased. To demand two years for the *usucapio* of land here would largely diminish the value of the institution and the jurists presumably have used a very sophisticated argument (from *usucapio hereditatis*) to reduce this period to one year. But there is no compelling reason to think that it was only after the disappearance of *usucapio hereditatis* that it was established that in *usucapio pro herede* land could be usucapted in one year—this interpretation could have occurred much earlier.

Gaius gives this account of *usureceptio*:

2. 59. Adhuc etiam ex aliis causis sciens quisque rem alienam usucapit. nam qui rem alicui fiduciae causa mancipio dederit vel in iure cesserit, si eandem ipse possederit, potest usucapere, anno scilicet soli si sit. quae species usucapionis dicitur usureceptio, quia id quod aliquando habuimus, recipimus per usucapionem. 60. Sed cum fiducia contrahitur aut cum creditore pignoris iure aut cum amico, qu*o* tutius nostrae res apud eu*m* essent, siquidem cum amico contracta sit fiducia, sane omni modo competit ususreceptio, si vero cum creditore, soluta quidem pecunia omni modo competit, nondum vero soluta ita demum competit, si neque conduxerit eam rem a creditore debitor, neque precario rogaverit ut eam rem possidere liceret; quo casu lucrativa usucapio competit. 61. Item, si rem obligatam sibi populus vendiderit eamque dominus poss*e*derit, concessa est ususreceptio; sed hoc casu praedium biennio usurecipitur. et hoc est quod vulgo dicitur, ex praediatura possessionem usurecipi; nam qui mercatur a populo praediator appella*tur*.

Thus, to take only *usureceptio* in *fiducia* for the moment, the debtor can usucapt the thing transferred in *fiducia* although he knows that it belongs to the creditor provided, where the debt has not been paid, that the thing has not been restored to his physical control by the creditor by way of *precarium* or *locatio*. Where the debt has been paid *usucapio* is allowed unconditionally, and the same is true of *usucapio* after *fiducia cum amico. Usureceptio*, even of land, requires only one year. As Wubbe has emphasized,[1] Gaius' treatment of *usucapio* shows that for *usureceptio* he is not thinking of the situation where, after the debt has been paid, the creditor returns the object to the debtor though without performing a *mancipatio* or going through an *in iure cessio*, but of the situation where the debtor acquires control of the thing without the co-operation of the creditor. Seizure of the thing given in *fiducia* by the debtor did not amount to *furtum*:

> G. 3. 201. Rursus ex diverso, int*er*dum alienas res occupare et usucapere concessum est nec creditur furtum fieri, veluti res hereditarias quarum heres non est nactus possessionem, nisi necessarius heres extet; nam necessario herede exta*n*te placuit nihil pro herede usucapi poss*e*. it*em* debitor rem quam fiduciae causa creditori mancipaverit aut in iure cesserit, ⟨*secun*⟩dum ea quae in superiore commentario rettulimus, sine furto possidere et usucapere potest.[2]

We can readily assume that Gaius' account gives the law as it was in the last two centuries of the Republic. *Fiducia* was well developed by the beginning of our period.[3]

There are, thus, four problems for *usureceptio*. First, how and why did it come to exist? Secondly, why did it continue in existence? Thirdly, why is it not *furtum* for the debtor to snatch the thing back from the creditor? Fourthly, why can land be usucapted after one year? These four problems are almost certainly very much intertwined.

The first problem, the reason for the existence of *usureceptio* is, this time, a real difficulty which is not explained by saying that at

[1] '*Usureceptio* und relatives Eigentum', *Tijd.* xxviii (1960) 13 ff. at pp. 14 ff.

[2] Wubbe, op. cit., p. 24, takes D. 13. 7. 22 pr. (Ulpian, 30 *ad ed.*) as showing Ulpian giving an *actio furti* against a debtor who seized back from the creditor his thing given in security. Thus, Ulpian's view would be different from Gaius'. But this is not necessarily the correct approach to the text. The factual situation envisaged is not described and Ulpian may have in mind the situation where the creditor returned the thing to the debtor under a *precarium* or *locatio*; that is, where the debtor cannot usucapt. If the debtor when called upon to return the thing to the creditor fails to do so, he might well commit *furtum* (when he contrectates).

[3] See now Watson, *Obligations*, pp. 172 ff.; Kaser, *Tijd.* xxxiv (1966) 416.

the time of its introduction *bona fides* and *iustus titulus* were not necessary for *usucapio*. The XII Tables laid down that *res furtivae* could not be usucapted[1] and one would have thought that for the debtor to seize back the thing given in *fiducia* would amount to *furtum* and hence there should be no *usureceptio*. If a pledge-debtor seized his *pignus* from the creditor he committed *furtum* even though he was the owner of the *pignus*:[2] *a fortiori* one would expect the debtor in *fiducia*, who was no longer the owner, to be liable for *furtum*.[3] But he was not. The absence of *furtum* here and the very existence of *usureceptio* are closely connected. Various explanations of *usureceptio* have been given. One explanation which formerly was very popular[4] was that *usureceptio* was intended to fit the paramount operation of the conveyance in security to its purpose. To this it has been rightly objected by Rabel[5] and Erbe[6] that at the time when *usureceptio* arose the full right of ownership of the creditor would not be restricted in this way. Erbe himself would explain *usureceptio* in terms of the underdeveloped theory of possession in early times.[7] He sees as a main case of *usureceptio* the situation where the creditor, after receiving payment of the debt, returns the thing to the debtor but fails to make *mancipatio* or *in iure cessio* of it. With the passage of a year, he says, the undisturbed and undisputed possession will become ownership since the legal position can no longer be examined. But this is not satisfactory. No particular explanation is really necessary for *usureceptio* in that situation. That situation in its essentials is really no different from other cases of *usucapio* by the bonitary owner. What does need to be explained, and is not covered at all on Erbe's view, is *usureceptio* where the debtor gets hold of the thing without the consent of the creditor and without the debt being paid to the creditor. A third view, proposed but rejected by Erbe,[8] is now brought forward and elaborated by Wubbe.[9] The solution, he says, is to be found in the doctrine of relative ownership, that is, in the view that in early law

[1] *Supra*, pp. 24 ff.

[2] Cf., e.g., G. 3. 200.

[3] Cf. Wubbe, op. cit., p. 19.

[4] See, for those who took this view, Erbe, *Die Fiduzia im römischen Recht* (Weimar, 1940), p. 66, n. 3.

[5] *Grundzüge des römischen Privatrechts*, 2nd edn. (Basel, 1955), pp. 100 f.

[6] Op. cit., p. 66.

[7] Op. cit., pp. 66 f.

[8] Op. cit., p. 66.

[9] Op. cit.

under the *legis actio* system, the judge in the action involving ownership did not have to decide who was the absolute owner, but only which of the parties had the better claim.[1] Where the debt was not repaid but the debtor has taken away the thing given in *fiducia* then, in Wubbe's opinion, the creditor has for one year the better claim, but thereafter the debtor has the better claim. Since the debtor has himself a kind of ownership in the thing there is no *furtum* and hence there can be *usureceptio*. At first sight this explanation has a certain plausibility but on closer examination it becomes untenable. To begin with, it raises more sharply than ever the problem of why it was *furtum* for the debtor to take away from the creditor something he had given as a *pignus*. Those who believe in the doctrine of relative ownership think that *pignus* is an instance where relative ownership plays an important role.[2] And one would think that a debtor who had given a *pignus* would be much more the owner than one who had given something in *fiducia*. On Wubbe's view, it seems incomprehensible that the law should be that the debtor who takes away his *pignus* is liable for *furtum* but not he who takes away a thing he had given in *fiducia*. Then, how is one to account for the survival of *usureceptio* when the concept of relative ownership disappeared as a result of the introduction of relevant *formulae* and when *bona fides* and *iustus titulus* became general requirements for *usucapio*? It would not be plausible to suggest legal conservatism as the answer. The legal framework surrounding the institution had changed so much, *usureceptio* was so unfavourably regarded,[3] and it would have been so easy for the jurists to interpret it away in situations where it seemed unjust (i.e. where the debtor had simply snatched the thing back without repaying the debt), that its survival—on Wubbe's view of *usureceptio*—seems impossible. Moreover, Wubbe takes for consideration as a case in practice that where the *vindicatio* is raised after the passing of one year, decision is given for the debtor and hence there is no *actio furti* against the debtor. But the fundamental case in practice, of course, would be very different, namely, where the *vindicatio* (and

[1] For a short and clear account of the general doctrine of relative ownership see Kaser, 'Der römische Eigentumsbegriff', *Rabels Zeitschrift* (1962), pp. 19 ff.

[2] Cf. Kaser, *RPR* i., pp. 126 f.

[3] At least in classical law: cf. Wubbe himself, op. cit., p. 24.

the *actio furti*) is brought shortly after the removal of the thing. The creditor will be the victor in the *vindicatio* and yet he will be refused the *actio furti*.[1] And there can be no explanation, on Wubbe's view, of the refusal of the *actio furti* here.

Two other apparent possibilities may be brought forward in order to be discarded. It might be thought that the purpose of *usureceptio*—like the reason for the survival of *usucapio pro herede*—was less the advantage of the acquirer than to penalize the person losing the ownership. The creditor, though owner, has a strong moral duty to look after the thing properly in the interests of the debtor. If he allows the thing to be taken away from him and makes no protest for a year then, it might be thought, he deserves to be deprived of his ownership, at least where the taker is the debtor. But this, of course, does not solve the problem of why during that year the creditor has no *actio furti* against the debtor. There is no reason for the creditor's being penalized if he is prepared to take active steps quickly enough. The other apparent but unreal possibility is that *usureceptio*, even where the debtor unilaterally seized the thing, arose as a juristic rule to meet the need for a legal presumption that, where the debtor was again in possession of the thing and there was no evidence of how this came about, then the debt had been paid and the thing had been returned informally. In early times in a legal system, especially where the judges are not professionals, presumptions—however reasonable—are very difficult to establish. But *usureceptio*, as we know it, is too clumsy and all-embracing for it to have developed this way. And, in any event, it is difficult to imagine that, where the facts were unclear, the judges would not tend to decide in favour of the debtor. Moreover any such need for a presumption would not have been for the situation where the debtor was again in possession of the thing without there being any evidence of a *mancipatio* to him, but where that was the case and in addition there was a dispute

[1] One can exclude the possibility that the fundamental case involves a situation where the thing has been transferred to an innocent third party for value, and that *usureceptio* was developed for his protection. Where the purchaser made no enquiries into the debtor's title he was no more deserving of special protection than any other purchaser in good faith of *res furtivae*; and similarly if he did make enquiries and found no evidence of remancipation and yet did not check with the creditor.

between the parties as to how this possession came about. And it is by no means clear that the presumption should strongly have been that the debt had been paid and the thing returned to the former debtor. For instance, apart even from ordinary cases of the debtor surreptitiously retaking what he might regard as his property, slaves given in *fiducia* might often secretively return to their former master.

A plausible solution of the *raison d'être* of *usureceptio* must satisfactorily account for this absence of *furtum*. The effect of the refusal of the *actio furti* should be noted. It means that there is no *legal* deterrent to the debtor simply seizing the thing back. The worst that can happen to the debtor, so far as the law is concerned, is that the creditor can bring a *vindicatio* and have the thing restored to him. Under the law the debtor cannot put himself into a worse position if he grabs the thing back. This aspect of *usureceptio* is so obvious and, prima facie at least, so appalling that it is virtually impossible to believe that it arose accidentally and yet was allowed to remain. It must, I submit, have been intended from the start and have been regarded as desirable. As for the means by which the institution came into existence, the only plausible explanation is that it was due to the jurists. Though Gaius gives explanations for both the existence and peculiarities of *usucapio pro herede*, he fails to do the same for *usureceptio* and so it seems reasonable to think he did not know of any.[1] Hence it seems unlikely that *usureceptio* was introduced and owed its peculiarities to a statute or edict. There is one hypothesis for the origins of *usureceptio* which—though it must of necessity be conjectural—does fit these requirements. It is submitted that *usureceptio* arose as an expression of the belief that the debtor should be allowed physical control of what was given in *fiducia*. In the Empire at least, it was customary though not invariable for what was given in *fiducia* to be returned to the custody of the debtor. Where this did not happen, the debtor would not be in the best position to repay his debt since the thing would usually be a *res mancipi* and hence of considerable importance for the debtor's earning capacity. In the

[1] Cf., e.g., Erbe, op. cit., pp. 65 f. (who, however, is apparently thinking only of the one-year period for the *usureceptio* of land); Wubbe, op. cit., p. 29.

circumstances, it would not be surprising if there was a feeling among the jurists that the debtor should be given back physical control even though it might be thought to be going too far to lay down a rule that the creditor must not retain possession. Thus, where the creditor in a *fiducia* retained the physical control of a thing and the debtor seized it back, the creditor, though owner, might be refused the *actio furti* on the ground that as against the debtor he had no legitimate financial interest in the custody of the thing.[1] The factors influencing this approach in *fiducia* would not operate with anything like the same force in *pignus*, both because the object given as a *pignus* would not usually be as important to the debtor's earning capacity and because, since ownership was not transferred to the creditor, his ability to safeguard his rights would not necessarily be so great.[2] From the proposition that it was not *furtum* for the debtor to take back what was given in *fiducia* it is but a short step to the rule that, if the debtor's control is not interfered with for a year, he can usucapt. In this context, just as in *usucapio pro herede*, it becomes reasonable for *usureceptio* of land to be completed in one year. The provision of the XII Tables, *usus auctoritas fundi biennium est*,[3] could easily be interpreted away, perhaps on the argument that that provision applied only to *usucapio* and that *usureceptio* was something different.[4] If it can be accepted that *usureceptio* served a purpose such as has been suggested, then its continued existence during the Republic and into the Empire presents no real puzzle.

The scope of *fiducia cum amico* is not clear. It is by no means certain whether, always or normally, the *amicus* was someone whom the debtor trusted with the thing more than he trusted the creditor

[1] Though in general the owner received as his damages in the *actio furti* a multiple of the value of the thing, not of his interest (cf. now, Watson, *Obligations*, p. 229), he had an *actio furti* only if he had a financial interest: G. 3. 203. *Furti autem actio ei competit cuius interest rem salvam esse, licet dominus non sit. itaque nec domino aliter competit quam si eius intersit rem non perire.*

[2] Especially if, as I have argued elsewhere, the creditor's real right against third parties was the *actio quasi Serviana* which developed after, and on the model of, the *actio Serviana* which lay against the debtor only: '*Actio Serviana* and *actio hypothecaria* (a conjecture)', *SDHI* xxvii (1961) 356 ff.

[3] Cicero, *top*. 4. 23.

[4] It is possible that the existence of a specific name for this institution indicates a desire to keep it separate from *usucapio*.

with it, or whether *fiducia cum amico* was frequently used outside the field of real security altogether where the transferor wished to accomplish something through a third party which, for practical or legal reasons, he could not himself directly accomplish.[1] In either case, the transferee would have no real financial interest in preventing the transferor's taking the thing back and one can see why in this case, too, the transferee would have no *actio furti* and the transferor would be permitted to usucapt.

The *ius praediaturum* is so complex and a matter of such controversy[2] that it would probably be pointless to look further for a reason for the *usureceptio* of G. 2. 61. But since it appears that only land can be involved here and it is likely that from quite early times the general opinion was that land could not be stolen, the problem of the existence of this *usureceptio* is probably not so great.[3]

But, as has been mentioned earlier,[4] in all other cases of *usucapio iustus titulus* and *bona fides* came to be essential. There is considerable controversy as to when these requirements were first demanded, though the dominant view regards the second century B.C. as likely. This seems quite plausible but we must consider whether there is any positive evidence which points to the existence of these requirements then.

To take *iustus titulus* (or *iusta causa*) first. The precise nature of this requirement is not in all details clear[5] but basically it means that to usucapt the possessor must prove that he obtained control of the thing by a legally recognized method, such as by sale, by gift, by dowry, and so on. It amounts to a further restriction on too easy *usucapio*. Two main arguments are produced for the view that it existed in the second century B.C. First, that its existence is a precondition of the *edictum Publicianum* and of the *regula*, *nemo sibi ipse causam possessionis mutare potest*,[6] and that this *regula* is one

[1] See most recently on this Wubbe, op. cit., pp. 24 ff.

[2] Cf. now, Wubbe, op. cit., pp. 30 f.

[3] For *usureceptio servitutis*, see Levy, '*Usureceptio servitutis*', now in *Gesammelte Schriften* (Cologne, Graz, 1963), ii. 149 ff.

[4] Cf. *supra*, pp. 31 f.

[5] Cf., e.g., Mayer-Maly, *RE* ixA. i, s.v. *usucapio* 1120 f.

[6] e.g., Kaser, *RPR*, i. 354 f.; 'Wesen und Wirkungen der Detention in den antiken Rechten', *Beiträge zur Rechtsforschung*, edit. by E. Wolff (Berlin, Tübingen, 1950), 1 ff. at p. 8.

of the *regulae* established by the 'Regularjurisprudenz'[1] of the second century B.C.[2] But, as we shall see later, it is very doubtful whether the *edictum Publicianum* was issued before the first half of the first century B.C. at the very earliest,[3] and the introduction of *iustus titulus* need not have occurred much before. And though the *regula* in question was the work of the *veteres* there is no evidence that it was due to the jurists of the second rather than of the first century B.C. There is no reason to think that *regulae* did not arise in the first century B.C. as well as in the second. Secondly, it is said that the *genera possessionum* of Quintus Mucius in D. 41. 2. 3. 23 (Paul, 54 *ad ed.*) are types of possession which rest upon the different *causae*.[4] This may or may not be so. What Quintus Mucius was thinking of as *genera*—apart from the instance we are told about—cannot now be discovered. He may have been thinking in terms such as *iusta possessio*, *iniusta possessio*, *possessio iussu magistratus*, and such concepts could exist long before the idea of *iusta causa*. Any possession not *iniusta* could have been regarded as *iusta* without any reference to a positive requirement such as *iustus titulus*. And the *genus possessionum* of which we are told—that given by a magistrate for the preservation of the object or because the other party would not give the *cautio damni infecti*—has no relevance for *usucapio*. And it could be regarded as a separate *genus* simply because it was due to the act of a magistrate and not to private behaviour, and again there would be no need for anything like a general idea of *titulus*. The positive arguments for holding that *iustus titulus* became a requirement in the second century B.C. are therefore not compelling.

There can be no doubt, however, that *iustus titulus* was demanded from the first century B.C. This would be shown by the *edictum*

[1] For this concept of 'Regularjurisprudenz', see Jörs, *Römische Rechtswissenschaft zur Zeit der Republik* (Berlin, 1888), i. 283 ff.; for criticisms of the term, see Schulz, *Roman Legal Science* (Oxford, 1953), pp. 66 f.

[2] e.g. Kaser, 'Wesen', p. 8; Hausmaninger, though he thinks *regulae iuris* began to be formulated in the second century B.C., does not seem positively to state that our *regula* is so early: '*Nemo sibi ipse causam possessionis mutare potest*', *Aktuelle Frage aus modernem Recht und Rechtsgeschichte: Gedächtnisschrift für Rudolf Schmidt* (Berlin, 1966), 399 ff. at p. 407.

[3] *Infra*, pp. 104 ff.; Kaser himself thinks 67 B.C. is not an improbable date: *EB*, p. 299, n. 17.

[4] Kaser, 'Wesen', p. 8. But see also on the text, Kaser, *EB*, pp. 338 f.

Publicianum if the generally accepted date of 67 B.C. is correct.[1] According to Lenel's reconstruction, which is not doubted, the edict ran:[2] *Si quis id quod mancipio datur traditum ex iusta causa et nondum usucaptum petet, iudicium dabo.* Again, and perhaps more important, there is the *regula, nemo sibi ipse causam possessionis mutare potest* which certainly does go back to the *veteres*:

D. 41. 2. 3. 19 (Paul, 54 *ad ed.*). Illud quoque a veteribus praeceptum est neminem sibi ipsum causam possessionis mutare posse.

D. 41. 2. 19. 1 (Marcellus, 17 *dig.*). Quod scriptum est apud veteres neminem sibi causam possessionis posse mutare, credibile est de eo cogitatum, qui et corpore et animo possessioni incumbens hoc solum statuit, ut alia ex causa id possideret, non si quis dimissa possessione prima eiusdem rei denuo ex alia causa possessionem nancisci velit.

I should hesitate to hazard an opinion on the original purpose and scope of this maxim but there is much to be said for Hausmaninger's view[3] that it was regarded as a general rule which was intended to stop any possessor whatever changing, *solo animo*, the existing reason for his possession for one which was more favourable to him. In classical law, as Kaser has emphasized,[4] its main use was to exclude *usucapio pro herede* where the person who wished to usucapt had been in physical control of the thing before the owner's death. But it might also be the reason why the debtor could not usucapt what he had given to the creditor in *fiducia* and which had been returned to his control under *locatio* or *precarium*. And Hausmaninger observes that it was also used to justify Cassius' decision that even if divorce takes place after there has been a gift from husband to wife, the wife still cannot usucapt.[5]

There are also a number of texts which show the existence and necessity of particular *iusti tituli*. Thus, D. 41. 6. 3 (Pomponius, 24 *ad Quintum Mucium*)[6] shows that Trebatius recognized the existence of a *titulus, pro donato*, for *usucapio*. The text, however, cannot show that a *iustus titulus* was required for *usucapio* since the

[1] But see *infra*, pp. 104 ff.

[2] *EP*, pp. 169 ff.

[3] *Die bona fides der Ersitzungsbesitzers im klassischen römischen Recht* (Vienna, Munich, 1964), pp. 60 f.

[4] Op. cit., p. 10.

[5] '*Nemo*', p. 403.

[6] Quoted and discussed, *infra*, pp. 231 f.

point at issue is really whether in the circumstances the wife could usucapt despite the *titulus* being a gift between husband and wife; that is, does the *causa* here exclude the *usucapio*, not is a *causa* required for *usucapio*.[1] *Vat. Fr.* 294, however, is more significant.

Papinianus libro xii responsorum. Quod pater filiae, quam habuit ac retinuit in potestate, donavit, cum eam donationem testamento non confirmasset, filiae non esse respondi; nam et peculia non praelegata communia fratrum esse constabat, Diversa ratio est contra legem Cinciam factae donationis. Tunc enim excepti*onem* voluntatis perseverantia doli replicatione perimi*t*; cum pater filiis, quos habuit ac retinuit in potestate, donat, nihil prodest non mutari voluntatem, quoniam quod praecessit totum inritum est. Unde cum filius in divisione bonorum penes fratrem quod pater donaverat errore lapsus reliquit, portionem eius non esse captam usu Servio Sulpicio placuit quod neque frater ipse donaverat neque pater donare poterat. Cur ergo quod vir uxori dedit, morte soluto matrimonio, si voluntas perseverarit, fini decimarum auferri non oportere, maximi principes nostri suaserunt et ita senatus censuit? sed nimirum liberi, qui repulsam donationis auctoritate iuris tulerunt, aliis rationibus ad bona patris perveniunt, ac plerique plus habere quam fratres iurgiis eiusmodi contendunt.

We are concerned only with the opinion of Servius expressed in the part *unde* to *poterat*. *Usucapio pro herede*, it will be noticed, is not brought into the discussion here and indeed it could not be. The *filius* to whom the gift had been made was in the *potestas* of his father—hence *neque pater donare poterat*—and so he and his brother would be *sui et necessarii heredes* whether the father made a will or not, and there could be no *usucapio pro herede* where there was a *heres necessarius* or *heres suus et necessarius*.[2] The situation is this: a father makes a gift to a son in his *potestas* and the gift is, of course, void.[3] The *pater* dies. We are not told whether he left a will or not but if he did he did not confirm the gift by his will. That son and

[1] Cf. Cicero, *de leg. ag.* 3. 3. 11: this text also shows that the concept of *causae possessionum* was recognized in 63 B.C. when this speech was delivered (or 60 B.C. when it was published); cf. Pernice, *Labeo* (Halle, 1895) ii. 1, 425 and n. 2. But it tells us nothing about the nature of such *causae* nor whether they were necessary for *usucapio*.

[2] Admittedly G. 2. 58 speaks only of a *necessarius heres*, but a *heres suus et necessarius* must also exclude *usucapio pro herede*: cf. de Zulueta, *Gaius* ii. 71, n. 3.

[3] Cf., e.g., Daube, 'Mistake of Law in Usucapion', *Cambridge Law Journal* (1958) 85 ff. at p. 90, n. 7.

his brother, who are the heirs, made a division of their father's property, but through a mistake (*errore lapsus*) the donee's brother leaves with him what had been given him by the father. According to Servius, the son cannot usucapt because his brother had not made him a gift and his father could not. This decision must rest on the total absence of a *iustus titulus*.[1] The text does not help us much with the problem whether for Servius a putative title[2] would or would not be sufficient for *usucapio*. It might be thought that, because the state of belief of the donee is not mentioned it was therefore irrelevant for Servius who, accordingly, must have held that a putative title was not sufficient for *usucapio*. But in fact it would appear that even if putative title were sufficient for *usucapio* the donee's state of mind would here still be irrelevant. If he thought that the gift to him from his *pater* was valid, then his error would be a mistake of law, not of fact.[3] It is difficult to see how he could have thought that the gift had been made to him by his brother. Daube has correctly pointed out that the brother's error of which we are told may be an error of law or an error of fact.[4] If the error were of law and was shared by the donee, then the donee would be regarding the gift as having been made by his father. If this error were not shared by the donee then there could be no question of putative title. If the error were one of fact, that is, where the donee's brother was unaware of or had forgotten about the gift, then it is hard to think that the donee could imagine that the invalid gift of his father was validly 'ratified' by his brother. Thus, if in any way the donee thinks there is a *iustus titulus* his error must be an *error iuris* not an *error facti*. Hence, if the text is authority for any proposition about putative title it is that if a person, as a result of *error iuris*, thinks wrongly that there

[1] Cf. Daube, op. cit., p. 90. The adequacy or inadequacy of *bona fides* has nothing to do with the matter here: cf. Daube, loc. cit.

[2] That is, where the person who wishes to usucapt thinks that there is *iustus titulus* but there is not.

[3] And in general a mistake of law would not help a person to usucapt: cf., e.g., Mayer-Maly, *Das Putativtitelproblem bei der usucapio* (Graz, Cologne, 1962), pp. 109 ff.

[4] Op. cit., p. 91: cf. Mayer-Maly, op. cit., p. 78, n. 13. Mayer-Maly, op. cit., p. 112, n. 27 seems to forget that Daube's point—correctly—is that the error of which we are told is that of the donee's brother.

is a *iustus titulus*, he cannot usucapt.[1,2] The important problem for putative title, namely, where due to an error of fact the person who wishes to be owner thinks mistakenly that there is a *iustus titulus*, just does not come within the scope of the facts of this case. A further text which gives the opinion of Servius scarcely takes us further.

D. 41. 5. 2. 2 (Julian, 44 *dig.*). Filium quoque donatam rem a patre pro herede negavit usucapere Servius, scilicet qui existimabat naturalem possessionem penes eum fuisse vivo patre. cui consequens est, ut filius a patre heres institutus res hereditarias a patre sibi donatas pro parte coheredum usucapere non possit.

In the text, *scilicet . . . patre* is generally and rightly regarded as an interpolation.[3] Some modern jurists think that the situation considered by Servius is the same as that of *Vat. Fr.* 294.[4] If this is correct, then since *usucapio pro herede* cannot really be under discussion,[5] the words *pro herede* must also be interpolated.[6] If the words *pro herede* are genuine, Servius must here be concerned with a different situation, this time where the *filius* was not the heir of the *pater* and there was no other *heres necessarius* or *heres suus et necessarius*.[7] On this view, the text would indicate that in the time of Servius, the rule expressed in the maxim, *nemo sibi ipse causam possessionis mutare potest*, already existed and applied to this sort of case.

There are two texts on *usucapio pro emptore*. In D. 41. 4. 2. 8 (Paul, 54 *ad ed.*) the sale is in fact valid and the purchaser can usucapt even though the thing does not belong to the seller.[8] In

[1] Cf. Mayer-Maly, op. cit., p. 112.

[2] Further to the text, see Mayer-Maly, op. cit., pp. 75 ff. and the authors he cites; and *infra*, p. 232.

[3] Cf. most recently Hausmaninger, *Die bona fides*, p. 64, n. 124. Even if the words were genuine they would not show that this was the reason which Servius gave for his decision rather than the one which Julian would attribute to him.

[4] They are referred to by Mayer-Maly, op. cit., p. 80, n. 18.

[5] Cf. *supra*, pp. 51 ff.

[6] But Siber alone would seem to hold *pro herede* an insertion: *ZSS* liii (1933) 127. Siber would also, arbitrarily, change the text so that *cui consequens* to the end would be giving us the opinion of Servius. There is no need, however, to decide whether he is right or not since if he is wrong that part of the text does not concern us, and if he is right it only tells us what we already know from *Vat. Fr.* 294.

[7] Cf. *supra*, pp. 51 f.

[8] On the text see now Watson, *Persons*, p. 135.

this respect the text shows only that a purchaser in good faith from a non-owner can usucapt. The other text, D. 41. 4. 2. 7 is more important.

Eius bona emisti, apud quem mancipia deposita erant: Trebatius ait usu te non capturum, quia empta non sint.

The text seems to be ignored in modern accounts of *iustus titulus* but would appear, none the less, to be relevant. You buy the *bona* of someone—probably a bankrupt—with whom slaves had been deposited. Trebatius held that you could not usucapt them because they had not been bought. The sale was of the *bona*, the slaves were not part of the *bona*, hence they did not fall within the sale. Since nothing is said of the purchaser's state of mind we can assume that it was irrelevant and that his belief that the slaves did belong to the person whose *bona* were sold would not allow him to usucapt. In this type of sale situation then, that is, where there is a valid sale but the objects under discussion were not in fact part of what was sold, a putative title resting on *error facti* will not suffice for *usucapio*. This decision should not be extended beyond sale since in classical law at least the law on *iustus titulus* was stricter in sale than in some other fields.[1,2]

The earliest date for which we have proof of the existence of the requirement of *bona fides* for *usucapio* is the last half century of the Republic. In D. 26. 8. 4 (Pomponius, 17 *ad Sab.*) we are told that Ofilius held that if I bought from a pupil with the authority of a tutor who was not *gerens* and I knew that another was *gerens* I could not usucapt. The sale itself, of course, would not be void.[3] *Vat. Fr.* 1 tells us that the *veteres* held that a person who knowingly bought a *res mancipi* from a woman without the authority of her tutor, or with the authority of someone who the buyer knew was not the tutor, did not buy in good faith. Nothing is expressly said

[1] Cf. Mayer-Maly, op. cit., pp. 139 ff.

[2] Thus in classical law, it would seem, most jurists (*plerique*) thought the heir could usucapt what he wrongly thought was part of the inheritance: D. 41. 5. 3 (Pomponius, 23 *ad Quintum Mucium*). Though this text comes from Pomponius commenting on Quintus Mucius there is no evidence that Mucius would have taken this view. G. 2. 50 is, of course, a different case since the sale or gift does have as an object the thing which we are told can be usucapted.

[3] See now on the text Watson, *Persons*, pp. 138 ff.

in the text about the attitude of the *veteres* here to *usucapio*, but the text must mean that they refused to permit *usucapio*.[1] A further text has been brought into the discussion of *bona fides* and *usucapio* in the Republic.[2]

D. 41. 2. 3. 3 (Paul, 54 *ad ed.*). Neratius et Proculus et solo animo non posse nos adquirere possessionem, si non antecedat naturalis possessio. ideoque si thensaurum in fundo meo positum sciam, continuo me possidere, simul atque possidendi affectum habuero, quia quod desit naturali possessioni, id animus implet. ceterum quod Brutus et Manilius putant eum, qui fundum longa possessione cepit, etiam thensaurum cepisse, quamvis nesciat in fundo esse, non est verum: is enim qui nescit non possidet thensaurum, quamvis fundum possideat. sed et si sciat, non capiet longa possessione, quia scit alienum esse. quidem putant Sabini sententiam veriorem esse nec alias eum qui scit possidere, nisi si loco motus sit, quia non sit sub custodia nostra: quibus consentio.

Brutus and Manilius, who were active around the middle of the second century B.C., held that a person who usucapted an estate has also usucapted *thensaurus* even though he does not know of the existence of the *thensaurus* in the land.[3] Mayer-Maly observes that the decision is based on the idea that the treasure shares the legal fate of the land, that there need be no special intention to possess or even knowledge of the treasure, and that the question whether there was *bona fides* is not put as such. He then himself raises the question whether the text is of no importance for the history of the requirement of *bona fides* or whether it permits the conclusion that *bona fides* was still not demanded in the time of Brutus and Manilius. He then gives the argument in favour of the second view. The form of the text, he thinks,[4] very strongly indicates that Brutus and Manilius would also have held that the possessor of the land had usucapted the treasure if he had known of the presence of the treasure in the land. Their view would then be opposed to that of Paul who held that if the possessor knew of the

[1] See now on the text Hausmaninger, op. cit., pp. 13 ff., whom I [*Persons*, p. 152, n. 1] follow completely.

[2] Mayer-Maly, 'Frühgeschichte III', pp. 104 ff.: cf. also the references he gives, ibidem, p. 105, n. 83.

[3] As Mayer-Maly says, op. cit., p. 105, though the text may have suffered alteration, it would appear that one can rely on this account of the opinion of Brutus and Manilius. *Longa possessione*, of course, is an interpolation.

[4] Op. cit., p. 106.

treasure he could not usucapt because he knew it belonged to another—that is, he lacked the necessary good faith. Hence Mayer-Maly postulates that it could be argued that in the time of Brutus and Manilius *bona fides* was still not demanded for *usucapio*. This view, however, he goes on, would in his opinion be wrong. And he suggests that the relevant factors for *bona fides* were different for Brutus and Manilius than for Paul. Paul excludes *bona fides* if one knows that a treasure lies in the soil; thus a positive content is given to *fides* and it is demanded that the person usucapting thinks with good reason that he is in a satisfactory position for becoming owner. On the other hand, says Mayer-Maly, for Brutus and Manilius it was enough that the possessor did not know of the rights of another, for, according to the essential part of the definition[1] which he regards as certainly ancient, only that *depositio pecuniae* is a *thensaurus* where the burial lies so far back that there is no memory of it and no one is any longer owner. He concludes that the narrowness of the old concept of treasure explains why Brutus and Manilius would allow the *usucapio* where the possessor of the land knew of the treasure without this conflicting with the demand for *bona fides* on the part of the person usucapting.

But these arguments of Mayer-Maly do not seem wholly satisfactory. The nature of the old concept of *thensaurus* cannot be by any means the whole answer. In practice, the problem of this part of the text could arise, at the most, in two ways. First, after the period of *usucapio* has run, someone else finds the *thensaurus* on the land but it is held that the owner of the land is owner of the *thensaurus* because he has usucapted. The whole doctrine of *thensauri inventio* would thus be here excluded and so it cannot have existed in the time of Brutus and Manilius. Secondly, after the period of *usucapio* has run, the *thensaurus* is found, its original owner is then discovered and he claims the *thensaurus* but is told that the owner of the land has usucapted the *thensaurus* and so is owner of it. Probably this latter is not a real way in which the problem could arise. One would imagine that if the person who buried the treasure or his heir appeared his ownership would not be ousted by any claims of the person in whose land the treasure

[1] D. 41. 1. 31. 1 (Paul, 31 *ad ed.*).

was buried. If the definition of *thensaurus* to which Mayer-Maly refers existed at this time its purpose would be to decide when the owner of the land owned treasure found on it, but it would have nothing to do with the doctrine of *thensauri inventio* which must be later.[1] There are, I think, two possible interpretations of this part of the text. One is that the opinion of Brutus and Manilius shows that *thensaurus*—however *thensaurus* might be construed—went with the land and legally is to be treated as part of the land. That is to say that on this view there would be *accessio* of the *thensaurus* to the *fundus*. Voci[2] argues that the idea that *accessio* is relevant here can be excluded on the ground that Brutus and Manilius would not have resorted to *usucapio* if *accessio* had been possible. But in the circumstances envisaged any argument for the owner of the land's ownership of the treasure would tend to fall into two parts: (*a*) ownership of the *thensaurus* goes by *accessio* with ownership of the land; (*b*) the land has been usucapted, hence so has the *thensaurus* whether the person who usucapted the land was aware of the *thensaurus* or not.[3] Likewise any argument in favour of the finder's ownership would be: (*a*) there is no *accessio* of *thensaurus* to land; (*b*) the land may have been usucapted but the *thensaurus* cannot have been. The law on *thensaurus* later changed and *accessio* ceased to be relevant for the ownership of the treasure. Hence Paul, who is concerned with *usucapio*, in giving the opinion of Brutus and Manilius would give their views on *usucapio* alone. Thus, on this view, no separate question of *bona fides* can be raised in respect of the *usucapio* of the treasure, so that the text does not help us to decide whether *bona fides* was or was not required around the middle of the second century B.C. The other explanation is independent of the idea of *accessio*. We do not know the circumstances in which Brutus and Manilius gave their opinion but it may well have been in reply to a specific question which had a form such as: 'Does a person who usucapts an estate usucapt treasure buried in the estate if he does not know of the existence of the treasure?' This could then give rise to a reply in the form:

[1] Cf. *infra*, p. 74.

[2] *Modi*, pp. 22 f.

[3] This is much more natural than simply: (*a*) ownership of the *thensaurus* goes by *accessio* with ownership of the land; (*b*) the land has been usucapted, hence the person who usucapted the land is owner of the treasure.

'A person who has usucapted the estate has also usucapted the treasure even though he does not know of its existence in the estate.' Such a reply, like the question, need not envisage the case where the person usucapting the estate knew of the treasure. *Quamvis*, 'even though', implies a sort of concession or that there is an easier case than the one under discussion. Here the *quamvis* may be due to the fact that for *usucapio* knowledge would in other circumstances be essential. It need not imply at all that in this situation (where knowledge of the presence of the treasure would also be knowledge that one had no title to it) knowledge of the existence of the treasure would, *a fortiori*, allow *usucapio*.[1] We would thus be freed from the necessity of thinking that a person would also usucapt if he did know both of the existence of the treasure and that he had no right to it. Now it is easy to imagine that in the time of Brutus and Manilius a person who in good faith bought an estate from a non-owner would usucapt not only the estate but also the movables, such as buckets, ropes, etc. which were on it and which for this purpose would be treated as part of the estate, without his having a separate knowledge of each individual thing and without his having a separate requisite intention of usucapting each thing. The general intention in respect of the *fundus* would be enough. Yet these things would not be part of the *fundus* by *accessio*, and if the purchaser for one reason or another knew he had no claim to a particular bucket or piece of rope he might not be able to usucapt it. Brutus and Manilius might regard the *thensaurus* as having a similar[2] legal relationship with the estate as the buckets and ropes had. That is, the general usucaption of the estate would allow *usucapio* of treasure buried in the land where the possessor had no specific knowledge of the existence of the *thensaurus*, but if he knew of the *thensaurus*, *usucapio* of it might be excluded since he would be aware that he was not entitled to it. On this interpretation, too, the text can tell us nothing about the requirement of *bona fides* for *usucapio* in the time of Brutus and Manilius.[3]

[1] *Sed et si sciat* need only imply that a more extreme case is being introduced. It is no evidence that that case had also been discussed by Brutus and Manilius.

[2] But not the same.

[3] D. 49. 15. 12. 9 (Tryphoninus, 4 *disp.*) should not be thought to provide

For *usucapio* to occur, the requisite degree of control over the thing had to be exercised for a period of two years for land, of one year for other things. The XII Tables' provision used the word *fundus* for land and this was interpreted to include *aedes*:

Cicero, *pro Caecina* 19. 54. Lex usum et auctoritatem fundi iubet esse biennium; at utimur eodem iure in aedibus, quae in lege non appellantur. . . .

Cicero, *top*. 4. 23. . . . Item: Quod in re pari valet, valeat in hac quae par est; ut: Quoniam usus auctoritas fundi biennium est, sit etiam aedium. At in lege aedes non appellantur et sunt ceterarum rerum quarum annuus est usus. Valeat aequitas, quae paribus in causis paria iura desiderat.

In *usucapio pro herede* and *usureceptio* following on *fiducia* land could be usucapted in one year.[1] In classical law the requisite control was *possessio*,[2] but this cannot always have been the case since *usucapio* is much older than the concept of *possessio*. Indeed, *possessio* as a term seems originally to have been restricted to situations involving public land. Early sources which may be relevant for *usucapio* use *uti* and *usus*.[3] As Kaser has observed,[4] a comparison of the interdict *uti possidetis* with the interdict *utrubi* shows that at the time when the latter was issued—probably in the third century B.C.[5]—the expression *possessio* had still not been extended to refer to movables. But the interdict *uti possidetis* shows that by the time it was introduced the term *possessio* was used of private land. Most writers have been content to regard *usus* and *possessio* as synonyms and to see little significance in the change of terminology, but Yaron[6] has convincingly argued that there was an important substantive difference between the two terms and that the replacement of *usus* by *possessio* was part of the reform of *usucapio*. He takes his stand on the literal meaning of *uti* and *usus*, and consequently holds that in early law it is not mere possession nor the

evidence for the requirement of *bona fides* in the Republic: cf Watson, *Persons*, p. 254, n. 6.

[1] Cf. *supra*, pp. 31 ff.

[2] For *possessio* see *infra*, pp. 81 ff.

[3] Cf. Kaser, *EB*., pp. 313 ff.; Yaron, pp. 209 ff.

[4] *EB*, p. 320.

[5] But see *infra*, pp. 86 ff. There is not enough similarity between these two interdicts for Kaser's suggestion, loc. cit., that *utrubi* is modelled on *uti possidetis*, to be compelling.

[6] Op. cit., pp. 209 ff.

abstract possibility of use resulting from possession which is important for *usucapio* but the actual, reasonable, suitable use of the land or chattel. This insistence on use, he observes, would, in a regime which had not yet worked out the requirements of *iusta causa* and *bona fides*, at least ensure that the owner may have occasion to come to know of the matter and be in a position to take steps to safeguard his rights. For at least most of our period, however, it would appear that *possessio* was required for *usucapio*. *Usucapio* of servitudes and of inheritances, so long as it lasted, and *usucapio* of freedom from servitudes are exceptional cases since these things being incorporeal could not be possessed.[1,2,3]

Usucapio was stopped by *usurpatio*, that is by an act of non-acquiescence by the owner. *Usurpatio* need not be actual deprivation of possession:

> Cicero, *de orat*. 3. 28. 110. Atque [hactenus loquantur] etiam hac *in* instituendo divisione utuntur, sed ita, non ut iure aut iudicio, vi denique recuperare amissam possessionem, sed ut [iure civili] surculo defringendo usurpare videantur. . .

Thus, a formal act—here the breaking of a twig—could be sufficient.[4,5,6]

[1] It will be noticed that Yaron's idea of *usus* may help to explain *usucapio servitutis*, *usucapio hereditatis*, and *usucapio libertatis*. Servitudes could be used, so could land in breach of a servitude, and one could, openly and reasonably, behave as heir: for the suggestion that even originally servitudes need not have been regarded as corporeal see *infra*, pp. 92 ff.

[2] It is not intended to go into the question of the meaning of *auctoritas*, since it is felt that this would throw no real light on *usucapio* in our period: but cf. the references given *supra*, p. 16, n. 2.

[3] Varro, *de re rust*. 2. 10. 4 and *Rhet. ad Herenn*. 4. 29. 40 tell us nothing more for *usucapio*.

[4] Cf. now Yaron, '*De usurpationibus*', to appear in *Studi Grosso*.

[5] *Pace* Costa [*Il diritto romano nelle comedie di Plauto* (Turin, 1890), p. 244, n. 18], who appears to be followed by Kaser [*EB*, p. 301, n. 26] and rather more cautiously by Mayer-Maly ['Frühgeschichte I', p. 23], there must be a legal reference in Plautus, *Am*. 375 *nam pugnis usu fecisti tuom*,' and 845 '*cave sis ne tu te usu perduis*'. It seems impossible to think of any meaning for *usu* which is unconnected with *usucapio*: cf. the translations of Nixon, 'Your fists have got a title to me by limitation', 'But just look out you don't lose your title to yourself by limitation': *Plautus* (London–Cambridge, Mass., 1937), i. 41, 49. The point of these legal jokes is obvious even though there appears to be nothing in them which could be useful for tracing the development of *usucapio*. Mayer-Maly also refers to *St*. 241.

[6] For *usus* in marriage see Watson, *Persons*, pp. 19 ff.

A rather special text which does not fall within any of the recognized modes of acquisition of ownership but may conveniently be dealt with here is D. 41. 1. 64 (Quintus Mucius Scaevola, *lib. sing. ὅρων*):

> Quae quisque aliena in censum deducit, nihilo magis eius fiunt.

With quite some emphasis (*nihilo magis*) Scaevola denies that a person becomes owner of things belonging to another which he registers on the census, that is, which for tax purposes he declares belong to him.[1] The question at issue is whether the entry on the census-list declaratory of the ownership of a certain thing is decisive of the ownership of that thing. But just as we know from Cicero, *pro Archia* 5. 11,[2] that in 63 B.C. the presence of a person's name on the census-list was not decisive of his citizenship, so Quintus Mucius held that the false attribution of ownership of a thing on the census-list did not transfer ownership. It is possible that Quintus Mucius' decision represents a refusal to allow the census to be used as a mode of transfer of ownership in the 'fictitious' way it was used for *manumissio censu*. One might compare the parallelism of *in iure cessio* and *manumissio vindicta* as 'fictitious' uses of *vindicatio* and *vindicatio in libertatem*.[3,4,5]

The remaining modes of acquisition of ownership were *iuris gentium*, that is they were available to peregrines as well as to Roman citizens.

Traditio

Traditio is the only mode (apart from *in iure cessio*) of voluntarily transferring ownership of corporeal *res nec mancipi*. In classical law it was transfer of ownership by delivery of the thing itself and,

[1] In modern times the text does not seem to have been regarded as interpolated. Cujas's emendation (cf. *Index Itp.*) of *deducit* to *dedicat* seems to miss the point of the text.

[2] Cf. Watson, *Persons*, p. 186.

[3] Whether originally only *res mancipi* were entered on the census-list does not concern us since it would appear that *res nec mancipi* were also entered from an early time: cf. Kaser, *EB*, pp. 174 ff.; Coli, *Iura* vii (1956) 81.

[4] The inferences which might be drawn from the text for the nature of the *liber singularis ὅρων* will be dealt with in a later volume on *Legal Science in the Later Roman Republic*.

[5] Cicero, *de invent.* 2. 51. 153 should not be thought of as picturing existing law in any way.

generally speaking, physical delivery was necessary. In the late Republic rather less was apparently demanded, and D. 18. 6. 1. 2 (Ulpian, 28 *ad Sab.*) and D. 18. 6. 15(14). 1 (Paul, 3 *epit. Alfeni*) show Trebatius and Alfenus respectively holding that goods were transferred to the seller as soon as he put his seal on them.[1] From these and from D. 41. 2. 51 (Iavolenus, 5 *ex post. Lab.*)[2]—which does not directly refer to the Republic—and D. 19. 1. 40 (Pomponius, 31 *ad Quintum Mucium*)[3] it would seem that one can deduce a rule for the later Republic that there is *traditio* when goods which are sold are precisely ascertained in the presence of the buyer though they remain under the physical custody of the seller. In classical law, though there were exceptions,[4] *traditio* usually demanded transfer of *possessio* and, as we shall see,[5] less[6] was demanded for the acquisition of *possessio* in the later Republic than in the Empire.[7] In the circumstances it would be of exceptional interest to know the attitude of the Republican jurists to *traditio longa manu* but we have no evidence for its existence or non-existence and the same is true of *traditio brevi manu*.[8]

Since *traditio* was a voluntary transfer of ownership, intention (of both parties) would be relevant, but we have no information on this, on *causa*, or on *error*.[9,10]

Occupatio

Occupatio was the acquisition of ownership of a *res nullius* by taking physical control of it. The most important text for the law of the later Republic is D. 41. 1. 5. 1 (Gaius, 2 *rer. cott.*).

[1] Both these texts have already been dealt with in detail: Watson, *Obligations*, pp. 59 f.

[2] Ibidem, p. 60.

[3] Ibidem, p. 61.

[4] And see for the Republic D. 34. 2. 4 (Paul, 54 *ad ed.*): *infra*, pp. 79 f.

[5] *Infra*, pp. 81 ff.

[6] At least in some situations.

[7] And the same was also true for *occupatio*: *infra*, p. 63.

[8] Nor have we evidence for *constitutum possessorium* which, however, is likely to be later and in classical law may have transferred only possession, not also ownership: cf. Watson, 'The Acquisition of Young in the *ususfructus gregis*', *Iura* xii (1961) 210 ff. at pp. 216 f. Against Thomas's criticism of the view that *constitutum possessorium* may have transferred only possession in classical law ('A Note on *summissio*', *RIDA* xi (1964) 255 ff. at pp. 259 f.) see now Watson, 'Acquisition of ownership by *traditio* to an *extraneus*', *SDHI* xxxiii (1967) 189 ff. at p. 209, n. 68; see also *infra*, p. 216, n. 2.

[9] Cf. Buckland, *Textbook*, pp. 227 ff.

[10] There is one text involving *error*, D. 18. 1. 18. 1 (Pomponius, 9 *ad Sab.*), but that concerns a very special situation: cf. Watson, *Obligations*, pp. 75, 83.

Illud quaesitum est, an fera bestia, quae ita vulnerata sit, ut capi possit, statim nostra esse intellegatur. Trebatio placuit statim nostram esse et eo usque nostram videri, donec eam persequamur, quod si desierimus eam persequi, desinere nostram esse et rursus fieri occupantis: itaque si per hoc tempus, quo eam persequimur, alius eam ceperit eo animo, ut ipse lucrifaceret, furtum videri nobis eum commisisse. plerique non aliter putaverunt eam nostram esse, quam si eam ceperimus, quia multa accidere possunt, ut eam non capiamus: quod verius est.

For Trebatius, ownership of a wild animal was acquired as soon as it was so wounded that it could be caught and the hunter remained owner so long as he kept in pursuit. If he gave up the pursuit he ceased to be owner, and anyone could take the animal and thereby become its owner. The authenticity of this part of the text seems generally accepted.[1] But the view which prevailed in classical and Justinianic law, as this text itself shows, was that the hunter only became the owner of the animal when he captured it. In this situation, too, lower standards were set in the Republic, at least by some jurists, for the acquisition of ownership.[2]

In contexts relating to *occupatio*,[3] three Digest texts[4]—none of which refers to the Republic—and one each from Gaius' Institutes[5] and Justinian's Institutes[6] tell us that what is taken from the enemy belongs to the person who takes it.[7] Other texts, both for the Republic and the Empire, show that such booty does belong to the

[1] Cf. Voci, *Modi*, p. 13. Against Di Marzo's doubts of the genuineness of the reference to Trebatius, *BIDR* x–xi (1948) 8 and 32, n. 41, see Wolff, *Studi Arangio-Ruiz* (Naples, n.d.) iv. 174, n. 9. For the aspects of the text which touch on *furtum* see now Watson, *Obligations*, pp. 225 f.

[2] Plautus' *Rudens*, 969 ff. shows that a person who caught fish in the sea became the owner; but see on the text Wolff, *ZSS* lxxxi (1964) 335, n. 5; most recently Harrison, *The Law of Athens : The Family and Property* (Oxford, 1968), p. 245 n. 1. For *occupatio* cf. Kaser, 'Die natürlichen Eigentumserwerbsarten im altrömischen Recht', *ZSS* lxv (1947) 219 ff. at pp. 220 ff.

[3] Cf. De Francisci (discussing G. 2. 69), *Atti del reale istituto veneto* lxxxii (1923) 968, n. 2; Bona, 'Preda di guerra e occupazione privata di *res hostium*', *SDHI* xxv (1959) 309 ff. at p. 341.

[4] D. 41. 1. 5. 7 (Gaius, 2 *rer. cott.*); 41. 2. 1. 1 (Paul, 54 *ad ed.*); 41. 2. 3. 21 (ibidem).

[5] G. 2. 69.

[6] J. 2. 1. 17.

[7] Those (e.g. Meylan, 'La baguette, symbole de la propriété civile dans la Rome des origines', *Mélanges Guisan* (Lausanne, 1950) pp. 21 ff. at p. 26) who simply hold that what was taken from the enemy in battle belonged to the State fail to give weight to the clear meaning of these texts.

individual yet on the other hand a number of texts make it plain that the booty goes to the State. The whole problem has recently been investigated with great thoroughness by Bona[1] and his work makes a very convenient starting place. His treatment of the texts is excellent and his conclusions on them can be accepted in large measure. But his general conclusions are not wholly persuasive. He holds that very probably at the beginning booty did not become *res publica* but belonged automatically—and not only in the abstract but also in practice—to the person who took it from the enemy.[2] The next stage was, he suggests, that the Roman State intervened to limit quantitatively the right of the individual to things of which he had physically taken control, and to advance its own claim to a determinate part of the booty, probably to the part which in historical times the general habitually reserved to the treasury—prisoners of war and the city's public treasure.[3] For some time, the introduction of these measures left unchanged the title in accordance with which the individual acquired ownership of his share of the booty, that is at first the right of the State to booty was parallel to that of the individual. But in time the right of the State prevailed and was extended to all booty, but magistrates, under their discretional power, were allowed to let the soldiers have, from time to time, that share of the booty which appeared proper.[4] In the late Republic, he goes on, the principle that the individual acquired what he took from the enemy was devoid of any real content but the principle continued to exist in the abstract. The State became the owner of booty and the contrary principle of acquisition by the individual existed in practice only in these marginal cases where one cannot speak of *praeda*.[5] The sole case where the abstract principle of individual *occupatio* existed in practice was where goods belonging to the enemy were on Roman soil at the beginning of hostilities and were seized.[6] Apart from the one text on that particular situation all the others from the Empire which talk of ownership going to the individual are expressed in abstract, not concrete, terms.[7] They are, in effect,

[1] Op. cit. [2] Op. cit., p. 360. [3] Op. cit., p. 361.
[4] Ibidem. [5] Op. cit., p. 362.
[6] This is based on D. 41. 1. 51. 1 (Celsus, 2 *dig.*): op. cit., p. 363.
[7] Op. cit., pp. 364 ff.

to be regarded as survivals representing the earlier position. Finally, he argues that in postclassical and Justinianic times the law remained basically the same.[1] The difficulty with this view—which, admittedly, conforms to the texts—is to understand how, when the State became legally the owner of all *praeda*, the legal principle—even the abstract legal principle—that what an individual took from the enemy was his property could survive. It would just no longer represent the law. And in such an obvious case the survival of an obsolete, and yet often repeated, statement of the law is incomprehensible.[2] I would like to suggest that there is a simpler explanation which is also in conformity with the texts. The fundamental texts are G. 4. 16 and Polybius, *Histories* 10. 16, the former because, as Bona argues, it gives the original Roman position, the latter because it shows how the later modifications came about and indicates their scope.

G. 4. 16. . . . festuca autem utebantur quasi hastae loco, signo quodam iusti dominii, qua*n*do iusto dominio ea maxime sua esse credebant, quae ex hostibus cepissent; unde in centumviralibus iudiciis hasta proponitur.

Gaius is describing the *legis actio sacramento in rem* and he says that the rod which was laid on the object claimed, such as a slave, represented a spear, the symbol of lawful ownership, because they (i.e. the early Romans) considered to be pre-eminently theirs by lawful ownership what they took from the enemy. And, concludes Gaius, it is for this reason that a spear is displayed in centumviral cases. Thus, in Gaius' view, in early times when these procedures were introduced, the instance *par excellence* of the acquisition of private ownership was what a man took from the enemy. It is quite possible that Gaius' explanation of the *festuca*[3] and of the *hasta* in the centumviral court[4] is wrong, but still it is

[1] Op. cit., pp. 368 ff.

[2] That the principle of private acquisition appears so often in the abstract is not necessarily significant. The Digest title on the acquisition of ownership, D. 41. 1, is unique in that the main statement of the law is taken from institutional works. The first 16 fragments are from such books.

[3] Cf. Meylan, op. cit., and the references he gives (to which might be added Nisbet, *JRS* viii (1918) 1 ff.).

[4] Cf., e.g., Kunkel, *An Introduction to Roman Legal and Constitutional History* (Oxford, 1966), p. 82.

extremely likely that in early law the individual acquired ownership of what he took from the enemy. The text, at the very least, shows that it was Gaius' firm conviction that this was the case. Moreover this corresponds to what one would expect the position in very early law to be, and according to Polybius this was the general rule among the Greeks.[1] The other fundamental text is Polybius 10. 16.

Καὶ τῆς μὲν κατὰ τὴν Ἰβηρίαν Καρχηδόνος τοῦτον τὸν τρόπον ἐγένοντο κύριοι Ῥωμαῖοι· εἰς δὲ τὴν ἐπαύριον ἀθροισθείσης εἰς τὴν ἀγορὰν τῆς τε τῶν στρατευομένων παρὰ τοῖς Καρχηδονίοις ἀποσκευῆς καὶ τῆς τῶν πολιτικῶν καὶ τῶν ἐργαστικῶν κατασκευῆς, ταῦτα μὲν ἐμέριζον οἱ χιλίαρχοι τοῖς ἰδίοις στρατοπέδοις κατὰ τὸ παρ' αὐτοῖς ἔθος. 2. ἔστι δὲ παρὰ Ῥωμαίοις τοιαύτη τις ἡ περὶ τὰς τῶν πόλεων καταλήψεις οἰκονομία. ποτὲ μὲν γὰρ ἑκάστης σημαίας πρὸς τὴν πρᾶξιν ἀπομερίζονταί τινες τῶν ἀνδρῶν κατὰ τὸ μέγεθος τῆς πόλεως, ποτὲ δὲ κατὰ σημαίας μερίζουσιν αὐτούς. 3. οὐδέποτε (δὲ) πλείους ἀποτάττονται πρὸς τοῦτο τῶν ἡμίσεων· οἱ δὲ λοιποὶ μένοντες κατὰ τὰς τάξεις ἐφεδρεύουσι, ποτὲ μὲν ἐκτὸς τῆς πόλεως, ποτὲ δὲ πάλιν ἐντός, ἀεὶ πρὸς τὸ δεικνύειν. 4. τῆς δὲ δυνάμεως διῃρημένης αὐτοῖς κατὰ μὲν τὸ πλεῖον εἰς δύο στρατόπεδα Ῥωμαϊκὰ καὶ δύο τῶν συμμάχων, ποτὲ δὲ καὶ σπανίως ἀθροιζομένων ὁμοῦ τῶν τεττάρων, πάντες οἱ πρὸς τὴν ἁρπαγὴν ἀπομερισθέντες ἀναφέρουσι τὰς ὠφελείας ἕκαστοι τοῖς ἑαυτῶν στρατοπέδοις, 5. κἄπειτα πραθέντων τούτων οἱ χιλίαρχοι διανέμουσι πᾶσιν ἴσον, οὐ μόνον τοῖς μείνασιν ἐν ταῖς ἐφεδρείαις, ἀλλὰ καὶ τοῖς τὰς σκηνὰς φυλάττουσι τοῖς τ' ἀρρωστοῦσι καὶ τοῖς ἐπί τινα λειτουργίαν ἀπεσταλμένοις. 6. περὶ δὲ τοῦ μηδένα νοσφίζεσθαι μηδὲν τῶν ἐκ τῆς διαρπαγῆς, ἀλλὰ τηρεῖν τὴν πίστιν κατὰ τὸν ὅρκον, (ὃν) ὀμνύουσι πάντες, ὅταν ἀθροισθῶσι πρῶτον εἰς τὴν παρεμβολήν, ἐξιέναι μέλλοντες εἰς τὴν πολεμίαν, 7. ὑπὲρ τούτου δὲ τοῦ μέρους εἴρηται πρότερον ἡμῖν διὰ πλειόνων ἐν τοῖς περὶ τῆς πολιτείας. 8. λοιπὸν ὅταν οἱ μὲν ἡμίσεις τράπωνται πρὸς τὰς ἁρπαγάς, οἱ δ' ἡμίσεις διαφυλάττοντες τὰς τάξεις ἐφεδρεύωσι τούτοις, οὐδέποτε κινδυνεύει Ῥωμαίοις τὰ ὅλα διὰ πλεονεξίαν. 9. τῆς γὰρ ἐλπίδος τῆς κατὰ τὴν ὠφέλειαν οὐκ ἀπιστουμένης ἀλλήλοις, ἀλλ' ἐπ' ἴσης ἑστηκυίας τοῖς μένουσι κατὰ τὰς ἐφεδρείας καὶ τοῖς διαρπάζουσιν, οὐδεὶς ἀπολείπει τὰς τάξεις· ὃ μάλιστα τοὺς ἄλλους εἴωθε βλάπτειν.

Polybius is discussing the capture of Cartagena in 209 B.C. by Scipio. Polybius himself lived from about 203 to about 120 B.C. so he is describing quite recent events. The Romans, he says, have a system for collecting booty. A certain number of men from each

[1] *Histories* 10. 17. 1.

maniple or even certain whole maniples, but never more men than comprise half of the force, are detailed to collect the booty while the remainder of the force carry out other tasks. The men so detailed bring the booty back, each to his own legion, and the booty is sold and the tribunes divide the profits equally among everyone, including those who were left behind, those who were ill, and those who were absent on special service. No one, he says, appropriates any of the loot, but they all keep the oath which they gave when setting out for a campaign. Presumably this is the oath which Polybius describes in 6. 21. 1, 2, 3, and which is given by each man to obey the officers and to execute their orders so far as is in his power. The purpose of this conduct in the army is to avoid a disaster through greed when everyone abandons his duty in order to acquire loot. The Roman system ensures that all will get their share of the booty and consequently no one leaves his allotted post. Thus, by the end of the third century B.C. at the latest, the taking of booty from the enemy was in practice normally regulated by this system, which was enforced by the commanding officer in virtue of his *imperium* and the oath which the troops had given to obey the orders of their officers.[1] The system, of course, has no effect whatever on the strict legal position. In theory a man is still the owner of whatever he takes from the enemy, but the military orders do prevail in the individual situations. The system will tend to have the following consequences. First, in every case where it is operated the individual soldier will either not become owner by *occupatio* of what he takes from the enemy because he has not the intention of becoming owner, or, at the very least, he will cease to be owner when all the booty is stacked together for the purpose of division. Secondly, the general as commanding officer will have very considerable discretion in his handling of the booty. He will be able to decide how many of the captives should be set free and not retained as slaves. He will also, inevitably, want to dedicate part of the spoils to the gods in thanksgiving and to give part to the State even if only for ostentation. It cannot surprise us if certain kinds of booty such as slaves began to be regarded as

[1] The charge of *peculatus* in 391 B.C. against Camillus might suggest that it is much earlier: *infra*, p. 68.

traditionally going to the State. It would come to be felt that the State had an interest in the booty. Whether the concept was that the State was owner of the booty which was collected together or only had a claim to be given ownership of a part at the discretion of the general is not very material here and probably cannot be discovered. It is worth mentioning, however, that apparently no text actually says that moveables taken from the enemy become, *ipso facto*, the property of the Roman State. The nearest the sources come to this is a text from such a weak authority for legal concepts as Livy who declares that when Syphax was conquered and captured, he himself, his wife, kingdom, land, towns, the men who lived there, and everything belonging to Syphax therefore were the booty of the Roman people (*praeda populi Romani*).[1] It is, of course, natural that conquered territory should become the property of the State.[2] Thirdly, since the booty collected together cannot be said to be the property or at the risk of any private individual or individuals, a person who takes any part to which he is not entitled cannot be liable for *furtum*. But some action must be found both against a person who removes part before distribution or sale and against the general who retains for himself a totally disproportionate share. Because of the State's interest it was not unreasonable to regard these offences as *peculatus*. For *peculatus* it was not necessary that there should be theft of something belonging to the State—for instance, an interest in receiving ownership of the thing was sufficient.[3,4] The earliest case of *peculatus* which has come down to us, that of the Dictator Camillus in 391 B.C., was for retaining bronze doors which had been part of booty,[5] and this might indicate that the development which has been suggested occurred early.

All the texts, both for the Republic and for the Empire, which

[1] 30. 14. 8.

[2] Cf. Livy, 3. 71. 7: cf. Bona, op. cit., p. 325, n. 56.

[3] A very clear text for the early Empire (Labeo) is in D. 48. 13. 11(9). 3 (Paul, *sing. de iud. publ.*).

[4] For the concept of *peculatus*, cf., e.g., Mommsen, *Römisches Strafrecht* (Berlin, 1899), pp. 764 ff.; Brecht, *RE*, supplement 7, 817 ff.

[5] Plutarch, *Cam.* 12; Pliny, *NH* 34. 3. 13; cf. Mommsen, op. cit., p. 765, n. 5; Kunkel, *Untersuchungen zur Entwicklung des römischen Kriminalverfahrens in vorsullanischer Zeit* (Munich, 1962), p. 35.

we have on things taken from the enemy are in harmony with this suggested development.

Plautus, *Captivi* 110.

> HEGIO: Advorte animum sis: tu istos captivos duos,
> heri quos emi de praeda de quaestoribus,
> is indito catenas singularias
> istas, maiores, quibu' sunt iuncti, demito . . .

452 . . . HE. edepol rem meam
> constabilivi, quom illos emi de praeda a quaestoribus . . .

Two captives forming part of the booty were sold by the quaestors, that is, on behalf of the State.[1] Presumably we are to imagine that they were handed over to the State by the victorious general.

Varro, *de re rust.* 2. 10. 4. . . . In emptionibus dominum legitimum sex fere res perficiunt: si hereditatem iustam adiit; si, ut debuit, mancipio ab eo accepit, a quo iure civili potuit; aut si in iure cessit, qui potuit cedere, et id ubi oportuit; aut si usu cepit; aut si e praeda sub corona emit; tumve cum in bonis sectioneve cuius publice veniit.

Full legal ownership of a slave can be acquired if he is purchased from booty *sub corona*.[2] Again this is a State sale. It is worth noticing, *en passant*, that Varro is concerned with the acquisition of ownership and that purchase *sub corona* is put on a level with *in iure cessio* and *mancipatio*: hence for acquisition of ownership by the individual from the State in such cases there is no need for a ceremony such as *mancipatio* or *in iure cessio*.[3]

Cicero, *de invent.* 1. 45. 84. . . . Enumeratio vitiosa intellegitur, si aut praeteritum quiddam dicimus, quod velimus concedere, aut infirmum aliquid adnumeratum, quod aut contra dici possit, aut causa non sit, quare non honeste possimus concedere. Praeteritur quiddam in eiusmodi enumerationibus: quoniam habes istum equum, aut emeris oportet aut hereditate possideas aut munere acceperis aut domi tibi natus sit aut, si eorum nihil est, subripueris necesse est: si neque emisti neque hereditate venit neque donatus est neque domi natus est: necesse est

[1] On these texts cf. now Bona, op. cit., pp. 316 f.: cf., Plautus, *Pers.* 501 ff., 520 ff. Plautus, *Epid.* 43, 64, 107, 608, 621, show only that a captive has been bought by an individual: but cf. Bona, op. cit., p. 317. Plautus, *Am.* 193, *Men.* 134, *Ps.* 1170 would not seem to help.

[2] We need not concern ourselves with the exact procedure of a sale *sub corona*.

[3] In general on the text see now Bona, op. cit., pp. 318 f.

ergo subripueris. 85. Hoc commode reprehenditur, si dici possit ex hostibus equus esse captus, cuius praedae sectio non venierit; quo inlato infirmatur enumeratio, quoniam id sit inductum, quod praeteritum sit in enumeratione. . . .[1]

Cicero is discussing faulty enumeration and gives as an example the instance where someone argues that if a person possessed a horse which he did not buy nor inherit nor receive as a gift and it was not born on his farm, then he must have stolen it. Cicero points out that a proper answer can be returned to this if it can be said that the horse was captured from the enemy and that there was no sale of this booty. The person possessing the horse is thus represented as having it lawfully and he has acquired it either by *occupatio* when he took it from the enemy or by its being assigned to him at the division of the booty. There was no sale of this booty and there is no indication that the State was involved in any way. *Pace* Bona,[2] Cicero *de off.* 1. 7. 20, 21 would seem to be relevant.

> De tribus autem reliquis latissime patet ea ratio, qua societas hominum inter ipsos et vitae quasi communitas continetur; cuius partes duae: iustitia, in qua virtutis splendor est maximus, ex qua viri boni nominantur, et huic coniuncta beneficentia, quam eandem vel benignitatem vel liberalitatem appellari licet. Sed iustitiae primum munus est, ut ne cui quis noceat, nisi lacessitus iniuria, deinde ut communibus pro communibus utatur, privatis ut suis. 21. Sunt autem privata nulla natura, sed aut vetere occupatione, ut qui quondam in vacua venerunt, aut victoria, ut qui bello potiti sunt, aut lege, pactione, condicione, sorte; ex quo fit, ut ager Arpinas Arpinatium dicatur, Tusculanus Tusculanorum; similisque est privatarum possessionum discriptio. Ex quo, quia suum cuiusque fit eorum, quae natura fuerant communia, quod cuique optigit, id quisque teneat; e quo si quis sibi appetet, violabit ius humanae societatis.

Bona says that Cicero is not thinking in terms of positive law,[3] and he follows the opinion of Costa who considers that Cicero is reporting in chronological order the modes of acquisition of ownership. This, says Costa, is dominated both by the Roman tradition of the historical relationship between peaceful *occupatio* and *occupatio* in

[1] The reading *praedae sectio non venierit* does not appear in all the MSS. but it must be original: cf. now Bona, op. cit., pp. 320 f.

[2] Op. cit., pp. 322 ff.

[3] 'Non ci muoviamo sul terreno del diritto positivo, ma su un terreno più ampio in cui confluiscono elementi filosofici, sociologici, giuridici che la mente eclettica dell'oratore cerca di fondere in un tutto organico': op. cit., p. 323.

war, and the assigning of the things so acquired to the members of the political group which is doing the occupying by means of a sovereign act of that group (*lege*). He claims that this sovereign act of acquisition is historically earlier than the acquisition of ownership by any other mode which depends on agreement among the members of the group (*pactione*, *condicione*), or by succession from one group to another (*sorte*).[1] But this view cannot be correct. It should be noticed to begin with that Cicero is not concerned with modes of acquisition of ownership but, if we wish to talk in legal terms, with *causae*. Apart from this, however, the opinion of Costa and Bona is flatly contrary to the Latin. In the part of the text which mainly concerns us, *sunt autem privata nulla natura*, *sed aut vetere occupatione*, *ut qui quondam in vacua venerunt*, *aut victoria*, *ut qui bello potiti sunt*, *aut lege*, *pactione*, *condicione*, *sorte*, the *causae* are divided into three groups each introduced by *aut*: *aut vetere occupatione* . . . *aut victoria* . . . *aut lege*, *pactione*, *condicione*, *sorte*. On the view that the text is giving a historical sequence of the ways of acquiring ownership, there should be no such division between *occupatio* in peace and *occupatio* in war; and more important, there should be such a division between *lex* on the one hand and *pactione*, *condicione*, *sorte* on the other. The significance of the divisions is very different: *aut vetere occupatione*—acquisition of *res nullius*; *aut victoria*—acquisition of *res hostiles*;[2] *aut lege*, *pactione*, *condicione*, *sorte*—acquisition of things already owned within the State. That in the whole passage in general Cicero is contrasting *res communes* and *res privatae*[3] should not mislead us. Here, in *sunt* . . . *sorte*, Cicero

[1] Costa, *Cicerone*, pp. 91 f.: 'La successione storica, qui rappresentata, dei modi d'acquisto della detta signoria, prescinde dal particolare atteggiamento che questi assunsero nel diritto positivo di Roma; ma essa è tuttavia dominata dalla tradizione romana circa lo storico rapporto intercedente fra l'*occupatio* pacifica o guerresca e l'attribuzione delle cose occupate a membri del gruppo politico occupante per atto sovrano de questo (*lege*); e circa la storica precedenza di codesta attribuzione a qualsivoglia altro modo d'acquisto, dipendente da convenzione fra i membri del gruppo (*pactione*, *condicione*), o di successione dell'uno all'altro gruppo (*sorte*).'

[2] That *res hostiles* under Roman law are technically *res nullius* should not be pressed. Cicero was quite capable of seeing the common-sense distinction between things 'owned' by an enemy and things which had no owner.

[3] Cf. Bona, op. cit., p. 323.

is only thinking of how one becomes the individual owner of a thing since by nature all things are *communia*. If this interpretation so far is correct, then it means that taking from the enemy was a way in which the individual acquired ownership directly, since if the State acquired it thus and the individual acquired it in some way from the State there could be no reason for the enunciation of *aut victoria* separate from *aut lege*, *pactione*, *condicione*, *sorte*.

Cicero, *ad fam.* 2. 17. 4. Rationes mei quaestoris nec verum fuit me tibi mittere, nec tamen erant confectae; eas nos Apameae deponere cogitabamus. De praeda mea praeter quaestores urbanos, id est populum Romanum, teruncium nec attigit nec tacturus est quisquam. Laudiceae me praedes accepturum arbitror omnis pecuniae publicae, ut et mihi et populo cautum sit sine vecturae periculo. Quod scribis ad me de drachmum CCCIↃↃↃ, nihil est quod in isto genere cuiquam possim commodare; omnis enim pecunia ita tractatur, ut praeda, a praefectis, quae autem mihi attributa est, a quaestore curetur.

In this letter from 50 B.C., Cicero says that no one has touched or will touch his booty except the *quaestores urbani*, that is, he says, the Roman people. So this time all the booty goes to the State but there is no indication that the State was automatically the owner. Nor can one draw any conclusion from the fact that part of the booty was assigned to Cicero. Probably this is to be understood as meaning that a share was assigned to him by the magistrates. This need mean no more than that Cicero voluntarily—so far at least as the law was concerned—gave all the booty to the State, and the magistrates in turn distributed part to those who had taken part in the campaign.[1]

Cicero, *ad Att.* 5. 20. 5. Nos Pindenissum, quod oppidum munitissimum Eleutherocilicum omnium memoria in armis fuit; feri homines et acres et omnibus rebus ad defendendum parati. Cinximus vallo et fossa; aggere maximo, vineis, turre altissima, magna tormentorum copia, multis sagittariis, magno labore apparatu, multis sauciis nostris incolumi exercitu, negotium confecimus. Hilara sane Saturnalia militibus quoque exceptis ⟨captivis⟩,[2] reliquam praedam concessimus. Mancipia venibant Saturnalibus tertiis; cum haec scribebam, in tribunali res erat

[1] Cf. on the text, Bona, op. cit., p. 324.

[2] *Captivis* must be the correct reading but the MSS. have variously *quibus*, *equibus*, and *equis*: cf. the text and the apparatus criticus given by Watt, *M. Tulli Ciceronis Epistulae* (Oxford, 1965), II. i. 181.

ad HS CXX. Hinc exercitum in hiberna agri male pacati deducendum Quinto fratri dabam; ipse me Laodiceam recipiebam.

This time Cicero tells us in a letter of 51 B.C. after the capture of Pindenissum that, with the exception of the captives, he granted the rest of the booty to the soldiers. The captives were sold. This letter shows the discretion of the commanding officer in respect of the booty. Presumably the money from the sale of the captives would go to the State but again we have no evidence that the captives or the other booty belonged to the State.

Cicero, *de leg. agr.* 1. 4. 12. Audite, audite vos qui amplissimo populi senatusque iudicio exercitus habuistis et bella gessistis: quod ad quemque pervenerit ex praeda, ex manubiis, ex auro coronario, quod neque consumptum in monumento neque in aerarium relatum sit, id ad decemviros referri iubet! Hoc capite multa sperant; in omnis imperatores heredesque eorum quaestionem suo iudicio comparant, sed maximam pecuniam se a Fausto ablaturos arbitrantur. Quam causam suscipere iurati iudices noluerunt, hanc isti decemviri susceper*unt*: idcirco a iudicibus fortasse praetermissam esse arbitrantur quod sit ipsis reservata.

2. 22. 59. . . . Vix iam videtur locus esse qui tantos acervos pecuniae capiat; auget, addit, accumulat. 'AURUM, ARGENTUM EX PRAEDA, EX MANUBIIS, EX CORONARIO AD QUOSCUMQUE PERVENIT NEQUE RELATUM EST IN PUBLICUM NEQUE IN MONUMENTO CONSUMPTUM', id profiteri apud decemviros et ad eos referr*i* iubet. Hoc capite etiam quaestionem de clarissimis viris qui populi Romani bella gesserunt, iudiciumque de pecuniis repetundis ad decemviros translatum videtis. Horum erit nunc iudicium quantae cuiusque manubiae fuerint, quid relatum, quid residuum sit; in posterum vero lex haec imperatoribus vestris constituitur; ut, quicumque de provincia decesserit, apud eosdem decemviros quantum habeat praedae, manubiarum, auri coronarii, profiteatur.

Cicero tells us of a provision of the *lex agraria* which was unsuccessfully proposed by P. Servilius Rullus at the end of 64 B.C., that generals at the end of their term of office must declare to the *decemviri* and hand over to them the *aurum*, *argentum ex praeda*, *ex manubiis*, *ex coronario* which they had not paid into the public treasury or used to commemorate the victories (*neque in monumento consumptum*). Cicero's attack on this provision shows that it was not part of the existing law. The texts also indicate that it was customary for generals to hand over part of the booty to the

State and to expend part in commemorating their victories, but they do not further our knowledge of the legal situation.[1]

Thensauri inventio

D. 41. 2. 3. 3 (Paul, 54 *ad ed.*), which has already been discussed,[2] shows that in the time of Brutus and Manilius ownership of *thensaurus* went with ownership of the land. There is no evidence that the position ever changed before the reform of Hadrian.[3]

Accessio

Accessio is the acquisition of ownership of a thing by the accession of that thing to something already owned by the acquirer. There are a number of distinct cases,[4] not all of which are directly evidenced for the Republic, though it would be surprising if they did not already exist. One important group of cases is that of incorporation in an immoveable. In connection with *damnum infectum*, Ulpian discusses in D. 39. 2. 9. 2 (53 *ad ed.*) the situation where part of your land falls on to my land[5] and he goes on: *ita demum autem crustam vindicari posse idem Alfenus ait, si non coaluerit nec unitatem cum terra mea fecerit.*[6] Thus, where part of your land collapses on to mine you can bring a *vindicatio* (and so you must have retained ownership of it) unless it has united with my land. Union will give me ownership of what was previously yours.

[1] Cicero, *in Verr.* II. 1. 59. 154 does not seem helpful for *praeda*. The titles of two of Cato's speeches, *uti praeda in publicum referatur* and *de praeda militibus dividenda*, have survived: cf. Malcovati, *Oratorum romanorum fragmenta liberae rei publicae*, 2nd edn. (Turin, 1955), pp. 42 and 91. The titles are suggestive but nothing positive can really be deduced from them. A complete list of the Livy passages concerning *praeda* is given by Fabia, *Mélanges Appleton* (Lyon–Paris, 1903), pp. 307 ff. The texts from Gaius' Institutes and the Digest which are directly relevant to the question of the acquisition of booty in the Empire have already been cited with the exception of D. 48. 13. 15 (13) (Modestinus, 2 *de poenis*). That tells us that a person who takes away property captured from the enemy *lege peculatus tenetur*. The other texts all tell us that what a person takes from the enemy becomes his property.

[2] Cf. *supra*, pp. 55 ff.

[3] J. 2. 1. 39. The literary texts produced by Rotondi, *Scritti giuridici* (Milan, 1922), iii. 344, have no probative force: cf. Voci, *Modi* p. 22.

[4] Cf. Buckland, *Textbook*, pp. 208 ff.; Kaser, *RPR* i, pp. 360 ff.

[5] The text is quoted and discussed, *infra*, pp. 148 f.

[6] For the genuineness of this part of the text see now Kaser, *ZSS* lxv p. 229, n. 29.

What constitutes union is not stated[1] but we have evidence in a different case.

D. 6. 1. 5. 3 (Ulpian, 16 *ad ed.*). De arbore, quae in alienum agrum translata coaluit et radices immisit, Varus et Nerva utilem in rem actionem dabant: nam si nondum coaluit, mea esse non desinet.

This text is generally regarded as interpolated[2] but no one seems to have questioned what is the main point of the text for us, namely that Alfenus would not give a *vindicatio* where a tree which was planted in another's field puts forth roots. Thus, for Alfenus where the transplanted tree puts forth roots it becomes the property of the owner of the field into which it has been put. There are, however, strong arguments for holding that Alfenus and Nerva did not give an *actio utilis in rem.*[3] But whether they simply denied an *actio in rem* or gave a personal *actio utilis* probably cannot now be determined.[4] This kind of *accessio* was known as *implantatio* and was akin to *satio* where seeds belonging to one person were sown in another's land. Daube has shown that it is very likely that as a mode of acquisition of ownership *implantatio* was recognized before *satio.*[5]

D. 41. 1. 16 (Florentinus, 6 *inst.*). In agris limitatis ius alluvionis locum non habere constat: idque et divus Pius constituit et Trebatius ait agrum, qui hostibus devictis ea condicione concessus sit, ut in civitatem veniret [venirent *Mommsen*], habere alluvionem neque esse limitatum: agrum autem manu captum limitatum fuisse, ut sciretur, quid cuique datum esset, quid venisset, quid in publico relictum esset.

Alluvio was acquisition by the imperceptible deposit of soil along a person's boundaries due to the action of a river. This text shows

[1] In classical law it seems that in the case of *avulsio*, that is, where the river carries off a piece of your land and deposits it on my land, the piece of land remains yours until trees on it put forth roots into my land: D. 41. 1. 7. 2 (Gaius, 2 *res. cott.*).

[2] To the references in the *Index Itp.* and *Supplementum* add Kaser, *RPR* i. 228, n. 26.

[3] Cf. for the difficulties, in addition to the references given *supra* n. 2, de Zulueta, *Gaius* ii. 78, and Arangio-Ruiz, *Istituzione di diritto romano*, 14th edn. (Naples, 1960), p. 192, n. 1, both of whom are concerned with G. 2. 78.

[4] But this aspect of the text will be examined in a chapter on decretal actions in the Republic in a later volume, *Legal Science in the Later Roman Republic.*

[5] '*Implantatio* and *satio*', *Acta juridica* (1958) 181 ff.; *Iura* xi (1960) 106, n. 108.

both that *alluvio* existed in the time of Trebatius and that it did not apply to *ager limitatus*. *Ager limitatus* was land whose boundary was defined by straight lines and not by natural features such as the bank of a river. Where, as was normally the case apart from land granted by the State, land was defined by its natural boundaries, a change in these boundaries would result in a change in ownership.

D. 41. 1. 38 (Alfenus Varus, 4 *dig. a Paulo epit.*). Attius fundum habebat secundum viam publicam: ultra viam flumen erat et ager Lucii Titii: fluit [fluit *del. Haloander*] flumen paulatim primum omnium [primum omnium—populi Romani eum *Mommsen*: omnium—omnis *Milan Digest*] agrum, qui inter viam et flumen esset, ambedit et viam sustulit, postea rursus minutatim recessit et alluvione in antiquum locum rediit. respondit, cum flumen agrum et viam publicam sustulisset, eum agrum eius factum esse, qui trans flumen fundum habuisset: postea cum paulatim retro redisset, ademisse ei, cuius factus esset, et addidisse ei, cuius trans viam esset, quoniam eius fundus proximus flumini esset, id autem, quod publicum fuisset, nemini accessisset [homini cessisset *Mommsen*]. nec tamen [tamen—iam *Mommsen*] impedimento viam esse ait, quo minus ager, qui trans viam alluvione relictus est, Attii fieret: nam ipsa quoque via fundi esset.

Though the facts of the situation are not absolutely clear, there is little doubt about the legal propositions which we can deduce from the text. It would seem that we are not given all the relevant facts at the beginning of the text though this is soon remedied.[1] On one side of the river is the land of Lucius Titius, on the other first the land of someone who is not named,[2] then a public road, and then the land of Attius. The river erodes first the land between the public road and the river and then the public road itself. To judge from the answer of Servius (or Alfenus), though this fact is not given in the statement of the case, the erosion of the land on one side of the river is coupled with accretion to the land of Lucius Titius on the other side of the river. The facts are not those of temporary flooding but of a river changing its course. At this stage the person who is not named has lost ownership of all his land, since it has been carried away or submerged by the river. Lucius Titius' ownership

[1] Cf. de Zulueta, *Digest 41, 1 & 2* (Oxford, 1950) pp. 70 f.

[2] It may be that it is unnecessary to introduce a further party and that the land between the road and the river also belonged to Attius. The *omnium* of the MSS. cannot be correct.

is extended to what has acceded by *alluvio* to his land. The river then gradually returns to its former channel. Lucius Titius loses ownership of what he had gained. On the other side of the river there is no question of the ownership of the person who is not named reviving. His title was completely wiped out when his land ceased to exist above water. The *via*, however, is accepted as continuing to exist as a public road. The difficult question is the ownership of the land between the public road and the river. It is held that this accedes to Attius and the presence of the public road is no obstacle to this since the road itself is part of the land of Attius. The road, that is, may be public, but ownership of it subsists in the owner of the land over which it runs.[1]

D. 41. 1. 24 (Paul, 14 *ad Sab.*). In omnibus, quae ad eandem speciem reverti non possunt, dicendum est, si materia manente species dumtaxat forte mutata sit, veluti si meo aere statuam aut argento scyphum fecisses, me eorum dominum manere,

26 pr. (ibidem). Sed si meis tabulis navem fecisses, tuam navem esse, quia cupressus non maneret, sicuti nec lana vestimento facto, sed cupresseum aut laneum corpus fieret. Proculus indicat hoc iure nos uti, quod Servio et Labeoni placuisset: in quibus propria qualitas exspectaretur, si quid additum erit toto cedit, ut statuae pes aut manus, scypho fundus aut ansa, lecto fulcrum, navi tabula, aedificio cementum: tota enim eius sunt, cuius ante fuerant.

It is not clear whether *Proculus indicat hoc iure nos uti, quod Servio et Labeoni placuisset* should be attached to what precedes or to what follows it since the text here is not really in proper form.[2] So we cannot tell whether Servius was concerned with *specificatio*, that is the creation of a *nova species*, or with *accessio*. If the former, his opinion would be that the maker of the *nova species* became its owner, not the person who previously owned the raw materials.[3,4]

[1] Cf. de Zulueta, loc. cit. See most recently on the text, Sargenti, 'Il regime dell'alveo derelitto nelle fonti romane', *BIDR* lxviii (1965) 195 ff. at pp. 204 ff. There is no way of checking the hypothesis that the nucleus of D. 7. 4. 23 (Pomponius, 26 *ad Quintum Mucium*) goes back to Quintus Mucius: cf. Sargenti, op. cit., pp. 201 ff.

[2] Cf., e.g., Kaser, *RPR* i. 243. He would attach *Proculus, etc.* to what precedes but, given his own opinion of the state of the text, this can hardly be other than arbitrary.

[3] There is no indication whether any of the instances given in the text go back to Servius.

[4] D. 19. 2. 31 (Alfenus, 5 *dig. a Paulo epit.*) and D. 34. 2. 34 pr. (Pomponius,

Acquisition through intermediaries

Whatever was acquired by a person *in potestate* or by a slave went to the *paterfamilias* or *dominus*. This can give rise to difficulties where the slave is owned by more than one master or is not really a slave but is a *liber homo bona fide serviens*.

D. 45. 3. 6 (Pomponius, 26 *ad Sab.*). Ofilius recte dicebat et per traditionem accipiendo vel deponendo commodandoque posse soli ei adquiri, qui iussit: quae sententia et Cassii et Sabini dicitur.

The text cannot originally have run like this.[1] Perhaps the most widely accepted reconstruction is that of Lenel:[2] *Ofilius recte dicebat et [per traditionem] ⟨fiduciae causa mancipio⟩ accipiendo vel [deponendo commodandoque] ⟨cum creditore vel cum amico contractae⟩ posse soli ei adquiri qui iussit: quae sententia et Cassii et Sabini dicitur*. Beseler suggests:[3] *Ofilius [recte] dicebat ⟨servum communem⟩ et ⟨mancipio⟩ [per traditionem] accipiendo ⟨et stipulando⟩ [vel deponendo commodandoque] posse soli ei adquir⟨ere⟩[i] qui iussit: quae sententia et Cassii et Sabini ⟨fuit⟩ [dicitur]*. Whether either of these is absolutely accurate or not does not really concern us since what is for us the main point of the text is unchallenged. It tells us that where a slave who is owned by more than one master takes something under an order from one master he acquires ownership for that master alone.

D. 26. 8. 12 (Julian, 21 *dig.*). Si servus communis tuus et Titii a pupilla tua te auctore aliquam rem per traditionem acceperit, tota ad Titium pertinebit. *Marcellus notat*: nam quodcumque ad omnes dominos non potest pertinere, id pro solido ad eum, cui adquiri potest, pertinere veteres comprobaverunt.

We are given no real indication of the circumstances in which the *veteres* used the rule attributed to them by Marcellus, but they

ad Quintum Mucium) show that in the Republic where goods were handed over under a contract of *locatio operis faciendi*, the recipient acquired ownership: cf. Watson, *Obligations*, pp. 106 ff.

[1] Cf. now, in addition to the references given in the *Index Itp.*, Erbe, *Die Fiduzia im römischen Recht* (Weimar, 1940), pp. 143 f.; Beseler, *ZSS* lxvi (1948) 610; Bretone, *Servus communis* (Naples, 1958), pp. 87 ff.

[2] *Pal.* ii. 136: cf. Erbe, op. cit., p. 143 and n. 6.

[3] Loc. cit.: followed by Bretone, op. cit., p. 87.

held that whatever could not be acquired for all of the masters was acquired *pro solido* for him who could acquire it.[1]

D. 41. 1. 19 (Pomponius, 3 *ad Sab.*) and D. 28. 5. 60(59) pr. (Celsus, 16 *dig.*), which have been dealt with in an earlier volume,[2] tell us that Trebatius held that the supposed master did not acquire an inheritance which was accepted at his command by a *liber homo bona fide serviens*. But the discussion of this case suggests that it was already accepted that there were circumstances in which one did acquire through a *liber homo bona fide serviens*.

In classical law delivery to a representative who was not in the *potestas* or *dominium* of his principal did not give his principal ownership.[3] It appears that this may not always have been the position.

D. 34. 2. 4 (Paul, 54 *ad ed.*). Cum quidam libertum suum in Asiam misisset ad purpuras emendas et testamento uxori suae lanam purpuream legasset, pertinere ad eam, si quam purpuram vivo eo libertus emisset, Servius respondit.

The text has excited very little discussion and is usually cited only as an instance of a *legatum quod eius* (sc. *uxoris*) *causa emptum paratumve esset*.[4] Ferrini,[5] indeed, uses the text for the proposition that a *legatum rerum uxoris causa emptarum* was valid even though the thing had not been handed to the woman: it would suffice that the thing was intended for her use. But there is no textual justification for regarding the situation as involving such a legacy. It is not said that the *libertus* was sent to buy the purple for the use of the wife and we are told that the legacy was of *lana purpurea*, not that it was of the *lana purpurea quae eius causa empta est, erit*. Moreover, there is nothing in the original context of Paul's 54th book on the Edict, which deals with *possessio* and *usucapio*,[6] to indicate that it was a legacy of that type.[7] But if, as would appear, the legacy were simply of the testator's *lana purpurea*, only the purple wool which

[1] See now on the text, Bretone, op. cit., pp. 60 f.

[2] *Persons*, pp. 222 ff.

[3] G. 2. 95: cf., e.g., Kaser, *RPR* i, pp. 227 f.

[4] Voci, *Diritto ereditario romano*, ii, parte speciale (Milan, 1963), p. 303, n. 181; Levy, *Iura* xiv (1963) 17.

[5] *Opere* (Milan, 1929), iii. 117, n. 1.

[6] Lenel, *Pal.* i. 1069.

[7] Further, its inclusion in the title D. 34. 2, would not justify the conclusion that it was a legacy of that type for the compilers.

he owned at the time of his death would fall within the *legatum*. The legacy would not include purple wool which he had a rightful claim to but did not own.[1] Hence, too, the *vivo eo* of the text. Thus, it seems that in the late Republic Servius at least held that the *patronus* would acquire ownership of what his *libertus* received on his behalf and acting under his instructions. The text stands alone and it would be rash to extend the rule to situations where the representative was not the *libertus* of his principal. It should be noticed that the *libertus* is not further described as being the *procurator* of the testator. The explanation of the rule probably is that the social bond between the *patronus* and his *libertus* was often very strong and the *libertus* frequently continued to live with the *patronus*.[2] In such circumstances, the *libertus* could be regarded as being still a member of the family of the patron and acquisition of ownership through him might be allowed even though usually it was not possible to acquire ownership *per extraneam personam*.[3] This seems to be another case where the requirements for the acquisition of ownership were less stringent in the later Republic than they were in classical law.[4]

We have one text concerning the retention of ownership:

D. 14. 2. 7 (Paul, 3 *epit. Alfeni dig.*). Cum depressa navis aut deiecta [disiecta *Mommsen*] esset, quod quisque ex ea suum servasset, sibi servare respondit, tamquam ex incendio.

According to Alfenus (or his master Servius), when a ship was sunk or was dashed to pieces, what each person saved from his own property in it he retained for himself. The circumstances envisaged are not those of the *lex Rhodia de iactu* since there was no *iactus*.[5,6]

[1] Cf. D. 34. 2. 34 pr. (Pomponius, 9 *ad Quintum Mucium*): Watson, *Obligations*, pp. 107 ff.

[2] Cf. Watson, *Persons*, p. 226.

[3] The earliest situation—it probably dates from the early Empire—where acquisition of possession *per extraneam personam* was permitted was *per procuratorem*: cf., e.g., Watson, 'Acquisition of Possession *per extraneam personam*', *Tijd.* xxix (1961) 22 ff. The usual explanation of this is that in early times a Roman would most often appoint as his *procurator omnium bonorum* one of his *liberti* and that at that time *liberti* were less independent of their *patronus* than was later the case: cf., e.g., Kaser, *RPR* i. 227 f.

[4] Cf. Watson, *SDHI* xxxiii, pp. 189 ff.

[5] Cf. de Sarlo, *AV*, pp. 112 f.; Osuchowski, *Iura* i (1950) 294.

[6] D. 5. 1. 76 (Alfenus, 6 *dig.*); D. 50. 16. 180. 1 (Pomponius, 30 *ad Sab.*) and Festus, s.v. *tuguria*, will be dealt with in a later volume on *Legal Science in the Later Roman Republic*.

3

POSSESSIO

ONE might describe possession non-technically as physical control over a thing, which one exercises either directly or through another person. More technically, *possessio* is that kind of control over a thing for the benefit of which the possessory interdicts were intended. According to the circumstances and the kind of interdict, the interdicts will allow a person to retain possession, to recover possession, or to acquire possession. Not all possessory interdicts are fashioned to protect the present possessor.

In classical law, and especially perhaps in later classical law, a person acquired possession when he had sufficient physical control over the thing (*corpus*) and had the requisite intention (*animus*).[1] The later Republican requirements for the acquisition of possession would appear to be less strict. It must be stressed that there is no sign in our very limited sources of a division of the necessary elements into *corpus* and *animus* but it is convenient and probably will not be anachronistic to consider the requirements in terms of the necessary physical control and of intention.

For the physical element we have no direct authority but it may be possible to draw support from *traditio* and from *occupatio*. In classical law it seems that in the straightforward case acquisition of ownership by *traditio* occurred when possession was transferred. Now in the Republic, though not later, *traditio* could occur when goods which were sold were precisely ascertained in the presence of the buyer even though they remained under the physical control of the seller.[2] If, in the straightforward case in the Republic, *traditio* required the acquisition of possession by the transferee, then in these circumstances here the buyer will have acquired possession. Likewise, in classical law, the *occupatio* of wild animals

[1] It is not intended here to consider specifically what counted as *corpus* and *animus* for the Empire.

[2] Cf. Watson, *Obligations*, pp. 59 ff.; *supra*, pp. 61 f.

required acquisition of possession. Trebatius held that a wild animal was acquired as soon as it was so wounded that it could be caught.[1] This decision did not prevail and later jurists required the actual capture of the animal. But if possession and ownership of wild animals were inseparable in the later Republic as they were later, then Trebatius would also have held that a person who so wounded an animal that it could be caught acquired possession of it and remained in possession so long as he continued in pursuit.

For the mental element we do have direct textual authority.

D. 41. 2. 1. 3 (Paul, 54 *ad ed.*). Furiosus, et pupillus sine tutoris auctoritate, non potest incipere possidere, quia affectionem tenendi non habent, licet maxime corpore suo rem contingant, sicuti si quis dormienti aliquid in manu ponat. sed pupillus tutore auctore incipiet possidere. Ofilius quidem et Nerva filius etiam sine tutoris auctoritate possidere incipere posse pupillum aiunt: eam enim rem facti, non iuris esse: quae sententia recipi potest, si eius aetatis sint, ut intellectum capiant.

The text has very frequently been regarded as interpolated[2] but the authenticity of the part which really concerns us, *Ofilius . . . iuris esse*, is widely accepted.[3] Thus, Ofilius (and Nerva the younger) would allow a *pupillus* to acquire possession even without the tutor's authority. *Pupillus* here means a pupil of any age whether *infantia maior* or still an *infans*.[4] This view in the text is then said to be acceptable in respect of children who are of an age *ut intellectum capiant*. This last part of the text has been held to be

[1] D. 41. 1. 5. 1 (Gaius, 2 *rer. cott.*); cf. *supra*, pp. 62 f.

[2] Cf., in addition to the references in the *Index Itp.*, Cannata, 'L'*animo possidere* nel diritto romano classico', *SDHI* xxvi (1960) 71 ff. at pp. 96 ff.; Watson, 'Acquisition of possession and usucapion *per servos et filios*', *LQR* lxxviii (1962) 205 ff. at p. 224 and n. 92; Tondo, 'Acquisto del possesso da parte del pupillo', *Studi Betti* (Milan, 1962) iv. 361 ff. at pp. 364 ff.

[3] Hägerström, *Der römische Obligationsbegriff im Lichte der allgemeinen römischen Rechtsanschauung* (Uppsala, Leipzig, 1927), i. 116 n., would alter *pupillum* to *infantem* but for our purposes this does not affect the significance of the text.

[4] This has been doubted and it has been suggested that *pupillus* was restricted to pupils who were *infantia maior* but the arguments of Tondo, op. cit., p. 368, against this idea are conclusive. Most recently, Gordon, 'Acquisition of Ownership by *traditio* and Acquisition of Possession', *RIDA* xii (1965) 279 ff. at pp. 280 f., has argued that in G. 2. 83 it is doubtful whether *pupillus* should be understood as meaning a child of any age under puberty because it should be read in the light of G. 3. 109. Gaius in 3. 109 says that when he said *pupillus* (in 3. 107) he meant one *qui iam aliquem intellectum habet*. But this qualification of Gaius simply shows that if there is no express qualification the natural meaning of *pupillus* is a child *sui iuris* of any age under puberty.

interpolated but in fact it corresponds to what we know from other texts was the view of Paul.[1] Thus, in the last century of the Republic there was a view—how widespread it was we cannot tell—[2] that even an infant could acquire possession without the authority of his tutor. On this view, very little weight is attached to the intention of the acquirer. [3,4,5]

A rather less strict attitude to possession is also apparent in D. 41. 2. 3. 5 (Paul, 54 *ad ed.*):[6]

> Ex contrario plures eandem rem in solidum possidere non possunt: contra naturam quippe est, ut, cum ego aliquid teneam, tu quoque id tenere videaris. Sabinus tamen scribit eum qui precario dederit et ipsum possidere et eum qui precario acceperit. idem Trebatius probabat existimans posse alium iuste, alium iniuste possidere, duos iniuste vel duos iuste non posse. quem Labeo reprehendit, quoniam in summa possessionis non multum interest, iuste quis an iniuste possideat: quod est verius. non magis enim eadem possessio apud duos esse potest, quam ut tu stare videaris in eo loco, in quo ego sto, vel in quo ego sedeo, tu sedere videaris.

The view of Labeo and Paul, which also appears to have been the general view in high classical law,[7] was that two people could not possess *in solidum* at the same time. Sabinus thought that the *precario dans* and the *precario accipiens* could both possess at the same time. Trebatius took a more general view, namely that one person could possess *iuste* another *iniuste*, but that two could not possess *iuste* or two *iniuste*.[8] D. 43. 26. 19 pr. (Julian, 49 *dig.*)

[1] See Watson, *Obligations*, pp. 222 ff.

[2] Cf. Cannata, op. cit., pp. 97 f.

[3] Though it does not concern us here, Paul's requirement of *tutoris auctoritas* for acquisition of possession by an *infans* represents a very anomalous use of *tutoris auctoritas* and is presumably an innovation to circumvent the infant's incapacity to acquire possession: cf. Watson, *Obligations*, pp. 223 f.

[4] Whether the justification in the text for the view of Ofilius and Nerva the younger, *eam enim rem facti, non iuris esse*, goes back to Ofilius or only to Nerva cannot now be determined.

[5] If the explanation given *supra*, pp. 55 ff., for the opinion of Brutus and Manilius in D. 41. 2. 3. 3 is wrong, and the *thensaurus* is not being usucapted as part of the land, then it might be arguable that for these jurists there was *possessio* of the *thensaurus* as a separate entity without knowledge and hence without intention.

[6] The substance of the text would seem to be trustworthy: see now Kaser, *EB*, pp. 349 ff.

[7] Cf. Kaser, loc. cit.

[8] The way that the text is framed suggests that Trebatius' opinion is a generalization of Sabinus: cf. Kaser, *EB*, p. 351.

indicates that Julian followed the opinion of Trebatius.[1] Kaser reasonably suggests[2] that for Trebatius a *iustus possessor* is one who enjoys interdictal possession but who cannot be attacked by interdict; and that a person possesses *iniuste* who holds *vi*, or *clam*, or *precario*. The view of Labeo and Paul is logical and reasonable. But that of Sabinus also makes good practical sense. The *precario accipiens* and the *precario dans* are in a settled relationship to one another. Whether one says that the *precario dans* possesses or not, he will win in the interdict in any dispute with the *precario accipiens*. In practical terms, Sabinus' opinion seems to mean that if the *precario accipiens* is ejected by a third party, both the *precario accipiens* and the *precario dans* will be able to bring an interdict against the intruder. More theoretically, one could justify the possession of the *precario dans* on the ground that he was possessing through the *precario accipiens*. It is the view of Trebatius which does not seem to make sense. In terms of the interdicts, it does not appear to make any practical difference whether when one person is ejected forcibly by another we say that the former continues to possess or that he has an interdict to recover possession. And Trebatius cannot be thinking of interdictal possession for the first possessor where the intruder is in turn ejected by a third person. Possession has to be conceded to this last—*iniusta possessio*—and since in Trebatius' opinion two people can possess *in solidum*, but not more than two and one of these must possess *iuste*, the other *iniuste*, then the person who posesses *iuste* (for the interdicts) is he who has just been ejected. Thus, the first possessor has no interdictal remedy. So far as I can see, this view of Trebatius—which Julian also held—is both illogical and pointless in terms of the interdicts. It can, however, make good sense in terms of *usucapio*. If a person who is usucapting loses possession *vi aut clam* then it would appear that his *usucapio* is broken. On the view of Trebatius, such a person would not lose possession and so his *usucapio* would continue.[3]

[1] Cf. Kaser, *EB*, p. 351. D. 43. 26. 15. 4 (Pomponius, 29 *ad Sab.*) might suggest that Pomponius was of the same opinion (or at least held the view of Sabinus): cf. Kaser, *EB*, pp. 351 f.

[2] *EB*, pp. 350 f.

[3] According to D. 41. 2. 25. 2 (Pomponius, 23 *ad Quintum Mucium*) some jurists held the view that if a person possesses land—land is not expressly men-

Possession was retained so long as one had sufficient physical control over the thing. This control could be exercised either directly by the possessor or through certain intermediaries, such as sons in power or slaves, or persons who held the thing from the possessor in terms of a legal institution which was acceptable for this purpose. Thus, a possessor continued to possess if he deposited the thing.

D. 41. 2. 3. 18 (Paul, 54 *ad ed.*). Si rem apud te depositam furti faciendi causa contrectaveris, desino possidere. sed si eam loco non moveris et infitiandi animum habeas, plerique veterum et Sabinus et Cassius recte responderunt possessorem me manere, quia furtum sine contrectatione fieri non potest nec animo furtum admittatur.

Even if the depositee decides to deny the deposit, the depositor according to the majority of the *veteres* will continue to possess. Only when the depositee actually commits theft by improperly moving the object will the depositor cease to possess.[1]

Cicero, *pro Caecina* 32. 94, tells us that a usufructuary has *possessio* and that a possessor continues to possess through a *colonus*. The latter statement would appear to be good law,[2] but not the former.[3,4]

tioned but is implicit as *ingressus* shows—by intention alone and someone else takes control of the land *clam*, the former does not at once lose possession but only when, on returning, he is repulsed, or ceases to possess *animo* because he thinks he will be repulsed by the intruder. The intruder will, of course, acquire possession when he enters with the requisite intention and has sufficient physical control, so it would seem that on this view, for a certain period, one person will possess *iuste*, another *iniuste*. It is difficult to see what advantage in respect of interdicts this approach will give to the *iustus possessor* but it could help him greatly with *usucapio* especially in respect of seasonal pastures where he might become aware of the intrusion only after a period of months and indeed only after the period remaining for *usucapio* had been completed. In the text it is said of this view, *quod quasi magis probatur*. Some scholars, notably Lenel, *Pal.* ii. 72, n. 7, regard this as an error (presumably due to the wrong extension of an abbreviation, *qm*) for *quod Quinto Mucio probatur*. This may be correct, but *quod quasi magis probatur* is not in itself suspicious and so the suggested reconstruction is too hypothetical for it to be accepted here that the view of Quintus Mucius is given: cf. Kaser, *EB*, p. 328, n. 30. There have been numerous suggestions of interpolation in the text but in the circumstances they do not concern us.

[1] Cf. now Watson, *Obligations*, pp. 221 f.

[2] Cf., e.g., for classical law, D. 41. 2. 30. 5 (Paul, 15 *ad Sab.*).

[3] Cf. Kaser, *EB*, pp. 338 f.

[4] For D. 41. 2. 3. 23 (Paul, 54 *ad ed.*) see *supra*, p. 49; for the *regula* of the *veteres*, *nemo sibi ipse causam possessionis mutare potest*, see *supra*, p. 50.

Possession was protected by interdicts[1] of which the most important probably were *utrubi* and *uti possidetis*. *Utrubi* lay in respect of moveables and by it the praetor forbade force to be used to prevent that party to the dispute leading the thing away who had possessed the thing for the greater part of the last year.[2] This interdict is not evidenced for the Republic but no conclusions should be drawn from this since the Digest title devoted to it, 43. 31, consists of only one short text of two fragments.[3] It is, however, widely thought that evidence for it exists in Plautus' *Stichus*[4]

696 SANGARINUS: mica uter utrubi accumbamus. STICHUS: abi tu sane superior.

This is to adopt the reading of Lindsay.[5] The manuscripts are corrupt: that normally designated as *P* has *amica*, and *A* has *m . . . cem*. Various other readings such as *amicam* have been adopted by modern scholars, but Lindsay's reading is the least drastic which avoids difficulties with scansion. The exact reading does not affect the point at issue. The two slaves, Stichus and Sangarinus, in love with the same slave girl, Stephanium, are arranging a feast *à trois*, and at this moment they are determining the seating plan.

750 STE. utrubi accumbo? SA. utrubi tu vis? STE. cum ambobus volo, nam ambos amo.

Stephanium asks where she is to sit. It is said that these lines certainly refer to the *interdictum utrubi* and that they contain a legal joke concerning which of the girl's admirers is to leave her to the other.[6] Further, it is argued that otherwise Plautus would not

[1] For the interdictal system see, above all, G. 4. 138 ff.: cf. Buckland, *Text-book*, pp. 729 ff.

[2] G. 4. 160: cf. Lenel, *EP*, pp. 488 ff.

[3] From Ulpian, 72 *ad edictum*.

[4] e.g. Ubbelohde in Glück's *Commentario alle pandette, libri xlii–xliv* (Milan, 1899), pp. 650 f.; De Martino, *La giurisdizione nel diritto romano* (Padua, 1937), pp. 116 f.; Biscardi, *La protezione interdittale nel processo romano* (Padua, 1938), pp. 103 f.; Kaser, *EB*, pp. 281 f.: *contra*, Kübler, *Geschichte des römischen Rechts* (Leipzig, 1925), p. 157, n. 3; Costa, *Il diritto privato romano nelle commedie di Plauto* (Turin, 1890), p. 457; *Storia del diritto romano privato*, 2nd edn. (Turin, 1925), p. 296.

[5] *T. Macci Plauti comoediae* ii (Oxford, 1905).

[6] Biscardi, loc. cit.

have insisted several times on a term, *utrubi*, which is not substantially helpful for the clarity and vividness of the text.[1] But even apart from any reference to the *interdictum utrubi*, *utrubi* is a perfectly natural word here and it does not appear to be unduly insisted on. And with its meaning, 'which of two' it does add to the text's vividness. Moreover, though there is of course a joke, it may be nothing more than the obvious coarse one. What is very much against the idea of a joke on the interdict is that *utrubi* by itself is a very ordinary word and the situation is not such that non-lawyers would naturally think, without prompting, of the interdict; and hence, if a legal joke were intended, far too many in the audience would miss it. Any reference to the interdict would have been—and easily could have been—more express. Thus, Stephanium could have begun: *utrubi vestrum*. Or the words *nec vi nec clam nec precario* might have been inserted. I submit the text ought not to be regarded as evidence for the existence of the interdict. But it can be argued that the absence of the term *possessio* from the interdict means that it goes back to a time before the word *possessio* was used in respect of moveables.[2]

Uti possidetis lay in respect of immoveables and we know that it did exist in the later Republic. We possess two slightly different versions of the interdict, one from Ulpian[3] and one from Festus,[4] of which the latter is probably an earlier formulation.[5] That version, which probably is not far different from that of the Republic even if it is not identical with it, runs: *Uti nunc possidetis eum fundum, quo de agitur, quod nec vi nec clam nec precario alter ab altero possidetis, ita possideatis. adversus ea vim fieri veto.* The text which we have concerns not the interdict itself but the *iudicium secutorium* which follows upon an alleged contravention of the interdict.[6]

D. 43. 17. 3. 11 (Ulpian, 69 *ad ed.*). In hoc interdicto condemnationis summa refertur ad rei ipsius aestimationem. 'quanti res est' sic accipimus 'quanti uniuscuiusque interest possessionem retinere' Servii

[1] De Martino, loc. cit.
[2] Cf. Kaser, *EB*, p. 320; *supra*, p. 59.
[3] D. 43. 17. 1 pr. (69 *ad ed.*).
[4] s.v. *possessio*.
[5] Cf. Lenel, *EP*, p. 470.
[6] For the *iudicium secutorium* see G. 4. 166 ff.

autem sententia est existimantis tanti possessionem aestimandam, quanti ipsa res est: sed hoc nequaquam opinandum est: longe enim aliud est rei pretium, aliud possessionis.

There have been various suggestions of interpolation but none appears really to affect us.[1] Servius, for a condemnation in the action in the terms *quanti res est*, 'whatever the matter in issue comes to', estimated that the value of possession was the worth of the thing. This punitive opinion appears to have been regarded as extreme by later jurists.[2] The *iudicium secutorium* was also called the *iudicium Cascellianum*,[3] presumably after the jurist Cascellius who was active in the first century B.C.[4]

Cicero's speeches not only show the existence of two other possessory interdicts, *de vi* and *de vi armata*, but they give the form which these interdicts had in his time. In 73 or 72 B.C. the date of the *pro Tullio*, the *interdictum de vi* ran: *Unde tu aut familia aut procurator tuus illum aut familiam aut procuratorem illius in hoc anno vi deiecisti, cum ille possideret, quod nec vi nec clam nec precario a te possideret, eo restituas.*[5] In later centuries the form of the interdict underwent changes.[6] In 69 B.C. the time of the *pro Caecina*, the *interdictum de vi armata* ran: *Unde tu aut familia aut procurator tuus illum vi hominibus coactis armatisve deiecisti, eo restituas.*[7] Previously, in 73 or 72 B.C., the interdict had had a different form, given by Cicero in the *pro Tullio* 12. 29 as: *Unde dolo malo tuo, M. Tulli, M. Claudius aut familia aut procurator eius detrusus est.*[8] Later the interdict underwent further modifications.[9] The difference in wording in the two interdicts involved that a person who had taken possession from the other by force, clandestinely, or by permission, and then was ousted by that other, could

[1] Add to the *Index Itp.*, Levy, *Nachträge zur Konkurrenz der Aktionen und Personen* (Weimar, 1962), pp. 57 f. and the references he gives, p. 58, n. 233.

[2] Cf. Levy, op. cit., p. 58.

[3] Cf. G. 4. 166*a*.

[4] Cf., e.g., Kaser, *RPR* i. 338; Kelly, *The Irish Jurist* i. (1966) 347.

[5] Cicero, *pro Tullio*, 19. 44 f.; *pro Caecina* 19. 55 f.; 20. 56 ff.; 30. 86 ff.; *de leg. agrar.* 3. 3. 11; *Rhet. ad Herenn.* 4. 29. 40; *lex agraria* (of 111 B.C.), line 18; cf. Lenel, *EP*, p. 462.

[6] Cf. Lenel, loc. cit.

[7] Cicero, *pro Caecina* 14. 41–17. 48; 19. 55; 21. 60 f.; 30. 88; *ad fam.* 15. 16. 3; cf. Lenel, *EP*, p. 467.

[8] Cf. Cicero, *pro Caecina* 17. 49; Lenel, *EP*, p. 467, n. 8.

[9] Cf. Lenel, *EP*, p. 467.

recover possession if he had been ousted by force of arms (*vi armata*) but not if he had been ousted simply by force (*vi*).[1] From the presence of the words *cum ego possiderem* (or *cum ille possideret*) in the *interdictum de vi* and their absence from the *interdictum de vi armata*, Cicero[2] tries to twist the meaning of the latter and to argue that a person who claims possession and is repulsed *vi armata* is entitled to the interdict even if he never had possession.[3]

Terence, *Eun.* 319 points to the existence in 161 B.C., the date of the play, of an interdictal clause about *vi, clam precario*,[4] but we cannot be precise about the interdict which is being thought of. Cicero, *de orat.* 1. 10. 41–4 shows that in 91 B.C., the year in which that dialogue is set, interdicts existed.[5]

In certain circumstances and under various edicts the praetor might order possession to be taken of a living person's goods.[6] The main one of these edicts for which we have evidence for the Republic is *Qui fraudationis causa latitabit*. This ran:[7] *Qui fraudationis causa latitabit, si boni viri arbitratu non defendetur, eius bona possideri vendique iubebo*. From D. 42. 4. 7. 13 (Ulpian, 59 *ad ed.*) we know that the *veteres* considered the import of *latitare*.

D. 42. 4. 7. 13 (Ulpian, 59 *ad ed.*). Illud sciendum est posse quem in eadem civitate esse et latitare, et in alia civitate et non latitare. etenim qui in alia civitate sit copiamque sui faciat in publico ibique pareat, an latitet, videamus. et hodie hoc iure utimur, ut sive quis eodem loci agat sive peregre agat, si tamen occursum creditoris evitet, latitare videatur. denique eum quoque, qui in foro eodem agat, si circa columnas aut stationes se occultet, videri latitare veteres responderunt, et posse quem adversus alterum latitare, adversus alterum non. constat autem, ut ipse eius possit bona vendere, adversus quem latitat.

Thus, the *veteres* did not demand that the person said to *latitare* be absent—it could be enough if, in the market, he hid behind pillars or stalls. And they considered that someone might *latitare* in

[1] Cf. G. 4. 154 f.

[2] *Pro Caecina*, 31. 91.

[3] Cf. Roby, *Roman Private Law* (Cambridge, 1902), ii. 519 ff.

[4] Cf., e.g., Kaser, *EB*, p. 278, n. 2.

[5] Cf., e.g., Biscardi, *La protezione interdittale nel processo romano*, pp. 100 ff.

[6] Cf. Lenel, *EP*, pp. 413 ff. *Bonorum possessio* of a deceased person will be discussed in a later volume on *Succession in the Later Roman Republic*.

[7] Cf. Lenel, *EP*, p. 415.

respect of one person and not of another.[1] A text of Cicero shows that the wording of this edict was not quite the same in his time.

> *pro Quinctio* 19. 60. Docui, quod primum pollicitus sum, C. Aquili, causam omnino, cur postularet non fuisse, quod neque pecunia debebatur et, si maxime deberetur, commissum nihil esset qua re ad istam rationem perveniretur. Attende nunc ex edicto praetoris bona P. Quincti possideri nullo modo potuisse. Recita edictum. QUI FRAUDATIONIS CAUSA LATITARIT. Non est is Quinctius; nisi si latitant qui ad negotium suum relicto procuratore proficiscuntur. CUI HERES NON EXSTABIT. Ne is quidem. QUI EXSILII CAUSA SOLUM VERTERIT. *Dici id non potest. QUI ABSENS IUDICIO DEFENSUS NON FUERIT.* Quo tempore existimas oportuisse, Naevi, absentem Quinctium defendi aut quo modo? tum cum postulabas ut bona possideres? Nemo adfuit; neque enim quisquam divinare poterat te postulaturum, neque quemquam attinebat id recusare quod praetor non fieri, sed *ex* edicto suo fieri iubebat. 61. Qui locus igitur absentis defendendi procuratori primus datus est? Cum proscribebas. Ergo adfuit, non passus est, libellos deiecit Sex. Alfenus; qui primus erat offici gradus, servatus est a procuratore summa cum diligentia.

This gives only the beginning of the edict but the word *latitarit* is used, not the *latitabit* of Hadrian's Edict.

The Cicero text also indicates the existence of two other edicts which granted possession of the goods of a living person. *Qui exsilii causa solum verterit*, it has been conjectured, has become the *Qui capitali crimine damnatus erit* of Hadrian's time.[2] It seems that the other edict, *Qui absens iudicio defensus non fuerit* can be conjectured from what Cicero says in the latter part of the text. At least in the Empire the edict seems to have continued: *et eius, cuius bona possessa sunt a creditoribus, veneant, praeterquam pupilli et eius, qui rei publicae causa sine dolo malo afuit.*[3,4]

[1] Beseler suggests that a passage may be missing before *et posse* and that possibly *veteres* was written by Justinian: *Beiträge* ii. 104. But there seems no particular reason to accept the latter point which is the one which mainly concerns us.

[2] Lenel, *EP*, pp. 421 ff.; Solazzi, *Il concorso dei creditori* (Naples, 1937), i. 107: cf. Kaser, *ZPR*, p. 303, n. 31.

[3] Cf. Lenel, *EP*, pp. 415 f.

[4] The rights and duties of a person in possession *ex edicto* were governed by edicts; cf. Lenel, *EP*, pp. 423 ff. For the most important, *Quemadmodum in possessione esse oporteat*, see, above all, Cicero, *pro Quinctio*, 27. 84.

4

VINDICATIO, ACTIO PUBLICIANA, ACTIO AD EXHIBENDUM

SINCE this book is concerned with legal rules and not primarily with legal concepts and is restricted historically to the period from around 200 B.C. to the end of the Republic, it is not appropriate to discuss systematically Kaser's important concept of ownership in early Roman law. The concept is complex and has many ramifications, but the fundamental points are now simply and clearly set out in 'Der römische Eigentumsbegriff', *Rabels Zeitschrift* (1962), pp. 19 ff. at pp. 20–9; and in an English version, 'The Concept of Roman Ownership', *Tydskrif vir Hedendaagse Romeins-Hollandse Reg* (1964), pp. 5 ff. at pp. 6–10.[1] But I am not quite convinced on some of the basic points and perhaps a few words might not be out of place at the beginning of this chapter.

(*a*) Kaser thinks that until late in the second century B.C. ownership was not 'institutionalized', that the legal control was but a mere reflection of the protection granted by vindication, that it was not yet conceived of as a specific legal type nor contrasted with other types of legal power. In this it differed, he says, from the powers exercised over persons—persons in power were under *potestas* or *manus* or *mancipium*. His view on early ownership is conclusively proved, he claims, by the fact that until the first century B.C. there was no technical name—neither *dominium*[2] nor *proprietas*—for ownership. Early law was content with the vague phrase *meum esse* which expressed only the appropriation of the thing, not the content and limits of the power over it. But this argument does not seem to me to be wholly persuasive. First, there

[1] Also in *Rapports généraux au vi^e Congrès international de droit comparé*, pp. 39–43.

[2] The earliest known use is in D. 8. 3. 30 (Paul, 4 *epit. Alfeni dig.*), which is discussed *infra*, pp. 184 ff.; cf. Daube, *Iura* xii (1961) 97.

can be another explanation of the absence of a technical term for ownership, namely that since it is the greatest right imaginable over a thing a technical name for it is not really needed. *Meum esse* is quite sufficient. It is lesser and restricted rights which need a technical name expressive of their content. Secondly, *meum esse* does not appear at all vague. Certainly it expresses the content and limits of the power over the thing just as much as *dominium meum esse* or *me dominum esse* would. A claim of *dominium* is no more and no less than a claim that it is mine. Thirdly, the claim *meum esse* was supported in the *actio sacramento in rem*,[1] in the *mancipatio*[2], and in *in iure cessio*[3] by the words *ex iure quiritium*. These words, though no doubt mainly concerned with the appropriation, would be largely meaningless if there was no technical content to *meum esse*.[4]

(*b*) Kaser claims that the uniformity of the early Roman power over things, however, went so far that ownership was the only real right which was recognized and so all real rights which later were thought of as restricted rights in another's thing were absorbed into ownership. This, he says, is particularly true of the four original servitudes which were in early times corporeal *res mancipi* in that ownership of the part of the land over which the way or aqueduct passed vested in the holder of the right. The enjoyment of the way or aqueduct was functionally divided between the limited owner and the other owner. Only later was a servitude recognized as a right *sui generis*. Now this argument is very logical since we know that these servitudes were created by *mancipatio*. Moreover there are signs that in Jewish law usufruct was not always distinguished from a right of ownership.[5] None the less, the argument need not be correct. As a social and economic fact those

[1] Cicero, *pro Murena* 12. 26. [2] Cf. G. 1. 119. [3] Cf. G. 2. 24.

[4] A friendly criticism of this paragraph has been that it fails to take account of the *vindicatio servitutis* where, again under the *legis actio*, the claim might be *meum esse*. But (i) the common view that servitudes were regarded as giving ownership could well be correct despite what is said *infra*, § *b*. If that view is correct then *meum esse* in the old *vindicatio servitutis* would be a claim of ownership. If that view is wrong then there is no good reason for thinking that *meum esse* was in the *vindicatio servitutis*. (ii) There is no real indication that *meum esse* was in the *legis act*fo claim for a servitude.

[5] Cf. Yaron, *Gifts in Contemplation of Death in Jewish and Roman Law* (Oxford, 1960) pp. 217 ff.

things which came to be legally recognized as the four original servitudes are of extreme importance in a primitive agricultural society. They will exist in practice by consent and without legal recognition. But naturally the need for legal protection will early be felt, and a method of creating them will have to come into existence. But how could they be created? Unless some totally new institution is invented there will have to be recourse to an existing method of transfer. *In iure cessio* is unlikely to have come under consideration since it is improbable that it existed at such an early date.[1] *Traditio* could not be used since, apart even from its informality, the thing to be transferred had to be handed over. Therefore, the corporeality of the thing had to be much in evidence. This leaves *mancipatio* as the only possible mode of transfer which could have been employed if servitudes were to come into existence.[2] And we know from G. 1. 121 that land to be transferred

[1] Perhaps it would be better to say that we cannot make a reasonable conjecture as to the time of introduction of *in iure cessio*. For the views which have been held see now Wolff, 'The constitutive effect of *in iure cessio*', *Tulane Law Review* xxx (1959) 525 ff. at pp. 525, n. 1. Kaser has shown (*EB*, p. 201,) that *Vat. Fr.* 50 does not necessarily mean that *in iure cessio* was mentioned in the XII Tables: hence, the text does not show that it existed in the time of the XII Tables. There is no logical reason for *in iure cessio* ever developing at all. It is, in its new use of an existing institution, a brilliant stroke presumably due to one individual and it could, on *a priori* grounds, have come into being at any time before the disappearance of the *legis actio* on which it is modelled. A slight argument in favour of a not too early date is this: it is a major 'breakthrough' in legal thinking and it must have won the sympathy of the praetors. Hence it is likely to have been thought of, and accepted, in a situation where no other way (or at least no other convenient way) to attain the desired result was available. But there are not many such situations which are early—thus, for instance, the direct creation of usufruct *inter vivos* and urban praedial servitudes do not seem to be early—and so in remote antiquity the need for it would be smaller than was later the case and hence the opportunities for its arising limited. Moreover, once it was introduced it might take some time for all the possible applications of it to be seen. Even if it were in existence before the four original servitude situations were common, its cumbrousness—especially in requiring the intervention of a magistrate—would make it very unattractive to farmers who would try other methods of making servitudes legally binding. It should not be forgotten that in very early times *mancipatio* was probably more flexible both in its form and in the kind of things which could be so transferred than it later became: cf., e.g., Kaser, *EB*, p. 168.

[2] At least as the only direct method. No doubt recourse could have been had to indirect methods. For instance, the owner of what was to be the dominant tenement could have mancipated it to the owner of what was to be the servient tenement, who could then remancipate it, with the right of servitude attached, to its former owner: or there could be *mancipatio fundi deducta servitute*.

by *mancipatio* did not have to be touched by the transferee and could even be at a distance.[1] Hence the corporeality of what was to be transferred was not necessarily much in evidence in *mancipatio*. One can go so far as to say that it was inevitable that individuals who wanted legal protection for servitude situations would try to create legal servitudes by *mancipatio*. Given the social importance of the four original servitude situations, the resulting need for a legal method of creating servitudes, the fact that no other possible direct method of creating servitudes existed, and that individuals must have tried to create servitudes by *mancipatio*, I think it could easily happen that 'servitudes' created by *mancipatio* would be given legal recognition even without there being the slightest feeling that the servitude was a corporeal thing or that what was being transferred was ownership of the land over which the way or aqueduct passed. A practical solution for a pressing problem could have been found with no real concern for abstract, theoretical matters.

(*c*) Kaser suggests that the lack of 'institutionalization' may further explain why early Roman ownership was actually a *relative* right, i.e. a mere reflection of the protection afforded by vindication. Under the old procedure by *legis actio sacramento in rem* both parties asserted '*meum esse aio*'. Both parties thus claimed to be owner, hence the judge could make only one decision, namely which party had the better right to the thing. He could not decide that neither had a right to it. Thus, he had to allot it to one or the other though a third party might later successfully vindicate it from that person. All of this seems to me to be unprovable. Even if one accepts that both parties to the action were placed on level terms, I can think of no good reason for holding that, for instance, where both parties were in bad faith and neither had any claim to the thing the judge none the less had to award it to one or the other. He could easily hold that both had given an *iniustum sacramentum* and so both would forfeit the amount of the oath. What happened to the thing under dispute might then depend on whether the judge was acting as *sequester* or had left it in the control of one of the parties. How far the judge might be willing to go to award the decision to someone who was not the owner but who had the

[1] Cf. Kaser, *EB*, pp. 224 f.

better claim can only be a matter of conjecture but it need not be very far. For instance, Kaser's own example is not convincing. He points out that in classical law the owner alone was entitled to the *vindicatio* but that to protect a person who had acquired a thing in good faith from a non-owner and who had lost control of it the *actio Publiciana* was introduced in the first century B.C.[1] But, he goes on, it cannot be doubted that the necessity to protect the *bonae fidei possessor* who had lost the thing against anyone who had a lesser right, e.g. a possessor in bad faith, must have been felt even before the introduction of the *actio Publiciana*. Since we do not know of any forerunner of the *actio Publiciana*, Kaser says that we are driven to the conclusion that the ancient *rei vindicatio* in the *legis actio sacramento* was admissible in these cases. This conclusion does not necessarily follow. The *bonae fidei possessor* who had lost possession might have been expected to use the *interdictum utrubi*[2] which is generally believed to have existed before 200 B.C.[3] This remedy might not cover every possible situation—though it would adequately cover most—but unfortunate gaps are not unusual in early law.[4] If the *malae fidei possessor* who had been ousted by the *interdictum* then insisted on bringing the *vindicatio* we cannot tell whether the judge would declare that the *bonae fidei possessor* had given a *iustum sacramentum* or whether he would hold that both parties had given an *iniustum sacramentum* but do nothing to deprive the *bonae fidei possessor* of his control of the thing. Further, one should remember that in early law it was in fact considerably easier to become owner by *usucapio* than it was in classical law,[5] so that there would be fewer cases where a person had a good right to have a thing but was not the owner.

But in any event, it is much more likely that the parties to the *legis actio sacramento in rem* were not placed on level terms and it

[1] For difficulties in dating the *actio Publiciana* see *infra*, pp. 104 ff.

[2] Even if this were not the original purpose of the interdict.

[3] Cf. Kaser, *RPR* i. 124 and n. 11. But for the absence of textual evidence on the point see *supra*, pp. 86 f.

[4] When one remembers that gap in the protection of an honest man dealing with a rogue which was not filled until the creation of the *actio de dolo* and the *exceptio doli* around 66 B.C., the *a priori* argument that in some other situation the necessity of protecting the honest man must have been felt and acted on before the first century B.C. loses much of its persuasiveness.

[5] Cf. *supra*, pp. 31 ff. and the references given.

was the plaintiff alone who had to prove his claim to be owner.[1] In this there is, I suggest, no difference between the *legis actio sacramento in rem* and the formulary *vindicatio*. On this view there can be no argument for holding that ownership was ever a relative, not an absolute, right.

Vindicatio

Around the end of the first half of the first century B.C. both the *legis actio sacramento in rem* and the *formula* of the classical *vindicatio* were in use contemporaneously. The continued existence of the former is shown by Cicero, *pro Murena* 12. 26, a speech which was delivered in the latter part of November, 63 B.C.

Cum hoc fieri bellissime posset: 'Fundus Sabinus meus est.' 'Immo meus', deinde iudicium, noluerunt. 'FUNDUS', inquit, 'QUI EST IN AGRO QUI SABINUS VOCATUR.' Satis verbose; cedo quid postea? 'EUM EGO EX IURE QUIRITIUM MEUM ESSE AIO.' Quid tum? 'INDE IBI EGO TE EX IURE MANUM CONSERTUM VOCO.' Quid huic tam loquaciter litigioso responderet ille unde petebatur non habebat. Transit idem iuris consultus tibicinis Latini modo. 'UNDE TU ME', inquit 'EX IURE MANUM CONSERTUM VOCASTI, INDE IBI EGO TE REVOCO.' Praetor interea ne pulchrum se ac beatum putaret atque aliquid ipse sua sponte loqueretur, ei quoque carmen compositum est cum ceteris rebus absurdum tum vero in illo: 'SUIS UTRISQUE SUPERSTITIBUS PRAESENTIBUS ISTAM VIAM DICO; ITE VIAM.' Praesto aderat sapiens ille qui inire viam doceret. 'REDITE VIAM.' Eodem duce redibant. Haec iam tum apud illos barbatos ridicula, credo, videbantur, homines, cum recte atque in loco constitissent, iuberi abire ut, unde abissent, eodem statim redirent. Isdem ineptiis fucata sunt illa omnia: 'QUANDO TE IN IURE CONSPICIO' et haec: 'ANNE TU DICAS, QUA EX CAUSA VINDICAVERIS?' Quae dum erant occulta, necessario ab eis qui ea tenebant petebantur; postea vero pervolgata atque in manibus iactata et excussa, inanissima prudentiae reperta sunt, fraudis autem et stultitiae plenissima.

G. 4. 16 confirms the substantial accuracy of this account of the form of the *legis actio*. A further text of Cicero, *in Verr*. II. 2. 12. 31, from a speech intended to be delivered in the latter part of 70 B.C. proves that a *formula* already existed.

[1] See Watson, 'Towards a new hypothesis of the *legis actio sacramento in rem*', *RIDA* xiv (1967), 455 ff. But far from being a new hypothesis it was expounded over 50 years ago by Abǵarowicz, *Essai sur la Preuve dans la rei vindicatio* (Paris, 1912); cf. contra, Kaser, *EB*, pp. 8 n. 6, 52 n. 4, *ZPR*, p. 75 n. 64. What appears to be Kaser's objection is, I think, dealt with in Watson, op. cit. p. 457.

Si vero illud quoque accedit, ut praetor in ea verba iudicium det ut vel L. Octavius Balbus iudex, homo et iuris et offici peritissimus, non possit aliter iudicare,—si iudicium sit eius modi: L. OCTAVIUS IUDEX ESTO. SI PARET FUNDUM CAPENATEM, QUO DE AGITUR, EX IURE QUIRITIUM P. SERVILI ESSE, NEQUE IS FUNDUS Q. CATULO RESTITUETUR: non necesse erit L. Octavio iudici cogere P. Servilium Q. Catulo fundum restituere, aut condemnare eum quem non oporteat? Eius modi totum ius praetorium, omnis res iudicaria fuit in Sicilia per triennium Verre praetore. Decreta eius modi: SI NON ACCIPIT, QUOD TE DEBERE DICIS, ACCUSES; SI PETIT, DUCAS. C. Fuficium duci iussit petitorem, L. Suettium, L. Racilium. Iudicia eius modi: qui cives Romani erant *iudicabant* si Siculi essent, cum Siculos eorum legibus dari oporteret; qui Siculi, si cives Romani essent.

If we leave aside the insertion of the name of the defendant instead of the name of the plaintiff (which need not concern us) we have here in essentials the *formula* of the classical *vindicatio*.[1] Again, if we ignore this change of name, Cicero is not giving us a *formula* which was restricted to the Edict of Verres as governor of Sicily. Capena is in southern Etruria and *ex iure Quiritium* shows that he is thinking of Roman, not of provincial law. Nothing in either text seems to indicate why the *legis actio* and the *formula* claiming civil law ownership could exist contemporaneously and the question will not be discussed here.[2] The fact seems to fit all the theories on the development of procedure in the later Republic.[3,4]

[1] For which see Lenel, *EP*, pp. 185 f. Further evidence that the *vindicatio* already had a clause for the restitution of the thing is in D. 6. 1. 57 and *h.t.* 58, which are discussed *infra*, pp. 100 ff.

[2] But it will be in a subsequent volume on *Legal Science in the Later Roman Republic*.

[3] Though for Kaser the *formula* could not give rise to a *iudicium legitimum* but only to a *iudicium imperium continens*: *Studi Albertario* i, especially pp. 28 and 53 ff. He observes that, with the exception of the *condictio*, the *legis actio* procedure was regarded as the normal in the time of Cicero and that the *formula* was used only in special circumstances (p. 53) and he claims that this is inexplicable on Wlassak's view [see for Wlassak's view the pages cited by Kaser, p. 28, n. 1] that both procedures were on an equal footing. Kaser suggests (pp. 53 f.) that the main factor for preferring the *legis actio* procedure was that the decision there had 'rechtsgestaltende Kraft' and was decisive even against third parties; and that this was not the case with the *formula*. The latter, he says, could not have this effect if the formulary *vindicatio* was only a procedure of the praetor or other magistrate and so the judgement could not give civil law ownership. ['Das Urteil der im Formularprozess geltendgemachten *actio in rem* hatte dagegen die rechtsgestaltende Wirkung nicht. Es konnte sie nicht haben, wenn

[*Footnotes continued overleaf.*

The *vindicatio* extended to all fruits and accessories which came into existence after *litis contestatio* but it did not cover those which were in existence before.[1]

D. 6. 1. 33 (Paul, 21 *ad ed.*). Fructus non modo percepti, sed et qui percipi honeste potuerunt aestimandi sunt: et ideo si dolo aut culpa possessoris res petita perierit, veriorem putat Pomponius Trebatii opinionem putantis eo usque fructuum rationem habendam, quo usque haberetur, si non perisset, id est ad rei iudicandae tempus: quod et Iuliano placet. hac ratione si nudae proprietatis dominus petierit et inter moras usus fructus amissus sit, ex eo tempore, quo ad proprietatem usus fructus reversus est, ratio fructuum habetur.

Thus, Trebatius held that where, due to the negligence or fraud of the possessor, the thing was destroyed (or lost), the other party was entitled to receive as fruits what would have come into existence up to the time when judgement was given.[2]

D. 22. 1. 19 pr. (Gaius, 6 *ad legem XII tab.*) concerns a different matter:

Videamus, an in omnibus rebus petitis in fructus quoque condemnatur possessor. quid enim si argentum aut vestimentum aliamve similem rem, quid praeterea si usum fructum aut nudam proprietatem, cum alienus usus fructus sit, petierit? neque enim nudae proprietatis, quod ad proprietatis nomen attinet, fructus ullus intellegi potest, neque usus fructus rursus fructus eleganter computabitur. quid igitur, si nuda proprietas petita sit? ex quo perdiderit fructuarius usum fructum, aestimabuntur in petitione fructus. item si usus fructus petitus sit, Proculus ait in fructus perceptos condemnari. praeterea Gallus Aelius putat, si vestimenta aut scyphus petita sint, in fructu haec numeranda esse, quod locata ea re mercedis nomine capi potuerit.

mit der formularen *vindicatio* nur ein amtsrechtlicher Prozess eingesetzt werden konnte, aus dem auch das Urteil nur amtsrechtlich wirkte und daher kein quiritisches Eigentum schaffen konnte.'] But this argument fails to convince. On Kaser's own view, only *legis actiones* were effective against third parties (cf. p. 53), so a judgement under a *formula*, whether the action was a *iudicium legitimum* or a *iudicium imperio continens* could not be effective against third parties. Hence if the reason why in Cicero's time the *legis actio* was regarded as the normal action was due to the fact that it was used because its judgement was effective against third parties, this preference would be given to the *legis actio* even if the action under a *formula* was a *iudicium legitimum*.

[4] One may presume that the *formula in rem per sponsionem* was also in existence before the end of the Republic: cf. G. 4. 91–4.

[1] Cf., e.g., Buckland, *Textbook*, p. 675.

[2] Cf. on the text, Reggi, *AG* cxlii (1952) 102 f.

Lenel[1] correctly regards this as relating to the provision of the XII Tables, *Si vindiciam falsam tulit, si velit is . . . tor arbitros tris dato, eorum arbitrio . . . fructus duplione damnum decidito.*[2] In our knowledge of the wording of this provision there are two gaps, each of about four or five letters. The meaning of the provision is by no means clear and there have been numerous hypotheses.[3] Perhaps the most satisfactory is that recently defended by Kaser,[4] namely that the party to an action who was given interim possession and who, knowing that he was not entitled to the thing, removed it temporarily *ex iure* for the period of the action, was liable to a penalty of double the fruits.[5] Within the framework of this provision, then, our text tells us that Gallus Aelius held that if an action were brought for clothes or drinking goblets the money which would have been made if these things had been hired out is to be counted as *fructus*. That sum would, of course, be doubled for the penalty.[6]

From at least the time of Hadrian a defendant might use the *exceptio doli* to recover at least some of his expenditure on the thing.[7] But there is no sign that the *exceptio doli* was so used earlier and we can at least presume that until the *exceptio* was issued around 66 B.C. by Aquillius Gallus[8] there was no way in which the defendant could recover any expenses which he had incurred on the thing.

[1] *Pal.* i. 245, n. 3; cf. most recently, Kaser, '*Vindicia falsa* und *fructus duplio*', *Iura* xiii (1962) 22 ff. at pp. 49 f.; Santoro, 'XII Tab. 12. 3', *Annali Palermo* xxx (1967) 1 ff.

[2] Festus, s.v. *vindiciae*.

[3] For literature see Kaser, op. cit., p. 22, n. 1; Santoro, op. cit., p. 6, n. 1.

[4] Loc. cit.

[5] He would reconstruct the provision: *Si vindiciam falsam tulit, si velit is ⟨prae⟩tor arbitros tres dato; eorum arbitrio ⟨reus⟩ fructus duplione damnum decidito. ⟨Prae⟩tor* would seem to be the only reasonable reconstruction for the first gap. But ⟨*reus*⟩ is rather unconvincing. It is obviously the defendant who must pay up and so there is not the slightest necessity to express *reus*. The superfluous precision of *reus* is all the more odd in view of *tulit* and *velit* where the person who takes and the person who wishes are different yet no attempt is made to clarify who they are. For other arguments against this reconstruction, see Santoro, op. cit., pp. 34 ff.

[6] Cf. Kaser, op. cit., p. 50. For the question whether in an action *per formulam* the provision was applied to the *formula petitoria* as well as to the *formula per sponsionem* see Kaser, op. cit., pp. 51 f.

[7] D. 6. 1. 37 (Ulpian, 17 *ad ed.*); *h.t.* 48 (Papinian, 2 *resp.*); *h.t.* 65 (*idem*); C. 3. 32. 5 [Gordian, A.D. 239].

[8] See now Watson, *Obligations*, pp. 258 f.

By what is probably more than just a coincidence we have two texts in which Alfenus (or Servius) discusses the problem where the possessor is sued by two different people at the same time in respect of a thing or slave and at least one of these actions is a *vindicatio*, and the defendant loses the first action.

D. 6. 1. 57 (Alfenus, 6 *dig.*). Is a quo fundus petitus erat ab alio eiusdem fundi nomine conventus est: quaerebatur, si alterutri eorum iussu iudicis fundum restituisset et postea secundum alterum petitorem res iudicaretur, quemadmodum non duplex damnum traheret. respondi, uter prior iudex iudicaret, eum oportere ita fundum petitori restitui iubere, ut possessori caveret vel satisdaret, si alter fundum evicisset, eum praestare.

Here both actions are *vindicationes*. So that the defendant will not suffer a double loss, the *iudex* in the first action is to declare that the defendant is to restore the *fundus* to the plaintiff if the plaintiff gives a *cautio*. This *cautio*, as Levy emphasizes,[1] can only be to make good the sum of the *condemnatio* in the second *vindicatio* if the defendant loses that too. It may well be that *vel satisdaret, si alter fundum evicisset, eum praestare* is interpolated[2] and since this point has no great significance for us here this part of the text will be left aside. The substance of the text is identical with one of Neratius, D. 5. 3. 57 (7 *membran.*), with the sole distinction that the latter text concerns two *hereditatis petitiones*.

D. 6. 1. 58 (Paul, 3 *epit. Alfeni dig.*). A quo servus petebatur et eiusdem servi nomine cum eo furti agebatur, quaerebat, si utroque iudicio condemnatus[3] esset, quid se facere oporteret. si prius servus ab eo evictus esset, respondit, non oportere iudicem cogere, ut eum traderet, nisi ei satisdatum esset, quod pro eo homine iudicium accepisset, si quid ob eam rem datum esset, id recte praestari. sed si prius de furto iudicium factum esset et hominem noxae dedisset, deinde de ipso homine secundum petitorem iudicium factum esset, non debere ob eam rem iudicem, quod hominem non traderet, litem aestimare, quoniam nihil eius culpa neque dolo contigisset, quo minus hominem traderet.

[1] *Nachträge zur Konkurrenz der Aktionen und Personen* p. 30. See also p. 31 for Levy's suggestion of the *cautio* which would be given if the defendant had not yet let himself in for the second action.

[2] Cf. Levy, op. cit., p. 29.

[3] *Condemnatus* cannot have been the original reading but must have been substituted for something like *contra se pronuntiatum* or *iudicatum*: cf. now Levy, op. cit., p. 48, n. 198.

This time, the other action is an *actio furti noxalis*. For the *vindicatio*, the significant situation is, of course, where the *actio furti* is the first to be decided.[1] This time, where the plaintiff wins in the *vindicatio* the judge is not to make a *litis aestimatio* because the defendant did not deliver the slave. This means that no *cautio* was to be exacted from the victorious plaintiff in the *actio furti*. It would thus appear that there is a significant difference between the effect in the two texts of the successful *vindicatio* where it is the second action. In D. 6. 1. 57 *litis aestimatio* will be made if there is no delivery, in D. 6. 1. 58 there will be no *litis aestimatio*. How is this difference to be explained? Levy suggests that the reason for the decision in D. 6. 1. 58, *quoniam nihil eius culpa neque dolo contigisset, quo minus hominem traderet*, does not go back to Alfenus since in his time it was not yet established that the defendant in the *vindicatio* was liable if he lost possession *dolo* or *culpa*.[2] By this Levy seems to mean—witness his acceptance of the decision in D. 6. 1. 57—that in the time of Alfenus there would generally be *litis aestimatio* if the defendant lost possession even without *dolus* or *culpa*. But in the present case, he suggests, there is no *litis aestimatio* because the slave is in the hands of the person to whom the owner would himself have had to deliver him unless he paid the penalty under the *actio furti*.[3] Thus, in Levy's view, it seems that the difference between the two decisions is due not to any theoretical distinction but to a common-sense juristic approach in D. 6. 1. 58. But there are weighty objections to Levy's view of the difference. First, the explanation given for the decision in D. 6. 1. 58 that the slave is already there where the owner would have to deliver him unless he paid the penalty in the *actio furti* is not satisfactory. It ignores the possibility that the *actio furti* was wrongly decided and that it would or could have been more strongly defended by the true owner. It also ignores a much more fundamental point. A defendant who is suffering defeat in an *actio furti noxalis* and who is facing a *vindicatio* for the same slave—

[1] For the situation where the *vindicatio* is the first to be decided see, most recently, Watson, *Obligations*, p. 279.

[2] Levy is not suggesting interpolation—though others have done—but only that the reason is Paul's: op. cit., p. 50.

[3] Op. cit., p. 49.

which he might very well feel that he would also lose—may reasonably decide to surrender the slave noxally even though the sum in which he would otherwise be condemned is far less than the value of the slave. This course of noxal surrender would not have been followed by the successful plaintiff in the *vindicatio* if he had been the person sued by the *actio furti*. Moreover, if one holds that the decision that, in this case, there should be no *litis aestimatio* has a common-sense basis, and that factors which came into existence after *litis contestatio* are taken into account, it is difficult to see how one can, at the same time, think that the idea was not yet in existence that the possessor might not be condemned if he had lost possession without *dolus* or *culpa*. That, after all, is the classic situation where factors arising after *litis contestatio* are treated as relevant. Secondly, Levy's examination of the *cautio* in D. 6. 1. 57 does not seem to cover all of the problems. If the defendant is here liable to suffer *litis aestimatio* in the second *vindicatio* if he does not hand over the *fundus* which he no longer has, then some protection for him, such as the *cautio*, is necessary. And the position of the plaintiff in the second *vindicatio* is satisfactory. The same cannot be said, without further investigation, for the successful plaintiff in the first *vindicatio*. If the defender loses the second *vindicatio* and pays the *litis aestimatio* to the plaintiff, the first plaintiff will have to pay up under the terms of the *cautio*. And there seems no ordinary action which he can bring for recovery against the plaintiff in the second *vindicatio* on the ground that the second case was wrongly decided.[1] Yet, prima facie, one might think that the second *vindicatio* is quite likely to be wrongly decided since the defendant, who in view of the *cautio* can suffer no financial loss if the decision is against him, may not exert himself to the utmost. The solution surely is that the plaintiff will only win his action if he can prove that he is owner, and it is not enough to show that the defendant has no title. Hence the decision in favour of the plaintiff in the first *vindicatio* means that the plaintiff in the

[1] It would be far-fetched to suggest that a *condictio* might be available. (The situation has nothing in common with that of, for instance, D. 12. 1. 9. 8 and 45. 1. 126. 2 (cf. Watson, *Contract of Mandate in Roman Law* (Oxford, 1961), pp. 82 ff.) since the *datio* by the defendant to the plaintiff in the second *vindicatio* was not made in the name of the plaintiff in the first *vindicatio*.)

second *vindicatio* to be successful must show that that first decision was wrong. It is for this reason that the *cautio* given by the first plaintiff to the defendant is satisfactory even from the former's point of view although there is no normal action against the second plaintiff for recovery. We can be sure that in practice it was possible for the first plaintiff to defend his title in the second *vindicatio*. Of these two objections to Levy's opinion, the first demands a new explanation of the decisions and the second opens the way to it. I should like to suggest the following explanation. In the time of Alfenus (or Servius), as later, the relevant moment for the facts on which *condemnatio* depended was *litis contestatio*. But some of the difficulties inherent in this attitude were becoming apparent and answers to the difficulties were being found. It is for this reason that we have two texts where the Republican jurist considers the situation where the same defendant was faced at once with two actions, at least one of which was a *vindicatio*. One answer which was then given to some of the difficulties was to hold that loss of the *res* after *litis contestatio* by the defendant without *culpa* or *dolus* could free him from having to undergo *litis aestimatio*. So in D. 6. 1. 58, *quoniam nihil eius culpa neque dolo contigisset, quo minus hominem traderet*, can go back to the Republican jurist. It should be noticed that Levy's objection to the existence of this ground of decision is apparently based only on his interpretation of D. 6. 1. 57.[1] But this ground of decision had not yet hardened into a firm rule[2] and a different answer might be given in other situations if it were felt to be more appropriate. This is the case with the decision in D. 6. 1. 57. In the situation there, if the second *vindicatio* is to be successful, the plaintiff must show that the decision in the first *vindicatio* was completely wrong. Since that second

[1] Op. cit., p. 50 and n. 202.

[2] Even once this ground of decision had been suggested, objections might be found to it. Thus, in the context of the *actio ad exhibendum*, Ulpian tells us that Pomponius thought that a defendant who had lost possession without *dolus* or *culpa* might none the less be blamed for not having restored (or exhibited) at once, but allowing *litis contestatio* to take place: D. 10. 4. 7. 5 (24 *ad ed.*). There have been suggestions of interpolation, but it is difficult to see why anyone would in a text of Ulpian ascribe the argument to Pomponius if he had not said anything of the kind: cf. now Marrone, '*Actio ad exhibendum*', *Annali Palermo* xxvi (1957) 177 ff. at p. 660, n. 142.

vindicatio has passed the stage of *litis contestatio* it seems most reasonable to allow that action to continue and to decide the question of ownership finally in it rather than to break it off and begin a new action against the first plaintiff. The informality of the proceedings before the judge will allow the first plaintiff to defend his title.[1]

Actio Publiciana

The *actio Publiciana* is generally said to be Republican and to date from the first half of the first century B.C. 67 B.C. is now the date regarded as by far the most likely since we know from Cicero[2] that in that year a Quintus Publicius was one of the praetors.[3] Perhaps this opinion is correct, but it must be emphasized that we have no direct evidence for the existence of the action before the time of Neratius[4] who was active around the closing decades of the first century A.D. and the opening decades of the second century A.D.[5] Bonfante has suggested that our earliest allusion is to the time of Sabinus and is in D. 6. 2. 15 (Pomponius, 3 *ad Sab.*).[6] But the fact that the *actio Publiciana* is mentioned in a text from Pomponius' commentary *ad Sabinum* by no means indicates that the action existed in the time of Sabinus and there is nothing positive in the text itself to link the giving of the action with Sabinus. Lombardi thinks that the earliest allusion is to the *veteres* in

[1] For D. 39. 2. 9. 2 (Ulpian, 53 *ad ed.*) see *supra*, p. 74 and *infra*, pp. 148 f.; for D. 6. 1. 5. 3 (Ulpian, 16 *ad ed.*), *supra*, p. 75. D. 50. 16. 25. 1 (Paul, 21 *ad ed.*) will be considered in a later volume on legal science. D. 5. 1. 76 (Alfenus, 6 *dig.*) would not seem to tell us anything significant for *vindicatio*.

[2] *Pro Cluentio* 45. 126: cf. Broughton, *The Magistrates of the Roman Republic* (New York, 1952), ii. 143.

[3] Cf., e.g., among recent writers, Kaser, *EB*, p. 299, n. 17 ('nicht unwahrscheinlich'); Wubbe, *Res aliena pignori data* (Leiden, 1960), p. 213 (who gives 66 B.C. as the date of Publicius' praetorship); 'Quelques remarques sur la fonction et l'origine de l'action Publicienne', *RIDA* viii (1961) 417 ff. at p. 437; Lombardi, *Dalla fides alla bona fides* (Milan, 1961), p. 243; Sturm, 'Zur ursprünglichen Funktion der *actio Publiciana*', *RIDA* ix (1962) 357 ff. at p. 358, n. 2.

[4] D. 6. 2. 9. 4 (Ulpian, 16 *ad ed.*); *h.t.* 17 (Neratius, 3 *membran.*).

[5] Cf. Kunkel, *Herkunft und soziale Stellung der römischen Juristen* (Weimar, 1952), pp. 144 f.

[6] He actually refers to D. 6. 2. 16, but this must be a mistake: II. ii. 327 and n. 8.

V.F. 1, where *bona fide emere* appears as a standard idea in matters relating to possession, and so with respect either to the *actio Publiciana* or to *usucapio*.[1] But there is no indication in the text that the *actio Publiciana* was being thought of here by the Republican jurists, and so the text is not helpful.[2] The action is certainly edictal and J. 4. 6. 4 tells us that Publicius was a praetor, but so far as our direct evidence goes there is nothing to exclude the possibility that the action was first introduced in A.D. 93 when Publicius Certus was praetor.[3] Are there, however, any factors which compel us to accept that the *actio Publiciana* is Republican? An argument has been drawn from the name.[4] Actions named after the person who introduced them are rare but (at least) three of them, the *actiones Calvisiana*, *Fabiana*, and *Rutiliana*, can be dated, it is said, to the first half of the first century B.C.[5] But the basis of any argument here is very fragile. The *actio Rutiliana* cannot really be later than 118 B.C., the latest possible date when the jurist P. Rutilius Rufus can have been praetor.[6] Though it is very likely that the *actiones Fabiana* and *Calvisiana* are Republican, this cannot be proved; far less can they be attributed with any degree of confidence to a particular period of the Republic. They may even be much earlier than the beginning of the first century B.C.[7] Even if we ought to leave aside the very enigmatic *actio Pauliana* which is certainly much later than the Republic, the clarity of the image is further obscured by the two *actiones Servianae*. There is no direct evidence that the *actio Serviana* for *pignus* existed in the Republic, but we have indications that some action of at least somewhat similar scope existed in the time of Cato.[8] So this *actio Serviana* may be much earlier than the first half of the first century

[1] Op. cit., p. 244.

[2] Unless one could show that *bona fides* for *usucapio* became necessary only after the introduction of the *actio Publiciana*. Lombardi, op. cit., p. 245, thinks that this was probably the position but his arguments are very hypothetical.

[3] Cf. Schuster, *RE* xxiii. 2, 1903 f. Our information on the names of praetors in the first century A.D. is very incomplete, and there could have been dozens called Publicius.

[4] Lombardi, op. cit., p. 244; cf. Wubbe, *Res*, p. 213—who, however, is trying to establish the date of the *actio Serviana*.

[5] So Wubbe (who also adds the *actio Publiciana*), loc. cit.

[6] Cf. Broughton, op. cit., i. 527.

[7] Watson, *Persons*, p. 234.

[8] Cf. Watson, *Obligations*, pp. 180 f.

B.C. or it may even be later. For the *actio Serviana* of the *bonorum emptor* there can be even less precision of dating. An argument from the name for ascribing the *actio Publiciana* to the Republic will have force only if it can be shown that conditions in the Empire were such as to militate against the use of the name of the magistrate introducing it.[1] But the number of *senatusconsulta* from the Empire which bear the name of the proposer can rule out this idea. Perhaps more significant for the choice of name is that these actions which bear the proposer's name tend to be given for complicated factual situations and it would not be easy to find a simple name which would clearly indicate their content.[2] This leaves, for the attribution of the *actio Publiciana* to the early first century B.C., the usually unexpressed arguments from the original function of the action and the general development of Roman law. The *actio Publiciana* was intended to let at least certain deserving non-owners who had lost possession recover possession or be awarded damages.[3] The original form of neither the edict nor the *formula* is clear. But even if the original function were certain we would not be much further forward. A remedy does not by any means necessarily arrive within a reasonable time after circumstances make it desirable.[4] To later generations the need may appear much greater and the way to the remedy much more obvious than it was to contemporaries. But even before the *actio Publiciana*, the deserving non-owner who lost possession would have some remedy in many circumstances by, for instance, the *actio furti*, the *interdictum utrubi*, or the *interdictum uti possidetis*. In the present situation there is no legal innovation which can serve as a *terminus ante quem* for the *actio Publiciana*. That apparently by far the greater part of the *edictum perpetuum* was created during the later Republic cannot raise a strong presumption that any particular edict for

[1] Cf. Lombardi, loc. cit.

[2] Thus a significant number of them have fictions. Where the *actio* bears the name of the person who introduced it, it is unlikely that he invented the name.

[3] For views held, see Sturm, op. cit., and the authors he cites. I would accept Sturm's arguments (especially those under § 5, pp. 383 ff.) against Wubbe, 'Quelques remarques', who thinks that the *actio* was intended to protect even owners who had had possession for less than the period of *usucapio* and who otherwise would have to prove that their predecessor was owner.

[4] Witness, e.g., the *actio de dolo*.

whose existence in the Republic we have no evidence was none the less in existence. It must be stressed, however, that nothing which has been said here should be taken to indicate a positive belief of the author that the *actio Publiciana* arose only in the Empire. Rather, I feel only that it is extremely suspicious that an action which is thought to be so important should not be evidenced until the end of the first century A.D. if it really was introduced as early as 67 B.C.[1]

Actio ad exhibendum

We have textual evidence in D. 19. 1. 17. 6 for the existence of the *actio ad exhibendum* in the time of Aquilius Gallus.[2] How much earlier than the first half of the first century B.C. it is can only be a matter of conjecture.[3] The *formula* is very much disputed as is even the question whether the action was civil or praetorian.[4] Since no text directly touches on these questions for the Republic, the problems will be left aside here. The action lay to a person who had an interest in a thing which someone else possessed[5] or had fraudulently brought it about that he no longer possessed, and was to compel the defendant either to produce the thing in court or suffer a financial condemnation in the amount of the plaintiff's interest. The *actio ad exhibendum* seems to have been allowed only as a preliminary to another action.[6] But as we shall see from D. 10. 4. 19, there are some indications that this requirement was not expressly stated in the *formula*.

[1] Since it is not certain that the action existed in the Republic its details will not be examined here.

[2] Cf. Burillo, 'Contribuciones al estudio de la *actio ad exhibendum* en derecho clasico', *SDHI* xxvi (1960) 190 ff. at p. 217 and n. 89.

[3] Cf., above all, Girard, *Manuel élémentaire de droit romain*, 8th edn. by Senn (Paris, 1929), p. 673, n. 4.

[4] A recent detailed discussion, with full citation of literature, is Burillo, op. cit., who opposes the generally held view that the action certainly was civil law. Kaser, 'Die *formula* der *actio ad exhibendum*', *RIDA* xiv (1967), 263 ff., appeared too late for consideration.

[5] Texts from the beginning of the Empire would indicate that at least some jurists held that the defendant had to have *possessio*, not just *detentio*: e.g. D. 10. 4. 15 (Pomponius, 18 *ad Sab.*), referring to Labeo; *h.t.* 5 pr. (Ulpian, 24 *ad ed.*) referring to Celsus. The latter text, which shows Celsus going to considerable lengths in arguing that even a person who does not have *possessio* can be sued, is especially significant.

[6] Cf., e.g., Kaser, *RPR* i, p. 365.

There are two texts for our period:

D. 19. 1. 17. 6 (Ulpian, 32 *ad ed.*). Si ruta et caesa excipiantur in venditione, ea placuit esse ruta, quae eruta sunt, ut harena creta et similia: caesa ea esse, ut arbores caesas et carbones et his similia. Gallus autem Aquilius, cuius Mela refert opinionem, recte ait frustra in lege venditionis de rutis et caesis contineri, quia, si non specialiter venierunt, ad exhibendum de his agi potest neque enim [enim *del. Mommsen*] magis de materia caesa aut de caementis aut de harena cavendum est venditori quam de ceteris quae sunt pretiosiora.

Aquilius Gallus held[1] that in the sale of an estate a clause excluding *ruta et caesa* was pointless because if they were not specifically included in the sale the seller (who had transferred the estate to the buyer) could bring an *actio ad exhibendum* for them. Here the *actio ad exhibendum* is preliminary to a *vindicatio*.

D. 10. 4. 19 (Paul, 4 *epit. Alfeni*). Ad exhibendum possunt agere omnes quorum interest. sed quidam consuluit, an possit efficere haec actio, ut rationes adversarii sibi exhiberentur, quas exhiberi magni eius interesset. respondit non oportere ius civile calumniari neque verba captari, sed qua mente quid diceretur, animadvertere convenire. nam illa ratione etiam studiosum alicuius doctrinae posse dicere sua interesse illos aut illos libros sibi exhiberi, quia, si essent exhibiti, cum eos legisset, doctior et melior futurus esset.

Although the text has been held to be interpolated,[2] the most modern opinion is—rightly—that both the substance and the form are genuine;[3] the tenor of the text is exactly what one would expect from a Republican jurist replying to a question. There is nothing suspicious in the *reductio ad absurdum* since Daube has proved that that form of argument was well known to jurists long before the Byzantine period.[4] The text, of course, shows that the plaintiff need not claim to be the owner of the thing in question. It also

[1] Bremer, who regards *quia . . . agi potest* as interpolated [*Iurisprudentiae antehadrianae quae supersunt* (Leipzig, 1901), II. i. 293] seems to be alone in suspecting the substance of the text: cf. now, Burillo, op. cit., p. 217.

[2] Beseler, *Beiträge*, i. 7; v. 25; *ZSS* lvii (1937) 5; Schulz, *RLS*, p. 206, n. 1. Against Beseler's suggestion that in its original setting D. 10. 4. 19 dealt with the *actio furti non exhibiti* see most recently Yaron, *Tijd.* xxiv (1966) 519, n. 31.

[3] Cf. Marrone, '*Actio ad exhibendum*' pp. 266 ff. and p. 279; Burillo, op. cit., pp. 239 ff.

[4] In a lecture, 'Le raisonnement par l'absurde chez les juristes romains', delivered at the Institut de droit romain of the University of Paris on 18 April 1958.

shows that by no means every financial interest in the production of the thing would be sufficient to permit the granting of the action. The most significant thing about the text is that Alfenus (or Servius), despite the almost polemical nature of what is said and the wealth of argumentation, does not attempt to define more exactly what kind of interest will be sufficient for the action. It would seem that the rule that the *actio ad exhibendum* could be brought only where it was intended as a preliminary to a further action in respect of some thing had not yet been consciously formulated or else tended to be ignored. If, as many believe, the plaintiff claimed, according to the *formula*, to be owner, or even to be about to bring a *vindicatio* for the thing,[1] then Marrone may well be right in thinking that it was Servius who began the doctrine that certain interests less than ownership could be sufficient.[2]

[1] e.g. Lenel, *EP*, p. 223; Marrone, op. cit., p. 499; Kaser, *Labeo* v (1959) 223 f.

[2] This is not the way Marrone formulates his opinion but it does, I think, express his thought.

5

BOUNDARIES AND DIVISION

IT is reasonable to treat boundary questions and the division of property together since the action for regulating boundaries, the *actio finium regundorum*, and the divisory actions, the *actio familiae erciscundae* and the *actio communi dividundo*, all have the very unusual characteristic that the judge (or judges) is to condemn either party to the action (or any of them where there are more than two) to give whatever is proper to the other (or others).[1] Moreover, the actions appear together in the Digest: the *actio finium regundorum* in title 10. 1, the *actio familiae erciscundae* in title 10. 2, and the *actio communi dividundo* in title 10. 3.

D. 2. 1. 11. 2 (Gaius, 1 *ad ed. prov.*). Si una actio communis sit plurium personarum, veluti familiae erciscundae, communi dividundo, finium regundorum, utrum singulae partes spectandae sunt circa iurisdictionem eius qui cognoscit, quod Ofilio et Proculo placet, quia unusquisque de parte sua litigat: an potius tota res, quia et tota res in iudicium venit et vel uni adiudicari potest, quod Cassio et Pegaso placet: et sane eorum sententia probabilis est.[2]

This text brings the *actiones finium regundorum*, *familiae erciscundae*, and *communi dividundo* together. § 2, like the preceding *principium* and § 1, discusses the question of the competence of magistrates in cases above a certain (unknown) value.[3] Ofilius (who was followed by Proculus) held that for this purpose what was to be considered was the *singulae partes* since each person was litigating for his own share. But the view of Cassius and Pegasus which prevailed was that the relevant sum for this purpose was the value of *tota res*. There is considerable dispute as to the time when a limitation on magisterial competence with regard to value was

[1] For Lenel's reconstruction of the *formulae*, see *EP*, pp. 206 ff.

[2] The interpolations suggested in the text do not concern us: cf. *Index Itp.*

[3] Cf. Pugliese, *Il processo civile romano II, Il processo formulare* (Milan, 1963), i. 145 ff., especially at p. 146.

introduced.[1] The matter need not detain us here, but our text shows that the limitation existed in the time of Ofilius.

Boundaries[2]

The *actio finium regundorum* dates back to the XII Tables.

Cicero, *de leg.* 1. 21. 55. . . . Ex hac autem non rerum, sed verborum discordia, controversia nata est de finibus: in qua quoniam usucapionem XII tabulae intra quinque pedes esse noluerunt, depasci veterem possessionem Academiae ab hoc acuto homine non sinemus; nec Mamilia lege singuli, sed ex iis tres arbitri fines regemus.

Under the XII Tables proceedings were before three *arbitri*, and in this it differed from the *actio familiae erciscundae* and the *actio communi dividundo* which were heard before one judge only. It is this which indicates that, unlike these last two actions,[3] proceedings were not *per iudicis postulationem*.[4] The *lex Mamilia* which apparently instituted proceedings before a single *iudex* seems to be the agrarian law of Julius Caesar, probably of 59 or 50 B.C.,[5] of which we have three chapters.[6]

D. 10. 1. 13 (Gaius, 4 *ad legem XII tab.*). Sciendum est in actione finium regundorum illud observandum esse, quod ad exemplum quodammodo eius legis scriptum est, quam Athenis Solonem dicitur tulisse: nam illic ita est: ἐάν τις αἱμασιὰν παρ' ἀλλοτρίῳ χωρίῳ ὀρύττῃ, τὸν ὅρον μὴ παραβαίνειν· ἐὰν τειχίον, πόδα ἀπολείπειν· ἐὰν δὲ οἴκημα, δύο πόδας. ἐὰν δὲ τάφον ἢ βόθρον ὀρύττῃ, ὅσον τὸ βάθος ᾖ, τοσοῦτον ἀπολείπειν· ἐὰν δὲ φρέαρ, ὀργυιάν. ἐλαίαν δὲ καὶ συκῆν ἐννέα πόδας ἀπὸ τοῦ ἀλλοτρίου φυτεύειν, τὰ δὲ ἄλλα δένδρα πέντε πόδας.

The XII Tables are not expressly mentioned but the text comes from Gaius' fourth book on the XII Tables and Gaius' reference to the modelling of a provision on the law of Solon can leave no

[1] Cf., e.g., Pugliese, loc. cit.; Kaser, *ZPR*, p. 128.

[2] See most recently Broggini, 'Regolamento di confini: diritto romano', in *Novissimo digesto italiano*.

[3] G. 4. 17a.

[4] Cf., e.g., Buckland, '*Finium regundorum*', *RHD* xv (1936) 741 ff.; Broggini, *Iudex arbiterve* (Cologne, Graz, 1957), p. 167: but Kaser would appear not to exclude the possibility that proceedings were *per iudicis postulationem*; *RPR* i. 125, nn. 6, 9: most recently, indeed, he inclines to think that that was the procedure; *ZPR*, p. 42, n. 12 and p. 79.

[5] Cf., e.g., Rotondi, *Leges*, pp. 388 f.; Herrmann, 'La date de la *lex Mamilia*', *RIDA* i (1948) 113 ff.

[6] Cf. Blume, Lachmann, Rudorff, *Die Schriften der römischen Feldmesser* (Berlin, 1848), i. 263 f.; Bruns, no. 15.

doubt that the jurist is in fact thinking of the XII Tables. The veracity of the text is very much doubted and it has been subjected to a two-pronged attack. The first prong denies the plausibility of an embassy's being sent, before the passing of the XII Tables, by the Romans to Athens and other Greek states to study the laws of Solon;[1] the second denies that the provisions given in the text could have formed part of the XII Tables. The question of the accuracy of the first prong of the attack need not detain us. The second prong of the attack on the accuracy of the text is that the provisions quoted are inappropriate for Latium of the fifth century B.C. Thus, Wieacker[2] and Ciulei[3] declare that it is hard to imagine fig and olive trees in Latium at that time. But even leaving aside all question of the accuracy of this opinion—and there can be doubts of its validity[4]—the point seems misconceived. Gaius is not telling us that the XII Tables reproduced the provisions of the law of Solon here, but that the law of Solon *quodammodo*, 'in a certain way' or 'to some extent',[5] provided the model for the XII Tables' provision. The Latin part of the text might be translated: 'In an action for regulating boundaries we must remember to observe that provision which was in a way [*or*, to some extent] drawn up on the model of the law which Solon is said to have laid down at Athens. For that law runs thus: . . .'[6] The XII Tables' provision, therefore, could be thought by the Romans to be modelled on the law of Solon without having all or most or even any of the latter's

[1] e.g., Arangio-Ruiz, *Storia del diritto romano*, 7th edn. (Naples, 1960), p. 56; Kaser, *Römische Rechtsgeschichte* (Göttingen, 1950), p. 57; Wieacker, 'Zwölftafelprobleme', *RIDA* iii (1956) 459 ff., who at p. 468, n. 25 suggests that the contrary view of Wenger, *Die Quellen des römischen Rechts* (Vienna, 1953), p. 365 f., is too tolerant of the Roman 'Annalistik'; Ogilvie, *A Commentary on Livy 1–5* (Oxford, 1965), pp. 449 f. Wieacker, 'Die XII Tafeln in ihrem Jahrhundert', *Fondation Hardt: Entretiens sur l'Antiquité classique, XIII* (Vandoeuvres–Genève, 1967), pp. 293 ff., appeared too late for consideration.

[2] Loc. cit.

[3] '*Finium regundorum*', *ZSS* lxxxi (1964) 303 ff. at p. 307.

[4] For the state of the question, see, on figs, Olck, *RE* vi. 2100 ff.; on olive trees, Pease, *RE* xvii. 1998 ff.; and the references they give.

[5] Cf. Lewis and Short, *A Latin Dictionary* (Oxford, reprinted 1951), s.v. *quodammodo*.

[6] Cf. the translation of Warmington: 'We must remember, in an action for the marking of boundaries, that we must not overlook that old provision which was drawn up in a manner after the pattern of the law which Solon is said to have laid down at Athens. In that law occurs the following . . .'; *Remains of Old Latin* (London, 1938), iii. 467.

particular rules.[1] This reasoning also removes force from Ciulei's arguments from the fact that the provisions mentioned in the text were not observed at Rome;[2] from, in his view, an apparent clash with the XII Tables' provision on the lopping off of overhanging branches;[3] and from the fact that according to Festus[4] the *ambitus* was to be two and a half feet and not the two feet mentioned in D. 10. 1. 13. Wieacker has a further argument, namely that the law of Solon is not directly concerned with the separation of boundaries. Prima facie this argument seems reasonable but it probably has no force. We know from other sources that the XII Tables contained a provision on *ambitus*. Apart from D. 10. 1. 13 we have no evidence on the action available for this provision. Of the private law actions known to us no other seems to be as appropriate as the *actio finium regundorum*. There is, I submit, no good reason to doubt Gaius' statement that the provision of the XII Tables said to be modelled on the rule of Solon quoted in the text was actionable by the *actio finium regundorum*. This is the sort of thing which we might expect him to know. The accuracy of his knowledge here has nothing to do with his views on the history of the XII Tables. The text can be taken, I submit, as showing that the *actio finium regundorum* did appear in the XII Tables and that that action could be used to enforce certain provisions concerning operations at the extreme edge of one's land. It also shows that these provisions of the XII Tables were still valid in the time of Gaius—how far they were rigidly observed is, of course, another matter—and hence also in our period. But it gives no indication of the contents of these Roman provisions.

[1] We can be fairly certain that D. 10. 1. 13 is giving us at least fairly accurately the main provisions of the law of Solon: cf. Plutarch, *Solon*, cap. 23; *P. Hal.* 1, lines 84 ff.; Ciulei, op. cit., p. 306.

[2] Ciulei's argument here is also weak in that we know from other sources, namely Varro, *de ling. lat.* 5. 22, Festus, s.v. *ambitus*, Volusius Maecianus, *de assis distr.* 46, that the XII Tables did contain a rule that buildings were not to be erected closer than two and a half feet to boundaries. These texts, however, by themselves would not tell us that the provision was still in existence in the later Republic.

[3] But in any event there is no conflict. A tree planted at least five feet from the boundary would frequently overhang. It should not be forgotten that Latium was then rich in numbers and varieties of trees: cf. Tenney Frank, *An Economic History of Rome*, 2nd edn. (Baltimore, 1927), pp. 5 ff.

[4] s.v. *ambitus*.

D. 10. 1. 13 may in fact help us to explain what seems to be the greatest problem in the *actio finium regundorum*, namely its restriction by juristic interpretation to the country. Two texts from Cicero's *topica*—a work in which he particularly shows his legal skill—state expressly that the *actio finium regundorum* does not apply in the city.[1] That this was the result of juristic interpretation emerges from a text of Paul, D. 10. 1. 4. 10 (23 *ad ed.*).

> Hoc iudicium locum habet in confinio praediorum rusticorum: nam in confinio praediorum urbanorum displicuit, neque enim confines hi, sed magis vicini dicuntur et ea communibus parietibus plerumque disterminantur. et ideo et si in agris aedificia iuncta sint, locus huic actioni non erit: et in urbe hortorum latitudo contingere potest, ut etiam finium regundorum agi possit.

Just as *placere* indicates a decision of a jurist or jurists so, one should imagine in a context like this, does *displicere*. Again, the argument for the rule, *neque enim confines hi, sed magis vicini dicuntur*, is so feeble and irrelevant[2] that it is hard to believe that it would have been produced had it been totally unnecessary, as it would have been if the scope of the action was dictated by the statute. Rather, it is what one might expect where a rule had to be twisted for some particular reason.[3] The same applies to the last clause of that sentence, *et ea communibus parietibus plerumque disterminantur*. The clause—if it were not for the *plerumque*—might explain why the *actio finium regundorum* was not useful in the city, but it would not tell us why it was in fact excluded from operation in the city. The *plerumque*, indeed, indicates that city properties were not always separated by common walls, and one can think of many situations where the *actio finium regundorum* would be appropriate. It is, of course, this which raises the problem. The very nature of the *actio finium regundorum* with the power of the judge to condemn either (or any) party and even, where desirable, to rearrange

[1] These are 4. 23 and 10. 43, both quoted *infra*, p. 172.

[2] Any such argument from the meaning of words should be based on *fines* which does occur in the name of the action. But *fines* was used of boundaries in respect of houses as well as of land: cf. Bruns, no. 133 (sale of half of a house, *cum . . . finibus*).

[3] But Arangio-Ruiz regards this part of the text as interpolated, apparently because of the switch from *confinium* to *confines*: *BIDR* xxxii (1922) 21; but the change is understandable.

the boundaries, means that in the right circumstances this could be much more flexible and generally useful than any other possible remedy. Accordingly, one would think that only for the most pressing reason would its scope be restricted. Yet it was deliberately interpreted by the jurists so that its use was excluded from the city.[1] Why did they do this? The answer, I suggest, is to be found in the XII Tables' provision on *ambitus*.[2] This, as we know from the archaeological evidence, was not observed in the cities and towns.[3] Indeed, in areas of dense population it can never have been anything other than an extreme inconvenience. But we know from D. 10. 1. 13—unless we deny Gaius' accuracy on the point—that *ambitus* was regulated by the *actio finium regundorum*. This gives the jurists a very good practical reason for holding that the *actio finium regundorum* applies only in the country. If it does not apply in the city and town then neither does *ambitus*. On this interpretation the non-observance of *ambitus* in the cities is not due, at least by the last century of the Republic, to neglect of the law but to the interpretation of the relevant provision as relating only to the country. No argument against this interpretation can be drawn from Cicero, *top*. 4. 24, though that text may throw some light on the date of the jurists' restrictive interpretation.

> Quae autem adsumuntur extrinsecus, ea maxime ex auctoritate ducuntur. Itaque Graeci talis argumentationes ἀτέχνους vocant, id est artis expertis, ut si ita respondeas: Quoniam P. Scaevola id solum esse ambitus aedium dixerit, quantum parietis communis tegendi causa tectum proiceretur, ex quo tecto in eius aedis qui protexisset, aqua deflueret, id tibi ius videri.

At the most, for our present purposes, the text shows that *ambitus* is connected with buildings. This, of course, we knew already. There is nothing in the text to prove—though the mention of a common wall may be suggestive—that P. Scaevola is thinking of buildings in the town rather than in the country. In any event, it

[1] The last part of D. 10. 1. 4. 10 shows it being widened again to allow its use inside the city.

[2] And the other similar provisions, if there were any.

[3] Cf., e.g., Rudorff, 'Über die Gränzscheidungsklage', *Zeitschrift f. geschichtliche Rechtswissenschaft* (1842), x. 343 ff.; Ciulei, '*Finium regundorum*', 306.

seems impossible to make sense out of the text. How can one declare that 'that alone is the *ambitus* of a house, so far as a roof projects for the purpose of protecting a common wall, from which roof water flows on to the house of him who did the protecting'? It is for this reason that it has been suggested that the text is corrupt.[1] In fact, however, it is unlikely that this part of the text is corrupt, and its whole point is its very absurdity. Cicero is considering arguments taken *extrinsecus*, that is from outside the case. These, he says, are called by the Greeks ἄτεχνοι, that is, without art (of the orator presumably)[2] and we are told that they take their strength above all from authority. Thus, for example, he goes on, since P. Scaevola declares *ambitus* to be such and such, that is to be regarded by you as being the law. The best illustration of a statement which takes its strength *ex auctoritate* would be one made by a prominent person and which looks absolutely absurd. If a statement is completely absurd the only possible reason for giving any weight to it would be the authority of the person responsible for it. Thus it is suggested that Publius Scaevola's statement looked as absurd to Cicero as it does to us. Of course it probably was not absurd in the context in which it was made. One practical solution may tentatively be offered. It may be felt that the reference to a common wall indicates that Scaevola was concerned with town property. If so, I would suggest that P. Scaevola (consul in 133 B.C.) was writing before the *actio finium regundorum* was interpreted as being restricted to the country and hence he was faced with the legal problem of getting round the XII Tables' provision on *ambitus* which was so inconvenient in towns and which was so frequently disregarded in practice. His solution was to give *ambitus*—not defined by the XII Tables though declared to be of two and a half feet—such a restricted meaning that in practice it properly could be, and had to be, ignored.[3]

[1] Cf. Hubbell, *Cicero de inventione, de optimo genere oratorum, topica* (London and Cambridge, Mass., 1949), pp. 398 f.

[2] Cf. Aristotle, *Rhet.* $1355^{a}55$; $1375^{b}22$.

[3] Nothing for law can be deduced from Terence, *Heaut.* 499 ff. There is a dispute between neighbours *de finibus* but there is no direct evidence as to which action is being brought. Even if there were legal implications it would seem impossible here to determine whether the law was Attic or Roman. The play seems to be set in the country. D. 8. 5. 17 pr. (Alfenus, 2 *dig.*) concerns an over-

The *actio finium regundorum* also governed the rule of the XII Tables mentioned in Cicero, *de leg*. 1. 21. 55[1] that the five *pedes* separating *fundi* could not be usucapted.[2]

We learn from D. 43. 27. 1. 8 (Ulpian, 71 *ad ed.*) and 43. 27. 2 (Pomponius, 34[3] *ad Sab.*) that the XII Tables also contained a provision that where a tree overhung a neighbour's property the neighbour was entitled to have the offending branches cut off up to a height of fifteen feet. We have no direct evidence as to whether the neighbour could himself cut off the branches or could compel the owner to do so. D. 43. 27. 2 has been taken by Arangio-Ruiz[4] and Perozzi[5] to mean the latter and for that very reason they hold it interpolated. The text runs:

> Si arbor ex vicini fundo vento inclinata in tuum fundum sit, ex lege duodecim tabularum de adimenda ea recte agere potes ius ei non esse ita arborem habere.

But in fact these scholars appear to have mistranslated the text. *Ex lege duodecim tabularum* cannot be taken with *agere potes*. One cannot translate: 'You can properly sue under the law of the XII Tables for its removal' since one could not then accommodate in the sense the remainder of the text, *ius ei non esse ita arborem habere*. *Recte agere potes* must be taken with what comes after. One should translate: 'By virtue of the XII Tables' provision for its removal, you can properly bring an action that he has no right to have the tree thus.' The action which is being considered, as the *ius ei non esse* shows, is the *actio negatoria*.[6] The XII Tables' provision is brought into issue merely as showing that (where there is no servitude) it is not allowed to have a tree overhanging one's neighbour's property. But on this interpretation, *ex lege duodecim*

hanging wall but it is discussed in a context concerned with servitudes: cf. *infra*, pp. 195 f.

[1] Quoted *supra*, p. 111.

[2] Cf. now Mayer-Maly, *ZSS* lxxviii (1961) 256 f.; Yaron, p. 196, n. 15 and p. 200, n. 20.

[3] Lenel believes that the text comes from Pomponius' 33rd book *ad Sabinum*: *Pal.* ii. 144.

[4] *BIDR* xxxii (1922) 25.

[5] *Istituzioni di diritto romano*, 2nd edn. (Milan, 1927), p. 630, n. 1.

[6] Presumably it is for this reason that Lenel, loc. cit., would place the fragment in Pomponius' book 33 *ad Sabinum*, which was concerned with servitudes.

tabularum de adimenda ea, which stands by itself, gives no indication of whether the injured neighbour has to sue the owner to compel the removal of the tree (or its offending branches) or whether he himself is allowed to do the necessary pruning.

D. 43. 27. 2, however, does provide evidence that the XII Tables' provision was not abolished. It was supplemented by two interdicts. The first ran: *Quae arbor ex aedibus tuis in aedes illius impendet, si per te stat, quo minus eam adimas, tunc, quo minus illi eam arborem adimere sibique habere liceat, vim fieri veto.*[1] Since the meaning of this was discussed by Rutilius who was active in the second half of the second century B.C.,[2] the interdict is early.

D. 43. 27. 1. 2 (Ulpian, 71 *ad ed.*). Si arbor aedibus alienis impendeat, utrum totam arborem iubeat praetor adimi an vero id solum, quod superexcurrit, quaeritur. et Rutilius ait a stirpe excidendam idque plerisque videtur verius: et nisi adimet dominus arborem, Labeo ait permitti ei, cui arbor officeret, ut si vellet succideret eam lignaque tolleret.

Rutilius' view which we are told was generally accepted was that if a tree overhung a neighbour's house the whole tree was to be taken out by the roots: it was not just to be lopped in so far as it did overhang. This interdict, which applies only when trees overhang houses is a big modification of the provision of the XII Tables. The other interdict which may have been issued at the same time or later[3] applies where a tree overhangs land and is closer in substance to the provision of the XII Tables. It ran:[4] *Quae arbor ex agro tuo in agrum illius impendet, si per te stat, quo minus pedes quindecim a terra eam altius coerceas, tunc, quo minus illi ita coercere lignaque sibi habere liceat, vim fieri veto.* Like the XII Tables it concerns the lopping of branches up to a height of fifteen feet. The praetor says that if it is due to the owner of the overhanging tree that it is not pruned up to a height of fifteen feet, then he forbids force to be

[1] Cf. Lenel, *EP*, p. 487; D. 43. 27. 1 pr. (Ulpian, 71 *ad ed.*).

[2] Cf., e.g., Münzer, *RE* iA. 1269 f.; Kunkel, *Herkunft und soziale Stellung der römischen Juristen* (Weimar, 1952), p. 15. He stood for the consulship in 115 B.C.

[3] It is in fact not directly evidenced for the Republic but it would be most implausible to suggest that it dates from the Empire.

[4] D. 43. 27. 1. 7; cf. Lenel, loc. cit.

used to stop the neighbour performing such pruning and keeping the wood.[1] It is from time to time suggested that the relevant texts are ambiguous and that the interdict (and hence presumably the XII Tables) could be referring not to branches up to fifteen feet from the ground but to branches higher than fifteen feet from the ground.[2] Most recently, Ceglie has maintained that in fact the texts are not ambiguous and can only mean branches higher than fifteen feet from the ground.[3] But this is just not so.

D. 43. 27. 1. 7. Deinde ait praetor: 'Quae arbor ex agro tuo in agrum illius impendet, si per te stat, quo minus pedes quindecim a terra eam altius coerceas, tunc, quo minus illi ita coercere lignaque sibi habere liceat, vim fieri veto.' 8. Quod ait praetor, et lex duodecim tabularum efficere voluit, ut quindecim pedes altius rami arboris circumcidantur: et hoc idcirco effectum est, ne umbra arboris vicino praedio noceret. 9. Differentia duorum capitum interdicti haec est: si quidem arbor aedibus impendeat, succidi eam praecipitur, si vero agro impendeat, tantum usque ad quindecim pedes a terra coerceri.

Quo minus pedes quindecim a terra eam altius coerceas in the interdict can only mean 'that you do not prune it fifteen feet up from the ground'. There seems no way in which the accusative *pedes quindecim* can be fitted in to give the other meaning. 'That you do not prune it higher than fifteen feet from the ground' cannot explain the accusative. *Altius*, as often,[4] is not used here with a comparative sense. Moreover, an interpretation such as Ceglie's has to ignore completely the obvious meaning of the last clause of § 9, *tantum usque ad quindecim pedes a terra coerceri.*[5]

[1] For this interpretation of the interdict, see the authors cited by Ceglie, 'Sull'*interdictum de arboribus caedendis*', *Labeo* iii (1957) 363 ff. at p. 364, n. 2.

[2] Cf. for last century, Dirksen, *Zeitschrift f. geschichtliche Rechtswissenschaft* (1816), ii. 423; Vangerow, *Lehrbuch der Pandekten*, 7th edn. (Marburg, Leipzig, 1876), pp. 545 f.

[3] Op. cit. He also refers to B. 60. 13. 7–9 (which might support him—though it seems to talk of the pruning of overhanging trees which are higher than fifteen feet, not of pruning branches higher than fifteen feet) and to P.S. 5. 6. 13 and Festus, s.v. *sublucare.*

[4] Cf. Lewis and Short, *A Latin Dictionary* (Oxford, reprinted 1951), s.v. *alo.* The verb and its derivatives abound in peculiarities.

[5] Dr. John Pinsent has observed to me that the fifteen feet may be related to the height a man can prune with a pruning hook. Pruning hooks longer than about nine feet cannot be manipulated.

The XII Tables (7. 10) also contained a provision that the owner be allowed to collect *glans* which fell onto a neighbour's land.

Pliny, *N.H.* 16. 5. 15. . . . cautum est praeterea lege XII tabularum, ut glandem in alienum fundum procidentem liceret colligere.

This provision came to be supplemented by an *interdictum de glande legenda* which ran:[1] *Glandem, quae ex illius agro in tuum cadat, quo minus illi tertio quoque die legere auferre liceat, vim fieri veto. Glans* was understood by the jurists as including all fruits.[2] We have no direct evidence that this *interdictum* was Republican but—especially in view of the interdicts *de arboribus caedendis*—it would be most implausible to suggest that it was not. A more important matter is the meaning of the word *glans*. It would appear that non-legal writers use the word *glans* in respect of natural fruits only of the fruit of the tree genus *quernus*, that is of the *quercus* and *ilex*. For them, that is, it has the meaning of 'acorn'. It is only the jurists who use the word *glans* in respect of natural fruits to include all fruits.[3] Hence we can deduce that at the time of the XII Tables the provision 7. 10 was meant for acorns—important for feeding pigs—and for acorns alone. Presumably, in the economic conditions then prevailing this was the situation which needed to be regulated. But the interdict also uses the word *glans*. Unless the interdict is so early that the same primitive economic conditions were prevailing—which is most unlikely—this means that *glans* must have been already interpreted under the XII Tables' provision to mean any fruit. Once a legal term has been satisfactorily interpreted there is a natural tendency for subsequent legislation, etc. to keep to the term, even though to the uninitiated the term may be misleading.[4] Though the date of the *interdictum* is unknown, this interpretation had been given to *glans* in the XII Tables by the time of Servius:

D. 18. 1. 80. 2 (Labeo, 5 *post. a Iavoleno epit.*). Silva caedua in quinquennium venierat: quaerebatur, cum glans decidisset, utrius esset. scio Servium respondisse, primum sequendum esse quod appareret

[1] D. 43. 28. 1 pr. (Ulpian, 71 *ad ed.*); Lenel, *EP*, p. 487.

[2] D. 50. 16. 236. 1 (Gaius, 4 *ad XII Tab.*); 43. 28. 1. 1 (Ulpian, 71 *ad ed.*).

[3] For all this see *TLL*, s.v. *glans*.

[4] For instance compare the continuing deliberate use in British statutes of 'in the course of employment'.

actum esse: quod si in obscuro esset, quaecumque glans ex his arboribus quae caesae non essent cecidisset, venditoris esse, eam autem, quae in arboribus fuisset eo tempore cum haec caederentur, emptoris.

In this very different context—the interpretation of what was included in a sale of *silva caedua*—Servius uses the word *glans* to mean fruit and the meaning cannot be restricted to acorns. Pliny the Elder mentions a number of trees which might be grown for their wood, *silva caedua*,[1] and among these the following also had importance for their fruit: chestnut, peach, hazel, and apple. The totally unnecessary choice in our text of the word *glans* to mean fruit could only have been made if it was absolutely natural for the jurist to use *glans* with this wider meaning. But such a meaning of *glans* which is restricted to juristic usage can only be the direct result of interpretation in circumstances which did call for such a meaning. And these circumstances can only be the scope to be attributed to the XII Tables' provision. Hence, *glans* in the XII Tables had been given the meaning of fruit by the jurists by the time of Servius at the latest. This is an example of deliberate misinterpretation of a provision to widen its scope.

Lastly, a further provision of the XII Tables (6. 7) forbade the dislodging of a beam fixed in buildings or vineyards. The provision continued to exist in classical law but there is no specific authority for the state of the law in our period.[2]

Division

The *actio familiae erciscundae* was available where there was more than one heir and it was desired to divide the *hereditas*. As in the *actio finium regundorum* and the *actio communi dividundo*, all the parties were in the position of both plaintiff and defendant.[3] The action goes back to the XII Tables[4] which authorized procedure *per iudicis postulationem*,[5] and it is clear that it was in existence before the *actio communi dividundo*.[6] There are three texts which

[1] *N.H.* 17. 20. 147, 151.

[2] Cf. now, in general, Melillo, *Tignum iunctum* (Naples, 1964).

[3] Cf. D. 10. 2. 2. 3 (Ulpian, 19 *ad ed.*).

[4] D. 10. 2. 1 pr. (Gaius, 7 *ad ed. prov.*).

[5] G. 4. 17a.

[6] Cf. for all, Berger, *Zur Entwicklungsgeschichte der Teilungsklagen im klassischen römischen Recht* (Weimar, 1912), pp. 1 ff.

directly concern the action for our period but two of these, Cicero, *pro Caecina* 7. 19 and the *lex Rubria*, cap. xxiii, do not tell us anything which we do not already know.[1] The remaining text is D. 10. 2. 16. 6 (Ulpian, 19 *ad ed.*).

> Item si servus hereditarius propriam rem heredum unius subripuerit, Ofilius ait esse familiae erciscundae actionem et communi dividundo furtique actionem cessare. quare agentem familiae erciscundae iudicio consecuturum, ut aut ei servus adiudicetur aut litis aestimatio in simplum offeratur.

A first difficulty with the text, as Berger points out,[2] is to determine whether *et communi dividundo* is to be taken with *esse familiae erciscundae actionem* or with *furtique actionem cessare*. Either appears possible but the position of the phrase with reference to the word *actionem* which occurs twice makes it much more natural to take it with *furtique actionem cessare* as do Berger and Kübler.[3] It would be extremely forced to take it with *esse familiae erciscundae actionem* though the corresponding passage of the Basilica[4] will allow the *actio familiae erciscundae* and the *actio communi dividundo*. Biondi, who alone seems to have regarded the text as interpolated, first suggested[5] that *et communi dividundo furtique actionem cessare* was an addition. He has two arguments. To begin with, the mention of the *actio communi dividundo* is, he says, certainly not in the right place. Admittedly the position is not particularly happy but the argument does not seem a strong one for interpolation. Then he thinks *furtique actionem cessare* looks Byzantine and he refers one to a few pages earlier.[6] There in arguing for an interpolation in D. 9. 2. 27. 1 he declared that the form *cessare actionem* was a favourite of the compilers. To support this, he refers to Justinianic constitutions where it occurs, to Digest texts where it is, he thinks, interpolated, and to interpolations in analogous phrases such as *cessare legem*. The fragility of this argument is easily demonstrated. For Digest texts in which he claims *cessare actionem* is interpolated, he gives only four instances, of which our

[1] Cicero, *de orat.* 1. 56. 237 also mentions the action.

[2] Op. cit., p. 163, n. 1.

[3] Whose opinion is communicated by Berger, loc. cit.

[4] 42. 3. 16.

[5] '*Iudicia bonae fidei*', *Annali Palermo* vii (1918) 112.

[6] To p. 109, n. 1.

present text, D. 10. 2. 16. 6, is one. But the *Vocabularium Iurisprudentiae Romanae*[1] lists sixty-six places where the phrase occurs. With so many instances it would be surprising if none at all were interpolated,[2] but there have to be many more than four before one can allege that the phrase is a favourite of the compilers and hence suspicious in itself. In fact, the large number of instances of the phrase makes the idea of general interpolation very difficult to accept since it would be hard to see why the compilers would have needed to insert the phrase so often. Thus, the arguments for this suggested interpolation are not persuasive. Even if they were, this would not change the main point of the text that in the circumstances envisaged the *actio familiae erciscundae* is appropriate. In a later study,[3] Biondi goes even further and holds the whole text from *familiae erciscundae* to the end an interpolation which replaced an original *furti noxalem actionem*. He gives no positive argument—apart from referring to his earlier work on the text—but his opinion on the text really rests on his belief that in classical law the *actio noxalis* was given between co-owners.[4] To demonstrate the weakness of his case here, it is enough to look at the two texts which he thinks have survived uninterpolated and show the classical law in its purity. Of these the first, D. 4. 9. 6. 1 (Paul, 22 *ad ed.*), says nothing of a noxal action between co-owners and I cannot see how the text can be understood as indicating that such actions were possible.[5,6] The second text, D. 9. 4. 10 (Paul, 22 *ad ed.*), does, as Biondi suggests, concern the *formula noxalis ex lege Aquilia*. But when the text is put in its original context[7] it emerges that the noxal action in question is not between co-owners. Thus, again, the arguments for the interpolation of D. 10. 2. 16. 6 are not satisfying and it seems better to regard it, with Berger, as genuine.

1 (Berlin, 1903) i. 115.

2 This, of course, is not to say that I would necessarily accept as interpolated those listed by Biondi.

3 'Le *actiones noxales* nel diritto romano classico', *Annali Palermo* x (1925) 119 f.

4 Ibidem, pp. 116 ff.

5 Biondi (ibidem, p. 117) simply says: 'Il testo è notevole: come l'actio servi nomine si esercita dal dominus per il delitto commesso dal proprio schiavo, cosi l'azione nossale si potra esercitare dal condomino contro il socius.'

6 This is so whether one takes both, either or none of the *mihi* as original.

7 See Lenel, *Pal.*, i. 1011.

The text tells us that Ofilius held that if a *servus hereditarius* stole a thing belonging to one of the heirs, the *actio familiae erciscundae* would lie, but not the *actio communi dividundo* nor the *actio furti*. In the *actio familiae erciscundae* the thievish slave is either to be adjudged to the victim or *litis aestimatio in simplum* is to be offered. In these circumstances, therefore, the *actio familiae erciscundae* is —sensibly—given the function of a noxal action.[1]

The *actio communi dividundo*, though later than the *actio familiae erciscundae*, was in existence in the late Republic and in all probability is much earlier. A *lex Licinnia*[2] of unknown date[3] authorized for this action the *legis actio* procedure *per iudicis postulationem*. It was available in all cases for the division of common property except where the co-ownership was the result of an *hereditas* coming to co-heirs. As in the *actio familiae erciscundae* the *iudex* had very considerable discretion. We know from D. 10. 3. 26 (Alfenus Varus, 2 *dig.*) that if a common slave broke his leg while he was with one of his masters and this was due to that master's fault, a proper action for compensating the other owner was the *actio communi dividundo*.[4] The judge, no doubt, would adjudge to the innocent owner the value which his share would have had apart from the accident.[5] Two other relevant texts, D. 33. 2. 31 (Labeo, 2 *post. a Iavoleno epit.*)[6] and Cicero, *ad fam.* 7. 12. 2, do not really tell us anything significant for the action.[7]

[1] Cf. Berger, op. cit., pp. 163 f.

[2] G. 4. 17a.

[3] Cf., e.g., Rotondi, *Leges*, p. 481.

[4] Cf. Lenel's reconstruction of the *formula*: *EP*, p. 211.

[5] Cf. now on the text, Watson, *Persons*, p. 181. For *damnum* to a common thing see in general, Berger, op. cit., pp. 111 ff. And probably one can deduce from D. 10. 2. 16. 6, *supra*, pp. 122 ff., that where a *servus communis* stole from one of his owners that owner could obtain recompense by the *actio communi dividundo*.

[6] Quoted and discussed *infra*, p. 217.

[7] In D. 19. 2. 35. 1 (Alfenus, 8 *quaest.*) the reference to an *actio communi dividundo* does not seem to go further back than Julian. Nothing for the *actio communi dividundo* can be deduced from Plautus, *Merc.* 451 ff.; nor from Festus, s.vv. *posticam lineam* and *postica*.

6

DAMNUM INFECTUM

IN a topic so complicated as *damnum infectum* it seems wisest to begin with some preliminary points on the aspect we know most about—the edict of the urban praetor—even although it is not absolutely certain that it was in existence in the Republic. There was also an old remedy involving a *legis actio* which we know survived in theory in the time of Gaius, and an edict of the peregrine praetor—probably rather different from that of the urban praetor—which existed by 42 B.C. at the latest.

Lenel's reconstruction of the *edictum praetoris urbani*, the accuracy of which is not doubted, runs:[1] *Damni infecti suo nomine promitti, alieno satisdari iubebo ei, qui iuraverit non calumniae causa id se postulare eumve cuius nomine aget postulaturum fuisse, in eam diem, quam causa cognita statuero. si controversia erit, dominus sit nec ne qui cavebit, sub exceptione satisdari iubebo. de eo opere, quod in flumine publico ripave eius fiet, in annos decem satisdari iubebo. eum cui ita non cavebitur, in possessionem eius rei, cuius nomine, ut caveatur, postulabitur, ire et, cum iusta causa esse videbitur, etiam possidere iubebo. in eum, qui neque caverit neque in possessione esse neque possidere passus erit, iudicium dabo, ut tantum praestet, quantum praestare eum oporteret, si de ea re ex decreto meo eiusve, cuius de ea re iurisdictio fuit quae mea est, cautum fuisset. eius rei nomine, in cuius possessionem misero, si ab eo qui in possessione erit, damni infecti nomine non satisdabitur, eum, cui non satisdabitur, simul in possessione esse iubebo.* Lenel shows that two clauses must have dropped out, one on *opus quod in via publica fiet* which is related to that on *opus quod in flumine publico ripave eius fiet*, and one on the situation where it was impossible for the person who wanted to be put into possession to go before the praetor. This latter must have come in front of the last sentence.

[1] *EP*, pp. 371 ff.

Although formal proof is probably impossible, there is very strong reason to believe that this edict existed in the Republic. There are in the Digest at least ten texts where the view of Republican jurists is referred to on *damnum infectum*.[1] These must have been regarded as still having relevance for later law. It is difficult to believe that they were in the main concerned with the position under the *legis actio* which, although it survived to the time of Gaius, was never used because the legal position under the edict was *commodius* and *plenius*.[2] There must have been considerable differences between the two, not just in procedure, but, as the *plenius* shows, also in substance. These differences would tend to limit the use made of texts on the *legis actio* in discussions of the law under the edict, even where the point at issue was the same in both systems. Further, what the Republican texts show most is the tremendous breadth of situation which was protected. It is even harder to believe that the texts which go back to Republican discussions referred originally to the edict of the peregrine praetor. On the whole, Roman jurists concentrate on the law used at Rome for Romans and, although on occasion they might have to deal with the *edictum praetoris peregrini*, the remains of Republican discussions here are too extensive for it to be in the least plausible that they were all or mainly concerned with the peregrine praetor's edict. There is also the general point that by far the greatest period for the development of the Edict of the urban praetor was the last two centuries of the Republic. But it must be admitted that there is no evidence for the proposition that the urban praetor's edict is very old. The argument might be used that in one of the *cautiones* proposed by the *praetor urbanus* the ways of causing the damage are listed, *quid ibi ruet scindetur fodietur aedificabitur*, and that the list is unnecessary, is reminiscent of the list in Chapter 3 of the *lex Aquilia*, and points to the great antiquity of the *cautio*.[3] And if it could be shown that the *cautio* could have nothing to do with the *legis actio* procedure, the conclusion would be that the *edictum praetoris urbani* must be old. But, in fact, one cannot argue very much from the

[1] D. 8. 5. 17. 2; 39. 2. 9. 2; *h.t.* 24. 4, 5, 12; *h.t.* 25; *h.t.* 43 pr., 1, 2; 39. 3. 3. 2.

[2] G. 4. 31.

[3] Cf. now Lenel, *EP*, p. 552, n. 1; followed by Karlowa, *Römische Rechtsgeschichte* (Leipzig, 1901), ii. 1241.

form of the *cautio*. Unnecessary listing of this kind is no sure guide to antiquity. Thus, the *lex Quinctia de aquaeductibus* of 9 B.C. gives a list in respect of repairing damaged aqueducts, etc.: *id omne sarcire reficere restituere aedificare ponere excidere demolire damnas esto.*[1]

The urban praetor's edict is couched in extremely general terms. It is, of course, concerned with *damnum*, i.e. financial loss, feared from a thing, but nothing is said of its being a neighbouring thing nor whether it is moveable or immoveable and, if the former, whether it is stationary or on the move, nor whether the threatened loss is due to a fault in the thing itself or in work done to the thing, nor whether some physicial injury, as well as financial loss, must be threatened. If protection for *damnum infectum* is limited then this must be due either to the way the edict is interpreted[2] or to the *cautiones*. So far as the latter are concerned, let it be said that we do not know whether before Julian the list issued by the praetor was regarded as exhaustive—variants at least were permitted[3]—and whether we have a complete list of those issued.[4] Very little on the forms of the *cautiones* has survived in the commentaries of the jurists and this little would tend to be on the most important *cautiones* so that it is quite possible that there was a number of others. It should be noticed, too, that in the normal course of events attention would be fixed on the case of an immoveable or stationary object falling on to a neighbour's property since only then, usually, can an individual foresee financial loss to him from an inanimate thing.

Before discussing individual cases and rules, it is as well to see how much can be known of the *legis actio* and the *edictum praetoris peregrini.*

The *legis actio*: Only one text, G. 4. 31, is certainly concerned with this:[5]

[1] Sometimes unnecessary listing is indicative of late formulation: cf., for oriental documents, Yaron, *Bibliotheca Orientalis* xv (1958) 18.

[2] Cf. the *actio de dolo*: see now Watson, *Obligations*, pp. 258 ff.

[3] D. 39. 2. 30. 2 (Ulpian, 81 *ad ed.*).

[4] Cf. Lenel, *EP*, pp. 551 ff. And of course the phrase *operis vitio* in a *cautio* could enable cases to be covered where the damage feared was not from an immoveable or stationary object.

[5] D. 43. 8. 5 (Paul, 16 *ad Sab.*) is almost certainly concerned with the *legis actio* for *damnum infectum*: cf. *infra*, pp. 131 ff.

Tantum ex duabus causis permissum est [id legis actionem facere] lege agere: damni infecti et si centumvirale iudicium fu*tu*rum *est*. sane qu*idem*, cum ad centumviros it*ur*, ante lege agitur sacramento apud praetorem urbanum vel peregrinum [praetorem]. damni vero infecti nemo vult lege agere, sed potius stipulatione qua*e* in edicto proposita est obligat adversarium suum, *id*que et commodius ius et plenius est. per pignoris *capionem* . . .

In the time of Gaius there were only two situations where one could proceed by *legis actio*: for *damnum infectum* and where the case was to go before the centumviral court. The survival of the *legis actio* procedure in the latter case does not appear too surprising —the centumviral court was concerned with questions of succession and to these the Romans attached particular importance and it is known that the Centumvirs had great prestige.[1] And in any event, this *legis actio* seems to have lost much of its formality.[2] But the other exception, *damnum infectum*, is not at all easy to explain, especially since there is no proof of the nature of the *legis actio* involved. A few preliminary points might help to clear the ground. First, it would be too simple to attribute the survival of the *legis actio* to the fact that when the *legis actiones* were abolished the praetor had not created a more up-to-date remedy for *damnum infectum*. Generally speaking, what one would have expected under such circumstances would be the substitution of a praetorian procedure although the substance of the law was unchanged. This must have happened in many instances. The only case where this objection would not apply is where the *legis actio* involved is outside the direct control of the praetor, which can be true only of the *legis actio per pignoris capionem*. This is the procedure thought of, for instance, by Lévy-Bruhl who does in fact attribute the survival of the *legis actio* to the absence at the appropriate time of a better praetorian procedure.[3] But this is open to the objection that if the procedure is not under the direct control of the praetor it can survive, at least in theory, even if the praetor had earlier created a better procedure. Hence the survival of this *legis actio* has nothing to do with the existence or non-existence at the relevant time of a better praetorian remedy. Secondly, no reason can be seen in the

[1] Cf. Lévy-Bruhl, *Recherches sur les actions de la loi* (Paris, 1960), pp. 325 f.
[2] Ibidem, pp. 151 f.
[3] Ibidem, p. 328.

nature or substance of threatened damage which would lead it to be singled out for the survival of its *legis actio*. The survival must be due rather to chance and it seems plausible to hold that this chance must be connected with the procedure, i.e. with the kind of *legis actio*, involved. On purely *a priori* grounds one would expect this kind of *legis actio* to have two characteristics. First, it should be capable of being overlooked. The reason for this statement is that although no proof is possible it seems much more likely that the *lex Aebutia* and the two *leges Iuliae* abolished the *legis actiones* not individually but by types. The kind of *legis actio* most likely to be overlooked would be that *per pignoris capionem*, not only because it seems to have contained only a few remedies, but also because it was not universally agreed that it did count as a *legis actio*.[1] Secondly, it should not be under the direct control of the praetor or he would refuse to allow it.[2] And Gaius says that the *legis actio* was not used, not because of any obstruction by the praetor but because the party wishing a remedy preferred to proceed under the Edict. This argument, too, points to the *legis actio per pignoris capionem* which was performed outside court and without magisterial intervention.[3] Further arguments also suggest that the procedure was a *legis actio per pignoris capionem*. Thus Paul tells us that *nulla legis actio prodita est de futuro*.[4] Yet any protection for *damnum infectum* must be *de futuro*, and Gaius tells us that there was a *legis actio* for *damnum infectum*. The only explanation which seems to avoid a direct substantive conflict is that the procedure involved was *per pignoris capionem* which for Gaius was a *legis actio*, but which perhaps for Paul, as certainly for some other jurists,[5] was not a *legis actio*. Again, the procedure *per pignoris capionem* seems very well adapted to the circumstances.[6] Further,

[1] Cf. G. 4. 29.

[2] Cf., e.g., the disappearance of the XII Tables' provision for *membrum ruptum*. Even if, in fact, *talio* was never exacted, the plaintiff had under this remedy a strong chance of getting greater financial compensation than he would under the Edict. The provision never seems to have been abolished and its disappearance would seem to be due to the praetor not allowing an action on it rather than to the plaintiff always preferring the provision of the Edict.

[3] G. 4. 26–9.

[4] *Vat. Fr.* 49 (Paul, 1 *man.*): cf. Lévy-Bruhl, op. cit., pp. 326 f. But what this means is doubtful.

[5] Cf. G. 4. 29.

[6] Cf. Lévy-Bruhl, op. cit., p. 327.

G. 4. 31 ends with the words *per pignoris* before the manuscript becomes illegible and no one doubts that Gaius was going to say something about the *legis actio per pignoris capionem*. What, of course, cannot be ascertained is whether this is a continuation of the discussion of *damnum infectum* or the beginning of a new topic. Finally, one might give as an argument in favour of the *legis actio* being *per pignoris capionem* the fact that no argument specifically points to some other particular *legis actio*.[1] The main argument against this view of the *legis actio* is that in G. 4. 27 and 28 Gaius gives us a list of *legis actiones per pignoris capionem* which, it is said, appears to be taxative and which does not include *damnum infectum* which is all the more surprising since it would be the only one left in existence.[2] But there is really nothing in these texts to suggest that the list is taxative,[3] and since Gaius was going to deal in some detail with *damnum infectum* in § 31 there was no particular reason for him to mention it in § 27 or § 28. Again, it might be objected that on the view here proposed the other cases of *legis actiones per pignoris capionem* ought to have survived, at least as theoretical possibilities. But factors totally unconnected with procedure might have led to the disappearance of these rights. One must not forget that at some time the military tribune became responsible for soldiers' pay; that the attitude to *publicani* hardened—witness the edicts *Quod familia publicanorum furtum fecisse dicetur*,[4] *Quod publicanus vi ademerit*,[5] and *Quod publicanus illicite exegerit*—[6] and the right of self-help given them by the censors might have been taken away from them to be replaced by the legal form with a fiction of which Gaius speaks,[7] and which presumably is also censorial;[8] and that attitudes to *dapes* also changed.[9] It should, at any rate, be significant that, with the exception of the case of the

[1] For other hypotheses see Bonfante II. i. 329 ff.: Branca, *Danno temuto* (Milan, 1937), pp. 31 f.; *Iura* xii (1961) 305 f.; Mozzillo, *Contributi allo studio delle stipulationes praetoriae* (Naples, 1960), pp. 54 ff. Most recently, Kaser, *ZPR*, p. 25, n. 13, would exclude the *legis actio per pignoris capionem* as a possibility.

[2] Bonfante, op. cit., pp. 329 f.: cf., e.g., de Zulueta, *Gaius* ii. 249.

[3] Cf. Lévy-Bruhl, op. cit., pp. 327 ff.

[4] Cf. Lenel, *EP*, pp. 335 ff.

[5] Ibidem, pp. 387 f.

[6] Ibidem, p. 388.

[7] G. 4. 32.

[8] Cf. Lenel, *EP*, pp. 388 f.

[9] Cf. Latte, *Römische Religionsgeschichte* (Munich, 1960), pp. 375 ff.

publicani which was a matter of censorial regulation rather than of civil law, no new remedy appeared, so far as we know, to take the place of these *legis actiones per pignoris capionem*. The *legis actio* for *damnum infectum* must have been less convenient and narrower in its scope than the procedure offered by the praetor, but this is no argument against the *legis actio* being *per pignoris capionem*. We do not really know anything about the conditions for the *legis actio* and it may easily have been the case, for instance, that a certain time had to elapse before there could be a seizure of a *pignus* and the amount to be seized might have been restricted.

To conclude. Although certainty is not possible, the balance of probability is very much in favour of the idea that the *legis actio* was *per pignoris capionem*.

A text which, in all probability, was concerned with the *legis actio* for *damnum infectum* is D. 43. 8. 5 (Paul, 16 *ad Sab.*).

> Si per publicum locum rivus aquae ductus privato nocebit, erit actio privato ex lege duodecim tabularum, ut noxa domino caveatur.

The codex Florentinus originally had *carveatur* but the first reviser deleted the first *r*. Cuiacius, on the basis of a now lost codex of the Basilica, altered the reading to *sarciatur* which has been followed by other scholars, notably Mommsen,[1] who calls attention to the appropriateness for *noxa* of the verb *sarcire*. But despite such distinguished support the reading *sarciatur* cannot be maintained. Palaeographically it is not very easy, since it demands the substitution of *s* for *c*, *c* for *v*, and *i* for *e*. *Caveatur* which involves merely the deletion of that *r* is much simpler. Again, it is difficult to make legal sense of *sarciatur*. So far as one can tell, there are only two possible actions which might be under discussion, the *legis actio* for *damnum infectum* or the *actio aquae pluviae arcendae*. In the former action there can have been no compensation for loss suffered unless some previous positive step had been taken[2] and there is no sign in the

[1] *Digesta Iustiniani Augusti* ii (Berlin, 1870), *ad h.l.* See also the authors referred to by Mozzillo, op. cit., pp. 68 f. For other views on the text see, in general, Mozzillo, pp. 68 ff.

[2] So much could be asserted with confidence even if we had no indication of what that step was, since otherwise the *legis actio* would have had advantages not shared by the proceedings under the urban praetor's edict and it would not have fallen into disuse: cf. *infra*, pp. 139 ff.

text of any such step if *sarciatur* is the reading accepted. Likewise, the *actio aquae pluviae arcendae* was aimed at warding off future injury[1] and did not give compensation except for loss suffered after *litis contestatio*.[2] But *ut noxa domino caveatur* does make legal sense for *damnum infectum* with the meaning 'that a stipulation be given to the owner in respect of the injury'. This does involve holding that under the old procedure for *damnum infectum*, as under the Edict, a *cautio* was somehow involved, but there is no *a priori* objection to that. It seems, though, that for two reasons one can exclude the idea that the *actio aquae pluviae arcendae* is the action referred to. First, there is no place for a *cautio* in connection with that remedy. Burckhard[3] very ingeniously tried to avoid this difficulty by suggesting a different interpretation of *ut noxa domino caveatur* which would not imply the presence of a *cautio*. He pointed out a non-technical meaning of *cavere alicui aliquid*: to keep something away from someone. He gave the example from Cato, *de agri cult.* 5. 7, *scabiem pecori et iumentis caveto*, and one might give other examples from later writers, such as Pliny the Elder, *N.H.* 20. 89. 244, *ipsa herba . . . cavenda . . . exulceratae vesicae et renium vitiis*.[4] Our text would then mean that if an aqueduct is likely to injure a private citizen, he will have an action under the XII Tables to keep the harm from him. The text would then be saying the sort of thing one might expect to hear about the *actio aquae pluviae arcendae*. None the less the interpretation is most implausible. No other Digest text exemplifies this usage, and the technical legal senses of *cavere* as 'to take a stipulation' and 'to lay down' or 'decide' are so overwhelmingly common[5] as to make it virtually impossible for *cavere* to be used in a legal text with the meaning Burckhard would ascribe to it especially if, as here, that usage would result in ambiguity in the text. Nor can it be suggested that *ut noxa domino*

[1] Cf. *infra*, pp. 154 ff.

[2] Cf., e.g., D. 39. 3. 6. 6 (Ulpian, 53 *ad ed.*). But Kaser, *Ius*, p. 219, does regard *noxiam sarcire* as appropriate to the *actio aquae pluviae arcendae*.

[3] Continuation of Glück, *Commentario alle pandette XXXIX*, 3 (Milan, 1905), pp. 39 ff.

[4] Cf. from the same work at 23. 57. 106, *caventur* (i.e. a kind of pomegranate) *aeque vomitionibus ac bilem reicientibus*.

[5] Cf. *Vocabularium Iurisprudentiae Romanae* (Berlin, 1903), i. 641 ff., s.v. *caveo*.

caveatur is a (modernized) quotation from the XII Tables and that the verb was used here in this connection before it became so heavily technical. The verb used in this clause of the XII Tables for warding off damage was not *cavere* but *arcere*, as both the name, *actio aquae pluviae arcendae*, and numerous texts show. The second reason why the *actio aquae pluviae arcendae* cannot be the action given here is that that action was given only for work done on private ground and not for work on public ground, whereas what is under discussion is a *per publicum locum rivus aquae ductus*, i.e., a channel of an aqueduct running through public land. It is the water from the aqueduct in public land which threatens the damage and even if another (non-dangerous) part of the aqueduct is on private land this could not alter the fact that the water threatens to do damage because of *opus in publico factum*. A *cautio* for *damnum infectum* could, of course, be taken in respect of *opus in publico factum*.[1] The suggestion could be made, however, that two arguments point to the *actio aquae pluviae arcendae* rather than to the *legis actio* for *damnum infectum*. One is that in book 16 *ad Sabinum*, which is the one from which our text is taken, Paul discussed the *actio aquae pluviae arcendae*,[2] whereas he had dealt with *damnum infectum* in book 10.[3] The other is that it is strange that Paul should refer to the action from the XII Tables for *damnum infectum* which was never used instead of the perfectly good praetorian remedy, but that it would not be odd for him to refer to the remedy of the XII Tables for *aqua pluvia arcenda* since it had not been replaced by an edict. But neither of these arguments would have much substance. As for the former, nothing would have been more natural than to bring in the fact that a remedy under *damnum infectum* could be given precisely because it is in contrast to the *actio aquae pluviae arcendae*. And for a similar reason of contrast reference would be made to the XII Tables' provision on this subject and not to the Edict simply because it was the same XII Tables which established the *actio aquae pluviae arcendae*.

It might be suggested that the *carveatur* of the text originally read *arceatur* and that therefore the text was concerned with the

[1] Cf. Lenel, *EP*, p. 551.
[2] Cf. Lenel, *Pal.* i. 1291 f.
[3] Cf. ibidem, 1280.

actio aquae pluviae arcendae. The emendation of *arceatur* is easier than *sarciatur* though more difficult than *caveatur*. Indeed, *caveatur* is so much the obvious reconstruction that positive external reasons (as was the case with *sarciatur*) have to be adduced before any weight can be given to a different suggestion. And the second objection to the *actio aquae pluviae arcendae* being the action in question would still stand.

Therefore, it very much looks as if D. 43. 8. 5 is referring to the *legis actio* for *damnum infectum*, and hence it is most probable that this action goes back to the XII Tables and that a *cautio* was somehow involved in it.

Edictum praetoris peregrini: The evidence for an edict of the peregrine praetor is in the *lex Rubria de Gallia Cisalpina* which dates from between 49 and 42 B.C., 49 B.C. itself being the most likely.[1]

xx. Qua de re quisque, et a quo, in Gallia Cisalpeina, damnei infectei ex formula restipularei satisve accipere volet, et ab eo quei ibei i(ure) d(eicundo) ⟨*p*(*raerit*)⟩ postulaverit, idque non k(alumniae) k(aussa) se facere iuraverit: tum is, quo d. e. r. in ius aditum erit, eum, quei in ius eductus erit, d. e. r. ex formula repromittere et, sei satis darei debebit, satis dare iubeto decernito. Quei eorum ita non repromeisserit aut non satis dederit, sei quid interim damni datum factumve ex ea re aut ob e(am) r(em) eove nomine erit, quam ob rem, utei damnei infectei repromissio satisve datio fierei ⟨*iubeatur*⟩, postulatum erit: tum mag(istratus) prove mag(istratu) IIvir IIIIvir praefec(tus)ve, quoquomque d. e. r. in ius aditum erit, d. e. r. ita ius deicito iudicia dato iudicar*e*que iubeto *c*ogito, proinde atque sei d. e. r., quom ita postulatum esset, damn[*e*]i infectei ex formula recte repromissum satisve datum esset. D. [*e. r.*] quod ita iudicium datum iudicareve iussum iudicatumve erit, ius ratumque esto, dum in ea verba, sei damnei infectei repromissum non erit, iudicium det itaque iudicare iubeat: 'I(udex) e(sto). S(ei), ant*e*quam id iudicium q. d. r. a(gitur) factum est, Q. Licinius damni infectei eo nomine q. d. r. a(gitur) eam stipulationem, quam is quei Romae inter peregreinos ius deicet in albo propositam habet, L. Seio repromeississet: tum quicquid eum Q. Licinium ex ea stipulatione L. Seio d(are) f(acere) oport*e*ret ex f(ide) b(ona) d(um)*t*(*axat*) HS e(ius) i(udex) Q. Licinium L. Seio, sei ex decreto IIvir(ei) IIIIvir(ei) praefec(tei)ve Mutinensis, quod eius ⟨*is*⟩ IIvir IIIIvir praefec(tus)ve ex lege Rubria, seive id pl(ebei)ve sc(itum) est, decreverit. Q. Licinius eo nomine

[1] Cf. Hardy, *Six Roman Laws* (Oxford, 1911), pp. 110 f.

qua d. r. a(gitur) L. Seio damnei infectei repromittere noluit, c(ondemnato); s(ei) n(on) p(aret), a(bsolvito)'; aut sei damnei infectei satis datum non erit, in ea verba iudicium det: 'I(udex) e(sto). S(ei), antequam id iudicium q. d. r. a(gitur) *f*actum est, Q. Licinius damnei infectei eo nomine q. d. r. a(gitur) ea stipulatione, quam is quei Romae inter peregrinos ius deicet in albo propositam habet, L. Seio satis dedisset: tum q(uic)q(uid) eum Q. Licinium ex ea stipulatione L. Seio d(are) f(acere) oporteret ex f(ide) b(ona) d(um)t(axat) , e(ius) i(udex) Q. Liciniu*m* L. Seio, sei ex decreto IIvir(ei) IIIIvir(ei) praef(ectei)ve Mutinensis, quod eius is IIvir IIIIvir praefect(us)⟨*ve*⟩ ex lege Rubria, seive id pl(ebei)ve sc(itum) est, decreverit, Q. Licinius eo nomine q. d. r. a(gitur) L. Seio damnei infectei satis dare noluit, c(ondemnato); s(ei) n(on) p(aret), a(bsolvito)'; dum IIvir IIIIvir i(ure) d(eicundo) praefec(tus)ve d. e. r. ius ita deicat curetve, utei ea nomina et municipium colonia locus in eo iudicio, quod ex ieis quae proxsume s(cripta) s(unt) accipie⟨⟨n⟩⟩tur, includ*a*ntur concipiantur, quae includei concipei s(ine) d(olo) m(alo) oporteret debebitve, ne quid ei quei d. e. r. aget petetve captionei ob e(am) r(em) aut eo nomine esse possit: neive ea nomina, qua⟨*e*⟩ in earum qua formula ⟨⟨quae⟩⟩ s(upra) s(cripta) s(unt), aut Mutina⟨*m*⟩ in eo iudicio includei concipei curet, nise⟨*i*⟩ iei, quos inter id iudicium accipietur leisve contestabitur, ieis nominibus fuerint, quae in earum qua formula s(upra) s(cripta), *s*(*unt*), et nisei sei Mutinae ea res agetur; neive quis mag(istratus) prove mag(istratu), neive quis pro quo imperio potestateve erit, intercedito neive quid aliud facito, quo minus de ea re ita iudicium detur iudiceturque.

An enormous literature has been produced on the question why in a charter for the Roman citizens of Gallia Cisalpina the *formulae* proposed should refer back to the *stipulatio* of the peregrine praetor.[1] It is not intended to go fully into the views expressed since the truth seems to be that too many factors are unknown for even a clear balance of probabilities to emerge. What seems to me, however, to be the most plausible view is that, for some reason or another, the peregrine praetor had jurisdiction over the citizens of Gallia Cisalpina.[2] But for the *formulae* to show that the *stipulatio* which was regarded as appropriate to Cisalpine Gaul was that proposed by the peregrine praetor is no direct evidence that

[1] See now Serrao, *La 'iurisdictio' del pretore peregrino* (Milan, 1954), pp. 87 ff., and the authors he cites.

[2] Cf. Serrao, op. cit., pp. 97 ff.; Wieacker, 'Zum Ursprung der *bonae fidei iudicia*', *ZSS* lxxx (1963) 1 ff. at p. 16; Frederiksen, 'The *Lex Rubria*: Reconsiderations', *JRS* liv (1964) 129 ff. at p. 133.

the peregrine praetor had jurisdiction. That stipulation may have been regarded merely as a convenient standard. Even the presence of a reference to that stipulation in the fiction does not imply the peregrine praetor's jurisdiction—the validity of such a stipulation, if it had been given, would rest not upon the peregrine praetor's jurisdiction, but upon the normal rules of *stipulatio*. And other possibilities abound. Thus it could be that at the time the *lex* was passed the urban praetor's edict was not in existence.[1] The usual objection to this is that there is evidence for the earlier existence of the *cautio*, especially in the old form *si quid ibi ruet scindetur fodietur aedificabitur*, and that this must be a creation of the urban praetor.[2] But first, the arguments for the antiquity of this *cautio* are by no means conclusive,[3] and secondly (and this is much more important), there is no good reason for assuming that the old non-praetorian procedure did not involve a *cautio*[4] whose form might have been adopted by a *cautio* of the urban praetor. The contrast in G. 4. 31 between *damni infecti lege agere* and *stipulatione quae in edicto proposita est obligare adversarium* does not in any way whatever imply that no *cautio* was involved in the former procedure. Again, it could be that the provisions of the urban praetor's edict and those of the edict of the peregrine praetor were not identical[5] and that for some reason those of the latter were here thought preferable. It is not necessarily a strong argument against this view that since it was probably intended that Gallia Cisalpina would soon cease to be a province and would be incorporated into Italy, the law applied in the *lex* would correspond as closely as possible to the law applied in Italy to Roman citizens. It would not be unnatural for a draftsman—even with the knowledge that his work would be shortlived—to insert the provisions he thought best. Another possible view is based on the fact that in the *lex Rubria* the magistrates are not given the right to order *missio in possessionem* if no *stipulatio* or *satisdatio* is given in respect of

[1] Cf. Burckhard, continuation of Glück, *Commentario alle pandette, XXXIX*, 2 (Milan, 1905), ii. 88 ff.

[2] Cf. Serrao, op. cit., p. 90 and p. 99, n. 36.

[3] Cf. *supra*, pp. 126 f.

[4] Even if the arguments on D. 43. 8. 5 (*supra*, pp. 131 ff.) are not acceptable.

[5] Cf., e.g., Puchta, *Zeitschrift f. geschichtliche Rechtswissenschaft* (1884), x. 211 ff.

damnum infectum, whereas *missio in possessionem* is provided for in the edict of the urban praetor. The suggestion is[1] that there was no provision for *missio in possessionem* under the edict of the peregrine praetor—*missio in possessionem*, it is said, is here impossible because the *missio ex secundo decreto* should lead to *usucapio* which was not open to peregrines[2]—and so this edict became the model for the *lex Rubria*, *missio in possessionem* being also impossible for the municipal magistrates because they had no *imperium*[3] and *missio in possessionem* is said in D. 2. 1. 4 (Ulpian, 1 *ad ed.*) to be more a matter of *imperium* than of *iurisdictio*.[4] But one cannot properly estimate the strength of this view. It has been objected to it[5] that on the simplest view of chapter xxi of the *lex Rubria* the local magistrates could order *missio in possessionem*. And if D. 2. 1. 4 says *missio in possessionem* is *imperii magis quam iurisdictionis* it says exactly the same about the right to demand a praetorian stipulation, and yet the right to demand the *cautio damni infecti* is given to the local magistrates by the *lex Rubria*. On the other hand, chapter xxii of the *lex Rubria* would appear to show that there was at least great reluctance to allow the right of *missio in possessionem* to the local magistrates. Again, it is objected that it is not clear that the *praetor peregrinus* did not have *missio* and that it certainly was later available to *peregrini*.[6] And there really is no justification for holding that the provisions of the *lex Rubria* on *damnum infectum* are identical with those of the peregrine praetor. But against that one might think that, at least, any right which the peregrine praetor had to order *missio in possessionem* would still be different from that of the urban praetor, because, since *peregrini* could not usucapt, there was no place for the *missio ex secundo decreto*.

To conclude. It is submitted that all in all it is extremely unwise to draw any conclusions[7] as to the history and nature of the edicts of the urban and peregrine praetors on *damnum infectum* from the acceptance of the *cautiones* of the latter as the standard for liability

[1] Karlowa, *Römische Rechtsgeschichte* ii. 1239 f.

[2] Karlowa, op. cit. (Leipzig, 1885), i. 471 f.

[3] Ibidem; cf. also now Bonifacio, *Iura* vi (1955) 243.

[4] Cf. Lenel, *EP*, p. 53; Pugliese, *Il processo civile romano II, Il processo formulare* (Milan, 1963), i. 118 ff.

[5] Frederiksen, op. cit., p. 133.

[6] Ibidem, p. 133, n. 23.

[7] Apart, that is, from the existence of the peregrine praetor's edict.

in the *lex Rubria* for the situation where no *stipulatio* or *satisdatio* had been given.

Chapter xx of the *lex Rubria* has been accorded a position of central importance in the history of the concept of *bona fides* since it seems to be universally accepted that the *formulae* given in it show that the peregrine praetor gave an action which contained the words *ex fide bona* in respect of his *stipulatio damni infecti*.[1] Thus Wieacker, who does not attribute great importance to the *praetor peregrinus* in the development of the concept of good faith,[2] none the less says that the *intentio* of the *actio ficticia*, *ex ea stipulatione . . . oporteret ex fide bona*, can only mean that if a peregrine in Rome had given the *promissio* laid down by the *praetor peregrinus*, he would have been judged in a *iudicium* whose *intentio* would run: *quidquid ex ea stipulatione Nm Nm Ao Ao dare facere oportet ex fide bona*.[3] But such a conclusion is, in fact, far from certain. The *tum quicquid eum Q. Licinium ex ea stipulatione L. Seio d(are) f(acere) oporteret ex f(ide) b(ona) d(um)t(axat) HS* can stand by itself and be completely independent of the edict of the peregrine praetor. It contains in the words *ex fide bona* its own basis of liability. The relevance of the peregrine praetor's edict may easily be restricted to the form of the *stipulatio*. That is to say that the *formula* of the *lex Rubria* would mean that if before the action Q. Licinius had not given the stipulation he was to be condemned in a sum equal to what it would be proper for him to give or do in accordance with good faith if he had given a stipulation in a particular form of words (namely, that to be found in the *stipulatio* of the peregrine praetor). The subjunctive *oporteret* is just as appropriate on this view as it is on the hypothesis that the peregrine praetor's *intentio* where the promise had been given was *quidquid . . . dare facere oportet ex fide bona*. Thus, *ex fide bona* in the *formula* may be the invention of the draftsmen of the *lex Rubria* and not of a *praetor peregrinus*. Chapter xx of the *lex Rubria* may suggest, but it is certainly not proof—and there is no proof elsewhere—that it was the peregrine praetor who put *ex fide bona* in the *intentio* of an

[1] Cf., e.g., Lenel, *EP*, p. 4, n. 1; Kunkel, *Festschrift Koschaker* (Weimar, 1939) ii. 1 ff., 9 f.; Wieacker, op. cit., pp. 15 ff., and the references he gives.

[2] Ibidem.

[3] Ibidem, p. 16.

action on a *stipulatio*. The measure of liability under the *stipulatio* of the urban praetor was *quanti ea res erit*[1] and it may have been the same under the *stipulatio* of the peregrine praetor.

It must be said, therefore, that the differences between the urban praetor's provisions for *damnum infectum* and those of the peregrine praetor are not necessarily anything like as great as one might imagine at first sight. It cannot be clearly shown that the peregrine praetor did not grant *missio in possessionem*, though it is certainly unlikely that he could grant *missio ex secundo decreto*. Likewise, it cannot be established that liability under the peregrine praetor's stipulation was *quidquid . . . dare facere oportet ex fide bona* rather than the *quanti ea res erit* of the urban praetor.

Edictum praetoris urbani: What follows is basically a discussion of the individual texts which relate to *damnum infectum* in the Republic. It will be largely assumed—though it cannot be proved —that they were in fact written about the urban praetor's remedy, first, because, for the reasons given above,[2] it is very likely that they were; secondly, even if they were not they must at least in substance fall within the scope of that remedy, otherwise the *legis actio* for *damnum infectum* would not, as Gaius alleges, have dropped completely out of use because no one wanted to use it. Whether written about the edict or not, the texts can tell us a lot about the edict.

The situations covered by the remedy for *damnum infectum* were very wide, as the Republican texts show. Since some of the *cautiones* seem to distinguish between a *vitium operis* and a *vitium aedium* or *loci* or *arborum* there has naturally been discussion as to whether one or the other was the earlier, at least so far as the praetorian remedy was concerned.[3] This aspect of the matter will be watched as we go along.

The text which is usually believed to give the earliest evidence of a *cautio*[4] for *damnum infectum* is Pliny the Elder, *N.H.* 36. 2. 5, 6.

CCCLX columnas M. Scauri aedilitate ad scenam theatri temporari et vix mense uno futuri in usu viderunt portari silentio legum. sed publicis

[1] D. 39. 2. 28 (Ulpian, 81 *ad ed.*).
[2] *Supra*, pp. 126 f.
[3] See above all the discussion in Bonfante II. i. 332 ff.
[4] That is, leaving aside D. 43. 8. 5. But see *supra*, pp. 131 ff.

nimirum indulgentes voluptatibus. id ipsum cur? aut qua magis via inrepunt vitia quam publica? quo enim alio modo in privatos usus venere ebora, aurum, gemmae? aut quid omnino diis reliquimus? 6. verum esto, indulserint publicis voluptatibus. etiamne tacuerunt maximas earum atque adeo duodequadragenum pedum Lucullei marmoris in atrio Scauri conlocari? Nec clam id occulteque factum est. satisdare sibi damni infecti coegit redemptor cloacarum cum in Palatium eae traherentur. . . .

Modern jurists take the Marcus Scaurus, *aedilis*, mentioned in the text as the aedile of 123 or 122 B.C.[1] But this is virtually impossible and a very much more likely candidate is Marcus Aemilius Scaurus who was aedile in 58 B.C.[2] First, Pliny goes on to say in 36. 3. 7 that L. Crassus, *orator*, had already installed foreign marble on the Palatine. L. Crassus, described simply as *orator*, can only be the consul of 95 B.C.[3] so a date as early as 122 B.C. for the situation in § 6 is almost out of the question. Secondly, Pliny cites the behaviour of Marcus Scaurus as an example of shameless extravagance, and the games of the aedile of 58 B.C. were notorious for that very fault.[4] Thirdly, although one cannot be more precise, a famous episode in the life of the aedile of 58 B.C. involved columns.[5] Thus Pliny is evidence for the existence of the *cautio* for *damnum infectum* in 58 B.C., not in 122 B.C. The text, none the less, has considerable interest. To begin with, the use of the verb *satisdare* makes it extremely likely that what was exacted was what appears in the edict as *alieno nomine satisdari* and not the *suo nomine promitti* and that, therefore, as early as 58 B.C. even non-owners could be made to give a *cautio* for *damnum infectum* in particular terms. In other words, this distinction between owners and non-owners had already been drawn.[6] Presumably the columns were regarded as public property. Then the passage shows that certain non-owners were regarded as having sufficient interest to demand the *satisdatio*. The person who asked for it, successfully, was the *redemptor*

[1] Cf. Karlowa, *Römische Rechtsgeschichte*, ii. 1241; Bonfante II. i. 332; Mozzillo, *Contributi allo studio delle stipulationes praetoriae*, p. 129.

[2] On him see Klebs, *RE* i. 588 ff.

[3] On him see Münzer, *RE* xiii. 1, 252 ff.

[4] Cf. Klebs, loc. cit.

[5] Cicero, *pro Scauro*, 22. 45.

[6] Even better evidence for the distinction having been drawn at least fifteen years before is in the next text to be discussed, Cicero, *in Verr.* II. 1. 56. 146.

cloacarum. Further, the *satisdatio* is in respect of a *facere*, against a *vitium operis*, and not against a *vitium aedium*, etc. Moreover, the *facere* guarded against is not concerned with work done to an immovable or even stationary object, but the very danger is that damage will be caused by the transportation of heavy objects. This is very far removed from what one might think of as the standard case of *damnum infectum*, one house falling on another.

Cicero, *in Verr*. II. I. 56. 146 now gives us earlier evidence for the *cautio* for *damnum infectum*.

> At ut videatur tamen res agi et non eripi pupillo: SI QUID OPERIS CAUSA RESCIDERIS, REFICITO. Quid erat, quod rescinderet, cum suo quemque loco lapidem reponeret? QUI REDEMERIT SATIS DET DAMNI INFECTI EI QUI A VETERE REDEMPTORE ACCEPIT. Deridet, cum sibi ipsum iubet satis dare Habonium. . . .

The situation in this text has been fully explained by Karlowa.[1] With the performance of repairs to public buildings, owners of neighbouring properties might feel that damage to their properties was threatened and would demand *satisdatio damni infecti* from the *redemptor*. The text of the contract (*lex operi faciundo*) proposed by Verres where a new *redemptor* was taking over the work included the term that the new *redemptor* was to make *satisdatio damni infecti* to those who had received such a *satisdatio* from the previous *redemptor*. The contract is to be dated to the years 73–70 B.C. when Verres was governor of Sicily. It shows that much of what was concluded from Pliny, *N.H.* 36. 2. 5, 6 to exist in 58 B.C. can be pushed back by about fifteen years. Already, non-owners in some cases had to give *satisdatio* for threatened damage arising *vitio operis*.

> Cicero, *top*. 4. 22. Ab efficientibus rebus hoc modo: Omnibus est ius parietem directum ad parietem communem adiungere vel solidum vel fornicatum. Sed qui in pariete communi demoliendo damni infecti promiserit, non debebit praestare, quod fornix viti fecerit. Non enim eius vitio qui demolitus est damnum factum est, sed eius operis vitio quod ita aedificatum est, ut suspendi non posset.

This text tends to be misquoted and misunderstood by jurists. Thus, instead of *non enim eius vitio qui demolitus est*, Karlowa[2] has

[1] Op. cit., ii. 1241: cf. Bonfante II. i. 334.

[2] Op. cit., ii. 1242.

non enim parietis vitio qui demolitus est and Bonfante[1] *non enim eius parietis vitio qui demolitus est*. Both likewise seem equally unaware that *demoliri* is a deponent verb and that the part cited means something like 'Not by the fault of him who demolished' and not something like 'Not by the fault of the wall which was demolished'. There is, therefore, *pace* these authors, nothing in the text about *parietis vitium* and so no justification for holding that Cicero knew about a *cautio* for *aedium vitium*. What the text does do, is throw vivid light on the limits of what counted as *operis vitium*.[2] Everyone, we are told, has the right to join at right angles a wall, whether solid or vaulted, to a common wall. But where one person, about to demolish a common wall, gave a *cautio damni infecti* to the other owner, he is not liable for any loss caused by the fault of the arch. For, it is said, the injury was caused not by the fault of the person demolishing the wall but by the fact that the arched wall was not built so as to be self-supporting. Thus where damage is suffered which would not have been suffered but for the conduct of a person who gave a *cautio damni infecti* which covered his actions, the *stipulatio* does not come into effect unless the damage can actually be attributed to fault on his part.

D. 8. 5. 17. 2 (Alfenus, 2 *dig.*). Secundum cuius parietem vicinus sterculinum fecerat, ex quo paries madescebat, consulebatur, quemadmodum posset vicinum cogere, ut sterculinum tolleret. respondi, si in loco publico id fecisset, per interdictum cogi posse, sed si in privato, de servitute agere oportere: si damni infecti stipulatus esset, possit per eam stipulationem, si quid ex ea re sibi damni datum esset, servare.

This text never seems to have been regarded as interpolated in substance.[3] De Sarlo seems to assume[4] that the wall in question is common but this seems to be excluded by the *secundum cuius parietem*. It is also difficult to reconcile with one of the hypotheses in the text, namely that the land on one side of the wall is *publicus*.

[1] II. i. 334.

[2] Admittedly, common walls tend to create particular problems (cf. *infra*, pp. 153 f.) but this should not affect the principle here.

[3] Cf. *Index Itp.*; recently on the text, De Sarlo, *AV*, pp. 81 ff.; Gandolfi, *Contributo allo studio del processo interdittale romano* (Milan, 1955), p. 108. But see Levy, *Gesammelte Schriften* (Cologne, Graz, 1963), i. 269; *West Roman Vulgar Law: The Law of Property* (Philadelphia, 1951), p. 77, n. 340.

[4] Loc. cit.

A man whose neighbour had made a manure heap against his wall, thus causing damp, asked how he could compel the neighbour to remove the heap. Alternative remedies, depending on the circumstances, are suggested.[1] The jurist then adds that if a *stipulatio damni infecti* had been taken the questioner could recover if he had suffered any loss. This situation, too, should be seen as concerning a *vitium operis*.

Not every case, though, where loss is caused by activity on neighbouring land gives rise to the remedy for *damnum infectum*.

D. 39. 2. 24. 12 (Ulpian, 81 *ad ed.*). Item videamus, quando damnum dari videatur: stipulatio enim hoc continet, quod vitio aedium loci operis damnum fit. ut puta in domo mea puteum aperio, quo aperto venae putei [tui *ins. Mommsen*] praecisae sunt: an tenear? ait Trebatius non teneri me damni infecti: neque enim existimari operis mei vitio damnum tibi dari in ea re, in qua iure meo usus sum. si tamen tam alte fodiam in meo, ut paries tuus stare non possit, damni infecti stipulatio committetur.

The text comes from Ulpian's commentary on the stipulations for *damnum infectum*.[2] He says we must see when *damnum* occurs, for the *stipulatio* covers loss caused *vitio aedium loci operis*. He then gives as a concrete case for discussion the situation where I open a well in my house which cuts off the springs to your well. Am I liable? Trebatius, he says, held I was not liable for *damnum infectum* for he did not regard *damnum* to be caused to you *operis mei vitio* where I used a right which I had. This is a perfectly straightforward decision. The rest of the text from *si tamen* is, in all probability, reporting the opinion of Trebatius. Although in classical Latin it is normal to put the apodosis in the subjunctive if the protasis is in the subjunctive, Ulpian habitually puts the apodosis in the indicative even if the protasis is in the subjunctive unless there is some other reason for the subjunctive in both clauses.[3] This part of the text tells us that if I dig so deeply on my land that your wall cannot stand you have an action against me on the *stipulatio damni infecti*. Again, it is the sort of decision one would expect.[4]

[1] See *infra*, pp. 177 ff.

[2] Cf. Lenel, *Pal.* ii. 883 f.

[3] As an examination of the texts of Ulpian will confirm.

[4] But it is not intended to work out the legal principle which distinguished the two cases.

More difficulty is experienced with the next text.

D. 39. 2. 25 (Paul, 78 *ad ed.*). Trebatius ait etiam eum accipere damnum, cuius aedium luminibus officiatur.

In the Digest it appears as a sort of appendix to *h.t.* 24. 12. It comes from Paul's commentary on the praetorian stipulations for *damnum infectum*[1] and there is no reason to believe that the opinion of Trebatius was expressed in a different context. Bonfante regards the substance of the text as interpolated[2] because it appears to conflict with the view expressed as being by Trebatius himself in *h.t.* 24. 12. But this is most implausible. It is very difficult to see why the compilers would insert the text into the long discussion from Ulpian 81 *ad edictum*, *h.t.* 24 and 26, if they had to interpolate the substance, and even more difficult to see how they could do this, taking the text as being relevant to *h.t.* 24. 12, and yet not notice a conflict between 24. 12 and their alterations to 25.[3] Perhaps the explanation is that neither in its original nor its present context did the text mean that Trebatius would give an action for *damnum infectum* where a neighbour's light was affected. *H.t.* 24. 12 shows him in effect considering when the action will lie and when it will not, although the neighbour has suffered loss. Where the supply of water to a well was cut off, he declares that the neighbour did not suffer *damnum operis mei vitio*. But he would have to concede that the neighbour did suffer *damnum* and that through my activity. Trebatius' original point which became the basis of *h.t.* 25 may well have been that another case of *damnum* to my neighbour through my activity which did not give rise to the action is where his light is affected. This would be a more extreme case, possibly even a *reductio ad absurdum*. Trebatius would then be making the same point which is made by Proculus—also, *inter alia*, in respect of building higher—in *h.t.* 26. Another possibility, which must be mentioned in order to be rejected, is that the text means that where there is a servitude of light, the owner of the dominant tenement can sue on a *stipulatio damni infecti* for any loss. But apart from the fact that the text says nothing about a servitude, this would

[1] Lenel, *Pal.* i. 1095.

[2] II. i. 344 f.

[3] Daube rightly treats the text as genuine: 'On the use of the term *Damnum*', *Studi Solazzi* (Naples, 1948), pp. 107 and 113.

offend against the principle evidenced in texts from the Empire that no action lies for *damnum infectum* if another remedy is available.[1]

D. 39. 3. 3. 2 (Ulpian, 53 *ad ed.*). Si vicinus, qui arvum solebat certo tempore anni rigare, pratum illic fecerit coeperitque adsidua irrigatione vicino nocere, ait Ofilius neque damni infecti neque aquae pluviae arcendae actione eum teneri, nisi locum complanavit eoque facto citatior aqua ad vicinum pervenire coepit.

The text has been held Justinianic from *nisi* to the end by Pernice[2] and Krüger.[3] That part is certainly an addition—though it may be a gloss—as the two indicatives instead of subjunctives show. The reason for the exclusion of the *actio damni infecti* and the *actio aquae pluviae arcendae* seems to be that it was established that the latter action, and hence also the former, did not lie where the damage was caused by certain agricultural processes on the neighbour's land.[4] A change of use, from arable land to pasture, involving a change in irrigation which resulted in injury to another did not give that person right to a remedy just as he would not have had one if the land had always been used as pasture. The question has been raised[5] whether Ofilius was concerned with the *legis actio damni infecti* or with the praetorian remedy, but, in truth, nothing in the text favours one or the other.

The remedies under *damnum infectum* were only available if the injured party had taken certain active steps before the damage occurred. There was, in principle, no remedy where one man suffered loss which was caused by another's property unless he had taken such steps. Very naturally, there were attempts to improve this position, and two texts which refer to the Republic occur in this context in Ulpian's *liber* 53 *ad edictum*, at D. 39. 2. 9. 1 and 2. They must be seen against their background in this part of Ulpian's commentary in *h.t.* 7 and *h.t.* 9.[6] At 7 pr. Ulpian gives the wording

[1] D. 39. 2. 13. 6; *h.t.* 18. 2; *h.t.* 18. 4; *h.t.* 20.

[2] In Bremer, *Iurisprudentiae antehadrianae quae supersunt* (Leipzig, 1896), i. 356.

[3] *Stereotype Digest*, *ad h.l.*

[4] Cf. Mozzillo, *Contributi allo studio delle stipulationes praetoriae*, p. 61 and the texts he cites, n. 17: cf. also *infra*, pp. 169 ff.

[5] Cf., most recently, Mozzillo, op. cit., pp. 61 ff.

[6] *H.t.* 8 (Gaius, *ad ed. praet. urb. tit. de damno inf.*) seems to have been inserted here wrongly. It is irrelevant to the topic under discussion: cf. Krüger, op. cit., *ad h.l.*

of the edict; in § 1 he says this edict is concerned with threatened damage; and § 2 raises the question whether any remedy is available if a house falls down when no *cautio* had been taken and the owner does not want to remove the rubble from his neighbour's land. The answer given is apparently Julian's whole system for dealing with the kind of situation which can be covered by the *cautio damni infecti* where no *cautio* was in fact taken before the damage occurred. This is that where the owner of the house which has fallen down wishes to take away any of it from his neighbour's land he is to be permitted to do so only if he takes away everything, what is useless as well as what is useful, and he must give a stipulation, not only against future but also against past loss. Hence, if the owner of the house which caused the damage wishes to recover any of it, the injured party can have himself put in the position he would have been in if he had taken the *cautio damni infecti* in time. But if, the text goes on, the owner of the house which fell does nothing, an interdict is to be given to the person on whose house the other's fell to compel him either to remove the debris—in which case, of course, the *cautio* mentioned above would have to be given —or to treat his whole house as *pro derelicto*. *H.t.* 9 pr. is mainly concerned with Julian's justification for his attitude and with Ulpian's approval of it. Then comes 9. 1.

De his autem, quae vi fluminis importata sunt, an interdictum dari possit, quaeritur. Trebatius refert, cum Tiberis abundasset et res multas multorum in aliena aedificia detulisset, interdictum a praetore datum, ne vis fieret dominis, quo minus sua tollerent auferrent, si modo damni infecti repromitterent.

The question is raised: *De his autem, quae vis fluminis importata sunt an interdictum dari possit, quaeritur*. This should mean, one would think, that what is at issue is whether the interdict which Julian gave where a house fell on a neighbour's is also available where a river carried off property belonging to one person and deposited it on the property of another and in the process the property of the former damaged the property of the latter. But what appears to be the answer in the text is not really an answer to that question.[1]

[1] But it never seems to have been held interpolated and it would be most implausible to suggest that it was.

Ulpian says that Trebatius declared that when the Tiber overflowed its banks and carried a large number of things belonging to many people against the buildings of others, the praetor issued an interdict to prevent force being used to stop the owners recovering their property provided they gave the *cautio damni infecti*. Thus, the interdict is given here for the benefit of those persons whose property has been the cause of the damage, not as in the situation discussed by Julian and presumably envisaged in Ulpian's question for the benefit of the persons whose property has been damaged. Probably the answer as we have it is primarily an argument in favour of an affirmative reply to the question, whether the form of the text is the result of Ulpian's answer being very elliptical or of it having been shortened by the compilers. But that Trebatius' opinion was of value even as an argument shows that—at least so far as Ulpian was aware—no direct affirmative argument had ever been given to his question. The context is concerned with recovery for *damnum iam factum* and this is true not only of what precedes our text, but also of *h.t.* 9. 2. The question in our text is also concerned with *damnum iam factum* and hence it would be natural to suppose that Trebatius' opinion also related to that point. But, in fact, Trebatius speaks only of a *cautio* for *damnum infectum* and there is really no justification for assuming that he intended it also to cover *damnum iam factum*. The relevance of Trebatius' opinion for Ulpian in the reply to his question is simply that first, a *cautio de damno infecto* is appropriate where the objects which pose the danger will cause the damage as a result of being carried off by a river and hence the decision given by Julian in the other case is equally appropriate here: and secondly, that this is a type of situation in which—though in a different way—a praetor had already intervened with an *interdictum*. The text, therefore, does not tell us of a Republican attempt to increase the range of protection round the remedies for *damnum infectum*. At the most in this connection it shows an attempt to increase the pressure on the owner of the threatening objects to give the *cautio* for the future. However, since this appears to be the kind of situation in which Julian would have exacted a stipulation in respect of the damage already done, and yet there is no sign of this stipulation, we can probably assume that that device had not yet been invented.[1] This is confirmed, to some extent, by *h.t.* 9. 2.

> Alfenus quoque scribit, si ex fundo tuo crusta lapsa sit in meum fundum eamque petas, dandum in te iudicium de damno iam facto, idque Labeo probat: nam arbitrio iudicis, apud quem res prolapsae petentur, damnum, quod ante sensi, non contineri, nec aliter dandam actionem, quam ut omnia tollantur, quae sunt prolapsa. ita demum autem crustam vindicari posse idem Alfenus ait, si non coaluerit nec unitatem cum terra mea fecerit. nec arbor potest vindicari a te, quae translata in agrum meum cum terra mea coaluit. sed nec ego potero tecum agere ius tibi non esse ita crustam habere, si iam cum terra mea coaluit, quia mea facta est.

Now this does show a Republican attempt to increase the range of protection round the remedies for *damnum infectum*. But it is much clumsier than Julian's position. Julian's attitude is that the owner of the ruin cannot get the debris back unless he gives a *cautio* for past, as well as threatened, damage. This means, in fact, that the praetor will not grant him a *vindicatio* unless he makes the necessary stipulation. But for Alfenus (who is followed by Labeo) if that person brings a *vindicatio* then a *iudicium de damno iam facto*[2] will be given against him. This *iudicium* can only be a decretal action. So, instead of refusing a *vindicatio* unless the requisite *cautio* is given, the praetor allows a *vindicatio* but, to redress the balance, then grants a decretal action against the plaintiff. This latter position is so much the clumsier that it would not have been invented if the former had ever been thought of. This, in turn, also suggests that the *cautio* of Trebatius mentioned in § 1 did not cover *damnum iam factum*. Something is not quite right with the present text from *arbitrio iudicis* to *prolapsa*. The accusatives and infinitives suggest a continuation of the indirect speech (and the accusative and infinitive construction is foreign to the compilers) but the indicatives are against this idea. One must accept, though, that whether *nam arbitrio iudicis . . . contineri* is an addition to the text or gives Alfenus' own opinion. it does show the law of Alfenus' time. If the

[1] Nothing in the text is indicative of which sorts of *vitium* will be covered by the *cautio*.

[2] Variant MSS. readings which suggest a *iudicium de damno infecto* appear incorrect: cf. Bonfante II. i. 366 f.

judge had been allowed to make *compensatio* in the *vindicatio*, the decretal *iudicium de damno iam facto* would have been totally unnecessary. *Nec aliter . . . prolapsa*, however, is more difficult. Beseler[1] has already suggested that it might be interpolated, first, because it does not fit logically into its present position and, secondly, because it says the surprising thing that the alternative 'all or nothing' is inserted by the praetor in the *formula* of the *vindicatio* rather than being exacted by the judge. The first of these objections is perfectly sound since Alfenus has been explaining the granting of the *iudicium de damno iam facto* and this point relates to the different question of the scope of the *vindicatio*. But a rather longer account by Alfenus might have been shortened. The second objection is not so certain. It is not clear from the text that 'all or nothing' was inserted in the *formula* rather than having been a requirement demanded by the praetor (who might have exacted a *cautio* to that effect) from the plaintiff before the action was allowed to proceed. It seems impossible to decide, even on a balance of probabilities, whether this part of the text gives the law in the time of Alfenus or not. In this text too there is no indication of the kind of *vitium* which caused the damage.

Naturally, an action could only be brought on the *cautio damni infecti* if the injury which followed was a result of a *vitium*.[2]

D. 39. 2. 43 pr. (Alfenus, 2 *dig*.). Damni infecti quidam vicino repromiserat: ex eius aedificio tegulae vento deiectae ceciderant in vicini tegulas easque fregerant: quaesitum est, an aliquid praestari oportet. respondit, si vitio aedificii et infirmitate factum esset, debere praestari: sed si tanta vis venti fuisset, ut quamvis firma aedificia convelleret, non debere. et quod in stipulatione est 'sive quid ibi ruet', non videri sibi ruere, quod aut vento aut omnino aliqua vi extrinsecus admota caderet, sed quod ipsum per se concideret.

D. 39. 2. 24. 4 (Ulpian, 81 *ad ed*.). Servius quoque putat, si ex aedibus promissoris vento tegulae deiectae damnum vicino dederint, ita eum teneri, si aedificii vitio id acciderit, non si violentia ventorum vel qua alia ratione, quae vim habet divinam. Labeo et rationem adicit, quo, si hoc non admittatur, iniquum erit: quo enim tam firmum aedificium

[1] *Beiträge* i. 19.

[2] For the Empire see above all D. 39. 2. 24. 3 (Ulpian, 81 *ad ed*.).

est, ut fluminis aut maris aut tempestatis aut ruinae incendii aut terrae motus vim sustinere possit?

These two texts should be taken together. It is quite likely that they both go back to the same discussion of Servius on the effect of *vis maior* where a *stipulatio damni infecti* had been taken. Mayer-Maly's interpretation[1] of the text is not wholly satisfactory. The *stipulatio* was given, wind then blew tiles off the roof of the house of the promisor, and the tiles damaged the property of the stipulator. Is there liability under the *repromissio*? Mayer-Maly argues that the wording of the *stipulatio*, *sive quid ibi ruet*, should leave no room for any doubt that there was liability, but that the obvious decision was overcome by Servius deciding that this clause applied only to damage arising from the sphere of influence of the promisor. The case would, thus, be a straightforward one of liability being excluded by *vis maior*. But there is much more to the problem than that. Mayer-Maly seems to be leaving out of account the other clause of the praetorian stipulation, *quod aedium loci operisve de quo agitur vitio*, which makes it clear that the damage must be due to a *vitium* affecting the property and not to external *vis*. And yet, the main discussions as we have them do raise, flatly, as a problem the question whether there is liability for external *vis*. Thus, Ulpian begins his discussion in *h.t.* 24. 3 with the question: *Haec stipulatio utrum id solum damnum contineat, quod iniuria fit, an vero omne damnum, quod extrinsecus contingat?* The problem, indeed, is a quite particular one, namely, how, in fact, can one take account of *vis maior* in this connection? The person who wants his neighbour to give him a *cautio damni infecti* must swear that he is not demanding it *calumniae causa*. That is, he must believe that there is a real threat that his property will be injured as a result of a *vitium operis, loci, aedificii*. If thereafter he does suffer injury from his neighbour's property, how is one to say that he did not suffer the injury from the *vitium* but from *vis extrinsecus*? To look at the particular instance—tiles blown off a roof by the wind—discussed by Servius. How can one ever decide that the tiles on this house which was in a dangerous condition have been blown off because

[1] 'Höhere Gewalt: Falltypen und Begriffsbildung', *Festschrift Steinwenter* (Graz, 1958), pp. 60 f.

the wind was of extraordinary force and would not equally have been blown off, because of the *vitium*, by a wind of normal strength?[1] The truth is that this matter of fact can never be properly ascertained, and hence a purely arbitrary answer has to be given to the question of legal liability. One might decide that, despite the extraordinary weather conditions, all damage was to be attributed to the *vitia* since a *cautio* had been taken because of their existence; or one might decide that, despite the existence of *vitia*, all damage was to be attributed to the extraordinary weather conditions; or one might try an equally arbitrary compromise solution.[2]

To turn now to a closer examination of *h.t.* 43 pr. Alfenus begins with a simple question. A *stipulatio damni infecti* was given to a neighbour. Tiles were blown off the building by the wind, fell on to the neighbour's tiles and broke them. Is there any liability? In the reply, Servius or Alfenus starts by declaring there is liability if the damage were caused by the *vitium* or weakness of the building. Nothing so far directly concerns *vis maior*. But, the reply goes on, if the force of the wind were so great that it might tear tiles off a house no matter how firm it was, there is no liability. Thus where there was *vis maior* and an arbitrary decision had to be given, the jurist decided that liability was excluded. But some justification has to be given. Reasonably enough, the jurist does not attempt to base his justification on the interpretation of the meaning of the clause, *quod aedium loci operisve de quo agitur vitio*—as argued above, in the case of extraordinary *vis venti* where there was also a *vitium*, one could not tell whether the damage was *aedium vitio* or *extrinsecus vi*. Instead, he argues from another clause of the *cautio*, *sive quid ibi ruet*, and says that a thing does not fall when it is pushed down by the wind or any external force. This is arbitrary and objectionable since it is based on a deliberate misinterpretation of the meaning of the clause, but it has the great merit that it brings

[1] In some other cases, of course, such as where the house is destroyed by an earthquake or where the injury which occurs is very different from that which was envisaged when the *cautio* was taken, the problem is nothing like so great.

[2] Cf. D. 39. 2. 24. 10 (Ulpian, 81 *ad ed.*). *Idem ait* [i.e. *Vivianus*], *si damni aedium mearum nomine tibi promisero, deinde hae aedes vi tempestatis in tua aedificia ceciderint eaque diruerint, nihil ex ea stipulatione praestari, quia nullum damnum vitio mearum aedium tibi contingit: nisi forte ita vitiosae meae aedes fuerint, ut qualibet vel minima tempestate ruerint. haec omnia vera sunt.*

into play as the sole consideration the question of whether there was *vis maior* or not, and leaves out of account the insoluble question of whether or not the injury is attributable to the *vitium* of the building.

H.t. 24. 4 shows Ulpian giving us a coarsened version of Servius' view. *H.t.* 43 pr. and 24. 4 do, however, also show that by this time *aedificii vitium*, as well as *operis vitium*, was covered by the *cautio*.

D. 39. 2. 24. 5. Idem Servius putat, si controversia aquae insulam subverterit, deinde stipulatoris aedificia ceciderint, nihil eum ex stipulatu consecuturum, quia id nec operis nec loci vitio factum est. si autem aqua vitiet fundamenta et sic aedificium ruisset, committi stipulationem ait: multum enim interesse, quod erat alioquin firmum, vi fluminis lapsum sit protinus, an vero ante sit vitiatum, deinde sic deciderit. et ita Labeo probat: etenim multum interesse, quod ad Aquiliam pertinet, sanum quis hominem occidat an vero factum inbecilliorem.

This follows upon § 4 and may equally be a coarsening of Servius' opinion. In the text Servius draws a distinction. If a flood of water overturns a tenement so that the house of the stipulator falls, the stipulator will not recover anything under the *stipulatio* since the damage was not caused by a *vitium* of the work or place. But if the water damages the foundations (i.e., of the tenement) and thus the stipulator's house falls down, there is an action on the stipulation. It makes a great deal of difference, it is said, whether it falls down by the force of the river, or whether it was damaged and then fell down. The idea seems to be that the former situation is one of *vis maior*, but in the latter fault attaches to the promisor because he should, after the flood, have put his house again into a sound condition. The form of the part of the text which interests us, i.e. as far as *deciderit*, does not appear to be perfect. The first *deinde* which seems to have a causal sense is strange, *aedificia* becomes *aedificium*, no indication is given as to whether the *fundamenta* are those of the *insula* or of the *aedificium*, the present tense, *vitiet*, is odd, and so is the indicative *erat*. *Quod erat alioquin firmum* may well be an addition[1] (which does not affect the substance) but the other flaws are more easily ascribed to a shortening of the text than to an alteration of the substance. The indicative, however, in the

[1] Cf. Guarneri Citati, *Annali Perugia* xxxvii (1924) 43 f.

clause, *quia id nec operis nec loci vitio factum est*, is not suspicious and the argument may go back to Servius. Ulpian frequently gives the indicative in such clauses (and thus shows his agreement) even where he is quoting the earlier jurist.[1] Two factors can explain the argument here from the absence of a *vitium* although this argument was so carefully avoided in § 4. First, once the existence of *vis maior* is established as being enough to exclude liability, it is natural to treat this as resulting from the clause of the stipulation relating to *vitium*. One no longer has to face the question whether the injury was caused by *vis maior* or by the *vitium*. Secondly, the present situation is much easier than the previous one to envisage as involving only *vis maior* and not also *vitium loci* or *operis*. It is reasonable to regard any flooding of a building, however slight, as involving *vis maior* but this is quite different from the blowing of a wind, which at its mildest is certainly not *vis maior* and where the point at which it is to be regarded as *vis maior* has to be fixed arbitrarily. § 5 also shows clearly that *vis maior* only excludes liability if the injury follows immediately upon the *vis*, not also if *vis maior* weakens the property of the promisor which eventually injures the property of the stipulator.

Although most of the texts show the *cautio* in operation in respect of *vitium operis*, *h.t.* 24. 4 and 5 show Servius also discussing it in respect of *vitium aedificii* and *loci*. More than that, there is no indication in any of the texts that at any earlier time the *cautio* would relate only to *vitium operis*.

Two texts concern a rather particular situation involving a common wall.

D. 39. 2. 43. 1 (Alfenus Varus, 2 *dig*.). Cum parietem communem aedificare quis cum vicino vellet, priusquam veterem demoliret [demolirent *Mommsen*], damni infecti vicino repromisit adeoque [ab eoque? *Best*] restipulatus est: posteaquam paries sublatus esset et habitatores ex vicinis cenaculis emigrassent, vicinus ab eo mercedem quam habitores non redderent, petere vult: quaesitum est, an recte petet. respondit non oportuisse eos, cum communem parietem aedificarent, inter se repromittere neque ullo modo alterum ab altero cogi potuisse: sed si maxime repromitterent, tamen non oportuisse amplius quam partis demidiae, quo amplius ne extrario quidem quisquam, cum parietem communem

[1] Cf. Magdelain, *Les Actions civiles* (Paris, 1954), p. 9.

aedificaret, repromittere deberet. sed quoniam iam in totum repromisissent, omne, quod detrimenti ex mercede vicinus fecisset, praestaturum.

It would seem that the text is interpolated from *si maxime* to *deberet* and that the words *in totum* are also an insertion.[1] Two neighbours wish to take down a common wall and replace it by a new one, and they take stipulations for *damnum infectum* from each other. After the wall is removed the tenants of one of the neighbours quit and he wishes to sue the other for the rent. Servius or Alfenus answers in the first place that the *cautio* should not have been given and could not have been compelled. Presumably, this is because they were involved in a joint effort. But, he goes on, since it was given, the whole of the loss of rent can be recovered.[2]

D. 39. 2. 43. 2. Idem consulebat, possetne, quod ob eam rem dedisset, rursus repetere, quoniam restipulatus esset a vicino, si quid ob eam rem, quod ibi aedificatum esset, sibi damnum datum esset, id reddi, cum et ipsam hanc pecuniam, quam daret, propter illud opus perderet. respondit non posse propterea, quia non operis vitio, sed ex stipulatione id amitteret.

This is a continuation of the above problem. The question was further raised whether the one who had to pay the *merces* to his neighbour could recover it under the terms of the stipulation which his neighbour had given him on the ground that he had suffered the *damnum* because of the building operation. But the jurist replies in the negative because the loss was not caused by *operis vitio* but by the giving of the *stipulatio*.[3,4,5]

[1] See now Daube, *Iura*, xii (1961) 102.

[2] See above all on the text Daube, loc. cit.

[3] Would the decision have been different if the *stipulatio* had been compellable?

[4] A number of texts, which do not refer expressly to the Republic, are said at times to be concerned with the *legis actio*: D. 39. 2. 6 (Gaius, 1 *ad ed. prov.*); 39. 3. 11. 3 (Paul, 49 *ad ed.*); 39. 3. 14. 2 (Paul, 49 *ad ed.*): cf. now Mozzillo, op. cit., pp. 54 ff. The present writer can see nothing in these texts indicative of the *legis actio* rather than of the praetorian procedure.

[5] There seem to be no texts for our period (or earlier) which concern *operis novi nuntiatio*: D. 39. 1. The general view, however, is that it is very odd: cf. now Cosentini, 'Appunti sull'*operis novi nuntiatio*', *Annali Catania* iv (1949–50) 297 ff.

7

ACTIO AQUAE PLUVIAE ARCENDAE

THIS action went back to the XII Tables:[1]

D. 40. 7. 21 pr. (Pomponius, 7 *ex Plautio*). . . . sic et verba legis duodecim tabularum veteres interpretati sunt 'si aqua pluvia nocet' id est 'si nocere poterit'. . . .

This tells us that the Republican jurists interpreted the words of the XII Tables *si aqua pluvia nocet* as *si nocere poterit*. The text might suggest that originally the plaintiff had to wait until damage occurred before he could sue and that the Republican jurists widened the scope of the action by allowing it to be brought even before any happened.[2] This view, however, is rather implausible, not because it seems unlikely that an action could be given here only if loss had occurred but because the combination that the plaintiff had to wait until he suffered injury and then—as was the case with this action—his damages only took account of threatened future injury and not of any past loss would seem to be incomprehensible. Greater evidence is needed before one can postulate here a case of deliberate juristic misinterpretation in order to widen the action's scope. The *actio* is not necessarily in direct conflict with the statement of Paul,[3] *nulla legis actio prodita est de futuro*, since although the action is given to prevent future damage, it is allowed on account of previous operations on the defendant's land.

The use of the words *aqua pluvia* in the XII Tables is confirmed by the attention paid to the interpretation of them in Cicero, *top.* 9. 38.[4] The action was, of course, an *actio civilis*[5] and there was no edict. According to Lenel's reconstruction, which does not seem

[1] Though D. 43. 8. 5 (Paul, 16 *ad Sab.*) is most probably concerned with the *legis actio* for *damnum infectum*: cf. *supra*, pp. 131 ff.

[2] Cf. Sargenti, *L'actio aquae pluviae arcendae* (Milan, 1940), p. 21.

[3] *Vat. Fr.* 49 (1 *man.*).

[4] Cf. *infra*, pp. 156 f. The text does not expressly mention the XII Tables.

[5] Lenel, *EP*, p. 375 and n. 4.

to be doubted, the *formula* ran: *Si paret opus factum esse in agro Capenate, unde aqua pluvia agro Ai Ai nocet, quam ob rem Nm Nm eam aquam Ao Ao arcere oportet, si ea res arbitrio iudicis non restituetur, etc.*

The water which threatened the damage had to be *aqua pluvia*, rain water. There are signs that the interpretation of this caused very considerable controversy.

Cicero, *top*. 9. 38. Sequitur is locus, qui constat ex eis rebus quae quodam modo adfectae sunt ad id de quo ambigitur; quem modo dixi in plures partes distributum. Cuius est primus locus ea coniugatione, quam [Graeci] *συζυγίαν* vocant, finitimus notationi, de qua modo est dictum; ut, si aquam pluviam eam modo intellegeremus quam imbri conlectam videremus, veniret Mucius, qui, quia coniugata verba essent pluvia et pluendo, diceret omnem aquam oportere arceri quae pluendo crevisset.

The text seems to point to a real juristic difficulty of interpretation, not just an imaginary one of Cicero. He represents that not only himself but also Trebatius, to whom the *topica* are dedicated, might think that *aqua pluvia* meant water which we see collected from rain. This is hardly flattering to Trebatius if the view expressed is too narrow ever to have been reasonably held by a jurist. The wider view that *aqua pluvia* meant any water which increased through rain is not only said to be that of Quintus Mucius but, on the more likely interpretation,[1] that jurist is represented as having given an argument for it. It would be slightly odd for Quintus Mucius to produce any argument at all if there was no legal difficulty and so it is all the more significant that he seems to use here an argument more abstract and apparently more artificial and forced than any other from him which has survived except for that in D. 32. 29. 1. The question at issue seems to have been whether *aqua pluvia* had to comprise only rain water or whether it was enough for the action that danger was threatened through water which

[1] The position of *quia . . . pluendo* before *diceret* might suggest the clause is telling us why Mucius said what he did and is not a reason he gave in saying it, but the imperfect subjunctive *essent* rather than the present indicative *sunt* implies that the reason was given by Mucius. Neither of these arguments, which tend in opposite directions, is conclusive, but I have consulted a number of Latin scholars who all felt—though with varying degrees of certainty—that the form of the text meant that the argument was Mucius'.

was swollen with rain water. That a real juristic difficulty was felt is confirmed by D. 39. 3. 1 pr. (Ulpian, 53 *ad ed.*).

Si cui aqua pluvia damnum dabit, actione aquae pluviae arcendae avertetur aqua. aquam pluviam dicimus, quae de caelo cadit atque imbre excrescit, sive per se haec aqua caelestis noceat, ut Tubero ait, sive cum alia mixta sit.

Rain water is described as water which falls from the sky and *imbre excrescit* whether it does damage by itself, as Tubero says, or whether it does damage when mixed with other water. In this connection the particular placing of *ut Tubero ait* can only mean that Tubero would only grant the *actio aquae pluviae arcendae* when the rain water, unmixed with other water, threatened damage, and not where the damage was feared through water swollen with rain.[1] The idea that damage which was threatened from a river swollen by rain was excluded from the scope of the *actio aquae pluviae arcendae* may seem to modern eyes to be excessively narrow but it obviously had some currency at the end of the Republic. It might be rash to assume that the narrow view was the older of the two.

But if some jurists took a very narrow view of the scope of the *actio aquae pluviae arcendae*, others, it would seem, took an exceptionally wide view.

D. 39. 3. 3 pr. (Ulpian, 53 *ad ed.*). Apud Trebatium relatum est eum, in cuius fundo aqua oritur, fullonicas circa fontem instituisse et ex his aquam in fundum vicini immittere coepisse: ait ergo non teneri eum aquae pluviae arcendae actione. si tamen aquam conrivat vel si spurcam quis immittat, posse eum impediri plerisque placuit. 1. Idem Trebatius putat eum, cui aquae fluentes calidae noceant, aquae pluviae arcendae cum vicino agere posse: quod verum non est: neque enim aquae calidae aquae pluviae sunt.

These texts have been interpreted in a large number of ways,[2] but I think it fair to say that no opinion would be regarded as at all satisfactory. The texts' difficulties cannot be removed by suggestions of alterations in the substance—thus, one of the most curious features, namely Trebatius' granting of an *actio aquae pluviae*

[1] *Contra*, Schönbauer, 'Die *actio aquae pluviae arcendae*', *ZSS* liv (1934) 233 ff. at p. 238.

[2] Cf. Sargenti, op. cit., pp. 33 ff. and the authors he cites; Bonfante II. i. 428, n. 6.

arcendae where hot water does damage, is treated as the unsuccessful view and so cannot be an invention of the compilers. And it is difficult to believe that a statement that this hot water was mixed with rain water has somehow accidentally dropped out. Both Ulpian and Justinian's compilers would have allowed an action for hot water mixed with rain water[1] so that we would have to say that any mention in Trebatius' opinion of rain water must have dropped out before *quod verum . . . sunt* was written. The inelegancies of the text, that is the rather inappropriate *ergo*[2] and the differences in mood in *conrivat* and *immittat*,[3] are most easily explained on the basis of a shortening of the text and scribal error and they do not justify the idea of changes in substance. A new approach to the text should, I submit, pay more attention than has hitherto been done to the word *placuit*. It is usually thought that just as in § 1 the view of Trebatius is corrected by Ulpian so in the *principium* it is corrected by the *plerique*.[4] This, I suggest, is not so and is belied by the use of *placuit*. The uses of *placuit* and *placet* are not the same. The latter, in the phrase *plerisque placet*, would mean simply that the present opinion of most jurists is being given. The use of the phrase *plerisque placuit* is different and more complex. It conveys a variety of shades of meaning. It can mean that in the past this particular view was held by the majority of jurists but is no longer.[5] But it can also at times be used to express living law where there is no longer a dispute. Thus the law might be given as settled, then we will be told *plerisque placuit*.[6] The implication here is that the legal position is no longer in dispute because at a time in the past most jurists agreed. Or a question might be posed, then *Cassius ait*, followed by a different view introduced by *sed plerisque placuit*.[7] Here *sed plerisque placet* would not be appropriate because it would imply, given the facts that the question for didactic purposes is first posed as if it could be a live issue (*quaeritur*) and the authority of Cassius, that the final answer could still be in doubt. *Sed plerisque placuit* here means that the issue is completely settled

[1] Cf. D. 39. 3. 1 pr. (Ulpian, 53 *ad ed.*).
[2] Cf. Sargenti, op. cit., p. 36.
[3] Cf. ibidem, p. 35.
[4] Cf. ibidem, p. 34.
[5] Cf. *plerisque placuerit* in D. 39. 2. 6 (Gaius, 1 *ad ed. prov.*).
[6] Cf. G. 3. 75.
[7] G. 3. 147.

against Cassius. What then is the significance in D. 39. 3. 3 pr. of *plerisque placuit* rather than *plerisque placet*? The implication is not, I suggest, that despite the authority of Trebatius the law is now settled in a different way because the majority took the opposite view. For that one would require a strongly adversative conjunction such as *sed*. Also, of course, the law cannot be settled if the text means that the *actio aquae pluviae arcendae* would be given since this seems contrary to the position of Ulpian in § 1. And if one says that what is settled is the giving of some remedy, presumably an interdict but not the *actio aquae pluviae arcendae*, then *a fortiori* there would not be a proper justification for *placuit* instead of *placet*. Rather, the implication is that, at one particular time, most jurists held this opinion and in the context this can only mean *apud Trebatium relatum*. That is, Trebatius gave this as the opinion of most jurists. Ulpian reports this majority view in direct speech even though he found it expressed in Trebatius: there is nothing odd in this. Thus, *si tamen, etc.* does not give a later correction to the view of Trebatius. It is, as the *si tamen* indicates, not a correction at all of Trebatius' view but a qualification which, in fact, is accepted by Trebatius himself as well as by the majority of jurists. The following situation was discussed. A man built a fuller's workshop around a spring which arose on his land and he began to send the spring water on to his neighbour's land. Trebatius said that the first man was not liable to the *actio aquae pluviae arcendae*. Then he adds qualifications. Most jurists, he says hold that if the man joins streams of water together or if he sends dirty water on to his neighbour's land he can be prevented (i.e. by the *actio aquae pluviae arcendae*. Trebatius' position seems to be this: A man is not liable to an *actio aquae pluviae arcendae* if he does nothing more than alter the direction of a spring which rises on his land and thus causes it to injure his neighbour. But if he does anything more to alter the character of the spring, such as to join more than one water channel together,[1] or if he makes the water foul, he will be liable to the *actio aquae pluviae arcendae*. Trebatius is trying to

[1] It is not clear whether the Latin means he joins the spring to other water courses, or joins together several streams resulting from the spring. There is no way to ascertain exactly what was meant.

make the scope of the action very much wider than would ever have been envisaged by the legislators. He recognizes—presumably because the statute says *aqua pluvia* and not just *aqua*—that not every case where water becomes dangerous because of work done on a neighbour's land is covered by the action but holds that the action does lie whenever danger is threatened because the volume of water running together is increased or the character of the water is artificially altered. It is easy to understand why such an attempt to widen the scope of the action was made.[1] The factual situation envisaged in § 1 is not wholly clear. *Aquae fluentes calidae* could refer either to a natural hot spring[2] or to water artificially heated. The use of the plural and of *fluentes* points—but by no means conclusively—to the former; but Trebatius' position would then be so extreme that one might prefer to revert to the latter. If we can accept the latter meaning, *idem Trebatius putat* would mean 'Likewise Trebatius thinks' and Trebatius would be giving a further qualification to his main view in the *principium*: water artificially heated must not be allowed to flow on to a neighbour's land and injure him. If we take the former meaning, *idem* must be used adversatively, 'And yet Trebatius thinks',[3] i.e. it is in apparent contradiction to what Trebatius held in the *principium*. Trebatius' view would then be almost unbelievably extreme—yet interpolation is out of the question. He would recognize that not all water can be understood by the term *aqua pluvia* but he would allow the qualifying adjective, *pluvia*, to exclude only naturally cold spring water. A person responsible for causing any other water to flow harmfully on to his neighbour's land would be held liable to the *actio aquae pluviae arcendae*.

It was not all rain water flowing from one man's land on to

[1] Probably the modern difficulties in interpreting the text arise from the feeling that Trebatius could never have had such an extreme view of the scope of the action. But that he had is shown by § 1, and it is § 1 which justifies this present interpretation of the *principium*. It is probably not the only example around this period of an attempt to make the scope of the *actio aquae pluviae arcendae* very much wider; cf. the attitude of Namusa in D. 39. 3. 2. 6 (Paul, 49 *ad ed.*): *infra*, pp. 161 ff.

[2] Cf. Schönbauer, op. cit., p. 242.

[3] Cf. Lewis and Short, *A Latin Dictionary* (Oxford, 1879, impression of 1951), s.v. *idem*.

another's and threatening damage which gave rise to the action. The danger had to arise from human activity on the former's land.

Cicero, *top*. 9. 39. Cum autem a genere ducetur argumentum, non erit necesse id usque a capite arcessere. Saepe enim citra licet, dum modo supra sit, quod sumitur, quam id ad quod sumitur; ut aqua pluvia ultimo genere ea est quae de caelo veniens crescit imbri; sed propiore, in quo quasi ius arcendi continetur [genus est, aqua pluvia] nocens; eius generis formae loci vitio et manu nocens, quarum altera iubetur ab arbitro coerceri, altera non iubetur.

Cicero is saying that of two kinds of *aqua pluvia nocens*, that which is *manu nocens* gives rise to the action, not that which arises *loci vitio*.[1] Here, too, in the later Republic a wider view was also taken.

D. 39. 3. 2. 6 (Paul, 49 *ad ed*.). Apud Namusam relatum est, si aqua fluens iter suum stercore obstruxerit et ex restagnatione superiori agro noceat, posse cum inferiore agi, ut sinat purgari: hanc enim actionem non tantum de operibus esse utilem manu factis, verum etiam in omnibus, quae non secundum voluntatem [mutata *ins. Mommsen*] sint. Labeo contra Namusam probat: ait enim naturam agri ipsam a se mutari posse et ideo, cum per se natura agri fuerit mutata, aequo animo unumquemque ferre debere, sive melior sive deterior eius condicio facta sit, idcirco et si terrae motu aut tempestatis magnitudine soli causa mutata sit, neminem cogi posse, ut sinat in pristinam locum condicionem redigi. sed nos etiam in hunc casum aequitatem admisimus.

Namusa held that if flowing water were blocked by filth and flooded the higher-lying ground, an action could be brought against the owner of the lower ground to allow the blockage to be removed. It was Namusa's opinion that the action lay not only where the water course was man-made, but also where it was natural. Labeo denied that the action would be given where the water course was natural. It is very difficult to believe that either

[1] Scherillo seems to be too positive in asserting that there is no doubt that this text derives from Quintus Mucius. His arguments are firstly its relationship with 9. 38 where Quintus Mucius is expressly cited, and secondly the mention here of *genera*: 'Note critiche su opere della giurisprudenza romana', *Iura* iii (1952) 180 ff. at p. 187. Although the opinion of Quintus Mucius on an aspect of this action is given in 9. 38 that does not necessarily mean that 9. 39 derives from that jurist, and although Quintus Mucius was interested in *genera*, distinctions of this kind are likely to occur quite independently of him in a work of the nature of the *topica*. Scherillo's main conclusion that this and a number of other texts in the *topica* come from Quintus Mucius, *liber singularis ὅρων*, will be opposed in a later volume on *Legal Science in the Later Roman Republic*.

the opinion of Namusa or of Labeo can be interpolated.[1] The meaning of the text can be clarified if we look at D. 39. 3. 2. 1.

Apud Labeonem proponitur fossa vetus esse agrorum siccandorum causa nec memoriam extare, quando facta est: hanc inferior vicinus non purgabat: sic fiebat, ut ex restagnatione eius aqua fundo nostro noceret. dicit igitur Labeo aquae pluviae arcendae cum inferiore agi posse, ut aut ipse purgaret aut te pateretur in pristinum statum eam redigere.

Labeo allows the *actio aquae pluviae arcendae* where the danger arises from a very old (*nec memoriam extare*, *quando facta est*) man-made ditch which is not cleared out. That is to say, Labeo will give this action in two different sets of circumstances, namely where men do something which results in threatened danger from water or where work of men is neglected and danger threatens from the very neglect.[2] Thus, his conflict with Namusa can only be over the case where no work of man is involved, which confirms that Namusa did allow the action in such circumstances. The action which Namusa will allow where a natural water course became blocked without human activity can only have as its object *ut sinat purgari* as the text says, or *ut aut ipse purget aut sinat purgari*, but not also *ut ipse purget* by itself. It seems inconceivable that the Romans would put a landowner to expense to protect his neighbour where damage was threatened by natural changes in the natural condition of the land. The view that in our text *ut sinat purgari* is interpolated[3] cannot be justified. And if it is genuine here there can be no *a priori* reason for thinking it interpolated in texts where it occurs where the damage is threatened as a result of neglect of earlier work of man.

It is usually thought that Namusa was attempting to widen the scope of the action and that his attempt was totally unsuccessful. Recently Sargenti has taken a different line.[4] He thinks, first, that the position of Namusa is a survival from an earlier period and that the jurists of the first century B.C. elaborated the primitive rules of the XII Tables and distinguished whether the damage could be

[1] Cf. Sargenti, op. cit., pp. 42 ff. For the interpolation of the end of the text which does not concern us see, among recent writers, Derine, *Iura* ix (1958) 42 ff.

[2] Though the actions may not have the same object.

[3] Beseler, *Beiträge* iii. 94.

[4] Loc. cit.

attributed to an *opus* or not and consequently changed the scope of the action. Secondly, he thinks that in the first century B.C., Namusa's opinion was not held by that jurist alone. His first point can neither be proved nor disproved, given the total absence of texts bearing on this question at an earlier period. But the balance of probability, I would suggest, is against Sargenti. On his view it would seem that the XII Tables would always allow a person to whom danger was threatened by water as a result of natural changes on a neighbour's land, at least where that land was lower-lying, to enter upon it to restore it to its previous condition. It is difficult to see how such a decemviral regulation could have defined more closely when a person could enter his neighbour's property where there was no *opus*. But it is very hard to imagine that such a wide general rule could ever have existed. It seems much more likely that originally only damage resulting from *opera* gave rise to an action but an attempt was made by at least one jurist to widen the scope of the action to damage arising from natural change and probably even then only in limited circumstances.[1] For his second point Sargenti refers in the first instance to D. 39. 3. 11. 6 (Paul, 49 *ad ed.*).

> Trebatius existimat, si de eo opere agatur, quod manu factum sit, omnimodo restituendum id esse ab eo, cum quo agitur: si vero vi fluminis agger deletus sit aut glarea iniecta aut fossa limo repleta, tunc patientiam dumtaxat praestandam.

But it is almost certain that Trebatius was not drawing a distinction between cases of *opus* on the one hand and cases where there was no *opus* on the other. He must have been at least including in the second group cases of natural change to the works of men, and like Labeo in *h.t.* 2. 1 would here have allowed the action *ad patientiam praestandam*. And he may have been thinking in this group of this class only. Thus, the use of *agger* to mean an artificial mound is much more common than its use to mean a natural mound.[2] *Fossa* means a man-made ditch.[3] What situation is envisaged by *glarea*

[1] The right to bring an action to be allowed to restore a neighbour's land to its previous condition does not fit neatly into the *formula*. We do not have enough information to say whether it would have fitted neatly into the relevant *legis actio* procedure.

[2] Cf. *TLL*, s.v. *agger*.

[3] Cf. D. 43. 14. 1. 5.

iniecta is not clear. The text, therefore, by no means necessarily shows that Trebatius would allow the *actio aquae pluviae arcendae* where the damage arose from natural changes affecting objects which were not man-made. The next text to which Sargenti refers does not support him at all.

D. 39. 3. 2. 4. Apud Ateium vero relatum est eam fossam, ex qua ad inferiorem fundum aqua descendit, cogendum esse vicinum purgare, sive extet fossae memoria sive non extet: quod et ipse puto probandum.

The ditch in question is clearly man-made as *sive extet memoria sive non extet* shows.[1]

So far we have seen the situations discussed for the action divided into three: where the danger threatened as a result of *opus factum*; where it threatened as the result of the deterioration of an earlier *opus*; and where it threatened although no *opus* was involved. The jurists do not seem to have been in agreement on these points as to what the law should be. But a further factor, namely the acquisition of a right of 'servitude' by lapse of time, was also treated as relevant for liability to the action though here, too, juristic opinion varied. A *lex Scribonia* which is apparently later than 69 B.C. but quite likely to date from 50 B.C.[2] abolished the usucaption of servitudes, but the classical jurists allowed lapse of time, at least in certain spheres including water rights, to have some effect.[3] The view of Labeo, Ulpian, and Paul[4] expressed in respect of the *actio aquae pluviae arcendae* was that *vetustas vicem legis tenet* and that in such circumstances[5] the lower ground was subject to the higher ground. For these jurists this seems to have meant that where an *opus* on the lower ground had enabled water to flow freely from the higher ground for a long time (*nec memoriam extare*,

[1] Sargenti would also argue (op. cit., pp. 46 ff.) that in Cicero, *top.* 9. 39, where the action is excluded when the damage threatens *vitio loci*, that *vitium loci* has a narrow meaning and the text does not mean that only damage which can be related to human activity is covered by the *actio*. But Cicero does seem to be dividing *aqua pluvia nocens* into two groups, *loci vitio nocens* and *manu nocens*, which, between them, would cover all situations.

[2] Cf. Rotondi, *Leges*, p. 414.

[3] Cf., above all, Bonfante, 'La "*longi temporis praescriptio*" delle servitù' *Scritti giuridici varii* (Turin, 1918), ii. 956 ff.

[4] Cf. D. 39. 3. 1. 23 (Ulpian, 53 *ad ed.*); *h.t.* 2 pr., 1 (Paul, 49 *ad ed.*).

[5] Provided, says Ulpian, the exercise was *neque vi neque precario neque clam*.

quando facta est) and the bad condition of the *opus* threatened to cause flooding on the higher ground, the owner of the higher ground had the *actio aquae pluviae arcendae* to be allowed to enter on his neighbour's land and restore the *opus* to its previous condition. At least two of the texts so far examined which concern Republican jurists seem to have involved the idea of a 'servitude' of lower ground to higher. Thus, in *h.t.* 2. 6, Namusa is shown to have held the opinion that if a water-course which enabled water to descend into lower ground is blocked, an action can be brought against the lower proprietor to compel him to let the water-course be cleared, whether the water-course be man-made or natural. Nothing is said in the text of the water-course having had to exist for any length of time. Here, as elsewhere in this long fragment from Paul, the fact that it is on the lower ground that the channel is blocked must be relevant to the decision. This is the much less common flood situation in practice—normally it is something on higher ground which leads to flooding of the lower ground—yet it cannot be said to appear in the text as the result of interpolations made to bring the text into line with others since Namusa's decision is not accepted. Accordingly Namusa was thinking of the 'servitude' situation. Whether his decision dates from before or after the *lex Scribonia* cannot be determined. If before, he need not have said anything about *vetustas* since that could quite easily have been assumed in the context. If after, lapse of time could have been regarded as irrelevant since there could no longer be usucaption of servitudes, and Namusa might have thought that the very nature of the situation of the land[1] gave a servitude right to the higher ground to have an *actio aquae pluviae arcendae* any time any change on the lower ground threatened to cause flooding. However this may be, Namusa's view is wider than that of Labeo, Paul, and Ulpian since he allows the action even if there was no *opus* on the lower ground. But it does seem now that we can restrict the wide view of Namusa that this action was available even if no *opus* were involved to the case where the flooding was threatened by lower ground to higher. The other text is *h.t.* 2. 4. The words *ex qua ad inferiorem fundum aqua descendat*—even apart from the context—

[1] *Natura loci*: cf. *h.t.* 2 pr.

proves that the situation under discussion involves a blockage in the lower ground. If the blockage were on the higher ground it would be irrelevant that the ditch normally took the water away through the low ground. This text, unlike the one giving the view of Namusa, is concerned only with an *opus* which in fact is in a state of disrepair. To take the text as it stands: For Ateius, this sort of 'servitude' right exists to protect the owner of the higher ground *sive extet fossae memoria sive non extet*. Again, there is no way of deciding whether the decision was given before or after the passing of the *lex Scribonia*. If before, the point could be that this kind of 'servitude' right derived from *natura loci* and was independent of *usucapio*. If later, Ateius might even be arguing that this kind of servitude existed, despite the *lex Scribonia*, because it had nothing to do with *usucapio* and it could be for this reason that he extends the right even to cases where *memoria extat*. Ateius seems to give the action to compel the neighbour to clean out his ditch. Bonfante,[1] however, holds *cogendum . . . extet* interpolated but, as Sargenti justly says,[2] any suggestions of alteration must be based purely on *a priori* grounds. And there was so much lack of agreement among the jurists, at least as to the scope of the action, that it is extremely implausible to hold that a certain view on this action could not have been held by at least one Republican or classical jurist. Ateius might very well have allowed the action to compel the neighbour to clear his *fossa* even if he had not made the *fossa*, although other texts might indicate that the action should only be given to compel the neighbour to permit his *fossa* to be cleared.[3] To begin with, the *clausula arbitraria* in the *formula* is more fitting for an action to compel than for an action to permit. Then, since the *cautio damni infecti* could be exacted where a building threatened to do damage even if it had not been erected by its present owner and even if no one knew when and by whom it had been erected, it might appear to some jurists not unreasonable that likewise for the *actio aquae pluviae arcendae* an owner (of lower ground) who had allowed his ditch to fall into a dangerous condition could be forced

[1] II. i., p. 432.

[2] Op. cit., pp. 114 f.

[3] Cf. *h.t.* 2. 1: but see also *h.t.* 2. 7. Both are held interpolated at the relevant places by Bonfante, loc. cit.

to restore it whether it was or was not known when it was made. Again, the wording of the *formula*, *si paret opus factum esse in agro Capenate, unde aqua pluvia agro Ai Ai nocet*, does not involve the maker's being the defendant, and it is not difficult to interpret it as including cases where the threat comes not from the making of the *opus* but from the disrepair of the *opus*. *H.t.* 11. 6 may or may not show Trebatius ignoring the question of a 'servitude' right and giving the *actio aquae pluviae arcendae* irrespective of whether the dangerous water arises from a fault of the upper or lower ground. Certainly the text makes no mention of upper or lower ground but it could be argued that in the context Trebatius was not concerned with the substance of the law but merely with the measure of damages. He might have meant only that where an action is brought when injury threatens through disrepair, the action will be to allow the plaintiff to repair, thus being in contrast with the object of the action for *opus factum*, and the circumstances in which the action would be allowed or not allowed are not considered.

The one remaining text is very much out of line with the others.

D. 39. 3. 2. 5. Item Varus ait: aggerem, qui in fundo vicini erat, vis aquae deiecit, per quod effectum est, ut aqua pluvia mihi noceret. Varus ait, si naturalis agger fuit, non posse me vicinum cogere aquae pluviae arcendae actione, ut eum reponat vel reponi sinat, idemque putat et si manu factus fuit neque memoria eius exstat: quod si exstet, putat aquae pluviae arcendae actione eum teneri. Labeo autem, si manu factus sit agger, etiamsi memoria eius non exstat, agi posse [ut reponi sinat, agi non posse *ins. Krüger*], ut reponatur: nam hac actione neminem cogi posse, ut vicino prosit, sed ne noceat aut interpellet facientem, quod iure facere possit. quamquam tamen deficiat aquae pluviae arcendae actio, attamen opinor utilem actionem vel interdictum mihi competere adversus vicinum, si velim aggerem restituere in agro eius, qui factus mihi quidem prodesse potest, ipsi vero nihil nociturus est: haec aequitas suggerit, etsi iure deficiamur.

We need not concern ourselves with the question of the interpolation of the last part of the text from *quamquam*.[1] The view ascribed to Alfenus which is our main interest has also been held not

[1] See most recently, Biondi, *Jus* ix (1958) 313; Mayer-Maly, *Österreichische Zeitschrift f. öffentliches Recht* ix (1958) 169 and n. 116.

to give the opinion of that jurist.[1] The idea of deliberate interpolation can be excluded since the view given as that of Alfenus is represented as the unsuccessful one. Apart from *a priori* arguments, there is nothing in the text which would justify the view that Alfenus' opinion has been accidentally changed. Certainly, though, Labeo's opinion is to some extent corrupt, but this is so whether or not Alfenus' opinion has also suffered. The simplest reconstruction is that of Krüger[2] who thinks that *ut reponi sinat, agi non posse* has dropped out immediately after *agi posse*. But this does not resolve all of the difficulties. The text has: *Labeo autem, si manu factus sit agger, etiamsi memoria eius non exstet, agi posse.* This appears to be a correction to the views of Alfenus, allowing the action to be brought where the *agger* is man-made even if it is not known when it was made. Thus, Labeo here appears to be accepting the view of Alfenus that the action can be brought where the *agger* is man-made and where it was known when it was made. But this is contrary to the implication of *h.t.* 2. 1, which very strongly suggests he allowed the action only when it was not known when the *opus* was made, and *h.t.* 2. 8 has point only if Labeo did draw a distinction between situations where *memoria exstat* and where *memoria non exstat*. So something more seems to be wrong with our present text. At first sight one might think that the defect could lie either in this part of the text or in the preceding part which gave the view of Alfenus but, in fact, no matter what precedes it, the *etiamsi* would suggest that Labeo would give the same decision in respect of a man-made *agger*, *sive memoria exstat sive memoria non exstat*, hence no amount of corruption of the view of Alfenus would explain the *etiamsi*. Accordingly, the peculiarity in this part of the text would not justify suspicions of corruption in the views attributed to Alfenus. The difficulty in still holding the views of Alfenus corrupt are two-fold. First, the objection to the

[1] Cf., above all, Karlowa, *Römische Rechtsgeschichte* (Leipzig, 1901), ii. 1256, who is opposed by Bonfante, continuation of Glück, *Commentario alle pandette, XXXIX, 3* (Milan, 1906), p. 490, n. 2; and Sargenti, *L'actio aquae pluviae arcendae*, p. 45, n. 2 and pp. 57 ff. Beseler, *ZSS* lxvi (1948) 608, who thinks the text has suffered much, would excise *vel reponi sinat* but none of his other suggested alterations affect the substance.

[2] *Stereotype Digest, ad h.l.*

text as it stands can only be the *a priori* one that Alfenus could never have held the views attributed to him, yet we know that on this subject of *aqua pluvia* there was a wide conflict of opinions and, moreover, Labeo must be correcting Alfenus, so the views of the latter cannot be the same as Labeo's.[1] Secondly, the amount of corruption which has to be postulated is very great.[2,3] The text should be treated as giving accurately the opinion of Alfenus. He held that, if the force of water destroyed an *agger* on a neighbour's land, no *actio aquae pluviae arcendae* lay if the *agger* were natural or if it were man-made but its construction was beyond the memory of man. The action, however, did lie if the *agger* were man-made and it was known when it was constructed. The first part of the decision, i.e. where the *agger* is natural, is the standard view. The rest is a reversal of what one might think the normal view. None the less, it is perhaps not so very difficult to understand. It does not seem unreasonable to assimilate the situation where a man-made *agger* is so old that no one knows when it was made to that where the *agger* is natural and to hold that, as in the latter, so in the former, the owner of the land is under no liability to his neighbour. And where the *agger* is man-made and recent, its lack of repair from which danger threatens a neighbour could, I feel, be brought under the terms of the *formula* although that was meant to cover cases of danger threatening as a result of new construction. On this view, of course, Alfenus was not thinking in any way of the action being given in respect of a 'servitude' right arising from *vetustas*, hence his views are unlikely to have applied only where damage was threatened by the lower to the higher ground. His approach, too, strongly suggests that he was writing after the passing of the *lex Scribonia*.

But not every *opus* which threatened damage from *aqua pluvia* gave rise to the action. Some agricultural processes were treated as exempt and there seems to have been lively discussion on how far the exemptions extended.

1 This is against Karlowa, loc. cit., whose reconstruction would make the views of Alfenus the same as those attributed to Labeo in other texts.

2 Especially since one cannot, as Karlowa does (cf. preceding note), simply turn around the decisions about man-made *aggera*.

3 This is against the suggestion of Sargenti, loc. cit.

D. 39. 3. 1. 3 (Ulpian, 53 *ad ed.*). De eo opere, quod agri colendi causa aratro factum sit, Quintus Mucius ait non competere hanc actionem. Trebatius autem non quod agri, sed quod frumenti dumtaxat quaerendi causa aratro factum solum excepit. 4. Sed et fossas agrorum siccandorum causa factas Mucius ait fundi colendi causa fieri, non tamen oportere corrivandae aquae causa fieri: sic enim debere quem meliorem agrum suum facere, ne vicini deteriorem faciat. 5. Sed et [et *del. Mommsen*] si quis arare et serere possit etiam sine sulcis aquariis, teneri eum, si quid ex his [si quid ex his *should be* si quos derexerit—*Mommsen*], licet agri colendi causa videatur fecisse: quod si aliter serere non possit, nisi sulcos aquarios fecerit, non teneri. Ofilius autem ait sulcos agri colendi causa directos ita, ut in unam pergant partem, ius esse facere. 6. Sed apud Servii auditores relatum est, si quis salicta posuerit et ob hoc aqua restagnaret, aquae pluviae arcendae agi posse, si ea aqua vicino noceret.

D. 39. 3. 3. 2 (Ulpian, 53 *ad ed.*). Si vicinus, qui arvum solebat certo tempore anni rigare, pratum illic fecerit coeperitque adsidua irrigatione vicino nocere, ait Ofilius neque damni infecti neque aquae pluviae arcendae actione eum teneri, nisi locum complanavit eoque facto citatior aqua ad vicinum pervenire coepit.

D. 39. 3. 24 pr. (Alfenus, 4 *dig. a Paulo epit.*). Vicinus loci superioris pratum ita arabat, ut per sulcos itemque porcas aqua ad inferiorem veniret: quaesitum est, an per arbitrum aquae pluviae arcendae possit cogi, ut in alteram partem araret, ne sulci in eius agrum spectarent. respondit non posse eum facere, quo minus agrum vicinus quemadmodum vellet araret. 1. Sed si quos sulcos transversos aquarios faceret, per quos in eius agrum aqua deflueret, hosce ut operiret, per [per *del. Mommsen*] arbitrum aquae pluviae arcendae posse cogere. 2. Sed et si fossas fecisset, ex quibus aqua pluvia posset nocere, arbitrum, si appareat futurum, ut aqua pluvia noceret, cogere oportere fossas eum explere et, nisi faceret, condemnare, tametsi antequam adiudicaret, aqua per fossas nunquam fluxisset.

In *h.t.* 1. 3[1] Quintus Mucius is reported as having held that the *opus* made by the plough for the sake of cultivation did not give rise to the action. Trebatius, however, would only exclude the action where the ploughing was for the production of grain (*frumenti dumtaxat quaerendi causa*). Presumably this means that Trebatius would allow the *actio aquae pluviae arcendae* not only where the ploughing would be deeper than was usual in the production of

[1] Which never seems to have been held interpolated. The reference in the *Index Itp.* to Beseler, *ZSS* lii (1932) 290 seems to be a mistake for D. 39. 1. 3. 3.

grain as, for instance, in vineyards and olive groves,[1] but also where the ploughing would be to the same depth as for grain but the intended crop was something else. Thus just as Trebatius took a much wider view than Quintus Mucius on what was to count as *aqua pluvia* for the action[2] so he took a much more restricted view on the nature of the *opera* which would exclude the action. Obviously, Trebatius was very much in favour of giving the action as wide a scope as possible.[3] *H.t.* 24 pr. which is concerned with the same question shows that for Alfenus where ploughing a field towards one side threatens to cause damage which would be avoided if the furrows pointed elsewhere, no action lies to the owner of the threatened land. This would appear to be so even if ploughing in the second direction were no less advantageous to the owner of the land.

In *h.t.* 1. 4 Mucius says that ditches (*fossae*) dug to dry the fields are *fundi colendi causa* (and so no action will lie) but they must not be dug to channel the water together. He qualifies this in § 5. If one can plough and sow, he says, even without *sulci aquarii*—presumably these are furrows intended to carry off water, but which are narrower and shallower than *fossae*[4]—then one will be liable, even if they were made *agri colendi causa*. But Ofilius says that *sulci* which are made *agri colendi causa* can be directed towards one side.[5] In *h.t.* 24. 1 Alfenus says that if one makes diagonal *sulci aquarii* through which water flows into another's field, the *arbiter* in the *actio aquae pluviae arcendae* can compel them to be filled in.[6] The situation is probably the same as that envisaged by Quintus Mucius in *h.t.* 1. 4 when he says *fossae* must not be made *corrivandae aquae causa*. But then in *h.t.* 24. 2 Alfenus goes further. *Sed et si* must introduce a more extreme case. Here he holds that the action will

[1] Cf. Columella, *de re rust.* 2. 2. 24.

[2] Cf. Cicero, *top.* 9. 38, and D. 39. 3. 3 pr.: *supra*, pp. 156 ff.

[3] See also on this text, Sargenti, op. cit., p. 74.

[4] Appears, e.g., from Columella, *de re rust.* 2. 8. 3; 11. 2. 82.

[5] The Latin here might suggest that they must be directed towards one side but this cannot be correct. Here, too, the position of *directos*, separated from *sulcos* by *agri colendi causa*, and its relationship to *ita, ut in unam pergant partem* make it impossible to regard it as meaning something like 'meeting at right angles' (see Cicero, *top.* 4. 22).

[6] That does seem to be the meaning of *operire* here, though normally that verb means 'to cover'.

lie if *fossae* are made whereby rain water might cause damage. Nothing is said this time of them being diagonal ditches and the possibility of that restriction can probably be excluded given the relationship with § 1 and the *sed et si*, and there is no sign in this text of Mucius' restriction in *h.t.* 1. 5 that the action will not lie if the ditches are necessary for ploughing or sowing.[1]

H.t. 1. 6 tells us that the pupils of Servius held that if a man planted willow groves and as a consequence water overflowed, an *actio aquae pluviae arcendae* could be brought if the water could injure a neighbour.

In *h.t.* 3. 2, *nisi* to the end of the text is certainly a later addition. Ofilius held that a change of use from ploughed land to pasture which involved a change in irrigation which injured a neighbour did not give rise to the action.

In the first century B.C. it seems to have been agreed—there is no sign of any dispute—that the action only lay where damage was threatened to a field and not where the danger was to a building or town.

D. 39. 3. 1. 17. Item sciendum est hanc actionem non alias locum habere, quam si aqua pluvia agro noceat: ceterum si aedificio vel oppido noceat, cessat actio ista, agi autem ita poterit ius non esse stillicidia flumina immittere. et ideo Labeo et Cascellius aiunt aquae quidem pluviae arcendae actionem specialem esse, de fluminibus et stillicidiis generalem et ubique agi ea licere. itaque aqua, quae agro nocet, per aquae pluviae arcendae actionem coercebitur.

Cicero, *top*. 4. 23. ... Ex comparatione autem omnia valent quae sunt huius modi: Quod in re maiore valet valeat in minore, ut si in urbe fines non reguntur, nec aqua in urbe arceatur. ...

Cicero, *top*. 10. 43. Alterum similitudinis genus conlatione sumitur, cum una res uni, par pari comparatur, hoc modo Quem ad modum, si in urbe de finibus controversia est, quia fines magis agrorum videntur esse quam urbis, finibus regendis adigere arbitrum non possis, sic, si aqua pluvia in urbe nocet, quoniam res tota magis agrorum est, aquae pluviae arcendae adigere arbitrum non possis.

But this rule is not likely to have been expressly stated in the provision of the XII Tables and it may be the result of juristic

[1] The substance is not affected by Arangio-Ruiz' suggestion that in the text *si appareat . . . noceret* and *tametsi* to the end are glosses: *BIDR* xxxii (1922) 36, n. 2.

interpretation. This would seem to emerge from the argument to it from the *actio finium regundorum* in the texts of Cicero. If the rule had been expressly laid down by statute, there could have been no place for the argument. One might be able to go further and say that since Cicero gives an argument from another action to justify the conclusion that the *actio aquae pluviae arcendae* only lies where fields might be injured, the rule for that action cannot be much older than the time of Cicero. Whether the argument from the *actio finium regundorum* to the *actio aquae pluviae arcendae* was used by the jurists one cannot really say,[1] but this argument, whether from the greater to the less or by analogy, does not, in itself, seem a particularly convincing one. There is no apparent reason why the two actions in this respect need have the same scope. The form of argument in Cicero and the *sciendum est* in D. 39. 3. 1. 17 indicate the complete acceptance of the rule at this time. The *formula* of the *actio*, however,[2] would also appear to contain the restriction to land, but whether this wording is the cause or effect of the restriction cannot be determined.

The action only lay for immission of *aqua pluvia* and was not given where someone stopped or reduced the flow of water on to his neighbour's land, even although the neighbour could have found the water beneficial.[3]

D. 39. 3. 1. 21. Sicut autem opus factum, ut aqua pluvia mihi noceat, in hanc actionem venit, ita per contrarium quaeritur, an posset aquae pluviae arcendae agi, si vicinus opus fecerit, ne aqua, quae alioquin decurrens agro meo proderat, huic prosit. Ofilius igitur et Labeo putant agi non posse, etiamsi intersit mea ad me aquam pervenire: hanc enim actionem locum habere, si aqua pluvia noceat, non si non prosit.

Where a servitude right of sending water on to one's neighbour's land existed, the neighbour could not on that account bring the *actio aquae pluviae arcendae*.

D. 39. 3. 2. 10 (Paul, 49 *ad ed.*). Illud enim verum puto, quod Ofilius scribit, si fundus tuus vicino serviat et propterea aquam recipiat, cessare aquae pluviae arcendae actionem, sic tamen, si non ultra modum noceat.

[1] Scherillo would attribute *top.* 10. 43, like many other texts in that work, to Quintus Mucius, *liber singularis ὅρων*: but see *supra*, p. 161, n. 1.

[2] Cf. *supra*, p. 156.

[3] Cf. Sargenti, op. cit., p. 102.

cui consequens est, quod Labeo putat, si quis vicino cesserit ius ei esse aquam immittere, aquae pluviae arcendae eum agere non posse.

It is generally thought[1]—rightly I believe—that *sic tamen si non ultra modum noceat* is an addition to the text, but this view has recently been disputed by Sargenti,[2] who would treat the phrase as being *sic tamen si non ultra modum servitutis noceat*. But even if the word *servitutis* could be implied this would be a very strange way to express the idea 'provided the servitude right is not exceeded and from this damage results'. It is much more natural to take the Latin as meaning 'provided no excessive harm occurs'.[3]

D. 39. 3. 11. 5 (Paul, 49 *ad ed.*). Si ex privato agro in agrum communem aqua immittatur, Ofilius ait socium cum eo agere posse.

According to Ofilius, where water flowed from land owned by one person on to land which he owned with another, the latter could bring the *actio aquae pluviae arcendae* against his co-owner. There is a difference here between this action and the *actio finium regundorum*. Pomponius held in D. 10. 1. 4. 7 (Paul, 23 *ad ed.*) that the latter action could not be given where one estate was owned by two persons in common and a neighbouring estate was owned by one of them alone.

The last text to be discussed in this context is D. 39. 3. 24. 3 (Alfenus, 4 *dig. a Paulo epit.*).

Lacus cum aut crescerent aut decrescerent, numquam neque accessionem neque decessionem in eos vicinis facere licet.

The text has received little attention but it has been held interpolated by Bremer,[4] who observes '*numquam! accessionem decessionem in eos facere!*', and by De Sarlo,[5] who thinks that the secondary proposition is strangely linked with the principal one: *numquam neque acessionem . . . licet, cum aut crescerent aut decrescerent*. Symptomatic, he thinks, is *licet* in face of *crescerent aut decrescerent*. But in fact De Sarlo misunderstood the text—and so perhaps did

[1] Cf. *Index Itp.*

[2] Op. cit., pp. 78 ff.

[3] It should be noticed that if Sargenti's interpretation of the text is correct, the text would be in harmony with D. 8. 3. 29 (Paul, 2 *epit. Alfendi dig.*): Sargenti, op.cit., p. 80.

[4] *Iurisprudentiae antehadrianae quae supersunt* (Leipzig, 1896), i. 191.

[5] *Alfeno Varo e i suoi digesta* (Milan, 1940), p. 56.

Bremer—as do Otto, Schilling, and Sintenis in their translation.[1] They translate it something like: 'Lakes may rise or fall but this neither increases nor decreases the property of the adjoining proprietors.' But the text can only mean something like: 'Although lakes might rise or fall, the adjoining proprietors are never allowed to make increases or decreases to their level.' That is, although the level of water in lakes might naturally alter, the surrounding proprietors are not allowed to do anything to alter the water level. The relation which the jurist had in mind between this proposition and the *actio aquae pluviae arcendae* is not here expressed but one can envisage several possibilities.[2]

[1] *Das Corpus Iuris Civilis* (Leipzig, 1832), iv. 73.

[2] Cicero, *pro Murena* 9. 22 tells us nothing of value for the action.

8

SERVITUDES

SERVITUDES were rights *in rem* vested in a person as owner of a *praedium* over a neighbouring *praedium*. For a right to be accepted as a servitude it had to fall within a recognized type or kind of servitudes. No text states this expressly for the later Republic but it can be deduced quite simply from the fact that we know that originally only a very small group of rights counted as servitudes and that, in all probability, even in classical law a servitude still had to fall within a recognized class.[1] Moreover, all the texts relating to the later Republic are concerned with what were well-recognized types of servitude. These are *iter*,[2] *actus*,[3] *via*,[4] *aquae ductus*,[5] *aquae haustus*,[6] *lumen*,[7] *prospectus*,[8] *cloaca*,[9] *aquam immittere*,[10] *servitus proiciendi protegendive*,[11] *stillicidium*,[12] *flumen*,[13] *pecoris ad aquam appellendi*,[14] and *oneris ferendi*.[15] But this is not to suggest that there was a closed list of servitudes. Rather, when a new situation came under discussion the jurists considered whether they were willing to recognize that a right of servitude could exist in such circumstances.

Doubt as to the accuracy of the proposition that a servitude had

[1] For this problem of the 'tipicità' of servitudes see the authors cited by Kaser, *RPR* i. 370, n. 6. D. 8. 5. 8. 5, the text which is mainly relied on to show that servitudes need not fall within a recognized type, is discussed *infra*, pp. 177 ff.

[2] D. 8. 3. 30; 43. 20. 8; 18. 1. 40. 1; 43. 19. 4 pr.; Cicero, *pro Caecina* 26. 74.

[3] Cicero, ibidem.

[4] D. 8. 3. 8.

[5] D. 43. 20. 8; 43. 21. 3 pr., 1; 43. 20. 1. 17; 8. 3. 15; 8. 3. 30 (?); Cicero, *pro Caecina* 26. 74; *ad Att.* 15. 26. 4; *ad Quintum fr.* 3. 1. 2(?).

[6] D. 8. 3. 30(?); 18. 1. 40. 1; Cicero, *pro Caecina* 26. 74; *ad Quintum fr.* 3. 1. 2(?).

[7] D. 8. 2. 16; 8. 2. 7(?); Cicero, *de orat.* 1. 39. 179.

[8] D. 8. 2. 16; 8. 2. 7(?).

[9] D. 43. 23. 2.

[10] D. 8. 3. 29(?); 39. 3. 2. 10.

[11] D. 8. 5. 17 pr. [cf. for the Empire D. 8. 2. 2. (Gaius, 7 *ad ed. prov.*)].

[12] D. 39. 3. 1. 17; Cicero, *de leg.* 1. 4. 14; *orat.* 21. 72; Varro, *de ling. lat.* 5. 27.

[13] D. 39. 3. 1. 17; Varro, *de ling. lat.* 5. 27.

[14] D. 43. 20. 1. 18.

[15] D. 8. 5. 6. 2; 8. 2. 33.

to enter a recognized class of servitudes might, prima facie, be raised by two texts.

D. 8. 5. 17. 2 (Alfenus, 2 *dig.*). Secundum cuius parietem vicinus sterculinum fecerat, ex quo paries madescebat, consulebatur [consulebat *Mommsen*], quemadmodum posset vicinum cogere, ut sterculinum tolleret. respondi, si in loco publico id fecisset, per interdictum cogi posse, sed si in privato, de servitute agere oportere: si damni infecti stipulatus esset, possit per eam stipulationem, si quid ex ea re sibi damni datum esset, servare.

D. 8. 5. 8. 5 (Ulpian, 17 *ad ed.*). Aristo Cerellio Vitali respondit non putare se ex taberna casiaria fumum in superiora aedificia iure immitti posse, nisi ei rei servitutem talem admittit. idemque ait: et ex superiore in inferiora non aquam, non quid aliud immitti licet: in suo enim alii hactenus facere licet, quatenus nihil in alienum immittat, fumi autem sicut aquae esse immissionem: posse igitur superiorem cum inferiore agere ius illi non esse id ita facere. Alfenum denique scribere ait posse ita agi ius illi non esse in suo lapidem caedere, ut in meum fundum fragmenta cadant. dicit igitur Aristo eum, qui tabernam casiariam a Minturnensibus conduxit, a superiore prohiberi posse fumum immittere, sed Minturnenses ei ex conducto teneri: agique sic posse dicit cum eo, qui eum fumum immittat, ius ei non esse fumum immittere. ergo per contrarium agi poterit ius esse fumum immittere: quod et ipsum videtur Aristo probare. sed et interdictum uti possidetis poterit locum habere, si quis prohibeatur, qualiter velit, suo uti.

In the latter, as in the former text, we are really concerned with the opinion of Alfenus. In the former a man builds a manure heap against his neighbour's wall[1] and Alfenus (or his master Servius) says that the neighbour should bring the *actio de servitute*[2] for its removal. In the latter, Alfenus allows the *actio negatoria* to stop a neighbour breaking stone on his own land in such a way that chips of stone fall on to my land.[3] It might be argued, then, that the

[1] The wall is not owned in common: cf. *supra*, pp. 142 f.

[2] The phrase *de servitute agere oportet* is held probably not to have been written by Alfenus: Perozzi, *Istituzioni di diritto romano*, 2nd edn. (Milan, 1927) i. 632, n. 1; Solazzi, *La tutela e il possesso delle servitù prediali* (Naples, 1949), p. 4; Levy, *West Roman Vulgar Law: The Law of Property* (Philadelphia, 1951), p. 77, n. 340. This does not affect the idea that the action in question is the *actio negatoria*.

[3] Wolff, *Iura* iii (1952) 135 f., would hold *idem ait . . . cadant* as a later scholion. Even if this is so—and I feel the emendation is unnecessary (cf. *infra*, pp. 179 f.) and Wolff's stylistic arguments unconvincing—the scholiast is most

texts show that Alfenus would recognize the validity of a right of servitude to build a manure heap against a neighbour's wall and of one to break stone on one's land in such a way that chips of stone fall on to a neighbour's land. These would, indeed, be very odd servitudes and they are not paralleled elsewhere.[1] There is however a much less extreme possibility. It will have been noticed that in both cases Alfenus is concerned not with the *actio confessoria*, i.e. that claiming a servitude, but with the *actio negatoria*, i.e. that denying a servitude. The Edict gave only a few forms for each of these actions and the forms had to be altered to meet the circumstances of the case.[2] An example for the *actio confessoria* is: *Si paret Aulo Agerio ius esse per fundum illum ire agere, quanti ea res paret, etc.* The *actio* does not expressly claim the right to a servitude, but naturally the *actio* would only be given if what was claimed could give rise to a right of servitude. The *actio negatoria* was the reverse: *Si paret Numerio Negidio ius non esse per fundum illum ire agere invito Aulo Agerio quanti, etc.* Again the *formula* does not expressly deny a right of servitude, but logically one would expect that, like the *actio confessoria*, it could only be used in circumstances where a right of servitude would be theoretically possible. But since the point of this latter action is the denial of the existence of a servitude, one can easily envisage that certain jurists might allow the action even in circumstances where no right of servitude could exist. That is, in the absence of some other action there would be a temptation to try to widen this action to turn it into a general action for nuisance. The extension is a very natural one and this, I submit, is what Alfenus was doing. There is no sign whatever of this approach outside of these two texts and so Alfenus' attempt to widen the scope of the *actio negatoria* appears to have awakened no response in later jurists apart from Aristo. There is, however, a text which shows Alfenus again making a wider

unlikely simply to have made up the view and attributed it to Alfenus. The view ascribed to him must be his own, especially since it accords with what he says in D. 8. 5. 17. 1 and 2.

[1] D. 8. 3. 3. 2 (Ulpian, 17 *ad ed.*) is concerned with a very different kind of situation from that in D. 8. 5. 8. 5 and one where one could much more easily imagine a servitude right developing. For D. 8. 5. 17. 2 see Solazzi, *Specie ed estinzione delle servitù prediali* (Naples, 1948), pp. 53 ff.

[2] Cf. Lenel, *EP*, pp. 191 ff.

use of the *actio negatoria* than ever seems to have been allowed later, and to this extent, the text is confirmation of the arguments on Alfenus' attitude in D. 8. 5. 17. 2 and *h.t.* 8. 5. But this time it appears that he was in agreement with the jurists of his time.

D. 8. 5. 17. 1. Cum in domo Gaii Sei locus quidam aedibus Anni ita serviret, ut in eo loco positum habere ius Seio non esset, et Seius in eo silvam sevisset, in qua labra et tenes [lenes *Hotoman*] cucumellas positas haberet, Annio consilium omnes iuris periti dederunt, ut cum eo ageret ius ei non esse in eo loco ea posita habere invito se.

All the *iuris periti*, we are told, gave Annius an action against Gaius Seius, *ius ei non esse in eo loco ea posita habere invito se*. This action is quite obviously the *actio negatoria*. But there is the peculiarity that it is given to the owner of the *praedium dominans* against the owner of the *praedium serviens* and its purpose is to stop the latter acting in a way which prevents the former from enjoying his servitude. One would, in fact, rather have expected Annius to be given the *actio confessoria*.[1] The granting of an *actio negatoria*, so far as I am aware, never reappears in these circumstances in any other text.[2] Moreover, in a way which is quite different from that in D. 8. 5. 8. 5 and *h.t.* 17. 2, we have here another instance where the *actio negatoria* is given where it would be quite impossible technically for the defendant to claim that he had a servitude right to do what he was doing. The conduct of Gaius Seius which is in question takes place on his own land and directly affects only his own land and no one can have a servitude over his own land.

This understanding of the attitude of Alfenus may lead to a better interpretation of the whole of D. 8. 5. 8. 5. This text occupies a central position in the discussion whether a right to be recognized as a servitude had to fall within an accepted class or not, and accordingly it has been much discussed.[3] It would, I think, none the less be true to say that no view has won anything like general acceptance. At the beginning of the text *nisi ei rei servitutem talem*

[1] Cf., for the Empire, D. 8. 5. 2. 1 (Ulpian, 17 *ad ed.*).

[2] A friend suggests, however, that where a servitude is negative it might be quite logical to give the owner of the dominant tenement the *actio negatoria*.

[3] Cf. Kaser, *RPR* i. 370, n. 6 and the authors he cites; Wolff, *Iura* iii (1952) 135 f.

admittit is not quite in perfect form. Mommsen's suggested emendation,[1] *nisi ei rei serviunt: nam servitutem talem admittit* is impossible because one can never then understand why later the text has *ergo per contrariam agi poterit ius esse fumum immittere: quod et ipsum videtur Aristo probare.*[2] The suggestion that the phrase is a complete interpolation[3] does, however, seem unnecessarily drastic. Perhaps the simplest solution is to regard *admittit* as a scribal error for *admittat*, of which the subject, expressed or implied, is the *superior*. That is, that the opinion of Aristo was that he did not think smoke from a cheese factory could lawfully be passed through the premises above unless the *superior* accepted such a servitude for that thing. Aristo's argument for this proposition falls into two parts. First, from *et ex superiore* to *id ita facere*. In this part he draws an argument by analogy from the fact that water cannot be sent *ex superiore in inferiora* (unless, that is, there is a servitude). Here he is considering the situation where a servitude could technically exist. Secondly, from *Alfenum denique* to *cadant* he argues, relying on the opinion of Alfenus in a different situation, that even where no servitude can exist the lower owner can be stopped from letting his smoke ascend into the premises above. Aristo, in fact, in giving his decision argues for it both where it might be thought that such a right of servitude could technically exist and where it might be thought that such a right of servitude could not technically exist. Aristo, therefore, is accepting (or at least using) Alfenus' wide and generally unsuccessful view of the *actio negatoria*. Ulpian, who does not share Alfenus' attitude, does not quite understand this, and so, after reporting that Aristo would allow the *actio negatoria* (*agique . . . ius ei non esse fumum immittere*), he says that, therefore, *per contrariam*, an *actio confessoria* could be brought, and he adds that this view seems to have Aristo's approval. The doubt in the text as to whether there could be a servitude such as this, and which obviously exercised both Aristo and Ulpian, shows that even in classical law a right, to be accepted as a servitude, had to fall within a recognized type.

[1] *Digesta Iustiniani Augusti* (Berlin, 1870), i. 270.

[2] Also see against this emendation the argument of Solazzi, *La tutela e il possesso delle servitù prediali*, p. 68.

[3] See, most recently, Solazzi, loc. cit.

In classical law servitudes are classed as rustic or urban.[1] There is no sign of the distinction in any of the numerous texts for the Republic and no particular reason to think that it then existed. The distinction could well be due to the classical jurists and even to the teachers among the classical jurists.[2] What are thought to be the main differences between rustic and urban servitudes, namely that the former are declared to be *res mancipi* while the latter are *res nec mancipi*[3] and that the former are lost by non-use while freedom from the latter must be positively usucapted by the servient tenement,[4] could grow up for individual servitudes and be originally independent of a classification into rustic and urban. None of our texts touch the problem of which servitudes are *res mancipi* or *res nec mancipi* so we may ignore the question whether only the four original rustic servitudes, *via*, *iter*, *actus*, and *aquae ductus*, or all the rustic servitudes were *res mancipi*. One text, however, does show that release from a servitude of light was achieved by positive *usucapio* by the servient tenement and not by mere non-use by the dominant tenement.

D. 8. 2. 7 (Pomponius, 26 *ad Quintum Mucium*). Quod autem aedificio meo me posse consequi, ut libertatem usucaperem, dicitur, idem me non consecuturum, si arborem eodem loco sitam habuissem, Mucius ait, et recte, quia non ita in suo statu et loco maneret arbor quemadmodum paries, propter motum naturalem arboris.

The kind of servitude involved is not expressly mentioned but the tenor of the text shows that it must either be *lumen* or *prospectus*. Freedom from the servitude can be usucapted by having a building on the servient tenement but, according to Quintus Mucius, not by having a tree there. The need for positive *usucapio* is shown not so much by the *ut libertatem usucaperem* as by the opinion of Quintus Mucius that having a tree on the servient tenement is not enough to secure release from the servitude. And yet the tree could effectively stop the exercise of the dominant tenement's right to light.

[1] The basis of the classification is very doubtful: cf., in addition to the references given by Kaser, *RPR* i. 370, n. 4, Bonfante III. 36 ff.

[2] Cf. Kaser, *RPR* i. 370.

[3] Cf. G. 2. 17; *Epit. Ulp.* 19. 1; F.V. 45 (by implication).

[4] Cf. Kaser, *RPR* i. 374, nn. 45, 46.

The text raises another point of interest which, although not strictly relevant to the present discussion, is best dealt with here. Quintus Mucius, who is followed by Pomponius, would not allow freedom from the servitude to be usucapted on account of a tree on the *praedium serviens*. Logically this should involve that these jurists would not regard the presence of a tree on the servient land as a breach of the servitude of *lumen* or *prospectus* since it should be the case that anything which amounts to a breach of the servitude on the part of the owner of the *praedium serviens* should be grounds for the *usucapio* of freedom from the servitude. But if this were the position of these jurists then they were in conflict with Javolenus and Ulpian. Javolenus in D. 8. 2. 12 (10 *ex Cassio*) says that *viridia* can cause a breach of a servitude of *prospectus* and Ulpian in *h.t.* 17 pr. (29 *ad Sab.*) says that the planting of a tree could be a breach of *lumen*. Neither of these texts considers the converse question whether the *viridia* or *arbor* could allow the *usucapio* of freedom from the servitude. The possibility must, however, be recognized that Quintus Mucius and Pomponius could be very illogical and could have considered the existence of the tree a breach of the servitude while maintaining that it was not enough to enable *usucapio* of freedom from the servitude. It is, in fact, quite difficult to envisage that any jurist could deny that there was a breach of a servitude of light where the light was blocked by a tree planted on the *praedium serviens*. The argument produced in the text for refusing to recognize *usucapio*, namely *quia non ita in suo statu et loco maneret arbor quemadmodum paries, propter motum naturalem arboris* is not very persuasive even in this context, but it would be a manifest absurdity to use it to deny breach of the servitude. There is, unfortunately, no way of telling whether the argument is Pomponius' own or goes back to Quintus Mucius. Though it can only be conjectural, I should like to suggest that the argument is not Mucius' and that his attitude was this: A tree when it grew enough would breach a servitude of *lumen* or *prospectus*. But he would not allow *usucapio* of freedom from the servitude because of the existence of the tree for the very practical reason that one could not reasonably tell when *usucapio* began. Was one to count the moment of planting as the beginning of *usucapio*? But for years the tree might not obscure *lumen* or *prospectus* at all. Was one to count *usucapio* as starting when the tree did begin to obstruct the *lumen* or *prospectus*? But, *ex post facto*, that moment could be impossible to determine.

It is reasonable to treat the four original rustic servitudes first and together, and *aquae haustus* along with them. Although *aquae haustus* is later and may never have been a *res mancipi* it is convenient to deal with it along with these others, partly because it apparently became more prominent than the other later rustic servitudes[1] and partly because it always involves a right of way, and also is not always easily distinguishable in the texts from *aquae ductus*.

Cicero, *pro Caecina* 26. 74. . . . Fundus a patre relinqui potest, at usucapio fundi, hoc est finis sollicitudinis ac periculi litium, non a patre relinquitur, sed a legibus; aquae ductus, haustus, iter, actus a patre, sed rata auctoritas harum rerum omnium ab civili iure sumitur.

Here, in effect, Cicero is listing what are for him the traditional typical servitudes. It will be noticed that of the original four *via* is omitted, and that *aquae haustus* is added. Probably little significance should be attached to this. At the most, the text might suggest that *aquae haustus* came to be associated mentally with the four original servitudes, perhaps because, one might expect, it was very common and it could often be thought of, non-technically, along with *aquae ductus*.[2] The absence of *via* from the list may be because it was regarded as nothing more than *iter* and *actus*.[3] No text, apart perhaps from Varro, *de ling. lat.* 5. 22, expressly mentions *via* for our period but Gaius says in D. 8. 3. 8 (7 *ad ed. prov.*) that the XII Tables laid down that the road was to be eight *pedes* wide on the straight and sixteen at the bends, and Javolenus tells us that this was the position in his time unless otherwise agreed.[4]

[1] e.g., it appears along with three of the four original servitudes in Cicero, *pro Caecina* 26. 74; it comes first in the list of the non-original rustic servitudes in D. 8. 3. 1. 1 (Ulpian, 2 *inst.*).

[2] e.g. D. 8. 3. 2. 1, 2 (Neratius, 4 *reg.*).

[3] Cf. D. 8. 3. 1 pr.: Kaser, *RPR*, i. 126. But a distinction could be found in that there was in the absence of the parties' agreement no statutory width for *iter* and *actus*—it had to be fixed by an *arbiter*—but there was for *via*: D. 8. 3. 13. 2 (Javolenus, 10 *ex Cassio*).

[4] D. 8. 3. 13. 3; cf. also D. 8. 1. 13 (Pomponius, 14 *ad Quintum Mucium*).

Of far greater significance in the discussion of the history of servitudes is D. 8. 3. 30 (Paul, 4 *epit. Alfeni dig.*).

Qui dua praedia habebat, in unius venditione aquam, quae in fundo nascebatur, et circa eam aquam late decem pedes exceperat: quaesitum est, utrum dominium loci ad eum pertineat an ut per eum locum accedere possit. respondit, si ita recepisset: 'circa eam aquam late pedes decem', iter dumtaxat videri venditoris esse.[1]

It seems now to be completely accepted that the four original servitudes were in early law regarded in some way as involving ownership over the objects of the servitudes.[2] The most powerful argument in favour of this proposition is that since (at least) these servitudes were *res mancipi* and could be transferred by *mancipatio* they must have been regarded as corporeal things. At some time, even these four servitudes came to be regarded as incorporeal.[3] But it has been suggested by Grosso[4] and Daube[5] that in this present text *aqua* is not to be equated with *aquae ductus*, the right to draw water, but that the vendor reserved for himself the ownership of the *fons*. Daube's argument, which at first appears very persuasive, seems less convincing on closer inspection. He says that the problem about the reservation of the strip of land seems the consequence of precisely the reservation of ownership of the water. 'If the first half had contemplated only a right to draw water, a servitude, it could hardly have been suggested that the second half, subordinate to the first, contemplated ownership.' But the difficulty, I suggest, is very different. As Daube himself points out, *aqua* denotes aqueduct in a number of texts.[6] (And, as

[1] Solazzi thinks (*SDHI* xviii (1952) 218 f.) that if *dominium loci* had really appeared in the text it would have been in apposition to the name of some other right, not just of *an ut per eum locum accedere possit*. Hence, he says, *dominium loci* must be interpolated and the text does not contain, as it otherwise would, the earliest use of the word to mean technically ownership. He would also reconstruct the text so that the servitude still has to be created. But his desire for balance in the style of Alfenus (or of his master Servius) seems exaggerated. The form of the question may also be as it was put by the person seeking advice.

[2] Cf., e.g., Kaser, *RPR* i. 126; but for the expression of a slight doubt, see *supra*, pp. 92 ff.

[3] G. 2. 17.

[4] *BIDR* xl (1932) 421 f.

[5] 'Slightly different', *Iura* xii (1961) 81 ff. at pp. 97 ff. And see now Colognesi, *Ricerche sulla struttura delle servitù d'acqua in diritto romano* (Milan, 1966), pp. 70 ff. especially at p. 75.

[6] e.g. D. 8. 5. 10; 8. 6. 7; *h.t.* 10; and a number of texts in title D. 43. 20.

we shall see, it could also denote *aquae haustus*.) There is thus no real difficulty in understanding a reservation of the *aqua quae in fundo nascitur* as technical and meaning a reservation of the right to an aqueduct (or *aquae haustus*). But the agreement then goes on to reserve *circa eam aquam late decem pedes*, a strip ten feet wide round that water, and there is no technical meaning for any of the other words or for the phrase itself such as applies to *aqua*. Thus it is, in fact, depriving the words of their natural meaning to hold that the reservation is only of a right of way and not of the ownership of the land. No doubt in the circumstances of the case—the reservation of the *circa eam aquam late decem pedes* being dependent on the reservation of the *aqua*—it was reasonable to raise the question of the interpretation of the reservation of the *decem pedes*, but there could only be a problem of interpretation if the reservation of the *aqua* was not a reservation of the ownership of the water. Alfenus' (or Servius') decision that *circa eam aquam late pedes decem* was a reservation only of an *iter* is conclusive proof that the reservation of *aqua* was not a reservation of ownership in the water.

There is, indeed, reason to think that in the earliest period the right to a servitude of *aquae ductus* (or of *aquae haustus*) did not reserve in any way ownership of the water to the owner of the dominant tenement. At first sight it is extremely odd that *aquae haustus* was not one of the original servitudes. Such a right must frequently have been wanted—much more often than *aquae ductus* where the situation of the servient tenement in relation to the dominant tenement must commonly have operated as a severe limitation. It would appear to be significant that *aquae haustus* was not one of the original servitudes, and most reasonable to attribute this to the absence of some feature which was then, but not later, considered to be essential for a servitude. What immediately springs to mind is that the four original servitudes must have been thought of as corporeal since they could be transferred by *mancipatio*. But if *aquae haustus* involved an *iter* plus ownership of the water, then it too could equally be classed as corporeal. If, however, it did not involve ownership of the water, then its corporeal aspect would be restricted to the *iter* and so it would not be a separate servitude. But if the ownership of the water was not here involved, then similarly in the case of *aquae ductus* there would be no question of the owner of the dominant tenement being owner of the water. The corporeal nature of the servitude would lie in the construction which carried the water. It is, in fact, difficult to believe that ownership of the water could be involved in *aquae haustus* or *aquae ductus*. A text from classical law, D. 1. 8. 2 (Marcian, 3 *inst.*), says that *aqua profluens* is common to all,[1] and there is no reason to believe that a different regime prevailed earlier.[2] And Ulpian tells us in D. 8. 3. 3 (17 *ad ed.*) that a *ius adeundi ad fontem* contained *haustus*.[3]

To return to D. 8. 3. 30. The text is concerned with the creation of a servitude of *aquae ductus* (or *aquae haustus*) and of an *iter* round the place where the water arises. The wording of the text suggests that the servitudes are already in existence (*utrum dominium loci ad eum pertineat an ut per eum locum accedere possit: iter dumtaxat videri venditoris esse*) and since servitudes could not be created simply by contract it appears that the servient *praedium* has already been transferred to the buyer by *mancipatio* or *in iure cessio* with reservation of the servitudes. It is quite likely, therefore, that *venditione* is an interpolation for *mancipatione*[4] but, whether this is so or not, what is involved is perfectly clear.[5]

D. 18. 1. 40. 1 (Paul, 4 *epit. Alfeni dig.*). In lege fundi aquam accessuram dixit: quaerebatur, an etiam iter aquae accessisset. respondit sibi videri id actum esse, et ideo iter quoque venditorem tradere oportere.

[1] Cf. J. 2. 1. 1.

[2] Though texts make a distinction between *flumina publica* and *flumina privata* there is no direct indication that the water of a *flumen privatum* was regarded as privately owned and not as *omnium communis*. The arguments adduced to show that *aqua profluens* means only water in a *flumen publicum* (see most recently, Colognesi, op. cit. pp. 52 ff. and especially p. 57 are indirect and extremely tenuous.

[3] If the slight doubt expressed earlier (*supra*, pp. 92 ff.), that servitudes even originally may never have been regarded as corporeals, is correct then the same explanation—that, since *aqua profluens* was common to all, *aquae haustus* was indistinguishable from a right of *iter* to the water—is appropriate.

[4] See on this point Solazzi, *Requisiti e modi di costituzione delle servitù prediali* (Naples, 1947), p. 99 and n. 42, who, however argues that *mancipatio* still has to take place. Daube, reasonably enough, simply assumes without question that *mancipatio* had taken place: op. cit., p. 97.

[5] I agree completely with Daube's explanation of the form of the text: op. cit., pp. 97 ff.

This text from the same book as the last is likewise concerned with a case where the servitudes have been created by *mancipatio* (or *in iure cessio*)[1]—hence *et ideo* to the end is interpolated[2]—but this time the estate which was sold is the dominant tenement and the servitudes over other land owned by the seller have been added to it.[3] One cannot argue from this either that *aquae haustus* must be a *res mancipi* or that *aquae haustus* is not involved, since it is apparent from D. 8. 4. 6 pr. which is concerned with servitudes on both rustic and urban *praedia* that urban servitudes, which are undoubtedly *res nec mancipi*, can be created in this way.

Again Grosso,[4] with whom Daube tends to agree,[5] argues that the classical jurists treated this as a case where the water on the servient estate passed into the buyer's ownership. But since *aqua* can designate the servitude of *aquae ductus* (and also *aquae haustus*) there is nothing in the text itself which points towards that conclusion, and since *aqua* in D. 8. 3. 30 must refer only to a servitude right of water and not to ownership it is most plausible to attribute to it a similar meaning here.[6] Grosso takes *iter aquae* together to mean 'aqueduct' as it frequently does, so that the question was whether the reservation of ownership of the water created a right to have an aqueduct. This, as Daube agrees, is a possible translation—but only if one can hold that the grant of *aqua* meant a grant of the ownership of the water. If, as I have argued, *aqua* means a servitude right of water then Grosso's translation is impossible —*etiam* is totally inappropriate since the sole grant would be of an aqueduct. One has, in fact, to accept the traditional view of *quaerebatur an etiam iter aquae accessisset* as meaning 'It was asked whether a right of way to the water was also included, or 'It was asked whether a right of way went with the right to the water'. This

[1] Again, Solazzi thinks that the servitudes still have to be created: op. cit., p. 99. But this is to ignore the tense of *accessisset*.

[2] Cf. now Daube, op. cit., p. 100, n. 34.

[3] For other instances of the creation of servitudes in this way see D. 8. 3. 32 (Africanus, 6 *quaest.*); 8. 4. 6 pr. (Ulpian, 28 *ad Sab.*): Cf. Daube, loc. cit.

[4] Op. cit., p. 421, n. 38.

[5] Loc. cit.

[6] It may be worth stating expressly that since, whatever the original implication may have been, the word *via* came to mean 'a servitude right of way', not 'ownership of a road', so the simple use of the word *aqua* in D. 8. 3. 30 and 18. 1. 40. 1 is no argument for holding that for the jurists of the period ownership of the water was involved.

means, of course, that *aqua* in the text is most plausibly taken to be a right of *aquae haustus*, so it appears that the word *aqua* can mean that just as it can mean the right of *aquae ductus*.[1] The text appears to tell us that Alfenus (or Servius) held that a grant of *aquae haustus* tacitly carried with it the right of *iter*.

The extent of these servitudes and the rights and duties of the parties are clarified by a number of texts.

D. 43. 19. 4 pr. (Venuleius, 1 *interd.*). Veteres nominatim adiciebant, ut ea quoque, quae ad refectionem utilia essent, adportanti vis non fieret: quod supervacuum est, quoniam qui adportari non patitur ea, sine quibus refici iter non possit, vim facere videtur, quo minus reficiatur.

The text, from Venuleius' first book on interdicts, is concerned with a question of right of way, and in particular with an *interdictum de itinere actuque*[2] which is the subject of the Digest title 43. 19. There were, in fact, two such interdicts,[3] and our text relates to the second which prohibits force to be used to stop repairs to a servitude right of way. The interdict runs:[4] *Quo itinere actuque hoc anno non vi non clam non precario ab illo usus es, quo minus id iter actumque, ut tibi ius est, reficias, vim fieri veto. Qui hoc interdicto uti volet, is adversario damni infecti, quod per eius operis vitium datum sit, caveat.* This interdict cannot be understood to have existed before the other *interdictum de itinere actuque* which accordingly must also be Republican. That interdict runs:[5] *Quo itinere actuque, quo de agitur, hoc anno nec vi nec clam nec precario ab illo usus es, quo minus ita utaris, vim fieri veto.* The present text says that the Republican jurists expressly added that force was not to be used against a person carrying things useful for the repair. Venuleius declares that this statement was unnecessary.

D. 43. 20. 8 (Scaevola, libro singulari ὅρων). Cui per fundum iter aquae debetur, quacumque vult in eo rivum licet faciat, dum ne aquae ductum interverteret.

The *cui* of the text is emended by Mommsen to *cuius*.[6] *Cui* is supported by the Basilica[7] but there are great difficulties in

[1] So it is not difficult to think that that might be what it means in D. 8. 3. 30.
[2] Cf. Lenel, *Pal.* ii. 1210.
[3] Cf. Lenel, *EP*, pp. 478 f.
[4] Following Lenel, *EP*, p. 479.
[5] Following Lenel, *EP*, p. 478.
[6] *Digesta Iustiniani Augusti* (Berlin, 1870) ii. 599.
[7] *Basilicorum Libri LX* (Leipzig, 1897), vii. 15[illegible].

accepting that the Digest text does have the correct reading. First, the imperfect subjunctive *interverteret* is incomprehensible. Secondly, the law which it expresses, namely that the person who has the right of *aquae ductus* can make the aqueduct wherever he pleases, seems unreasonable. Stated as it is, without qualification, it seems to conflict with the rule which we know existed in classical law that a servitude right had to be so exercised as to cause as little inconvenience as possible.[1] The substitution of *cuius* for *cui*[2] is the simplest alteration which would give a text with a satisfactory meaning.[3] The imperfect subjunctive, *interverteret*, following on the present indicatives, *vult* and *licet*, becomes explicable as a *coniunctivus irrealis*.[4] An instance parallel to what is being suggested is in Cicero, *de off*. 1. 25. 89.

. . . quae placet Peripateticis, et recte placet modo ne laudarent iracundiam et dicerent utiliter a natura datam.

'Which the Peripatetics accept, and would rightly accept if only they do not praise anger and say that it was given by nature to good purpose.' The text means, of course, that the Peripatetics do praise anger and say that it was given by nature to good purpose. Similarly I suggest in D. 43. 20. 8 which is to be translated: 'A person over whose estate a right of *aquae ductus* is due might properly make a water-course wherever on his land he wishes provided he were not to affect adversely the aqueduct.' Here, too, the meaning is that a particular case is under discussion where the actions of the owner of the servient tenement did adversely affect the aqueduct. The question put to Quintus Mucius may have been phrased as follows: 'I have a right of aqueduct over my neighbour's land and he has made a water-course on his land which adversely affects my aqueduct. Is he entitled to do this?' It may be objected to this approach that the nature of Quintus Mucius' *liber singularis* ὅρων as a

[1] Cf. Buckland, *Textbook*, p. 260 and the texts he cites, n. 10.

[2] A possible abbreviation of *cuius* could be *cuĩ*: cf. Cappelli, *Dizionario di abbreviature latine ed italiane*, 6th edn. (Milan, 1961), p. 61, where the particular example given is from the thirteenth century.

[3] This is not necessarily to say that the interpretation of the text which I favour is the same as Mommsen's.

[4] For the *modus irrealis* see Kühner–Stegmann, *Grammatik der lateinischen Sprache*, 4th edn. by Thierfelder (Munich, 1962), ii. 398 ff.

book of aphorisms is against the idea that Quintus Mucius was giving a reply to a particular problem, but it should be remembered that the general view seems to be that the book may be a later collection from Scaevola's *Ius civile* or from Pomponius' *libri ad Quintum Mucium.*[1] And elsewhere I have already argued that the formulation of D. 50. 17. 73 pr. from the same book is not at all what one would expect in an aphorism, and that the text can be explained if one concedes that Quintus Mucius was thinking in more concrete terms.[2] But whether the *liber singularis ὅρων* is a later compilation or not, D. 43. 20. 8 is so closely connected with D. 8. 3. 15 (Pomponius, 31 [32?—Lenel] *ad Quintum Mucium*) that there can be little doubt that D. 43. 20. 8 itself comes originally from Mucius' *libri iuris civilis.*[3] Hence there is no reason to hold that in its original context in the *libri iuris civilis*, D. 43. 20. 8 was not giving an answer to a particular problem, and that the imperfect subjunctive, *interverteret*, was inadvertently retained when the text was excerpted for the *liber singularis ὅρων*.

D. 8. 3. 15 is, in a sense, almost the converse of D. 43. 20. 8.

Quintus Mucius scribit, cum iter aquae vel cottidianae vel aestivae vel quae intervalla longiora habeat per alienum fundum erit, licere fistulam suam [suam *del. Krüger*] vel fictilem vel cuiuslibet generis in rivo ponere, quae aquam latius exprimeret, et quod vellet in rivo facere, licere, dum ne domino praedii aquagium deterius faceret.

A person who has a right of aqueduct over another's land (whether the right is to have water every day or only in the summer or at longer intervals) may place pipes whether made of clay or of any other sort in the water-channel to increase the flow of water and may do whatever he wishes with the water-channel provided he does not make the water-course worse for the owner of the land.

[1] Cf. Lenel, *Pal.*, i. 762, n. 7; H. Krüger, *Studi Bonfante* (Milan, 1930) ii. 336; Schulz, *RLS*, p. 94; *contra*, Scherillo, 'Note critiche su opere della giurisprudenza romana', *Iura* iii (1952) 180 ff. It would seem that Beseler also accepts the authenticity of this book; *ZSS* liv (1934) 325; and so does Stein, *Regulae iuris* (Edinburgh, 1966), pp. 38 f. But neither of these last two writers gives arguments or refers to the modern literature. The authorship of the *liber singularis ὅρων* will be discussed in a later volume on *Legal Science in the Later Roman Republic*.

[2] Watson, *Persons*, pp. 118 ff.

[3] Lenel, *Pal.* i. 762, n. 7; accepted even by Scherillo, op. cit., pp. 185 f.

D. 43. 21. 3 pr. (Ulpian, 70 *ad ed.*). Servius autem scribit aliter duci aquam, quae ante per specus ducta est, si nunc per apertum ducatur: nam si operis aliquid [aliud quid *Mommsen*] faciat quis, quo magis aquam conservet vel contineat, non impune prohiberi. ego et in specu contra, si non maior utilitas versetur adversarii. 1. Servius et Labeo scribunt, si rivum, qui ab initio terrenus fuit, quia aquam non continebat, cementicium velit facere, audiendum esse: sed et si eum rivum, qui structilis fuit, postea terrenum faciat aut partem rivi, aeque non esse prohibendum. mihi videtur urguens et necessaria refectio esse admittenda.

These texts are also concerned with aqueducts and in particular with the interpretation of the interdict *de rivis*.[1] That interdict runs:[2] *Rivos* [or *Rivum*] *specus septa reficere purgare aquae ducendae causa quo minus liceat illi, dum ne aliter aquam ducat, quam uti priore aestate non vi non clam non precario a te duxit, vim fieri veto*. The *principium* concerns us only so far as *non impune prohiberi* and this part of the text cannot be completely in proper order. It begins by saying that Servius held that it did amount to leading water *aliter* if one now channels it in uncovered pipes whereas previously it ran in covered pipes. But it then goes on—and the infinitive *prohiberi* shows that we still have indirect speech and hence the decision of Servius—to say 'for if anyone does anything to conserve or contain the water better he cannot be prevented with impunity'. The decision is not what one would expect after the first part of the text, and there is nothing in the text which attempts to justify the giving of the interdict despite the fact that the water is being conducted differently. Also water conveyed in an open conduit would not be conserved or contained better. Yet the two most obvious possibilities of error do not cure the text. First, the insertion of a *non* before *aliter* would not be satisfactory, both because the situation does appear to amount to conducting the water differently[3] and also because the reason given from *nam si* would not be appropriate. Secondly, the deletion of *non* before *impune* is impossible since *nam si* to *contineat* would then be nonsensical. A more plausible explanation is that the text has been shortened and that something has been excised between *ducatur*

[1] Cf. Lenel, *Pal.* ii. 831.

[2] Lenel, *EP*, p. 480.

[3] No contrary argument can be drawn from *h.t.* 1. 6 (Ulpian, 70 *ad ed.*).

and *nam si* which perhaps said that none the less the interdict would at times be given where some alterations were made which could not harm the servient tenement. *Nam si* would then explain in what circumstances the interdict might be given though there had been a change.

§ 1 is relevant to us as far as *non esse prohibendum*. *Audiendum esse* and *non esse prohibendum* show that, despite the infinitives, *si rivum* to *prohibendum* is dependent on *scribunt* and so gives us the opinion of Servius and Labeo. These jurists hold that a person who has a right of aqueduct is to be permitted to make the water-channel of cement where previously it was simply in the earth and did not retain the water. Likewise they hold that such a person may make all or part of the channel simply of earth where it was previously tiled. Beseler, however, holds *audiendum* to *aeque* interpolated.[1] The second situation, which is the converse of the first, he thinks is contrary to good sense, *faciat* should be *facere velit*, and *aut partem rivi* is 'kompletoman'. These arguments look persuasive but they may not be completely convincing. What is under discussion is the scope of the word *reficere* in the interdict, and it is not senseless to hold that where an aqueduct with a tiled channel needs repairing, a simple channel of earth—perhaps wanted for reasons of economy—is legally acceptable. Where repairing is being discussed it does not seem quite so much 'kompletoman' to bring in a reference to a part. And there is really no need to introduce *velle*. It is quite reasonable to say, in Latin as in other languages, 'Where someone does this, he is not to be prevented'.

So far as the first part of that text is concerned, the view of Servius may be in conflict with that of Ofilius which has come down to us in D. 43. 21. 1. 10 (Ulpian, 70 *ad ed.*).

> Si quis terrenum rivum Signinum, id est lapideum facere velit, videri eum non recte hoc interdicto uti: non enim reficit qui hoc facit: et ita Ofilio videtur.[2]

Si quis to *uti* is indirect speech, so that we are being given the opinion of some jurist whose name has not come down to us. But we are told that Ofilius held the same view, namely that a person

[1] *Subsiciva* (Leipzig, 1929), p. 13.

[2] *Id est lapideum* may be a gloss: cf. *Index Itp.*

who wishes to make a water-course which is simply a channel in the earth into a stone-built channel cannot properly use this interdict. Presumably, Ofilius' reason is that given in the text—though in direct speech—that this conduct is not *reficere*. It is, however, possible that there is no real conflict between Ofilius and Servius; that Ofilius was thinking of a situation where the original water-channel was satisfactory and in good order whereas Servius' point is that where the original water-channel in the earth is not satisfactory it is proper to make it satisfactory by making it of cement.

D. 43. 21. 3. 10. Si quis eum exportare [eum ea portare *Mommsen*] vehere, quae refectioni necessaria sunt, prohibeat, hoc interdictum ei competere Ofilius putat, quod est verum.

Another text dealing with the same interdict and hence with the servitude of *aquae ductus*. Ofilius thought the interdict would lie against someone who did not allow things necessary for the repair to be brought on to the land.[1]

D. 43. 20. 1. 17 (Ulpian, 70 *ad ed.*). Item quaeritur, si quis aquae, quam hoc anno ducebat, aliam aquam admiscuerit, an impune prohibeatur. et extat Ofilii sententia existimantis recte eum prohiberi, sed eo loci, in quo primum aquam aliam in rivum admittit: et [at *Mommsen*] Ofilius in tota aqua recte eum prohiberi ait. ego Ofilio adsentio non posse dividi, quia non potest ita in parte vis fieri, ut non in tota aqua fiat.

This text, too, concerns *aquae ductus*, but this time relates to a different interdict, *de aqua cottidiana et aestiva*.[2] This interdict runs:[3] *Uti hoc anno aquam, qua de agitur, non vi non clam non precario ab illo duxisti, quo minus ita ducas, vim fieri veto*. Since Gothofredus there has been general agreement that *Ofilii* is a scribal error for some other jurist's name.[4] Thus the unknown, probably Republican, jurist held that if the owner of the dominant tenement added other water (that is, on the servient land) to the water which he was conducting in that year he can rightly be stopped, but at the point at which he introduced the additional

[1] Cf. 43. 19. 4 pr. on an interdict *de itinere actuque*: *supra*, p. 188.
[2] Cf. Lenel, *Pal.*, ii. 828.
[3] Cf. Lenel, *EP*, p. 479.
[4] Cf., e.g., Mommsen, *Digesta Iustiniani Augusti*, ii. 596, n. 5; Lenel, *Pal.*, ii. 828, n. 2; Bonfante, *Milan Digest*, p. 1238, n. 5.

water into the water-course. Ofilius, with whom Ulpian agrees, said that he could be stopped in respect of all the water.[1,2]

To turn now to the remaining servitudes and first to *lumen* and *prospectus*. D. 8. 2. 7 (Pomponius, 26 *ad Quintum Mucium*), which concerns one or the other, has already been quoted and discussed.[3]

D. 8. 2. 16 (Paul, 2 *epit. Alfeni dig.*). Lumen id est, ut caelum videretur, et interest inter lumen et prospectum: nam prospectus etiam ex inferioribus locis est, lumen ex inferiore loco esse non potest.

Lumen is described as the right to see the sky. *Lumen* and *prospectus* are then distinguished and the distinction seems to be that for *lumen* the dominant tenement must be higher than the servient while this need not be so for *prospectus*.

Cicero, *de orat.* 1. 39. 179. Quo quidem in genere familiaris noster M. Buculeius, homo neque meo iudicio stultus et suo valde sapiens et ab iuris studio non abhorrens, simili [in re] quodam modo nuper erravit: nam cum aedis L. Fufio venderet, in mancipio lumina, uti tum essent, ita recepit; Fufius autem, simul atque aedificari coeptum est in quadam parte urbis, quae modo ex illis aedibus conspici posset, egit statim cum Buculeio, quod, cuicumque particulae caeli officeretur, quamvis esset procul, mutari lumina putabat.

In spite of its human interest, the text does not tell us very much about *lumen*. The reported declaration in the *mancipatio, uti tunc esset, ita recepit*, corresponds to a standard clause in a *mancipatio, uti nunc sunt, ut ita sint* which had the meaning that a certain servitude was due from a neighbour.[4] In this particular instance, the purchaser, L. Fufius, interpreted the clause as meaning that any new building in any part of the city which could be seen from his house amounted to a breach of the seller's warranty. Presumably he should only have been successful if he could have had, in theory, a servitude right of *lumen* in respect of the new building, but Cicero's words of good-natured contempt—even his *erravit*—for the seller,

[1] Despite its proximity, § 18 cannot be concerned with this interdict: cf. *infra*, p. 197.

[2] Cicero, *ad Att.* 15. 26. 4 and *ad Quintum fr.* 3. 1. 2 tell us nothing more though the former is concerned with *aquae ductus* (the land in question is the servient tenement) and the latter with some kind of servitude relating to water.

[3] *Supra*, pp. 181 f.

[4] D. 8. 2. 33 (Paul, 5 *epit. Alfeni dig.*); and, for the Empire, D. 8. 2. 17. 3 (Ulpian, 29 *ad Sab.*).

M. Buculeius, do not allow us to conclude that such a theoretical right could have existed. He may merely mean that such a clause which apparently implies that what appear to be exercised as servitude rights are in fact servitude rights is inappropriate for *lumina* and is easily capable of being misinterpreted by a purchaser.

A servitude right to channel off one's excess water on to a neighbour's land could exist.

D. 8. 3. 29 (Paul, 2 *epit. Alfeni dig.*). Qui duo praedia confinia habuerat, superiorem fundum vendiderat: in lege ita dixerat, ut aquam sulco aperto emptori educere in fundum inferiorem recte liceat: si emptor ex alio fundo aquam acciperet et eam in inferiorem ducere vellet, quaesitum est, an possit id suo iure facere nec ne. respondi nihil amplius, quam quod ipsius fundi siccandi causa derivaret, vicinum inferiorem recipere debere.

A person who owned two adjoining estates sold the higher one and imposed a servitude on the lower (*in lege ita dixerat*—so presumably the servitude was created by the *mancipatio* of the *praedium*) that the purchaser could drain off water, when the furrows were opened, on to the lower estate. The question was whether the purchaser, if he had to receive water from another estate could under this right drain even that water on to the lower estate. Alfenus (or his master Servius) replied that the owner of the lower estate need not accept more water than what the owner of the higher estate channelled off in order to dry his own land. The natural interpretation of this reply (though it is not the only possible one) is perhaps that the owner of the higher estate cannot drain on to the lower one the water he has had to receive.[1] This interpretation is strengthened by the presence of *ipsius*.

D. 8. 5. 17 pr. (Alfenus, 2 *dig.*). Si quando inter aedes binas paries esset, qui ita ventrem faceret, ut in vicini domum semipedem aut amplius procumberet, agi oportet ius non esse illum parietem ita proiectum in suum esse invito se.

This text, like the other fragments of this *lex*, is concerned with the *actio negatoria*,[2] but this time we know from a text of Gaius,

[1] For D. 39. 3. 2. 10 (Paul, 49 *ad ed.*), which also concerns this servitude, see *supra*, pp. 173 f.

[2] Cf. *supra*, pp. 177 ff.

D. 8. 2. 2 (7 *ad ed. prov.*), that there could be a *ius proiciendi protegendive*. The text tells us that an *actio negatoria* will be given where a wall bulges half a foot or more over on to a neighbour's house. In the text, *semipedem aut amplius* has frequently been held to be a Justinianic interpolation.[1] The main reason for this attitude seems to be that the very precise restriction that the overhang must be by half a foot or more is thought necessarily to be due to a legislator. But even if this be accepted,[2] it should be noted that there is not the slightest indication that this legislator was Justinian and there is no *a priori* reason to exclude the possibility that the provision was very old. Biondi[3] also seems to object to the *aut amplius*, but it seems perfectly in order to say that if the wall overhang by half a foot or more the *actio negatoria* will lie.

Two closely related servitudes were *flumen* and *stillicidium*. The former was the right to let water flow on to a neighbour's property, the latter to let it drip (from a height) on to his property.[4]

Varro, *de lingua latina*, 5. 27. Fluvius quod fluit, item flumen; a quo lege praediorum urbanorum scribitur ⟨⟨scribitur⟩⟩: 'Stillicidia fluminaqu⟨⟨v⟩⟩e ut ita cadant fluantque; inter haec quod inter⟨est⟩ quod stillicidium eo, quod stillatim cadit; flumen, quod fluit continue.

This text seems to give us the earliest evidence for the existence of servitudes apart from the four original ones. From D. 39. 3. 1. 17 (Ulpian, 53 *ad ed.*)[5] we learn that in the Republic the *actio negatoria* in respect of *stillicidium* and *flumen* could be brought both where the property suffering from the water was a house and where it was land.

For Cicero, *stillicidium* seems to have represented the epitome of legal pettiness.

de leg. 1. 4. 14. . . . Quamobrem quo me vocas aut quid hortaris? ut libellos conficiam de stillicidiorum ac de parietum iure? an ut stipulationum et iudiciorum formulas componam? Quae et scripta a multis

[1] Add to the references in the *Index Itp.*, Biondi, *Il diritto romano cristiano* (Milan, 1954), iii. 313 f. But Kaser is sceptical: *RPR* i. 345, n. 17.

[2] And perhaps it need not be. It may be that all Alfenus means is that where the overhang is very small, less than half a foot, the interest of the plaintiff is minute and is not worthy of protection, since the cost to the defendant would be so disproportionate: cf. Seidl, *Festschrift Lehmann* (Berlin, 1956) i. 108.

[3] Loc. cit.

[4] Cf. D. 8. 2. 20. 5 (Paul, 15 *ad Sab.*).

[5] *Supra*, pp. 172 f.

sunt diligenter et sunt humiliora quam illa quae a vobis exspectari puto.

orat. 21. 72. . . . Quam enim indecorum est, de stillicidiis cum apud unum iudicem dicas, amplissimis verbis et locis uti communibus: de maiestate populi Romani summisse et subtiliter! Hic genere toto.

One may suspect that *stillicidium* was singled out for this position at least partly because of its imposing name.

Another servitude right was that of driving animals to drink from water on a neighbour's land.

D. 43. 20. 1. 18 (Ulpian, 70 *ad ed.*). Trebatius, cum amplior numerus pecoris ad aquam appelletur, quam debet appelli, posse universum pecus impune prohiberi, quia iunctum pecus ei pecori, cui adpulsus debeatur, totum corrumpat pecoris adpulsum. Marcellus autem ait, si quis ius habens pecoris ad aquam appellendi plura pecora adpulserit, non in omnibus pecoribus eum prohibendum: quod est verum, quia pecora separari possunt.

This text, despite its position, cannot be discussing the interdict *de aqua cottidiana et aestiva* which was confined to *aquae ductus*.[1] The text, however, is brought in because of its analogy with § 17.[2] Trebatius held that if the holder of a servitude right to drive animals to water drove more animals than he was entitled to, he could properly be stopped. But Marcellus and Ulpian himself took the view that only those in addition to the permitted number could be stopped. The interdict in question would seem to be that *de fonte*[3] which runs:[4] *Uti de eo fonte, quo de agitur, hoc anno aqua nec vi nec clam nec precario ab illo usus es, quo minus ita utaris, vim fieri veto. de lacu puteo piscina item interdicam.*[5]

There could be a servitude right to pass a sewer through a neighbour's land.

D. 43. 23. 2 (Venuleius, 1 *interd.*). Quamquam de reficienda cloaca non etiam de nova facienda hoc interdicto comprehendatur, tamen aeque interdicendum Labeo ait, ne facienti cloacam vis fiat, quia eadem utilitas sit: praetorem enim sic interdixisse, ne vis fieret, quo minus

[1] *Supra*, pp. 193 f.

[2] *Supra*, pp. 193 f.

[3] For its applicability to *pecoris ad aquam adpulsus* see D. 43. 22. 1. 2. (Ulpian, 70 *ad ed.*).

[4] Lenel, *EP*, p. 480.

[5] The last sentence may be a later addition to the interdict since its form is different. It is not in itself evidenced for the Republic.

cloacam in publico facere liceret: idque Ofilio et Trebatio placuisse. ipse dicendum ait, ut ne factam cloacam purgare et restituere permittendum sit per interdictum, novam vero facere is demum concedere debeat, cui viarum publicarum cura sit.

This text, probably as a result of scribal error, is not quite in perfect form,[1] but it seems that we can reconstruct the opinion of Ofilius and Trebatius. The interdict under discussion is *de cloacis*, which runs:[2] *Quo minus illi cloacam, quae ex aedibus eius in tuas pertinet, qua de agitur, purgare reficere liceat, vim fieri veto. Damni infecti, quod operis vitio factum sit, caveri iubeo.* Although this interdict talks of cleaning and repairing an existing sewer, Ofilius and Trebatius were willing to interpret it so as to make it apply also to the making of a new sewer. Just as, presumably for reasons of utility, Ofilius and Trebatius were willing to widen the scope of the interdict beyond its ordinary meaning, so similarly the praetor omitted from the wording of this interdict the customary *nec vi nec clam nec precario ab illo usus es*.[3,4]

The servitude *oneris ferendi* is exceptional in that it offends against the maxim *servitus in faciendo consistere non potest*.

D. 8. 5. 6. 2 (Ulpian, 17 *ad ed.*). Etiam de servitute, quae oneris ferendi causa imposita erit, actio nobis competit, ut et onera ferat et aedificia reficiat ad eum modum, qui servitute imposita comprehensus est. et Gallus putat non posse ita servitutem imponi, ut quis facere aliquid cogeretur, sed ne me facere prohiberet: nam in omnibus servitutibus refectio ad eum pertinet, qui sibi servitutem adserit, non ad eum, cuius res servit. sed evaluit Servi sententia, in proposita specie ut possit quis defendere ius sibi esse cogere adversarium reficere parietem ad onera sua sustinenda. Labeo autem hanc servitutem non hominem debere, sed rem, denique licere domino rem derelinquere scribit.

D. 8. 2. 33 (Paul, 5 *epit. Alfeni dig.*). Eum debere columnam restituere, quae onus vicinarum aedium ferebat, cuius essent aedes quae servirent, non eum, qui imponere vellet. nam cum in lege aedium ita scriptum esset: 'paries oneri ferundo uti nunc est, ita sit', satis aperte significari in perpetuum parietem esse debere: non enim hoc his verbis dici, ut in perpetuum idem paries aeternus [aeternus *del. Mommsen*] esset, quod ne fieri quidem posset, sed uti eiusdem modi paries in perpetuum esset

[1] Cf. the attempts at reconstruction by Mommsen, op. cit., ii. 602, n. 4; *Milan Digest*, p. 1213.

[2] Cf. Lenel, *EP*, p. 481.

[3] Cf. D. 43. 23. 1. 7 (Ulpian, 71 *ad ed.*).

[4] See also Cicero, *pro Caecina* 13. 36.

qui onus sustineret: quemadmodum si quis alicui cavisset, ut servitutem praeberet, qui onus suum sustineret, si ea res quae servit et tuum onus ferret, perisset, alia in locum eius dari debeat.

Consequently there have been a great many suggestions as to the historical origins of this servitude, various attempts to explain its nature have been made and its very existence has even been denied.[1] But these suggestions and explanations are unsatisfactory since they are all too subtle and over-sophisticated. There is, I suggest, really no problem about the historical origins or nature of this servitude. The utility of having a right of support from a neighbour's wall is obvious. And it is equally obvious that such a right to be fully useful must be a real and not just a personal right. But in the Roman framework such a real right could only be a servitude or at least be like a servitude. In the circumstances, the recognition of a servitude of support was virtually inevitable—it would reflect nothing but discredit on the quality of the Roman jurists if no such right had been recognized. If this be accepted, then it should be observed that this servitude would give rise to practical difficulties absent from other servitudes and it is simply the attempts to meet these difficulties which account for the conflict of views between Gallus and Servius in D. 8. 5. 6. 2 and for the final position that the owner of the servient tenement is bound to keep the wall in sufficient repair. If this servitude were treated like any other, then the impracticable factual situation would arise that there would be two persons who were responsible for the upkeep of the wall or part of the wall, but neither was bound to, and neither had an action against the other to compel him to, repair, nor an action to recover expenses if he himself repaired. The owner of the servient tenement would, of course, be responsible for the upkeep of the wall in so far as he wanted to use it for any purpose, and in virtually every case where a servitude *oneris ferendi* came into existence the servient wall would have been there before, built for the purposes of the owner of the land. But as we have seen, especially from the texts concerning interdicts, the owner of the dominant tenement has the responsibility of seeing that the corporeal aspects of his servitude

[1] Cf., even for earlier views, Buckland, *Textbook*, pp. 259 f.; Solazzi, *Requisiti*, pp. 19 ff.; *Specie*, pp. 62 ff.

were kept in proper order. Accordingly, there was here a fruitful field for squabbles. An owner could feel great moral indignation if he repaired and the person in right of the servitude refused to make a contribution. And if the owner did repair, was he to be forced to repair in a way convenient to the person in right of the servitude despite the latter's refusal to contribute? Or the owner might fail to repair in the hope that the person in right of the servitude might find himself forced to carry out the repair to save his own building from collapse. And if the owner were willing to let the wall—which was also useful to him—fall into such disrepair that the servitude could not be exercised, was the other party to be forced either to repair or to allow *usucapio* of freedom from the servitude?[1] Hence, special rules of some sort were virtually a necessity. It could not be enough to let the difficulties be settled by contract which had only a personal and not a real effect since in time third parties would take over ownership of the *praedia*. It is against this background that we must see the dispute between Gallus and Servius. Gallus, apparently, wanted this servitude to be treated like the others in respect of repairs: the owner of the dominant tenement was not to be able to compel the owner of the servient tenement to repair. Because of the practical difficulties involved in treating this like other servitudes, Servius held that in this case an action could be brought to compel the owner of the servient land to repair the wall so that it would support the burden.[2] The dispute between Gallus and Servius does show that by the middle of the first century B.C. the servitude *oneris ferendi* was recognized. It seems very probable that when the servitude was first accepted it was regarded as being the same as others in respect of repairs, that Gallus was maintaining the original position, while Servius pressed for alteration.

D. 8. 2. 33 gives us again the opinion of Servius. Servius or Alfenus is also concerned with the correct interpretation of the clause '*paries oneri ferundo uti nunc est, ita sit*'. It is naturally and reasonably held that it means not that there must be the same wall

[1] For *usucapio* of freedom see D. 8. 2. 7 (Pomponius, 26 *ad Quintum Mucium*): *supra*, pp. 181 f.

[2] Labeo, of course, allows the defendant to relinquish the wall instead of repairing.

for ever, but that there must always be a wall capable of supporting the burden.[1,2]

Where the parties were Roman citizens and the *praedia* in question were in Italy[3] those servitudes which were *res mancipi* could be created by *mancipatio* and *in iure cessio* and those which were *res nec mancipi* could be constituted by *in iure cessio*.

D. 8. 4. 15 (Paul, 1 *epit. Alfeni dig.*). Qui per certum locum iter aut actum alicui cessisset, eum pluribus per eundem locum vel iter vel actum cedere posse verum est: quemadmodum si quis vicino suas aedes servas fecisset, nihilo minus aliis quot vellet multis eas aedes servas facere potest.

Here the *cessisset* and the *cedere* allude to an *in iure cessio*.[4] One can easily understand that doubt may have been felt whether, after *in iure cessio* of an *iter* or *actus* had been made, there could be further *in iure cessiones* of *iter* or *actus* over the same route. The owner of two estates might in the *mancipatio* of one either reserve a servitude right for the estate he was retaining[5] or grant a servitude over that one for the benefit of the estate being transferred.[6] Whether in D. 8. 2. 33[7] from *nam cum* a servitude in favour of the house being sold is being created or an existing one is being declared, the text has a special significance in that although a right declared in the *mancipatio* is under examination what is chosen as the basis of discussion is the wording not of the *mancipatio* but of the written document (*nam cum in lege aedium ita scriptum esset*) evidencing the *mancipatio*—a strong indication that in questions relating to the interpretation of the actual words used it was natural to turn to the written document as the most reliable evidence of the words

[1] According to Lenel, *ut servitutem . . . sustineret* is a gloss: *Pal.*, i. 51, n. 2.

[2] Cicero, *pro Rosc. Amer.* 9. 24 shows that there could be an *iter ad sepulchrum*. This was a real right but differed from a servitude in that there was no dominant tenement: see now, De Visscher, *Le Droit des tombeaux romains* (Milan, 1963), pp. 83 ff. and the authors he cites.

[3] Cf. G. 2. 29. We have no cases for our period of servitudes on land outside Italy or where the parties were not Roman citizens.

[4] Cf. Lenel, *Pal.* i. 45, n. 2; De Sarlo, *Alfeno Varo e i suoi digesta* (Milan, 1940), pp. 78 f.

[5] D. 8. 3. 30 (Paul, 4 *epit. Alfeni dig*).: *supra*, pp. 184 ff.

[6] D. 8. 3. 29 (Paul, 2 *epit. Alfeni dig.*): *supra*, p. 195.

[7] *Supra*, pp. 198 f.

used.[1] Although there is no direct evidence for the later Republic there is no reason to doubt that then, as later, servitudes could also be created by a legacy *per vindicationem* or by the decision of a *iudex* in a divisory action.[2] Until the *lex Scribonia*,[3] perhaps of 50 B.C., there could be *usucapio* of servitudes.

We have already seen from D. 8. 2. 7 (Pomponius, 26 *ad Quintum Mucium*)[4] that for the extinction of a servitude of *lumen* or *prospectus* it was not enough that there be non-use for the prescribed period but the servient tenement had to usucapt freedom from the servitude. D. 8. 6. 7 (Paul, 13 *ad Plautium*), on the other hand, shows that for the extinction of *aquae ductus* non-use for the prescribed period was enough.

Si sic constituta sit aqua, ut vel aestate ducatur tantum vel uno mense, quaeritur quemadmodum non utendo amittatur, quia non est continuum tempus, quo cum uti non [non *del. Mommsen*] potest, non sit usus. itaque et si alternis annis vel mensibus quis aquam habeat, duplicato constituto tempore amittitur. idem et de itinere custoditur. si vero alternis diebus aut die toto aut tantum nocte, statuto legibus tempore amittitur, quia una servitus est: nam et si alternis horis vel una hora cottidie servitutem habeat, Servius scribit perdere eum non utendo servitutem, quia id quod habet cottidianum sit.

We are interested only in the opinion of Servius[5] that if there is a right to draw water only at alternate hours or for one hour per day, the servitude will be lost by non-use, during the normal period for *usucapio*. Naturally, this situation could only be discussed when it was settled that in the ordinary case of *aquae ductus* where the water could be drawn continuously through the day non-use would lead to extinction.[6,7]

[1] Cf. D. 17. 1. 1. 2: Watson, *Contract of Mandate in Roman Law* (Oxford, 1961), pp. 61 f.

[2] Cf. Kaser, *RPR* i. 373.

[3] Cf. *supra*, pp. 22 ff., 164 ff.

[4] *Supra*, pp. 181 f.

[5] For suggestions of interpolations in other parts of the text see *Index Itp.*

[6] Nothing can be learned from D. 50. 16. 157 (Aelius Gallus, 1 *de verborum quae ad ius pertinent significatione*). '*Paries*' *est, sive murus sive maceria est.* 1. *Item 'via' est, sive semita sive iter est.* The conjunction of *paries* and *via* might lead one to think that he is considering the meaning of these words in connection with servitudes but his description of *via* is against this.

[7] Nothing more for servitudes can be deduced from D. 21. 2. 75 (Venuleius, 16 *stip.*); D. 18. 1. 59 (Celsus, 8 *dig.*); Cicero, *de orat.*, 1. 39. 178; *de off.* 3. 16. 67 [for all these, see Watson, *Obligations*, pp. 79 f.]; *de leg. agrar.* 3. 2. 9. For Cicero, *top.* 5. 27 see *supra*, pp. 14 f.

9

USUSFRUCTUS AND SIMILAR RIGHTS

Ususfructus

No reasonably satisfactory solution of the problem of the origins of usufruct has so far been advanced and it is not intended to go into the matter here.[1] It can, indeed, be shown that in all likelihood usufruct was already in existence by the beginning of the second century B.C. The evidence is in Plautus, *Casina*, 836 f.[2]

> LYSIDAMUS: meum corculum, melculum, verculum. OLYMPIO: heus tu, malo, si sapis, cavebis;
> meast haec. LY. scio, sed meus fructust prior.

Lysidamus and Olympio are both contending for the favours of the supposed slave girl. What is significant in the text is that when Olympio claims that the supposed girl is his—she has been promised to him in marriage[3]—Lysidamus concedes this and says, *scio, sed meus fructust prior*. There seems to be a deliberate contrast, for humorous purposes, between *mea est* and *meus fructus est*. Perhaps we should not take the legal joke so far as to see in *mea est* a reference to the form of the *vindicatio* and in *meus fructus est* a reference to the *vindicatio ususfructus*, but a claim to the right to the fruits is certainly put in opposition to a claim of 'ownership'. Even though this be accepted it might be suggested that the text is not good evidence for the existence of the legal institution of usufruct[4] but merely shows that it was known that there could be situations where one person was owner and another was entitled

[1] The most common view is that usufruct was introduced because of the growth of marriage *sine manu*: the widow in such a marriage had not entered her husband's *familia* and so did not, as she did if married *cum manu*, share in the succession with the *familia*. But the arguments adduced for this view are not valid: cf. Watson, *Tijd.* xxxi (1963) 614.

[2] Cf., e.g., Kaser, *EB*, p. 306, n. 10; Wesener, *RE* ix A, s.v. *usus fructus*, 1138.

[3] Cf. 67 ff.

[4] Masson would seem to deny any legal significance to the text: 'Essai sur la conception de l'usufruit', *RHD* xiii (1934) 3, n. 2.

to the fruits, e.g. where the owner sold to another his right to fruits;[1] or where a *res mancipi* was transferred by *traditio* but the recipient took a stipulation *uti frui habere possidere licere*.[2] Such a suggestion would not, I feel, have a great deal of force. Such separations of ownership and enjoyment are relatively much more technical and this aspect of the joke would not be readily understood by the audience if they were the situations in Plautus' mind. Where a non-jurist separates ownership from enjoyment and puts them in opposition it is most natural to believe that he is thinking of usufruct.[3]

The other text of Plautus, *Mercator* 830 ff., which is sometimes also adduced as evidence that usufruct then existed,[4] has little force.

> CHARINUS: Limen superum inferumque, salve, simul atque vale:
> hunc hodie postremum extollo mea domo patria pedem.
> usus, fructus, victus, cultus iam mihi harunc aedium
> interemptust, interfectust, alienatust. occidi!

It is, of course, true that *fructus* is not used in its 'objective' sense of 'fruits',[5] and that the words *usus* and *fructus* appear together. But we must not forget that the stipulation taken against eviction in sale normally ran something like *uti frui habere possidere licere* and that statutes granting enjoyment of land also spoke of *uti frui habere possidere* or had similar formulations[6] and that neither the stipulations nor the statutes are concerned with *ususfructus*. This usage, in all probability, is very old and shows that *usus* and *fructus* may be used in conjunction to mean something like 'use and enjoyment' without referring to usufruct and without implying its existence.[7]

[1] Cf. Cato, *de agri cultura* 150.

[2] For the meaning of the expression *uti frui habere possidere*, cf. Kaser, *EB*, pp. 321 f.

[3] Most recently against the idea of any reference to *ususfructus* in the text is Marrone, 'La posizione possessoria del nudo proprietario nel diritto romano', *Annali Palermo* xxviii (1961) 18, n. 6 (at p. 19). He says: 'Nel *Casina*, con le parole *meus fructust prior* Lisidano contende ad Olimpio l'amore di una donna, e a null'altro fa riferimento che al godimento (*fructus*), che egli pensa di avere della donna stessa.' But this is to ignore the contrast *mea est, meus fructus est*.

[4] e.g. Kaser, *EB*, p. 306, n. 10; Wesener, loc. cit.

[5] Cf. Bretone, *La nozione romana di usufrutto I, Dalle origini a Diocleziano* (Naples, 1962), pp. 39 ff.

[6] e.g. *lex agraria* (of 111 B.C.) 9, 10, 11, etc.; *lex Antonia de Termessibus* (of 71 B.C.) 24, 26, 31, 35.

[7] Cf. Marrone, loc. cit.; Bretone, op. cit.

A third text which on occasion is adduced as showing the early existence of *ususfructus*[1] is *fructus ovium hac lege venire oportet* from Cato, *de agri cultura* 150, which was written around 160 B.C. The whole text runs:

> Fructum ovium hac lege venire oportet. In singulas casei p.i.s. dimidium aridum, lacte feriis quod mulserit dimidium, et praeterea lactis urnam i. Hisce legibus agnus diem et noctem qui vixerit, in fructum, et Kal. Iun. emptor fructu decedat. Si interkalatum erit, K. Mais. Agnos xxx ne amplius promittat. Oves quae non pepererint, binae pro singulis in fructu cedent. Die lanam et agnos vendat, menses x ab coactore releget. Porcos scrarios in oves denas singulos pascat. Conductor ii menses pastorem praebeat. Donec domino satisfecerit, aut solverit, pigneri esto.

The text, as I think no one would deny, is concerned not with *ususfructus*, but with the sale of *fructus* of a flock. *Ususfructus* could not be created by sale, and all that is involved is a contractual, not a real, right, But does the text provide any indication that *ususfructus* either did then exist or did not exist? For the former view, all that the text can directly indicate is that the economic idea of *fructus* was in existence, but this is of little help since that concept must, logically, be prior in time to the legal right of *ususfructus*. No argument can be drawn from the clause *agnos xxx ne amplius promittat*.[1] The usufructuary did have—at least in classical law, for there is no direct evidence for the Republic—the duty of keeping up the flock in a *ususfructus gregis* but it is not surprising to find the same duty, with a certain restriction, suggested as a clause for the contract of the sale of *fructus* of a flock. It is natural for the seller of the *fructus* to want his flock kept up to strength and such a clause could easily develop as a common term in a sale of *fructus* even without the example of *ususfructus*.[2] Masson has produced an argument for holding that the text indicates that *ususfructus* did not then exist.[3] He says that if the legal theory of usufruct had existed it would not have been necessary to indicate in a *lex* what

[1] e.g. Kaser, loc. cit.; Wesener, loc. cit.

[2] The subject of *promittat* is *emptor*: cf. von Lübtow, 'Catos *leges venditioni et locationi dictae*', *Eos* xlviii (1957) 227 ff. at p. 347; followed by Watson, *Obligations*, p. 45, n. 5.

[3] Op. cit., p. 4, n. 1.

are the *fructus* of a flock (. . . *hisce legibus agnus diem et noctem qui vixerit*) nor even to make a special *lex*. But there is, I think, a special reason for specifying that a lamb which lives for a day and a night is to be regarded as part of the *fructus*. That clause is to be treated in conjunction with *oves, quae non pepererint, binae pro singulis in fructu cedent*. Sheep which do not produce young are to be counted two for one and the point of *hisce . . . in fructum* is that the only young which are to be counted are those which live for a day and a night.[1] Hence, this part of the text does not provide an argument for the view that *ususfructus* did not yet exist.

That *ususfructus*, however, did certainly exist by the middle of the second century B.C. is proved by the dispute between P. Scaevola (consul 133 B.C.) and M'. Manilius (consul 149 B.C.) on the one hand, and M. Brutus (praetor 142 B.C.) on the other, as to whether the *partus ancillae* was to be regarded *in fructu*.[2] The question seems to have been raised specifically in respect of usufruct.[3]

The normal method of creating a usufruct was by legacy.[4] It is sometimes said that originally usufruct was always created by legacy[5] but there is no indication that there ever was such a legal restriction on its creation. The sole text concerned with the Republic which shows usufruct being created by some other means is D. 40. 12. 23 pr. (Paul, 50 *ad ed.*) where the mode is *in iure cessio*.[6] Of the other modes possible in the Empire—by *adiudicatio* in a divisory action, by *mancipatio* or *in iure cessio* or *legatum* of a thing,

[1] Considerable difficulties arise if one accepts Thielscher's reconstruction of the text [*Des Marcus Cato Belehrung über die Landwirtschaft* (Berlin, 1963), p. 150]: *hisce legibus: agnus, diem et noctem qui vixerit. in fructum* ⟨*Kalendis Sextilibus emptor veniat*⟩ *et Kal*(*endis*) *Iun*(*iis*) *emptor fructu decedat*. No sense can now be made of *hisce . . . vixerit*. As von Lübtow points out [op. cit., p. 346] one cannot connect it with the preceding terms about what has to be given to the seller (though a more compelling argument would be that one should then have had the accusative *agnum*). But von Lübtow's own explanation, that *hisce . . . vixerit* is out of place and should come after *agnos xxx ne amplius promittat* seems far too drastic.

[2] Cicero, *de fin.* 1. 4. 12; D. 7. 1. 68 pr. (Ulpian, 17 *ad Sab.*): cf. *infra*, pp. 214 ff.

[3] Cf. D. 7. 1. 68 pr.: cf. Kaser, '*Partus ancillae*', *ZSS* lxxv (1959) 156 ff. at p. 159.

[4] Cicero, *top.* 3. 17; 4. 21; *pro Caecina* 4. 11; V.F. 68; 70; D. 32. 2. 31; 33. 2. 12; 35. 2. 1. 9. To judge from the texts concerned with the Empire in V.F. 41–93, the legacy was usually *per vindicationem*.

[5] Buckland, *Textbook*, p. 271.

[6] On the text see now Watson, *Persons*, pp. 166 ff.

deducto usu fructo—there is no sign, but that need not be significant.

The most common case would seem to be a legacy of usufruct by the testator to his widow. There is no reason to think that this happened always or even in the main where the marriage was *sine manu*. Where the marriage was *cum manu* a legacy of usufruct would also be desirable, for instance if the husband for any reason did want to make a will (for then the wife *in manu* would not succeed automatically to a share as on intestacy), or, where he had a number of children, if he wanted her to continue living in the matrimonial home in the style to which she was accustomed.[1,2]

Ususfructus was a very personal right and could not survive the usufructuary.[3] A definition of a later period runs: *Usus fructus est ius alienis rebus utendi fruendi salva rerum substantia.*[4] The requirement that the substance of the object of the usufruct be unimpaired had three important implications. First, the usufructuary's rights to make alterations in the object of the usufruct were restricted. There is no information on this proposition for the Republic. Secondly, there could be no usufruct in respect of things which are consumed by use. Thirdly, if the object of the usufruct perished, or if its character altered radically, no matter how this occurred, the usufruct would end.

The impossibility of having a usufruct over things which were consumed by use was altered at some point by a *senatusconsultum*. Kaser says that *ususfructus* must have originated with landed estates as the typical fruit-bearing things—the interdicts for the protection of *uti frui* are all framed on the interdicts for land, and also a formless mode of creation which would be appropriate for *res nec mancipi* was unknown, at least in the older law. All the same, he goes on, Cicero knew of a *bonorum suorum usufructum legare* and

[1] Cf. Watson, *Tijd.* xxxi (1963) 614.

[2] The line of Lucretius, *de rer. nat.* 3. 971, *Vitaque mancipio nulli datur, omnibus usu*, although obviously referring to *ususfructus* (as the contrast with *mancipium* shows) tells us nothing for the legal aspects of usufruct.

[3] No textual authority for the Republic, but none is needed. Nor are there any texts on the effect of *capitis deminutio* or of an attempt by the usufructuary to sell his usufruct.

[4] D. 7. 1. 1 (Paul, 3 *ad Vitellium*); J. 2. 4 pr. We need not consider here how far the definition is classical.

Gaius tells us of a *senatusconsultum, ut omnium rerum, quas in cuiusque patrimonio esse constaret, usus fructus legari possit*, but the dating of this is uncertain. This usufruct in the whole inheritance, he says, was understood as a usufruct in the individual things of the inheritance, and therefore presupposes a usufruct of moveables.[1] But this position, at least in some aspects, seems doubtful. Kaser seems to be saying, if I understand him correctly, that originally there could be neither a usufruct over moveables alone, nor a usufruct which included moveables; and that the first evidence of a usufruct which included moveables is in Cicero, *top.* 3. 17 and *pro Caecina* 4. 11, the Ciceronian texts to which he refers.[2] But Cicero's own *de fin.* 1. 4. 12 which is concerned with the dispute between P. Scaevola, M'. Manilius, and M. Brutus as to whether the *partus ancillae* was to count as *fructus* or not[3] shows that as early as the middle of the second century B.C. there could, at least, be usufruct which included moveables. And if Plautus, *Casina*, 836 f., does refer to *ususfructus*[4] (as Kaser himself thinks) then it must have been possible for usufruct to include moveables as early as the time of Plautus. It is also very doubtful whether the proposition—if this is Kaser's point—that even originally *ususfructus* was restricted to immoveables[5] is correct. The argument from the nature of the interdicts granted for the protection of usufruct is not very helpful. First, interdicts in general seem to have been thought of primarily—though by no means exclusively—as being for the protection of land.[6] It would not be surprising for

[1] Kaser, *RPR* i. 377: 'Dem Gegenstand nach dürfte der ususfructus von den Grundstücken als den typisch fruchttragenden Sachen ausgegangen sein; die zum Schutz des 'uti frui' geschaffenen Interdikte sind sämtlich den Grundstücksinterdikten nachgebildet, auch ist eine formlose Bestellungsart, wie sie den res nec mancipi angemessen wäre, mindestens dem älteren Recht unbekannt. Immerhin weiß schon Cicero von einem 'bonorum suorum usumfructum legare' und Gaius berichtet vom SC '*ut omnium rerum, quas in cuiusque patrimonio esse constaret, usus fructus legari possit*', doch ist die Datierung unsicher. Dieser Nießbrauch am Gesamtnachlaß wird als solcher an den einzeln darin enthaltenen Gegenständen aufgefaßt, er setzt mithin den Nießbrauch an beweglichen Sachen bereits voraus.'

[2] *RPR* i. 377, n. 12.

[3] Cf. D. 7. 1. 68 pr.: *supra*, p. 206 and nn. 2, 3: *infra*, pp. 215 ff.

[4] Cf. *supra*, pp. 203 f.

[5] Though apparently followed by Wesener, *RE*, ix A, 1154.

[6] See the interdicts in Lenel, *EP*, pp. 446 ff.

interdicts to protect the usufruct of a *fundus* only, even though there could be usufruct of moveables. Secondly, for Kaser's argument to have any force, the interdicts must have been issued before moveables could be included in a usufruct. As we have seen, moveables could be so included from around the middle of the second century B.C. at the latest. The interdicts in question are not evidenced before Ulpian and Paul,[1] that is, not before the end of the second century A.D. Even apart from the total lack of evidence for their existence in the Republic it is *a priori* extremely unlikely that they could have emerged before the middle of the second century B.C. It is very difficult to conceive of them as being early. They inevitably presuppose the recognition of *possessio* as a legal concept fundamental to the idea of interdictal protection; that the usufructuary has no *possessio*, and so cannot use the ordinary interdicts; but that, nevertheless, he deserves interdictal possession. Kaser's other argument—the absence of a formless mode of creation which would be in keeping for *res nec mancipi*—is, if anything, even less persuasive. Considering the incorporeal nature of usufruct, an informal mode of creation *inter vivos* is really out of the question. And the formality of the *legatum* is due to the nature of *legatum* and has nothing to do with *ususfructus* itself.[2]

There can be no doubt that the *senatusconsultum* to which Kaser refers caused usufruct (or quasi-usufruct) to be recognized in things consumed or diminished by use. And also it should be agreed that Cicero, *top*. 3. 17, does not accept the existence of such a usufruct (or quasi-usufruct):

> Ex contrario autem sic: Non debet ea mulier, cui vir bonorum suorum usum fructum legavit, cellis vinariis et oleariis plenis relictis, putare id ad se pertinere. Usus enim, non abusus, legatus est. [Ea sunt inter se contraria.]

The *topica* were written in 44 B.C.[3] Unfortunately, however, this does not enable us to conclude that the *senatusconsultum* was not

[1] V.F. 90; 91; 92; D. 43. 16. 3. 13–18 (Ulpian, 69 *ad ed.*); *h.t.* 9. 1 (Paul, 65 *ad ed.*).

[2] And I do not think it would ever be argued that the formalities of *legatum* show that originally there could only be a legacy of *res mancipi*.

[3] Perhaps the possibility that Cicero was concerned with a rule which was already out of date should not be ignored.

then in existence. The terms of the *senatusconsultum* are not clear. The implication of one text, D. 7. 5. 1 (Ulpian, 18 *ad Sab.*), is that the *senatusconsultum* laid down that there could be a usufruct of everything which was in someone's patrimony, and it was juristic interpretation of this which established that there could be a legacy of the usufruct in these things which are consumed or diminished by use. One cannot tell whether the text is closely following the wording of the *senatusconsultum* or not.[1] Nor if it is, can one know that legacies of a usufruct *omnium rerum* were previously impossible. Such legacies may very well have been possible (and even normal) but things which were consumed or diminished by use may have been treated as falling outside the legacy, and the point of the *senatusconsultum*—even framed in this way—may have been to extend the usufruct to things *quae usu tolluntur vel minuuntur*. Two other texts, however, *Epit. Ulp.* 24. 27 and J. 2. 4. 2, give the impression that the *senatusconsultum* expressly said that there could be a legacy of usufruct in such things provided a *cautio* was given to the heir. If this is how the *senatusconsultum* ran there is no reason to doubt that previously there could be legacies of *ususfructus omnium rerum* which, however, was not considered to extend to such things. There seems no way of deciding whether D. 7. 5. 1 or *Epit. Ulp.* 24. 27 and J. 2. 4. 2 give a more accurate picture of the tenor of the *senatusconsultum*, and so one cannot tell whether it existed in the Republic or not.[2] What one can say, however, is that legacies of *ususfructus omnium rerum* were certainly known sometime before 70 B.C.

Cicero, *pro Caecina* 4. 11. . . . Moritur Fulcinius—multa enim, quae sunt in re, quia remota sunt a causa, praetermittam—testamento facit heredem, quem habebat e Caesennia filium; usum et fructum omnium bonorum suorum Caesenniae legat ut frueretur una cum filio.

[1] Two other texts, D. 33. 2. 1 (Paul, 3 *ad Sab.*) and 35. 2. 69 (Pomponius, 5 *ad Sab.*), give no indication of how the *senatusconsultum* was framed and, in particular, do not show that the tenor was as suggested by D. 7. 5. 1: *contra*, Grosso, *Usufrutto e figure affini nel diritto romano*, 2nd edn. (Turin, 1958), p. 412.

[2] The general view is that the *senatusconsultum* dates from the Empire: e.g. Arangio-Ruiz, now *Istituzioni di diritto romano*, 14th edn. (Naples, 1960), p. 240; Grosso, op. cit., p. 411; *contra*, Volterra, *Nuovo digesto italiano* xii. 1. 33 (*senatusconsulta*, no. 40); non-committal, Kaser, *RPR* i. 377 and n. 14.

The *pro Caecina* was delivered in 69 B.C., and the present text tells us that Fulcinius left a legacy of the usufruct *omnium bonorum suorum* to his widow. By the time of the oration not only was Fulcinius dead but so also was his widow Caesennia, who had had time to remarry, so Fulcinius' will must have been composed at the latest before 70 B.C. Although such legacies were recognized so early, *top*. 3. 17, as we have seen, shows that in 44 B.C. they were not treated as including in the usufruct things which are consumed or diminished by use.

The remaining implication of the requirement that the substance of the object of the usufruct be unimpaired was that if the object of the usufruct perishes, or if its character alters radically, no matter how this occurs, the usufruct ends. For the proposition that the usufruct ends if its object completely and irrevocably perishes we have proof, if any is needed, in Cicero, *top*. 3. 15,[1] which says, *inter alia*, that if a slave who is the object of the usufruct should die, the heir is not bound to replace him. Where, however, what was in issue was the radical alteration of the character of the object of the usufruct there was much difficult learning and subtle distinctions. Two texts relate to our period.

D. 33. 2. 12 (Alfenus Varus, 2 *dig. a Paulo epit.*). Heres in fundo, cuius usus fructus legatus est, villam posuit: eam invito fructuario demolire non potest, nihilo magis quam si, quam arborem posuisset, ex fundo is evellere vellet: sed si antequam usufructuarius prohibuerit, demolierit, impune facturum.

All that interests us in the text at the moment is the fact that where a country house is built (by the heir) on an estate, the usufruct of the estate does not terminate. Since the heir cannot demolish the house against the wishes of the usufructuary, the usufructuary's rights, and so the usufruct, must still exist. The alteration to the object of the usufruct in this case is insufficiently radical. To judge from a text concerned with the Empire, D. 7. 1. 53 (Iavolenus, 2 *epist.*), the principle was that if *mutatio rei* occurred only for part of the object, the usufruct was not extinguished.[2] That text says that if the legacy of a usufruct of a tenement is left to anyone, he

[1] Quoted and discussed *infra*, p. 217.

[2] Cf. Grosso, op. cit., p. 384.

retains the usufruct of the whole ground (*totius soli*) so long as any part of the tenement remains.

D. 7. 1. 71 (Marcellus, 17 *dig.*). Si in area, cuius usus fructus alienus esset, quis aedificasset, intra tempus quo usus fructus perit superficie sublata restitui usum fructum veteres responderunt.

This text, if it is genuine, tells us in effect that the *veteres* held that if a piece of open ground (*area*) which was the object of usufruct were built on, the usufruct would cease to exist, but that if the building were removed within two years the usufruct would be restored (*restitui*). The text does not really make it plain with the verb *restitui* whether in the meantime the usufruct was quiescent, or whether it was fully extinguished but could be restored. The substance of the text is held interpolated by Guarneri Citati,[1] who with some slight hesitation is apparently followed by Grosso.[2] Guarneri Citati would excise *intra tempus quo usus fructus perit* and insert *non* before *restitui* so that the *veteres* would have been deciding that by the erection of the building on the *area*, the usufruct would be extinguished once and for all. The main argument for the interpolation is drawn from the catena, D. 7. 4. 5. 3 to 7. 4. 7.

(Ulpian, 17 *ad Sab.*). Si areae sit usus fructus legatus et in ea aedificium sit positum, rem mutari et usum fructum extingui constat. plane si proprietarius hoc fecit, ex testamento vel de dolo tenebitur.

7. 4. 6 (Pomponius, 5 *ad Sab.*). (sed et interdictum quod vi aut clam usufructuario competit)

7. 4. 7 (Julian, 35 *dig.*). nisi sublato aedificio usum fructum areae mihi cesserit, tempore scilicet quo usus fructus perit transacto.

In D. 7. 4. 7, *tempore scilicet quo usus fructus perit transacto* is said, rightly, to appear interpolated. So the similar idea in D. 7. 1. 71 can also be held interpolated.[3] Unfortunately, one cannot convincingly argue in so uncomplicated a fashion. It is, of course, true that *tempore scilicet quo usus fructus perit transacto* does look compilatorial but this may be due to nothing other than a shortening of the

[1] *Annali Messina* i. 99 ff.; *SDHI* iii (1937) 208 ff.

[2] Grosso, op. cit., pp. 384 ff.

[3] It should be noted that Grosso is much too cautious to accept the idea without reserve. He says (p. 386): 'Noi non riteniamo di poter senz'altro respingere la ricostruzione del Guarneri Citati.'

text with no alteration in substance. A splendidly clear example of this sort of thing appears in D. 9. 2. 27. 10 (Ulpian, 18 *ad ed.*) with its very odd *scilicet si paries exusta sit* which, however, as *Coll.* 12. 7. 8 shows, does correspond to part of the original text.[1] It would be risky enough to argue that in D. 7. 4. 7 itself the form of *tempore . . . transacto* means that the substance must also have been altered, but it is even more rash to use the argument to prove the substantive interpolation of D. 7. 1. 71 which does not look suspicious.[2] On the balance of probabilities, D. 7. 1. 71 would appear genuine in substance.[3]

The usufructuary's rights were to use the object of the usufruct and enjoy its fruits. What was to count as fruits was often a delicate question.

D. 7. 1. 9. 7 (Ulpian, 17 *ad Sab.*). Instrumenti autem fructum habere debet: vendendi tamen facultatem non habet. nam et si fundi usus fructus fuerit legatus et sit ager, unde palo in fundum, cuius usus fructus legatus est, solebat pater familias uti, vel salice vel harundine, puto fructuarium hactenus uti posse, ne ex eo vendat, nisi forte salicti ei vel silvae palaris vel harundineti usus fructus sit legatus: tunc enim et vendere potest. nam et Trebatius scribit silvam caeduam et harundinetum posse fructuarium caedere, sicut pater familias caedebat, et vendere, licet pater familias non solebat vendere, sed ipse uti: ad modum enim referendum est, non ad qualitatem utendi.

If the usufruct of an estate is left and there is a field whose wood for stakes, willows, or reeds were used by the testator for the needs of the estate (*in fundum*) then, the text says, the usufructuary can use but not sell them, unless a usufruct was left by legacy of a plantation of willows, a wood intended to provide stakes, or a bed of reeds. For, the text goes on—and this is the part which concerns us—, Trebatius writes that the usufructuary can cut wood which is meant for cutting and a thicket of reeds just as the testator did, and he can sell them even though the testator did not sell them but used them himself. Presumably, if the text is genuine, Trebatius would accept the distinction made in the preceding part of the

[1] On the texts, see now Watson, *Tijd.* xxx (1962) 290 ff.

[2] Though *tempus quo usus fructus perit* may originally have read *biennium*: cf. Lenel, *Pal.* i. 620, n. 3; Cavin, *L'Extinction de l'usufruit rei mutatione* (Lausanne, 1933), p. 86.

[3] Cf. Kaser, *RPR* i. 379, n. 39.

text. There is, however, the view that the substance of the text is interpolated and that Ulpian and Trebatius would only allow the usufructuary the right to sell if the testator had been accustomed to sell. This is the proposal of Riccobono, who reconstructs in this way V.F. 70 which corresponds to the latter part of the text.[1] But Grosso rightly points out[2] that V.F. 70 has such great lacunae that it permits the most different reconstructions and so it provides no support for the substance of the original text. Grosso also observes that Riccobono's view would take away from the Romans all the subtlety of analysis in the text.[3]

D. 7. 1. 11 (Paul, 2 *epit. Alfeni dig.*). Sed si grandes arbores essent, non posse eas caedere.

To judge from its present position after *h.t.* 10—which is all we have to go on—Alfenus was probably making the point that for the uses of the estate branches and even small trees could be cut down, but large trees could not be felled.

Incidentally, we know from D. 50. 16. 30 pr. (Gaius, 7 *ad ed. prov.*) what would count as *silva caedua* in the eyes of Servius: . . . *Servius eam esse, quae succisa rursus ex stirpibus aut radicibus renascitur*. Lenel[4] would place this text in that part of Gaius' 7th book on the provincial edict which dealt with servitudes, but it is not unlikely that at least the part of the text which is printed came from Gaius' discussion of usufruct in the same book.[5]

Where the usufruct of an *ancilla* was left, it was early discussed whether any child born to her belonged to the usufructuary or to the owner of the *ancilla*.

Cicero, *de fin.* 1. 4. 12. An partus sitne in fructu habendus, disseretur inter principes civitatis, P. Scaevolam, M'. Manilium, ab hisque M. Brutus dissentiet, quod et acutum genus est, et ad usum civium non inutile: . . .

[1] '*Vaticana Fragmenta* 70[1]', now in *Scritti di diritto romano* (Palermo, 1957), i. 187 ff. Riccobono's reconstruction of V.F. 70 is accepted by Girard, *Textes de droit romain*, 6th edn. by Senn (Paris, 1937), pp. 524 f.; and it also appears in *FIRA* ii. 478.

[2] *Usufrutto e figure affini nel diritto romano*, p. 126; followed by Wieacker, *Textstufen klassischer Juristen* (Göttingen, 1960), p. 288, n. 52.

[3] Op. cit., p. 129.

[4] *Pal.* i. 204.

[5] Cf. D. 7. 1. 9. 7 (Ulpian, 17 *ad Sab.*); *h.t.* 10 (Pomponius, 5 *ad Sab.*); *h.t.* 48. 1 (Paul, 9 *ad Plautium*); 7. 4. 10. 4 (Ulpian, 17 *ad Sab.*).

D. 7. 1. 68 pr. (Ulpian, 17 *ad Sab.*). Vetus fuit quaestio, an partus ad fructuarium pertineret: sed Bruti sententia optinuit fructuarium in eo locum non habere: neque enim in fructu hominis homo esse potest. hac ratione nec usum fructum in eo fructuarius habebit. quid tamen si fuerit etiam partus usus fructus relictus, an habeat in eo usum fructum? et cum possit partus legari, poterit et usus fructus eius.

Thus, around the middle of the second century B.C., P. Scaevola and M'. Manilius must have held that the child did belong to the usufructuary, but M. Brutus argued that it belonged to the owner of the *ancilla*. It has been suggested that the form of the Cicero text shows that the matter was still not settled in the first half of 45 B.C. when the *De finibus* was written[1] and Sturm goes so far as to hold that the text shows that Brutus' opinion was still isolated.[2] All this is completely unjustified. At the beginning of the *De finibus*, Cicero attempts a justification of the study of philosophy. One of his points is that law, a discipline of far less importance, is regarded as a perfectly proper study even by the most important men in the state. Hence the present text. Three leaders of the Roman State discussed and disagreed on a petty point of law. Which view prevailed—if either did—is not important for him.[3] Even if much closer to Cicero's own time leading jurists had pronounced on the question there would be no good reason to mention them. At any rate, as D. 7. 1. 68 pr. shows, the view of Brutus prevailed. Kaser suggests,[4] following Brini, that in this text the reason for the decision, though it is formulated as Ulpian's own assertion, could go back to Brutus. This is possible but not provable. Kaser further thinks that the reason relates to a concept of fruits which does not permit the fruit to have the same form as the producer of the fruit. Accordingly, he says, the young of animals should not be counted as fruit and, in fact, he goes on, Ulpian does not find it consistent (*tamen* in § 1) that the founders of the Sabinian school count the young of animals as fruit in the case of a usufruct. But the *tamen* in § 1 is capable of a simpler explanation. It is used merely to underline

[1] Arangio-Ruiz, *Ciceroniana, rivista di studi ciceroniani* i. (1959), 10; Sturm, *RIDA* ix (1962) 405.

[2] Loc. cit.

[3] This is not to bring Cicero's knowledge of law into question.

[4] '*Partus ancillae*', 157.

that the decisions in respect of *partus ancillae* and *fetus pecorum* are different. Nor is there any need for such an abstract interpretation of the reason for the decision in the *principium*. It may simply show the moral feeling or philosophical idea that a human being should not be regarded as *fructus*.[1] There are, as it happens, no texts on the ownership of *fetus pecorum*, but I have no doubt that they went to the usufructuary.[2] D. 33. 2. 12 (Alfenus Varus, 2 *dig. a Paulo epit.*)[3] says that if the heir erects a country house on the estate which is the object of the usufruct, he cannot demolish it against the wishes of the usufructuary, which suggests that the usufructuary is entitled to the use of the house.[4,5] In classical law the usufructuary was bound to keep premises in good repair and he was bound to cultivate land properly. But he was not liable to repair old buildings which collapsed.[6] There is no evidence for the existence of these obligations in the Republic but one can at least show that the duty to repair or rebuild did not lie on the owner.

[1] Cf. D. 22. 1. 28. 1 (Gaius, 2 *rer. cot.*). See now Watson, 'Morality, Slavery and the Jurists in the Later Roman Republic,' *Tulane Law Review* xlii (1968) 289 ff.

[2] In the case of *ususfructus gregis*—for which again we have no authority for the later Republic—the usufructuary was bound to keep up the flock. For the pre-Julian view of transfer in ownership in the *fetus*, see now Watson, 'The Acquisition of Young in the *ususfructus gregis*', *Iura* xii (1961) 210 ff. The first (and, I think, less likely) solution proposed in that note is followed by Thomas, 'A Note on *summissio*', *RIDA* xi (1964) 255 ff. Thomas's criticisms (pp. 259 f.) of my rejection (pp. 216 ff.) of *constitutum possessorium* as a possible mode of transferring ownership of the *fetus* from the usufructuary to the owner of the flock are not altogether to the point and he says nothing about my second and third arguments; and, *pace* Thomas (p. 264, n. 43), my reflections on *res mancipi* and *res nec mancipi* (pp. 217 f.) are only concerned with *constitutum possessorium*. This, however, is not the place to go into the matter, especially since I have nothing to add to my original statement. The main texts on *summissio* for later law are D. 7. 1. 68. 1; *h.t.* 69; *h.t.* 70 pr.–5; P.S. 3. 6. 20; J. 2. 1. 38.

[3] Quoted *supra*, p. 211.

[4] This remains true (cf. Marrone, *Annali Palermo* xxviii (1961) 63, n. 22) even if one accepts Riccobono's quite plausible reconstruction of the text [now, *Scritti di diritto romano* (Palermo, 1964), ii. 299 and nn. 176, 177]: *Heres in fundo, cuius usus fructus ⟨per vindicationem⟩ legatus est, villam posuit: eam invito fructuario demolire non potest, nihilo magis quam si arborem posuisset, ex fundo is evellere vellet: sed si [antequam usufructuarius prohibuerit] ⟨per damnationem fuerit usus fructus legatus et antequam usum fructum in iure cesserit⟩ demolierit, impune facturum.*

[5] No text tells us whether fruits were acquired by *fructuum perceptio* or *fructuum separatio*.

[6] Cf. Buckland, *Textbook*, p. 269 and n. 15.

Cicero, *top*. 3. 15. A similitudine hoc modo: Si aedes eae corruerunt vitiumve faciunt, quarum usus fructus legatus est, heres restituere non debet nec reficere, non magis quam servum restituere, si is cuius usus fructus legatus est deperisset.

Thus if a building falls or becomes defective[1] the *heres* is not bound to rebuild or repair, just as he is not bound to replace a slave who died.

A particular question of the extent of the usufruct occurs in D. 33. 2. 31 (Labeo, 2 *post. a Iav. epit.*):

Is qui fundum tecum communem habebat usum fructum fundi uxori[2] legaverat: post mortem eius tecum heres arbitrum communi dividundo petierat. Blaesus ait Trebatium respondisse, si arbiter certis regionibus fundum divisisset, eius partis, quae tibi optigerit, usum fructum mulieri nulla ex parte deberi, sed eius, quod heredi optigisset, totius usum fructum eam habituram. ego hoc falsum puto: nam cum ante arbitrum communi dividundo coniunctus pro indiviso ex parte dimidia totius fundi usus fructus mulieris fuisset, non potuisse arbitrum inter alios iudicando alterius ius mutare: quod et receptum est.

A person who owned an estate in common left a legacy of the usufruct of the estate to his wife. After his death his heir brought an *actio communi dividundo*. According to Trebatius, if the *arbiter* divided the estate into fixed parts, the widow would have a usufruct over all the part adjudged to the heir, none at all over the rest. Labeo took a different view.[3] Trebatius' opinion seems to be the more practicable.

[1] This is the meaning of *vitium facere*: cf. Heumann–Seckel, *Handlexikon zu den Quellen des römischen Rechts*, 10th edn. (Graz, 1968), p. 630, s.v. *vitium*.

[2] Some scholars would insert *per vindicationem* here: cf. most recently, Bretone, *La nozione romana di usufrutto, I, Dalle origini a Diocleziano*, p. 68 and n. 41. This does not affect the issue.

[3] Cf., for views on the text, Bretone, op. cit., pp. 68 ff. He himself takes this text as showing that for Trebatius usufruct was conceived of as *pars dominii*: but see Watson, *Tijd.* xxxi (1963) 614 f. The difference of opinion between Trebatius and Labeo will be considered again in a later volume on Legal Science. It is not intended here to enter into discussion of the Republican concept of *ususfructus*. I feel that we have not enough information to justify even the belief that a jurisprudential concept or concepts of usufruct existed at this time. The individual situations might have been decided without reference to any general concept. V.F. 68 and D. 35. 2. 1. 9, which do concern usufruct, will be dealt with in connection with the *lex Falcidia* in a later volume on Succession. D. 40. 12. 23 pr. (Paul, 50 *ad ed.*) does not show that there could be usufruct in a free man—the *in iure cessio* has made him a slave: for a full discussion of the text, see Watson, *Persons*, pp. 166 ff.

In the classical law, at the beginning of a usufruct created by legacy, the usufructuary had to give a praetorian stipulation, the *cautio usufructuaria*, that he would use the object of the usufruct *arbitratu boni viri* and that when the usufruct ended he would restore to the owner what then existed.[1] We do not know whether the *cautio* dates from the Republic or not. The usufructuary had for his protection the *vindicatio usufructuaria*, but we have no direct evidence for its existence in the Republic unless perhaps in Plautus, *Casina* 836 f.[2]

We have already seen some ways in which the usufruct would be terminated. Non-use of the object of the usufruct for the normal period of *usucapio* ended the usufruct during the Empire, and Cavin[3] suggests that D. 7. 1. 71[4] (which we have already considered to some extent and decided was probably genuine in substance) shows the same principle in our period. Guarneri Citati[5] has already objected to this that it would show two modes of extinction—*mutatio rei* and *non usus*—operating successively on the same right. It is indeed perfectly possible to treat the period of *usucapio* as relevant for extinction by *mutatio rei* without bringing in the idea of *non usus* at all. In most cases of *mutatio rei* there could be no doubt that the *ususfructus* was extinguished immediately and permanently. But some cases would not be so clear. For instance if a field were completely flooded there would be *mutatio rei*, but the flood waters might soon recede, *eodem impetu*, and nothing would be more reasonable in such circumstances than to decide that the usufruct continued.[6] But once the idea was admitted in cases of this sort it would be natural to extend it to other situations and to settle on an arbitrary time limit within which restoration of the thing would mean that the usufruct was not extinguished. And the most obvious arbitary time limit is the very short period of usucaption. Thus the decision in D. 7. 1. 71 could be reached without any reference to the rule that *ususfructus* was extinguished by *non*

[1] D. 7. 9: cf. Lenel, *EP*, pp. 538 f.; Kaser, *RPR* i. 378 f. and the references he gives.

[2] *Supra*, pp. 203 f.

[3] *L'Extinction de l'usufruit rei mutatione*, p. 86.

[4] Quoted *supra*, p. 212.

[5] *SDHI* iii (1937) 209.

[6] For this situation see D. 7. 4. 23 (Pomponius, 26 *ad Quintum Mucium*); *h.t.* 24 pr. (Iavolenus, 3 *ex post. Labeonis*).

usus, and even without the existence of any such rule. The usufruct was not affected by any change in the owner of the object of the usufruct. Thus it continued if the owner sold the property[1] or if he died.

Cicero, *top*. 4. 21. A repugnantibus: Si paterfamilias uxori ancillarum usum fructum legavit a filio neque a secundo herede legavit, mortuo filio mulier usumfructum non amittet. Quod enim semel testamento alicui datum est, id ab eo invito, cui datum est, auferri non potest. Repugnat enim recte accipere et invitum reddere.

This text is particularly strong proof of the last statement. The succession to the dead *filius* can only be under a clause of pupillary succession in the father's will. The testator left a legacy of the usufruct where the heir was the *institutus*, but he did not where the heir was the pupillary substitute. The *institutus* succeeded to the estate and the *ususfructus* came into being. The *institutus* then died and the estate went to the *substitutus*. The *ususfructus* was not extinguished despite the fact that the new owner succeeded to the estate under the will which created the usufruct and that the usufruct was not left as a legacy away from him. If the *institutus* had died before the testator the usufruct would never have come into being.[2]

In addition to usufruct there were three similar rights.

Usus[3]

This was *ususfructus* without *fructus*. The person to whom the right was granted was entitled to use the object of the *usus* but was not entitled to its fruits. There are two texts.

D. 7. 8. 4. 1 (Ulpian, 17 *ad Sab*.). Mulieri autem si usus relictus sit, posse eam et cum marito habitare Quintus Mucius primus admisit, ne ei matrimonio carendum foret, cum uti vult domo. nam per contrarium quin uxor cum marito possit habitare, nec fuit dubitatum. quid ergo si viduae legatus sit, an nuptiis contractis post constitutum usum mulier habitare cum marito possit? et est verum, ut et Pomponius libro quinto et Papinianus libro nono decimo quaestionum probat, posse eam cum

[1] Cf. Cicero, *pro Caecina* 7. 19.

[2] Cicero, *de leg*. 1. 8. 25; *ad fam*. 7. 29. 1; 7. 30. 2 tell us nothing for the law of usufruct.

[3] See now Grosso, *Usufrutto e figure affini nel diritto romano*, pp. 430 ff.

viro et postea nubentem habitare. hoc amplius Pomponius ait et cum socero habitaturam.

Quintus Mucius was the first to declare that if *usus* of a house was left to a woman she could inhabit it along with her husband.[1] On the other hand, it had never been disputed that if the *usus* of a house were left to a husband, his wife could live there with him. There is no sign that the rest of the text goes back to Republican roots.[2]

D. 7. 8. 2. 1 (Ulpian, 17 *ad Sab.*). Domus usus relictus est aut marito aut mulieri: si marito, potest illic habitare non solus, verum cum familia quoque sua. an et cum libertis, fuit quaestionis, et Celsus scripsit, et cum libertis: posse hospitem quoque recipere, nam ita libro octavo decimo digestorum scripsit, quam sententiam et Tubero probat. sed an etiam inquilinum recipere possit, apud Labeonem memini tractatum libro posteriorum, et ait Labeo eum, qui ipse habitat, inquilinum posse recipere: idem et hospites et libertos suos.

Tubero was of the opinion that the husband's freedmen could also live in the house with him and his *familia*.[3,4]

Habitatio[5]

This was really *usus* or a modification of *usus* of a house or lodging. It is clear that in the Republic there was some doubt as to whether a grant of *habitatio* was the same as a grant of *usus*.

D. 7. 8. 10. 3 (Ulpian, 17 *ad Sab.*). Utrum autem unius anni sit habitatio an usque ad vitam, apud veteres quaesitum est: et Rutilius donec vivat, habitationem competere ait, quam sententiam et Celsus probat libro octavo decimo digestorum.

Thus it was disputed among the Republican jurists whether a grant of *habitatio* was for one year or for life, and Rutilius declared it was for life. Buckland[6] very reasonably suggests that probably at first *habitatio* was meant to be only temporary and was not intended to create a right *in rem*.[7]

[1] This need not imply that *usus* was of very recent origin in the time of Quintus Mucius: *contra*, Buckland, *Textbook*, p. 273 and n. 3.

[2] Further to the text see Grosso, op. cit., pp. 437 f.

[3] Further to the text see Grosso, op. cit., pp. 436 f.

[4] Nothing legal can be deduced from Cicero, *de leg.* 1. 8. 25.

[5] See now Grosso, op. cit., pp. 494 ff.; Buckland, *Textbook*, p. 274.

[6] Loc. cit.

[7] D. 33. 2. 40. (Alfenus Varus, *8 dig. a Paulo epit.*) tells us nothing significant for *habitatio*.

Operae servorum vel animalium[1]

This also was a particular form of *usus* but it had one or two special rules. There is no evidence for its existence in the Republic. The only text which might possibly be called into service is D. 35. 2. 1. 9 (Paul, *libro singulari ad legem Falcidiam*). This text tells us that a certain opinion of the *veteres* about the legacy of usufruct is not followed but that it is necessary for *operae servi*. But there is no sign here that the *veterum sententia* necessarily referred to *operae servi* either expressly or impliedly.[2]

[1] See now Grosso, op. cit., pp. 504 ff.; Buckland, *Textbook*, pp. 274 f.

[2] So we need not enter into the discussion whether this part of the text (from *sed operis servi*) is interpolated.

10

THE INTERDICT *QUOD VI AUT CLAM*

A RESTITUTORY interdict was issued on account of work which was done on land either by force or by stealth.[1] The interdict was extensively commented on during the later Republic and it was in existence at least as early as the time of Quintus Mucius.[2] According to Lenel's reconstruction,[3] it ran: *Quod vi aut clam factum est, qua de re agitur, id, si non plus quam annus est cum experiendi potestas est, restituas.* The *formula arbitraria* and the *sponsio* are mentioned for this interdict by Cicero, *pro Tullio* 23. 53.[4]

Vis and *clam* were both given very wide meanings by the Republican jurists.[5]

D. 50. 17. 73. 2 (Quintus Mucius Scaevola, libro sing. *ὅρων*). Vi factum id videtur esse, qua de re quis cum prohibetur, fecit: clam, quod quisque, cum controversiam haberet habiturumve se putaret, fecit.

D. 43. 24. 1. 5 (Ulpian, 71 *ad ed.*). Quid sit vi factum vel clam factum, videamus, vi factum videri Quintus Mucius scripsit, si quis contra quam prohiberetur fecerit: et mihi videtur plena esse Quinti Mucii definitio.

D. 43. 24. 4 (Venuleius, 2 *interd.*). Servius etiam eum clam facere, qui existimare debeat sibi controversiam futuram, quia non opinionem cuius et resupinam existimationem esse oporteat, ne melioris condicionis sint stulti quam periti.

Quintus Mucius thought that something was done *vi* when a person did it after he had been forbidden. Though the text from Scaevola's *liber singularis ὅρων* does not mention this interdict, and

[1] Cf. in general on the interdict, Berger, *RE* ix. 1662 ff.; Bonfante II. i. 402 ff.; David, *Études sur l'interdit quod vi aut clam* [*Annales de l'Université de Lyon*, 3e sér., x (1947)].

[2] Cf. D. 43. 24. 1. 5; *h.t.* 5. 8; 50. 17. 73. 2.

[3] *EP*, pp. 482 f.

[4] Cf. Lenel, *EP*, p. 483. For the function of these in interdicts see the account of Gaius, G. 4. 162 ff.

[5] For *vis*, see now, in general, Mayer-Maly, *RE* X A. 311 ff.; for its interpretation in interdicts, ibidem, 323 ff.

the text of Ulpian does not expressly say that Scaevola defined *vis* in this context, it would be hard to believe that Quintus Mucius' definition of *vis* was not meant by him to apply to our interdict.[1] Mucius' definition of *vis* is extremely wide and would seem to include situations where no force was used. The definition in fact must represent a deliberate attempt to make the interdict very wide in its scope, whether one says that the credit for the attempt should go to Mucius or whether, as Stein would have it,[2] the definition derives from his observation of the various cases in which the praetor had held that possession was obtained *vi*.

Further clarification of the interpretation of *vis* in the Republic is given by D. 43. 24. 1. 7.

> Sed et si contra testationem denuntiationemque fecerit, idem esse Cascellius et Trebatius putant: quod verum est.

Cascellius and Trebatius thought a person acted *vi* who continued to act contrary to a *testatio*, a declaration made before witnesses, or a *denuntiatio*, an announcement.[3]

Quintus Mucius thought something was done *clam* if a person did it when he had, or thought he would have, opposition. One should probably understand that he did it without giving notice.[4] This definition seems straightforward enough. *Clam* does imply deliberate stealth and this is brought out in the definition by *cum controversiam haberet habiturumve se putaret*. Much more significant, not just for the interdict but also for the history of Roman law, is Servius' addition which is reported in D. 43. 24. 4.[5] In this text, *quia* to the end has frequently been held interpolated[6] but that part need not concern us at the moment. The first part of the text, *Servius etiam eum clam facere, qui existimare debeat sibi*

[1] Whether, for Quintus Mucius, this meaning of *vis* should be restricted to this context, as Mayer-Maly might be prepared to hold, op. cit., p. 326, or is wider in its application, as David maintains, op. cit., p. 25, need not concern us here.

[2] *Regulae iuris* (Edinburgh, 1966), p. 37.

[3] Cf. on the text, David, op. cit., pp. 26 f.

[4] Thus Mommsen suggests an emendation of the text: *clam, quod quis clam cum eo quocum controversiam*: *Digesta Iustiniani Augusti* (reprinted, Berlin, 1963), ii. 961.

[5] Cf. for the text in general, David, op. cit., p. 22.

[6] Cf. *Index Itp.*

controversiam futuram, does not seem to have been attacked. Indeed, it would be virtually impossible to do so without holding, in effect, that the whole text was a fabrication of the compilers. Servius would widen *clam* to include what was done without notice by one who ought to think that there would be opposition. Thus, Servius would widen the interdict even to cover certain cases where there was no deliberate wrongful conduct and in this he was followed by at least some later jurists.[1] This seems an instance of deliberate misinterpretation. But so far as I am aware the wider significance of the text has been overlooked. This is that an edictal provision explicitly framed in terms of deliberate wrongful conduct is interpreted, as early as the first century B.C., to include (grossly?) negligent behaviour. But if such a development could occur here, in the face of an edictal provision, it could also happen elsewhere. And so in other situations where it was established that liability was for *dolus* only, liability could be extended to cover cases of gross negligence. When proper consideration is given to D. 43. 24. 4, any *a priori* argument against the classicality of the concept[2] of *culpa lata* must lose its force.[3]

Those who hold the text interpolated from *quia* appear not to give any argument for their point of view. It would seem difficult to argue convincingly either for the text's genuineness or for interpolation. Even on the hypothesis of interpolation there would seem also to be present some scribal error in *quia . . . oportet*,[4] and scribal error might be enough to explain the awkwardness of this part of the text. In view of the usual meaning of *clam*, the argument *ne melioris condicionis sint stulti quam periti* is certainly inelegant, but the frame of mind behind the argument is reasonable and understandable.

[1] Cf. Celsus in D. 43. 24. 3. 7 (Ulpian, 71 *ad ed.*).

[2] If not against the term.

[3] Kaser, *RPR* i. 423 suggests that originally *dolus*, within the contractual system, meant deliberate breach of faith but that it was extended by the later Republic to include gross negligence. He gives as evidence of this Cicero, *pro Rosc. Am.* 38. 111. But there is, I think, no strong indication here of the inclusion of the concept of *culpa lata* within *dolus*. There is no evidence that liability for negligence in the *bonae fidei* contracts was the result of an interpretation of the meaning of *dolus*.

[4] Cf. the *apparatus criticus* given by Mommsen, op. cit., ii. 603.

A row of texts gives us further information on Servius' understanding of *clam.*

D. 43. 24. 5. 3 (Ulpian, 70[1] *ad ed.*). Sed et Servius recte ait sufficere feminae viro notum facere opus se facturum: vel denique sciente eo facere: quamquam etiam illud sufficiat celandi animum non habere. 4. Item ait, si quis in publico municipii velit facere, sufficere ei, si curatori rei publicae denuntiet. 5. Si quis, dum putat locum tuum esse, qui est meus, celandi tui, non mei causa fecerit, mihi interdictum competere. 6. Idem dicit et si servi mei vel procuratoris celandi causa factum sit, mihi interdictum competere.

§ 3 tells us that the jurist thought it was sufficient (to escape the charge of acting *clam*) that notice be given to a woman's husband, or that the work be done with his knowledge. Mommsen regards *vel* as having dropped out between *feminae viro.*[2] But the suggestion is unnecessary. *Vir* is frequently used with the meaning of husband.[3] Moreover, on this reconstruction one might have expected the text to read: *vel denique sciente ea eove facere.* The text ends that it is enough (for it not to be *clam*) that he had no intention of hiding the activity. This is held to be interpolated by Pringsheim[4] who says that *animum non habere* can never have the force of *denuntiatio.* But the objection is irrelevant. The text is not making *animum non habere* have the force of *denuntiatio*[5] and the immediately preceding part of the text had already passed beyond the discussion of *denuntiatio.* The text has three parts: for something not to be done *clam* it is sufficient that notice be given to the woman's husband, or that he be aware of the activity, or even that it be done with no intention of concealment. In favour of the genuineness of this last part of the text it should be noticed that it is in indirect speech. Indirect speech—which attributes this opinion directly to Servius—would be unnecessary for the compilers. This part of the text, though, should be read in conjunction

[1] It should be 71: cf. Lenel, *Pal.* ii. 835.

[2] Op. cit., ii. 604.

[3] Cf. *Vocabularium Iurisprudentiae Romanae* (Berlin, 1939), v. 1394 ff.

[4] Now in *Gesammelte Schriften* (Heidelberg, 1961), i 260; followed by Albertario, now in *Scritti di diritto romano* (Milan, 1936), iii. 223, n. 1; and, apparently, by David, op. cit., p. 22, n. 2.

[5] And there is no sign that a formal *denuntiatio* was required to prevent the interdict being given.

with Servius' view reported in *h.t.* 4. The person acting must not be one who ought to have thought that there would be opposition.

§ 4 is concerned with notice where work is to be done on land belonging to a *municipium*. Servius is made to say that the notice to the *curator rei publicae* is sufficient. But this must be an interpolation[1] since the office of *curator rei publicae* was a creation of the Emperors and is not securely evidenced before A.D. 113.[2] The person to whom Servius referred cannot now be discovered.[3]

§ 5 is in indirect speech and its positioning between §§ 4 and 6 permits the assumption that it too gives the view of Servius. The text says that if a person thinks the land is yours when it is mine, and acts to conceal his behaviour from you, not from me, the interdict is available to me.

§ 6 takes the matter slightly further and says that if he acts with the intention of concealing his activity from my slave or procurator I will have the interdict.

The wording of the interdict does not disclose who is the person against whom the interdict is to be brought, but much clarification was given by Quintus Mucius.

D. 43. 24. 5. 8. Haec verba 'quod vi aut clam factum est' ait Mucius ita esse 'quod tu aut tuorum quis aut tuo iussu factum est'.

The words *quod vi aut clam factum est* are to be interpreted *quod tu aut tuorum quis aut tuo iussu factum est*. It is widely thought that the text is not in perfect form—and especially that *fecisti* has dropped out after *tu*—but it seems completely accepted that the text gives the genuine thought of Quintus Mucius.[4] Labeo, as reported in § 9,[5] would take a broader view and include the heirs of those whom Quintus Mucius listed.[6]

[1] Cf. *Index Itp.*; David, op. cit., p. 23, n. 1.

[2] Cf. Mommsen, *Römisches Staatsrecht*, 3rd edn. (Leipzig, 1887), ii. 1082 ff., especially at p. 1083, n. 1.

[3] Bremer conjectures that it was a *servus publicus*: *Iurisprudentiae antehadrianae quae supersunt* (Leipzig, 1896), i. 237; Alibrandi suggests a *duovir*: *Opere giuridiche e storiche* (Rome, 1896), i. 480: cf. David, loc. cit.

[4] To the references in the *Index Itp.* add: Beseler, *Festschrift Schulz* (Weimar, 1951), i. 31; Beretta, *Studi Albertario* (Milan, 1953), ii. 150.

[5] Interpolated, according to Beseler, loc. cit.

[6] Cf. in general on D. 43. 24. 5. 8: David, op. cit., pp. 139 f.

The interdict did not expressly state who was entitled to it, but it certainly was not restricted to the owner of the land which was affected by the *opus*:

D. 43. 24. 13. 4 (Ulpian, 71 *ad ed.*). Unde apud Servium amplius relatum est, si mihi concesseris, ut ex fundo tuo arbores caedam, deinde eas alius vi aut clam ceciderit, mihi hoc interdictum competere, quia ego sim cuius interest: quod facilius erit admittendum, si a te emi vel ex aliquo contractu hoc consecutus sim, ut mihi caedere liceat.

Thus, according to Servius, the person to whom the owner of land accorded the right[1] to cut down trees has the *interdictum quod vi aut clam* against someone else who cuts them down.[2]

Again, although the *interdictum* was not specific, the classical jurists seem to have been agreed that it lay only in respect of *opus factum in solo*.[3] Trebatius seems to have taken a wider view.

D. 43. 24. 22. 3 (Venuleius, 2 *interd.*). Si stercus per fundum meum tuleris, cum id te facere vetuissem, quamquam nihil damni feceris mihi nec fundi mei mutaveris, tamen teneri te quod vi aut clam Trebatius ait. Labeo contra, ne etiam is, qui dumtaxat iter per fundum meum fecerit aut avem egerit venatusve fuerit sine ullo opere hoc interdicto teneatur.

As Labeo says, the *fundus* is not altered because manure was carried over it. Yet Trebatius allows the *interdictum* though there was no *opus*. Possibly even more surprising is that Trebatius will grant the interdict even though the person requesting it has suffered no financial loss. Presumably the object of granting the interdict here is to compel the 'wrongdoer' to remove the manure from its present place or else to suffer a monetary condemnation. Hence it is intended to act as a deterrent to stop him committing the 'offence' again.[4,5]

1 By *in iure cessio* according to Pernice, as reported by Bremer, loc. cit.

2 *Quod facilius* to the end is in direct speech and so, whether interpolated or not (cf. *Index Itp.*), it should not be attributed to Servius and hence need not be discussed here.

3 Cf., e.g., D. 43. 24. 7. 5, 6, 8, 9, 10 (Ulpian, 71 *ad ed.*); *h.t.* 8 (Venuleius, 2 *interd.*); *h.t.* 9 (Ulpian, 71 *ad ed.*); *h.t.* 10 (Venuleius, 2 *interd.*); *h.t.* 11 pr. (Ulpian, 71 *ad ed.*).

4 Cf. on the text G. Lombardi, *BIDR* xii–xiii (1948) 304 f.

5 In Cicero, *pro Tullio* 23. 53 the discussion of the *interdictum* is in respect of the demolition of a roof erected by the injured person on land which he claimed was his, but which was apparently the wrongdoer's: cf. David, op. cit., pp. 20 f.

On occasion a person against whom the interdict was brought and who acted *vi aut clam* might have the benefit of an *exceptio*. For the Republic there is only one text, D. 43. 24. 7. 4 (Ulpian, 71 *ad ed.*).

Est et alia exceptio, de qua Celsus dubitat, an sit obicienda: ut puta si incendii arcendi causa vicini aedes intercidi et quod vi aut clam mecum agatur aut damni iniuria. Gallus enim dubitat, an excipi oporteret: 'quod incendii defendendi causa factum non sit'? Servius autem ait, si id magistratus fecisset, dandam esse, privato non esse idem concedendum: si tamen quid vi aut clam factum sit neque ignis usque eo pervenisset, simpli litem aestimandam: si pervenisset, absolvi eum oportere. idem ait esse, si damni iniuria actum foret, quoniam nullam iniuriam aut damnum dare videtur aeque perituris aedibus. quod si nullo incendio id feceris, deinde postea incendium ortum fuerit, non idem erit dicendum, quia non ex post facto, sed ex praesenti statu, damnum factum sit nec ne, aestimari oportere Labeo ait.

It is widely accepted[1] that in the text *Celsus* is a scribal error for *Gallus* and that at least as far as *concedendum* the text is genuine in substance.[2] Thus where, to stop fires spreading, neighbouring houses were pulled down, Gallus hesitated over allowing the *exceptio*, *quod incendii defendendi causa factum non sit*. Servius would allow the *exceptio* to a magistrate but not to a private citizen. If something were done (by the private citizen) *vi aut clam* and the fire had not reached the neighbour's house, Servius says that recovery will be of the simple value. But if the fire had reached the neighbour's house, the sentence ends, he should be absolved. This last part of the sentence seems still to be concerned with the *interdictum quod vi aut clam*, but in view of what precedes the absolution cannot be due to the *exceptio*, but must be because there has been no financial loss caused by the act done *vi aut clam* since the house would have been destroyed anyway.

[1] But not by Lenel, *Pal.* i. 160; ii. 836.

[2] Cf. most recently on the text, Watson, *Obligations*, pp. 240 ff., which, however, is insufficiently precise and does not distinguish between the *interdictum quod vi aut clam* and the *actio legis Aquiliae*. But one can presume that the law in question is the same for both the *interdictum* and the *actio*.

11

DONATIO

THE *lex Cincia de donis et muneribus*[1] of 204 B.C. was a plebiscite of the tribune M. Cincius Alimentus[2] and the *suasor* was Q. Fabius Maximus.[3] It had two main provisions. First, it forbade gifts to be made to advocates for pleading cases.[4] Secondly, it forbade gifts of more than a certain (unknown) value except between certain specified classes; namely, between cognates up to second cousin, between *adfines*, to any female cognate if the gift were intended as *dos*, and by a *tutor qui tutelam gerit*.[5] The *lex* was *imperfecta*.[6]

Husband and wife were included among the *exceptae personae* so that gifts between them were valid.[7] None the less, gifts between husband and wife came to be void. It has often been maintained that this prohibition was due to the *lex Iulia et Papia* of Augustus,[8] but this seems impossible and the prohibition seems to extend back into the Republic and be due to custom.[9] The main arguments for this are[10] that Ulpian declares that the prohibition was introduced *moribus*,[11] that it was known to Alfenus[12] and Trebatius,[13] and that the texts adduced to show the origin of the prohibition in statute[14]

1 For the sources, see Rotondi, *Leges*, pp. 261 ff.

2 Cf. Livy, 29. 20. 11; Cicero, *de orat.* 2. 71. 286.

3 Cf. Cicero, *de sen.* 4. 10.

4 Cf. Cicero, *ad Att.* 1. 20. 7; Tacitus, *Ann.* 11. 5; 13. 42; 15. 20; Archi, *La donazione* (Milan, 1960), pp. 16 f.

5 For the provisions see V.F. 298–309.

6 Cf., e.g., Buckland, *Textbook*, pp. 254 f.; Biondi, *Successione*, pp. 637 ff.

7 V.F. 302 (Paul, 71 *ad ed.*).

8 For those who took this view see Scherillo, 'Sulle origini del divieto delle donazioni fra coniugi', *Studi Solmi* (Milan, 1941), i. 173.

9 Cf. Scherillo, op. cit.; Archi, op. cit., pp. 195 ff.; apparently also Biondi, op. cit., pp. 649 ff.

10 Cf., above all, Scherillo, op. cit.

11 D. 24. 1. 1 (Ulpian, 32 *ad Sab.*).

12 D. 24. 1. 38 (Alfenus, 3 *dig. a Paulo epit.*).

13 D. 41. 6. 3 (Pomponius, 24 *ad Quintum Mucium*); cf. 24. 1. 64 (Iavolenus, 6 *ex post. Labeonis*).

14 Plutarch, *Quaest. Rom.* 7; V.F. 273; *C. Th.* 5. 1. 9.

are far from probative.[1] Alfenus and Trebatius, it is true, lived into the Empire, and Trebatius would seem to have died only shortly after A.D. 4,[2] that is after the *lex Iulia de maritandis ordinibus* of 18 B.C. but before the *lex Papia Poppaea* of A.D. 9. But nothing indicates that Alfenus lived even until 18 B.C., and moreover the decisions in D. 24. 1. 38, as often in Alfenus, may go back to his master, Servius,[3] who died in 43 B.C. Perhaps the main argument for holding the prohibition Republican is this. The prohibition is either Republican or of Augustus' time and it was introduced *moribus*. Augustus was exceptionally interested in the reform of family law and he was responsible for a large number of important reforms which were introduced by statute. Other sources of law began to show a marked dependence on the will of the Emperor. In all these circumstances it seems most unlikely that a rule of family law so important as the prohibition of gifts between husband and wife would develop early in Augustus' reign independent of his legislation and as a result of custom.[4]

D. 24. 1. 38 pr. (Alfenus, 3 *dig. a Paulo epit.*). Servus communis viri et fratris eius puerum donavit uxori fratris: pro qua parte is servus qui donasset viri esset, pro ea parte munus non esse factum mulieris respondit.

A slave owned in common by two brothers gave a slave boy to the wife of one of his owners. Alfenus (or Servius) replied that for the proportion of the slave which belonged to the husband the gift was

[1] Nothing should be deduced from the *praesumptio Muciana*: cf. Scherillo, op. cit., p. 175. Even if it mainly concerns gifts by husband to the wife (which is doubtful: cf., e.g., Kaser, '*Praesumptio Muciana*', *Studi De Francisci* (Milan, 1956), i. 213 ff.), nothing in the *praesumptio*, so far as we know it, would allow the conclusion that the gifts were void or valid. Likewise nothing can be argued from the *lex Iulia repetundarum* of 59 B.C. which prohibited gifts to magistrates with certain exceptions, one of which was gifts from a wife: D. 48. 11. 1. 1 (Marcian, 14 *inst.*). This only means that a magistrate who accepted a gift from his wife was not subject to the *condemnatio in quadruplum* under the statute. It throws no light on whether the gift was itself valid or void.

[2] Cf., e.g., Sonnet, *RE* viA. 2259; Kunkel, *Herkunft und soziale Stellung der römischen Juristen* (Weimar, 1952), p. 28. D. 24. 1. 64, though it refers to Trebatius and concerns *donatio inter virum et uxorem*, relates to a factual situation of 16 B.C. (cf. Sonnet, loc. cit.) and hence should not be dealt with here.

[3] But the *respondit* of the *principium* is no help in deciding whether the jurist responsible was Servius or Alfenus: cf. von Lübtow, *Studi Betti* (Milan, 1962), iii. 369.

[4] It must be admitted, though, that it is not easy to see how the prohibition could develop *moribus*.

void. Since a slave, even one who had *libera administratio peculii*, could not make a gift without the consent of his *dominus*,[1] some reconstruction of the text, such as that of Beseler who inserts *comparavit et utriusque iussu* after *puerum*,[2] seems indicated.

D. 24. 1. 38. 1. Idem iuris erit, si ex tribus fratribus unus uxorem haberet et rem communem uxori donasset: nam ex tertia parte mulieris res facta non est, ex duabus autem partibus reliquis, si id scissent fratres aut posteaquam donata esset ratum habuissent, non debere mulierem reddere.

One of three brothers gave to his wife a thing owned in common by the brothers and it is held that one-third of it does not become the woman's property, but that she need not restore the remaining two-thirds, if the other brothers knew of the gift or later ratified it.[3]

There were, of course, exceptions to the prohibition of gifts between spouses. The only one evidenced for the Republic, and perhaps the only one in fact (apart presumably from gifts of small value), is where the donor does not become poorer by the gift.[4]

D. 41. 6. 3 (Pomponius, 24 *ad Quintum Mucium*). Si vir uxori vel uxor viro donaverit, si aliena res donata fuerit, verum est, quod Trebatius putabat, si pauperior is qui donasset non fieret, usucapionem possidenti procedere.

The text tells us that according to Trebatius, if one spouse gave the other something which belonged to a third party, the recipient could usucapt if the donor were not made poorer by the gift. The substance of the text is held interpolated by Beseler.[5] He thinks that in all cases of *traditio*, apart from *venditio* and *dotis datio*, the ground for *usucapio* is 'die von kausalem Konsense begleitete auf

[1] Cf., e.g., Buckland, *The Roman Law of Slavery* (Cambridge, 1908), pp. 204 f.

[2] *ZSS* xlv (1925) 445. He would also delete the second *fratris*.

[3] The whole text is held interpolated by Beseler, loc. cit.: *contra*, Burdese, *Autorizzazione ad alienare in diritto romano* (Turin, n. d.), p. 62, n. 8. *Pace Index Itp.*, Thayer, *Lex Aquilia* (*Digest IX*, 2 *ad legem Aquiliam*). *On gifts between husband and wife* (*Digest XXIV*, 1 *de donationibus inter virum et uxorem*) (Cambridge, Mass., 1929), p. 206, is non-committal.

[4] On the doctrine of *depauperatio–locupletatio* see in general Archi, op. cit., pp. 201 ff.

[5] *ZSS* xlv (1925) 226 f.; *ZSS* li (1931) 190.

Eigentumsübertragung abzielende Tradition'. Hence in our text the *donatio* is void but there is a real *consensus de donando* and this is enough for *usucapio*. If this view is correct then it should be irrelevant that the donor be made poorer, and so Beseler excises *si pauperior . . . fieret*. But this is unconvincing. If Beseler's view on *iustus titulus* is correct in general, then there would have to be an exception for *donatio inter virum et uxorem* where the rule was that such gifts were generally void. It would be nonsensical to have a rule that *donationes inter virum et uxorem* were void and yet allow the recipient to usucapt after one or two years.[1]

Naturally, a *paterfamilias* could not make a valid *donatio* to someone in his *potestas*.[2] And a person *in potestate* could not make a gift except with the approval of his *paterfamilias*.

Cicero, *de leg*. 2. 20. 50. . . . in donatione hoc eidem secus interpretantur: et quod paterfamilias in eius donatione, qui in ipsius potestate esset, approbavit, ratum est: quod eo insciente factum est, si id is non approbat, ratum non est. . . .

Even a *filius* who had full power to administer his *peculium* could not, it would seem,[3] make a gift from it.

Valerius Maximus, *Mem*. 8. 2. 2 concerns a *donatio mortis causa* made by C. Visellius Varro to his mistress, Otacilia Laterensis. Visellius, however, does not die and the gift is ineffective. It is possible, but by no means certain, that the gift would be void for immorality.[4]

[1] Beseler in *ZSS* li (1931) 190 suggests that the view of Trebatius did not prevail.

[2] See Servius in V.F. 294 (Papinian, 12 *resp*.): quoted and discussed *supra*, pp. 51 ff.

[3] To judge from classical texts: e.g. D. 39. 5. 7 pr. (Ulpian, 44 *ad Sab*.).

[4] On the text see now Watson, *Obligations*, pp. 32 ff.

INDEX OF TEXTS

LEGAL SOURCES

(*a*) PRE-JUSTINIANIC WRITERS AND COLLECTIONS

Codex Theodosianus
5. 1. 9 229 n. 14

Collatio
12. 7. 8 213

Gai Institutiones
1. 119 16 n. 4, 92 n. 2
1. 120 16 n. 4, 17 n. 5
1. 121 16 n. 4, 93
1. 122 16 n. 4
2. 2 1 n. 1
2. 3 1 n. 2
2. 8 1 n. 3
2. 10 1 n. 4
2. 12 1 n. 5
2. 13 14 n. 2
2. 14 14 n. 3
2. 15 17 n. 7
2. 16 17 n. 9
2. 17 181 n. 3, 184 n. 3
2. 24 21 n. 1, 92 n. 3
2. 27 17 f.
2. 28 14 n. 5
2. 29 17 n. 6, 201 n. 3
2. 45 26 ff., 30
2. 48 22 n. 3
2. 49 26, 28, 30 n. 7
2. 50 19 n. 2, 54 n. 2
2. 54 23 n. 4, 32, 40
2. 55 40
2. 58 51 n. 2
2. 59 41
2. 60 41
2. 61 41, 48
2. 69 63 n. 5
2. 78 75 n. 3
2. 83 82 n. 4
2. 95 79 n. 3
3. 75 158 n. 6
3. 107 82 n. 4
3. 109 82 n. 4
3. 147 158 n. 7
3. 200 43 n. 2
3. 201 42
3. 203 47 n. 1
4. 16 65, 96
4. 17 a. 111 n. 3, 121 n. 5, 124 n. 2
4. 26 129 n. 3
4. 27 129 n. 3, 130
4. 28 129 n. 3, 130
4. 29 129 nn. 1, 3, 4
4. 31 126 n. 2, 127 ff., 136
4. 32 130 n. 7
4. 91 97 n. 4 (at 98)
4. 92 97 n. 4 (at 98)
4. 93 97 n. 4 (at 98)
4. 94 97 n. 4 (at 98)
4. 138 ff. 86
4. 154 f. 89 n. 1
4. 160 86
4. 162 ff. 222 n. 4
4. 166 a. 88 n. 3

Pauli Sententiae
1. 17. 2 23 n. 7
3. 6. 20 216 n. 2
5. 6. 13 119 n. 3

Ulpiani Epitome
19. 1 181 n. 3
24. 27 210

Vaticana Fragmenta
1 31 n. 3, 54; 105
41–93 206 n. 4
45 181 n. 3
49 129 n. 4, 155 n. 3
50 21 n. 2
68 206 n. 4, 217 n. 3
70 206 n. 4, 214, 214 n. 1
90 209 n. 1
91 209 n. 1
92 209 n. 1
273 229 n. 14
294 40 n. 2, 51, 53, 232 n. 2
298–309 229 n. 5
302 229 n. 7

(*b*) Justinianic

Institutiones

2. 1. 1 186 n. 1
2. 1. 17 63 n. 6
2. 1. 38 216 n. 2
2. 1. 39 74 n. 3
2. 4 pr. 207 n. 4
2. 4. 2 210
2. 6. 2 26 n. 3
4. 6. 4 105

Digesta

1. 8. 2 186
1. 8. 6. 3 10 n. 1
2. 1. 4 137
2. 1. 11 pr. 110
2. 1. 11. 1 110
2. 1. 11. 2 110
4. 9. 6. 1 123
5. 1. 76 80 n. 6, 104 n. 1
5. 3. 57 100
6. 1. 5. 3 76, 104 n. 1
6. 1. 33 98
6. 1. 37 99 n. 7
6. 1. 48 99 n. 7
6. 1. 57 97 n. 1
6. 1. 58 97 n. 1, 100 f., 103
6. 1. 65 99 n. 7
6. 2. 9. 4 104 n. 4
6. 2. 15 104
6. 2. 16 104 n. 6
7. 1. 1 207 n. 4
7. 1. 9. 7 213, 214 n. 5
7. 1. 10 214, 214 n. 5
7. 1. 11 214
7. 1. 48. 1 214 n. 5
7. 1. 53 211
7. 1. 68 pr. 206 nn. 2, 3; 208 n. 3, 215
7. 1. 68. 1 215, 216 n. 2
7. 1. 69 216 n. 2
7. 1. 70 pr.–5 216 n. 2
7. 1. 71 212 f., 218
7. 4. 5. 3 212
7. 4. 6 212
7. 4. 7 212 f.
7. 4. 10. 4 214 n. 5
7. 4. 23 77 n. 1, 218 n. 6
7. 4. 24 pr. 218 n. 6
7. 5. 1 210; 210 n. 1
7. 8. 2. 1 220
7. 8. 4. 1 219 f.
7. 8. 10. 3 220
7. 9 218 n. 1
8. 1. 13 183 n. 4
8. 1. 14 pr. 23 n. 7 (and at 24)
8. 1. 15 pr. 23 n. 7 (at 24)
8. 1. 17 23 n. 7 (at 24)
8. 2. 2 176 n. 11, 196
8. 2. 7 24 n. 2, 176 nn. 7, 8; 181, 194, 200 n. 1, 202
8. 2. 10 182
8. 2. 16 176 nn. 7, 8; 194
8. 2. 17 pr. 182
8. 2. 17. 3 194 n. 4
8. 2. 20. 5 196 n. 4
8. 2. 33 176 n. 5, 194 n. 4, 198 ff.
8. 3. 1 pr. 183 n. 3
8. 3. 1. 1 183 n. 1
8. 3. 2. 1 183 n. 2
8. 3. 2. 2 183 n. 2
8. 3. 3 186
8. 3. 3. 2 178 n. 1
8. 3. 8 176 n. 4, 183
8. 3. 13. 2 183 n. 3
8. 3. 13. 3 183 n. 4
8. 3. 15 176 n. 5, 190
8. 3. 29 174 n. 3, 176 n. 10, 195, 210 n. 6
8. 3. 30 20 n. 7, 91 n. 2, 176 nn. 2, 5, 6; 184, 186 f., 187 n. 6, 188 n. 1, 201 n. 5
8. 3. 32 187 n. 3
8. 4. 6 pr. 187, 187 n. 3
8. 4. 15 201
8. 5. 2. 1 179 n. 1
8. 5. 6. 2 176 n. 15, 198 f.
8. 5. 8. 5 176 n. 1; 177, 178 n. 1, 179
8. 5. 10 184 n. 6
8. 5. 17 pr. 116 n. 3, 176 n. 11, 195
8. 5. 17. 1 177 n. 3 (at 178), 179
8. 5. 17. 2 10, 126 n. 1, 142, 177, 177 n. 3 (at 178), 178 n. 1, 179
8. 6. 7 184 n. 6, 202
8. 6. 8 184 n. 6
9. 2. 27. 1 122
9. 2. 27. 10 213
9. 4. 10 124
10. 1 110
10. 1. 4. 7 174
10. 1. 4. 10 114, 115 n. 1
10. 1. 13 111, 113 ff., 113 n. 1
10. 2 110
10. 2. 1 pr. 121 n. 4

10. 2. 2. 3 121 n. 3
10. 2. 16. 5 6 n. 5
10. 2. 16. 6 122 f., 124 n. 5
10. 3 110
10. 3. 6. 6 5 f.
10. 3. 10 pr. 6 n. 5
10. 3. 26 124
10. 4. 5 pr. 107 n. 5
10. 4. 7. 5 103 n. 2
10. 4. 15 107 n. 5
10. 4. 19 107 f.
11. 7 5 n. 3
11. 7. 2. 1 6 n. 3
11. 7. 5 8 n. 4
11. 7. 12. 4 7 n. 5
11. 7. 14. 11 7
11. 7. 16 7
11. 7. 40 10 n. 1
12. 1. 9. 8 102 n. 1
13. 7. 22 pr. 42 n. 2
14. 2. 7 80
17. 1. 1. 2 202 n. 1
18. 1. 18. 1 62 n. 10
18. 1. 40. 1 20 n. 7, 176 nn. 2, 6; 186, 187 n. 6
18. 1. 59 202 n. 7
18. 1. 80. 2 120 f.
18. 6. 1. 2 62
18. 6. 15 (14). 1 62
19. 1. 17. 6 107 f.
19. 1. 40 62
19. 2. 31 77 n. 4
19. 2. 35. 1 124 n. 7
21. 2. 75 202 n. 7
22. 1. 19 pr. 98
22. 1. 28. 1 216 n. 1
24. 1. 1 229 n. 11
24. 1. 38 229 n. 12, 230
24. 1. 38 pr. 230
24. 1. 38. 1 231
24. 1. 64 229 n. 13, 230 n. 2
26. 8. 4 31 n. 3, 54
26. 8. 12 20 n. 7, 78
28. 5. 60 (59) pr. 79
31. 49. 2 14
32. 2. 31 206 n. 4, 217
32. 29. 1 156
33. 2. 1 210 n. 1
33. 2. 12 206 n. 4, 211, 216
33. 2. 31 124
33. 2. 40 220 n. 7
34. 2 79 n. 7
34. 2. 4 62 n. 4, 79
34. 2. 34 pr. 77 n. 4, 80 n. 1
35. 2. 1. 9 206 n. 4, 217 n. 3, 221
35. 2. 69 210 n. 1
39. 1 154 n. 5
39. 1. 3. 3 170 n. 1
39. 2. 6 154 n. 4
39. 2. 7 145
39. 2. 7 pr. 145
39. 2. 7. 1 146
39. 2. 7. 2 146
39. 2. 8 145 n. 6
39. 2. 9 145
39. 2. 9 pr. 146
39. 2. 9. 1 145 f., 148
39. 2. 9. 2 74, 104 n. 1, 126 n. 1, 145, 147 f.
39. 2. 13. 6 145 n. 1
39. 2. 18. 2 145 n. 1
39. 2. 18. 4 145 n. 1
39. 2. 20 145 n. 1
39. 2. 24 144
39. 2. 24. 3 149 n. 2, 150
39. 2. 24. 4 126 n. 1, 149 f., 152 f.
39. 2. 24. 5 126 n. 1, 152 f.
39. 2. 24. 10 151 n. 2
39. 2. 24. 12 126 n. 1, 143 f.
39. 2. 25 126 n. 1, 144
39. 2. 26 144
39. 2. 28 139 n. 1
39. 2. 30. 2 127 n. 3
39. 2. 43 pr. 126 n. 1, 149, 151 f.
39. 2. 43. 1 126 n. 1, 153 f.
39. 2. 43. 2 126 n. 1, 154
39. 3. 1 pr. 157, 158 n. 1
39. 3. 1. 3 170
39. 3. 1. 4 170 f.
39. 3. 1. 5 170 ff.
39. 3. 1. 6 170, 172
39. 3. 1. 17 172 f., 176 nn. 12, 13; 196
39. 3. 1. 21 173
39. 3. 1. 23 164 n. 4
39. 3. 2 pr. 164 n. 4, 165 n. 1
39. 3. 2. 1 162 f., 164 n. 4, 166 n. 3, 168
39. 3. 2. 4 164 f.
39. 3. 2. 5 167
39. 3. 2. 6 160 n. 1, 161, 165
39. 3. 2. 7 166 n. 3
39. 3. 2. 8 168
39. 3. 2. 10 173 f., 176 n. 10, 195 n. 1
39. 3.3 pr. 157 ff., 160 n. 1, 171 n. 2

Digesta (cont.)
39. 3. 3. 1 157 ff., 160 n. 1
39. 3. 3. 2 126 n. 1, 145, 170, 172
39. 3. 6. 6 132 n. 2
39. 3. 11. 3 154 n. 4
39. 3. 11. 5 174
39. 3. 11. 6 163, 167
39. 3. 14. 2 154 n. 4
39. 3. 24 pr. 170 f.
39. 3. 24. 1 170 ff.
39. 3. 24. 2 170 f.
39. 3. 24. 3 174
39. 5. 7 232 n. 3
40. 7. 21 pr. 155
40. 12. 23 pr. 206, 217 n. 3
41. 1 65 n. 2
41. 1. 5. 1 62 f., 82 n. 1
41. 1. 5. 7 63 n. 4
41. 1. 7. 2 75 n. 1
41. 1. 14 pr. 13 n. 1
41. 1. 16 75
41. 1. 19 79
41. 1. 24 77
41. 1. 26 pr. 77
41. 1. 31. 1 56 n. 1
41. 1. 38 76
41. 1. 41 12, 12 n. 6 (at 13)
41. 1. 51. 1 64 n. 6
41. 1. 64 61
41. 2. 1. 1 63 n. 4
41. 2. 1. 3 82
41. 2. 3. 3 55, 74, 83 n. 5
41. 2. 3. 5 83
41. 2. 3. 18 85
41. 2. 3. 19 50
41. 2. 3. 21 63 n. 4
41. 2. 3. 23 49, 85 n. 4
41. 2. 19. 1 50
41. 2. 25. 2 84 n. 3
41. 2. 30. 5 85 n. 2
41. 2. 51 62
41. 3. 4. 6 26
41. 3. 4. 28 23 n. 7 (at 24), 24 n. 1
41. 3. 9 22 n. 3
41. 3. 33 pr. 26 n. 3
41. 3. 34 31 n. 3
41. 4. 2. 7 54
41. 4. 2. 8 31 n. 3, 53
41. 5. 2. 2 40 n. 2, 53
41. 5. 3 54 n. 2
41. 6. 3 50, 229 n. 13, 231
41. 10. 4 pr. 29
42. 4. 7. 13 89
42. 5. 29 12 n. 6 (at 13)
43. 8. 2. 2 11 nn. 3, 4
43. 8. 2. 5 11 n. 3
43. 8. 2. 7 11 n. 4
43. 8. 2. 17 11 n. 5
43. 8. 2. 18 11 n. 5
43. 8. 2. 39 11, 11 n. 9
43. 8. 5 127 n. 5, 131, 134, 136 n. 4, 139 n. 4, 155 n. 1
43. 14. 1. 5 163 n. 3
43. 16. 3. 13–18 209 n. 1
43. 16. 9. 1 209 n. 1
43. 17. 1 pr. 87 n. 3
43. 17. 3. 11 87 f.
43. 19 188
43. 19. 4 pr. 176 n. 2, 188, 193 n. 1
43. 20 184 n. 6
43. 20. 1. 17 176 n. 5, 193, 197
43. 20. 1. 18 176 n. 14, 194 n. 1, 197
43. 20. 8 176 nn. 2, 5; 188 ff.
43. 21. 1. 6 191 n. 3
43. 21. 1. 10 192
43. 21. 3 pr. 176 n. 5, 191
43. 21. 3. 1 176 n. 5, 191 f.
43. 21. 3. 10 193
43. 22. 1. 2 197 n. 3
43. 23. 1. 7 198 n. 3
43. 23. 2 176 n. 9, 197 f.
43. 24. 1. 5 222, 222 n. 2
43. 24. 1. 7 223
43. 24. 3. 7 224 n. 1
43. 24. 4 222 ff.
43. 24. 5. 3 225
43. 24. 5. 4 225 f.
43. 24. 5. 5 225 f.
43. 24. 5. 6 225 f.
43. 24. 5. 8 222 n. 2, 226, 226 n. 6
43. 24. 5. 9 226
43. 24. 7. 4 228
43. 24. 7. 5 227 n. 3
43. 24. 7. 6 227 n. 3
43. 24. 7. 8 227 n. 3
43. 24. 7. 9 227 n. 3
43. 24. 7. 10 227 n. 3
43. 24. 8 227 n. 3
43. 24. 9 227 n. 3
43. 24. 10 227 n. 3
43. 24. 11 pr. 227 n. 3
43. 24. 11. 1 12 n. 6 (at 13)
43. 24. 13. 4 227
43. 24. 22. 3 227
43. 26. 15. 4 84 n. 1

43. 26. 19 pr. 83
43. 27. 1 pr. 118 n. 1
43. 27. 1. 7 118 n. 4, 119
43. 27. 1. 8 117 ff.
43. 27. 1. 9 119
43. 27. 2 117 f.
43. 28. 1 pr. 120 n. 1
43. 28. 1. 1 120 n. 2
43. 31 86
45. 1. 126. 2 102 n. 1
45. 3. 6 78
48. 11. 1. 1 230 n. 1
48. 13. 11 (9). 3 68 n. 3
48. 13. 15 (13) 74 n. 1
49. 15. 12. 9 58 n. 3
49. 15. 27 30 n. 5
50. 16. 25. 1 104 n. 1
50. 16. 30 pr. 214
50. 16. 157 pr. 202 n. 6
50. 16. 157. 1 202 n. 6
50. 16. 180. 1 80 n. 6
50. 16. 236. 1 120 n. 2
50. 17. 73 pr. 190
50. 17. 73. 2 222, 222 n. 2

Codex
3. 32. 5 99 n. 7

(*c*) Byzantine

Basilica
42. 3. 16 122 n. 4
60. 13. 7 119 n. 3
60. 13. 8 119 n. 3
60. 13. 9 119 n. 4

Harmenopoulos
Ἑξάβιβλος
3. 3. 92 29 n. 3

Theophili Paraphrasis
2. 6. 2 26 n. 3

(*d*) Leges, Documents, Papyri, etc.

Bruns
no. 15 111 n. 6
no. 105 4 n. 2, 9 f.
no. 133 114 n. 2

FIRA iii
no. 72 4 n. 2, 9 f.

Leges

agraria
9 204 n. 6
10 204 n. 6
11 204 n. 6
18 88 n. 5

Antonia de Termessibus
24 204 n. 6
26 204 n. 6
31 204 n. 6
35 204 n. 6

duodecim tabularum
6. 7 121
7. 10 120
10 9 n. 6

Rubria
xx 134 f., 138
xxiii 122

Papyrus
P. Hal. 1, 84 ff. 113 n. 1

II. NON-LEGAL SOURCES

Aristotle

Rhetorica
1355ª55 116 n. 2
1375ᵇ22 116 n. 2

Arnobius
adversus gentes
7. 31 4

Cato
de agri cultura
5. 7 132
150 204 n. 1, 205

Cicero

Epistulae

ad Atticum
1. 1. 3 20 n. 7
1. 5. 6 31 n. 3, 37, 39
1. 20. 7 229 n. 4
4. 2. 3 4
5. 20. 5 73 f.
15. 26. 4 18, 176 n. 5, 194 n. 2

Cicero (*cont.*)
Epistulae (*cont.*)

ad familiares
2. 17. 4 — 72
7. 5. 3 — 17 n. 4
7. 12. 2 — 124
7. 29. 1 — 20 n. 7, 219 n. 2
7. 30. 2 — 219 n. 2
13. 8. 2 — 16 n. 2
15. 16. 3 — 88 n. 7

ad Quintum fratrem
3. 1. 2 — 176 nn. 5, 6; 194 n. 2

Orationes

p. Archia
5. 11 — 61

in Q. Caecilium divinatio
1. 3 — 2

p. Caecina
4. 11 — 206 n. 4, 208, 210
7. 19 — 122, 219 n. 1
13. 36 — 198 n. 4
14. 41 ff. — 88 n. 7
17. 49 — 88 n. 9
19. 54 — 16 n. 2, 22, 59
19. 55 — 88 n. 7
19. 55 f. — 88 n. 5
20. 56 ff. — 88 n. 5
21. 60 f. — 88 n. 7
26. 74 — 22, 24, 176 nn. 2, 3, 5, 6; 183, 183 n. 1
30. 86 ff. — 88 n. 5
30. 88 — 88 n. 7
31. 91 — 89 n. 2
32. 94 — 85

p. Cluentio
45. 126 — 104 n. 2

de domo
49. 127 — 4 n. 1
49. 128 — 4 n. 1
53. 137 — 4 n. 1

p. Flacco
32. 80 — 18
34. 84 — 37
34. 85 — 37, 39 f.

de haruspicum responso
7. 14 — 16 n. 2, 20 n. 7
14. 32 — 4, 22 n. 1

de lege agraria
1. 4. 12 — 73
2. 22. 59 — 73
3. 2. 9 — 202 n. 7
3. 3. 11 — 51 n. 1, 88 n. 5

p. Murena
12. 26 — 92 n. 1, 96

philippicae
3. 6. 16 — 29 n. 1
9. 6. 14 — 5
9. 6. 15 — 5

p. Quinctio
19. 60 — 90
19. 61 — 90
27. 84 — 90 n. 4

p. Roscio Amerino
9. 24 — 201 n. 2
38. 111 — 224 n. 3

p. Scauro
22. 45 — 140 n. 5

p. Tullio
12. 29 — 88
19. 44 f. — 88 n. 5
23. 53 — 222, 227 n. 5

in Verrem
II. 1. 42. 109 — 25
II. 1. 56. 146 — 140 n. 6, 141
II. 1. 59. 154 — 74 n. 1
II. 2. 12. 31 — 96 f.
II. 3. 40. 93 — 13 f.

Philosophica

Cato maior de senectute
4. 10 — 229 n. 3

de finibus bonorum et malorum
1. 4. 12 — 206 n. 2, 208, 214

de legibus
1. 4. 14 — 15 nn. 5, 6; 176 n. 12, 196 f.
1. 8. 25 — 219 n. 2, 220 n. 4
1. 21. 55 — 22 n. 4, 111, 117

2. 19. 47 15 n. 5
2. 19. 47 ff. 33 n. 1
2. 19. 48 32 f., 40
2. 19. 49 33
2. 20. 49 33 f.
2. 20. 50 35, 232
2. 21. 52 33 f.
2. 22. 55 8 nn. 1, 6
2. 22. 57 8
2. 23. 58 6, 9 nn. 1, 2
2. 24. 61 6 n. 4, 9 nn. 4, 5; 22

de officiis
1. 7. 20 70
1. 7. 21 70
1. 25. 89 189
3. 16. 67 202 n. 7

Tusculanae disputationes
3. 19 19 n. 1

Rhetorica

de oratore
1. 10. 41 ff. 89
1. 38. 173 15 nn. 5, 6
1. 39. 178 202 n. 7
1. 39. 179 176 n. 7, 194
1. 56. 237 122 n. 1
2. 24. 100 9
2. 71. 286 229 n. 2
3. 28. 110 60

de inventione
1. 45. 84 69 f.
1. 45. 85 70
2. 51. 153 61 n. 5

orator
21. 72 15 n. 6, 176 n. 12, 197

topica
3. 15 211, 217
3. 17 206 n. 4, 208 f., 211
4. 21 206 n. 4, 219
4. 22 141, 171 n. 5
4. 23 22, 47 n. 3, 59, 114 n. 1, 172
4. 24 115
5. 27 14, 24 n. 4, 202 n. 7
5. 28 19 ff.
6. 29 34 n. 2
7. 32 13
8. 36 17
9. 38 155 f., 161 n. 1, 171 n. 2
9. 39 161, 161 n. 1, 164 n. 1

10. 43 114 n. 1, 172, 173 n. 1
10. 45 18

Columella

de re rustica
2. 2. 2. 4 171 n. 1
2. 8. 3 171 n. 4
11. 2. 82 171 n. 4

Festus
s.v. ambitus 113 n. 2
s.v. bustum 6 n. 4
s.v. postica 124 n. 7
s.v. posticam lineam 124 n. 7
s.v. religiosum 3
s.v. religiosus 1 f., 9
s.v. rodus 17 n. 3
s.v. sublucare 119 n. 3
s.v. tuguria 80 n. 6
s.v. vindiciae 99 n. 2

Gellius

Noctes Atticae
4. 9. 7 3 n. 2
4. 9. 8 3
4. 9. 9 3
4. 9. 10 3
17. 7. 1 24
17. 7. 2 24
17. 7. 3 24
17. 7. 4 25 n. 4
17. 7. 5 25 n. 4
17. 7. 6 25 n. 4
17. 7. 7 25 n. 4
17. 7. 8 25 n. 4

Livy
3. 71. 7 68 n. 2
29. 20. 11 229 n. 2
30. 14. 8 68 n. 1

Lucretius

de rerum natura
3. 971 207 n 2

Macrobius

Saturnalia
3. 3. 2 4
3. 3. 4 9
3. 3. 5 3 n. 3
3. 3. 8 5

Plautus

Amphitruo
193 69 n. 1
375 60 n. 5
845 60 n. 5

Captivi
110 ff. 69
452 f. 69

Casina
836 f. 203, 208, 218

Epidicus
43 69 n. 1
64 69 n. 1
107 69 n. 1
608 69 n. 1
621 69 n. 1

Menaechmi
134 69 n. 1

Mercator
451 ff. 124 n. 7
830 ff. 204

Persa
501 ff. 69 n. 1
520 ff. 69 n. 1

Pseudolus
1170 69 n. 1

Rudens
699 ff. 63 n. 2

Stichus
241 60 n. 5
696 86
750 86

Truculentus
273 f. 17

Pliny the Elder

Naturalis historia
16. 5. 15 120
17. 20. 147 121 n. 1
17. 20. 151 121 n. 1
20. 89. 244 132
23. 57. 106 132 n. 4
36. 2. 5 139 ff.
36. 2. 6 139 ff.
36. 3. 7 140

Plutarch

Quaestiones Romanae
7 229 n. 14

Solon
23 113 n. 1

Polybius

Historiae
6. 21. 1 67
6. 22. 2 67
6. 22. 3 67
10. 16 65 f.
10. 17. 1 66 n. 1

Rhetorica ad Herennium
4. 29. 40 60 n. 3, 88 n. 5

Seneca

de beneficiis
6. 5. 3 40 n. 1

Tacitus

Annales
11. 5 229 n. 4
13. 42 229 n. 4
15. 20 229 n. 4

Terence

Eunuchus
319 89

Heauton timorumenos
499 ff. 116 n. 3

Valerius Maximus

Memorabilia
8. 2. 2 232

Varro

de lingua latina
5. 22 113 n. 2, 183
5. 27 176 nn. 12, 13; 196
5. 163 17 n. 3
6. 85 17 n. 4
9. 83 17 n. 3

de re rustica
2. 10. 4 20 n. 7, 21, 60 n. 3, 69

Volusius Maecianus

de assis distributione
46 113 n. 2

GENERAL INDEX

Accessio, 57, 74 ff.
actio: *ad exhibendum*, 91, 103 n. 2, 107 ff.; *aquae pluviae arcendae*, 131 ff., 145, 155 ff.; *auctoritatis*, 16, 16 n. 2, 17 n. 1; *Calvisiana*, 105; *communi dividundo*, 6, 110 ff., 121 ff., 217; *confessoria*, 178 ff.; *de modo agri*, 16; *de servitute*, 177; *Fabiana*, 105; *familiae erciscundae*, 6, 110 f., 121 f.; *finium regundorum*, 110 f., 113 ff.; *furti*, 42 n. 2, 45 ff., 101 f., 106, 122; *furti noxalis*, 101 f., 123; *in factum*, 6; *legis Aquiliae*, 6 n. 5; *legis Aquiliae noxalis*, 123; *negatoria*, 117, 177 ff., 195 f.; *Pauliana*, 105, *Publiciana*, 91, 95, 104 ff.; *Rutiliana*, 105; *Serviana*, 105 f.; *utilis*, 75; *utilis in rem*, 75.
acquisition *per extraneam personam*, 80, 80 n. 3.
actus, 176, 181, 183, 201.
adiudicatio, 206.
adoptio, 17 n. 5.
aestimatio litis, 101 f.
ager limitatus, 76.
alluvio, 75 ff.
ambitus, 113 ff.
aquae ductus, 176, 181, 183 ff., 197, 202.
aquae haustus, 24, 176, 183 ff.
aquam immittere, 176.
avulsio, 75 n. 1.

Boundaries, 110 ff.

Cautio, 100, 102 f.; *damni infecti*, 49, 126 ff., 131 ff., 146 ff.; *usufructuaria*, 218.
cessio in iure, 14, 16, 20 f., 43, 61, 69, 93, 93 n. 1, 186, 201, 206.
clausula arbitraria, 166.
cloaca, 176, 197.
coemptio, 17 n. 5.
condemnatio, 103.
condictio, 97 n. 3, 102 n. 1.
constitutum possessorium, 62 n. 8.
curator rei publicae, 226.

Damnum iam factum, 147 ff.
damnum infectum, 74, 125 ff.
damnum iniuria datum, 6 n. 5.
decemviri, 73.
divisory actions, 110 ff., 121 ff.
donatio, 229 ff.; *mortis causa*, 232.
dotis dictio, 231.

Edictum: *de damno infecto* (*praetoris peregrini*), 134 ff., *de damno infecto* (*praetoris urbani*), 125 ff., 139 ff.; *de sumptibus funerum*, 7; *Publicianum*, 49 f.; *quemadmodum in possessione esse oportet*, 90 n. 4; *qui absens iudicio defensus non fuerit*, 90; *qui capitali crimine damnatus erit*, 90; *qui exsilii causa solum verterit*, 90; *qui fraudationis causa latitarit*, 89 f; *quod familia publicanorum furtum fecisse dicetur*, 130; *quod publicanus illicite exegerit*, 130; *quod publicanus vi ademerit*, 130.
emptio sub corona, 69, 69 n. 2.
exceptio, 228; *doli*, 99.

Festuca, 65.
fiducia, 41 ff., 50.
flumen, 176, 196.
formula in rem per sponsionem, 97 n. 4, 99 n. 6.
furtum, 5, 42 ff.

Habitatio, 220.
hasta, 65.
heres necessarius, 51, 51 n. 2.
heres suus et necessarius, 51, 51 n. 2.

Iactus, 80.
implantatio, 75.
institutio, 219.
interdictum: *de aqua cottidiana et aestiva*, 193, 197; *de cloacis*, 198; *de fonte*, 197; *de glande legenda*, 120; *de itinere actuque*, 188; *de rivis*, 191; *de vi*, 89 f.; *de vi armata*, 89 f.; *ne quid in loco publico vel itinere fiat*, 10 f.; *quae arbor ex aedibus tuis*, 118; *quae arbor ex agro tuo*, 118 f.; *quod*

interdictum (cont.)
in itinere publico factum erit, ut restituetur, 11 f.; *quod vi aut clam*, 222 ff.; *uti possidetis*, 59, 86 f., 106; *utrubi*, 59, 86 f., 95, 106.
iter, 176, 181, 183, 185 f., 201.
iudicium imperium continens, 97 n. 3.
iudicium legitimum, 97 n. 3.
iudicium secutorium, 87 f., 87 n. 6.
ius praediaturum, 48.

Legatum, 206, 209; *per vindicationem*, 202, 206 n. 4; *quod eius causa emptum est*, 79; *ususfructus*, 207.
leges Iuliae, 129.
legis actio: *damni infecti*, 124 ff., 145; *per iudicis postulationem*, 111, 121, 124; *per pignoris capionem*, 128 ff.; *sacramento in rem*, 65, 94 ff.
lex: *Aebutia*, 129; *agraria*, 73; *Atinia*, 24 ff., 25 n. 5; *Aquilia*, 126; *a vicanis Furfensibus templo dicta*, 4 n. 2, 9 f.; *Cincia*, 229; *duodecim tabularum*, 6 n. 4, 8 f., 21 f., 26 ff., 43, 47, 59, 93 n. 1, 99, 111 ff., 115 ff., 133, 155, 162 ff.; *Iulia*, 30 f.; *Iulia de maritandis ordinibus*, 230; *Iulia et Plautia*, 30; *Licinnia*, 124; *Mamilia*, 111; *Papia Poppaea*, 230; *Plautia*, 30; *Rhodia de iactu*, 80; *Rubria*, 122, 134 ff.; *Quinctia de aquaeductibus*, 127; *Scribonia*, 15, 22 ff., 32, 164 ff., 202.
liber homo bona fide serviens, 78 f.
libertus, 79 f.
litis contestatio, 103 f., 103 n. 2.
locatio, 41, 50.
lumen, 176, 181 f., 194 f., 202.

Mancipatio, 16 ff., 20 n. 7, 43, 45, 69, 92 f., 184, 186, 194 f., 201, 206.
manumissio censu, 61.
manus, 37.
missio in possessionem, 137.

Occupatio, 62 ff., 81.
oneris ferendi, 176, 198 ff.
opera servorum vel animalium, 221.

Paries, 14 f.
partus ancillae, 206, 208, 214 ff.
patronus, 80.
pecoris ad aquam appellendi, 176, 197 n. 3
peculatus, 67 n. 1, 68, 68 n. 4, 74 n 1
petitio hereditatis, 100.
pignus, 43 f., 47.
possessio, 49, 59, 62, 79, 81 ff., 95, 209.
postliminium, 17.
praeda, 63 ff., 74 n. 1.
praesumptio Muciana, 230 n. 1.
precarium, 41, 50, 83 f.
procurator, 80.
prospectus, 176, 181 f., 194, 202.

Quaestores urbani, 72.

Regulae, 49 f.
relative ownership, 43 ff., 91 ff.
res, 1 ff.; *communes*, 71 f.; *divini iuris*, 1 ff.; *extra commercium*, 13 f.; *furtivae*, 24 ff., 45 n. 1; *hostiles*, 71, 71 n. 2; *humani iuris*, 1; *mancipi*, 17 f., 31, 61 n. 3, 181, 183 f., 187, 201, 204; *nec mancipi*, 14, 18 f., 61, 61 n. 3, 181, 187, 207, 209; *nullius*, 71, 71 n. 2; *privatae*, 1, 71; *publicae*, 1, 10 ff., 64; *quae tangi non possunt*, 13 f.; *quae tangi possunt*, 13 f.; *religiosae*, 1 ff., 8, 21; *sacrae*, 1 ff., 9 f., 21; *sanctae*, 1 ff., 9.

Sacra, 33 ff.
sacrilegium, 5,
satio, 75.
senatusconsultum, 208 ff.
sepulchra: *familiaria*, 8; *hereditaria*, 8.
sequester, 94.
servitudes, 15, 22 ff., 32, 92 f., 176 ff.; rustic, 181, 183; urban, 181.
servitus proiciendi protegendive, 176, 196.
stillicidium, 14 f., 176, 196 f.
specificatio, 77.
stipulatio: *habere licere*, 204; *praetoria*, 135 ff.
substitutio pupillaris, 219.

Thensauri inventio, 74.
thensaurus, 55 ff., 83 n. 5.
traditio, 14, 16, 31, 61 f., 81, 93, 202, 231.

Usucapio, 6 n. 4, 9, 15, 21 ff., 79, 95, 105, 117, 181, 231: *bona fides* in, 23 n. 5, 31 f., 32 n. 1, 43 f., 48 ff., 54 f., 84; *error facti* in, 52 ff.; *error iuris* in, 52 f.; *hereditatis*, 32 ff., 60 n. 1; *iusta causa* in, 31, 43 f.; *libertatis*, 32, 60 n. 1, 182, 200; *pro*

derelicto, 32 n. 1; *pro emptore*, 53 f.; *pro herede*, 31 ff., 46, 50 ff., 59; *servitutis*, 15, 22, 32, 60 n. 1, 164 ff., 202.
usureceptio, 31, 41 ff., 59; *servitutis*, 48 n. 3.
usurpatio, 59.
usus, 219 f.
ususfructus, 203 ff.; *gregis*, 205, 216 n. 2.
Venditio, 231.
via, 176, 181, 183, 187 n. 6.
vindicatio, 21 n. 5, 44 f., 61, 74 f., 91, 95 ff., 108, 203; *in libertatem*, 61; *servitutis*, 92 n. 4; *ususfructus*, 203, 218.
vis maior, 150 f.

PRINTED IN GREAT BRITAIN
AT THE UNIVERSITY PRESS, OXFORD
BY VIVIAN RIDLER
PRINTER TO THE UNIVERSITY